Mansfield College Lectures.

THE CHURCH

IN

THE ROMAN EMPIRE

BEFORE A.D. 170.

MANSFIELD COLLEGE LECTURES, 1892

THE CHURCH

IN

THE ROMAN EMPIRE

BEFORE A.D. 170

BY

W. M. RAMSAY, M.A.,

PROFESSOR OF HUMANITY IN THE UNIVERSITY OF ABERDEEN;
FORMERLY PROFESSOR OF CLASSICAL ARCHÆOLOGY, AND
FELLOW OF EXETER COLLEGE, OXFORD;
AUTHOR OF "THE HISTORICAL GEOGRAPHY OF ASIA MINOR," ETC.

WITH MAPS AND ILLUSTRATIONS

G. P. PUTNAM'S SONS

NEW YORK
27 WEST TWENTY-THIRD STREET

LONDON
24 BEDFORD STREET, STRAND

The Knickerbocker Press

To
A. M. R.

PREFACE.

THIS work originates from the invitation with which the Council of Mansfield College, Oxford, honoured me in the end of July 1891, to give a course of six lectures there in May–June 1892. The opinion of Dr. Fairbairn, Dr. Sanday, and other friends encouraged me to hope that faults of execution—of which I was and am painfully conscious—did not wholly obscure a good idea in them ; and it is at their advice that the present book appears. The lectures are almost entirely rewritten (except Chap. IX.), and are enlarged by the addition of Part I. and in other respects, which need not be specified ; but they retain their original character as lectures, intended rather to stimulate interest and research in students than to attain scientific completeness and order of exposition. They exemplify to younger students the method of applying archæological, topographical, and numismatic evidence to the investigation of early Christian history ; and, as I always urge on my pupils, their aim is to suggest to others how to treat the subject better than I can.

The books of the New Testament are treated here simply as authorities for history ; and their credit is estimated on the same principles as that of other historical documents. If I reach conclusions very different from those of the school of criticism whose originators and chief exponents are German, it is not that I differ from their method. I fully accept their principle, that the sense of these documents can be ascertained only by resolute criticism ; but I think that they have often carried out their principle badly, and that their criticism often offends against critical method. True criticism must be sympathetic ; but in investigations into religion, Greek, Roman, and Christian alike, there appears to me, if I may venture to say so, to be in many German scholars (the greatest excepted) a lack of that instinctive sympathy with the life and nature of a people which is essential to the right use of critical processes. For years, with much interest and zeal, but with little knowledge, I followed the critics and accepted their results. In recent years, as I came to understand Roman history better, I have realised that, in the case of almost all the books of the New Testament, it is as gross an outrage on criticism to hold them for second-century forgeries as it would be to class the works of Horace and Virgil as forgeries of the time of Nero.

Some German reviewers have taxed me with unfair depreciation of German authorities. The accusation must seem to my English friends and pupils a retribution for the persistence with which I have urged the necessity of studying German method. None admires and reverences German scholarship more than I do ; but it has not taught me to be blind to faults, or to be afraid to speak out.

I cannot sufficiently acknowledge my debt to various friends, chiefly to Dr. Sanday ; also to Dr. Hort, Dr. Fairbairn, Mr. Armitage Robinson, Mr. A. C. Headlam, etc. From the discriminating criticism of Mr. Vernon Bartlet I have gained much : the pages on 1 Peter were doubled in meeting his arguments. My old friend of undergraduate days, Mr. Macdonell, formerly of Balliol College, gave me especially great help throughout the first fourteen chapters. In the index I have been aided by my pupil, Mr. A. Souter, now of Caius College.

A special tribute is due to two writers. Lightfoot's *Ignatius and Polycarp* has been my constant companion ; yet my admiration for his historical perception, his breadth of knowledge and his honesty of statement, and my grateful recollection of much kindly encouragement received from him personally, do not prevent me from stating frankly where I am bound to differ from him. Mommsen's review of Neumann explained certain difficulties that long puzzled me ; and the lectures attempt, however imperfectly, to apply principles learned mainly from his various writings.

Of many shortcomings I regret most the following. An account of the organisations permitted by the Empire, especially the Augustales, would illustrate by contrast the position of the Church. The evidence of Hermas was omitted from ch. xiii., because I had to put him before A.D. 112, and this date would not be generally considered to strengthen my argument. The discussion of *Codex Bezæ* should have been concentrated in one chapter, and carried out to illustrate, by comparison with *Acta Theklæ*, the character of the Church in Asia about 130 A.D. In palliation of many faults I may plead the want of a good library and the pressure of other duties.

As the whole work is due to my explorations in Asia Minor, I hope it may stimulate the progress of discovery in that land, which at present conceals within it the answer to many pressing problems of history; and, perhaps, may even prevent my researches from coming to an end. Next to further exploration and excavation, the greatest *desideratum* is a society to study and edit the *acta* of the Eastern Saints.

ABERDEEN,
    January 23rd, 1893.

CONTENTS.

CHAPTER XII.

CHAPTER XIII.

CHAPTER XIV.

CHAPTER XV.

CHAPTER XVI.

CORRIGENDA.

N.B.—*Part I left my hands in October* 1892, *Part II in January* 1893.

Page 32, n*, I adhere to this against M. Bérard, *Bull. Corr. Hell.*, 1892, p. 420. An inscription just published in Lanckoronski, *Städte Pamphyliens*, II, p. 203, no. 58, will strengthen and make more precise the view which I have stated. "Royal Road" seems to have been a popular Asian term denoting a well-constructed highway: it perhaps arose from the Persian "Royal Road" (*Hist. Geogr.*, p. 27ff).

 46, *last* 14 *lines* are not needed for the argument, and I would omit them, until more evidence is found to justify the suspicion, which I still hold: the Greek is late and Asiatic.

 ,, 64, l. 2 *from foot, read* situation implied in Gal. iv. 13.

 ,, 71, l. 4 *from foot,* at Iconium *refer to* p. 46.

 ,, 101, l. 9f, *delete, and refer to date proposed on* pp. 167, 427.

 ,, 142, the references to cult of Zeus, etc., are only analogies, not direct arguments, for Artemis-cult. We find on gems μέγα τὸ ὄνομα Σαράπιδος, and in Aristides I., p. 467, μέγας ὁ Ἀσκληπιός

 ,, 477, n ‡, *add* On Michael of Poimanenon, see *Hist. Geogr.*, p. 157.

THE CHURCH IN THE ROMAN EMPIRE.

PART I.—EARLIEST STAGE:

ST. PAUL IN ASIA MINOR.

CHAPTER I.

GENERAL.

1. Plan of the Work.

IN view of the important part played by the churches of Asia in the development of Christianity during the period 70–170 A.D.,* the proper preliminary to the subject which is treated in this book would be a study of the social and political condition of Asia Minor about the middle of the first century of our era. Such a task is too great for the narrow limits of present knowledge. In place of such a preliminary study, it appeared a more prudent course to describe the travels of St. Paul in the country, as affording a series of pictures of single scenes, each simple and slight in character, and each showing some special feature of the general life of society.†

But while chronological considerations require that these chapters be placed as a preliminary part, they are, alike in conception and in execution, later than the body of the book. The writer, while composing the opening chapters, had the rest of the work already clear in his mind; and there has been unconsciously a tendency to write as if the views

---

* See below, p. 171.

† Perhaps at some later date, when the investigations, studies, and travel necessary for a projected historical work are completed, it may be possible to paint a general picture of the state of society in the first century.

stated in the main body of the work were familiar to the reader. In the preliminary part it is important to observe any faint signs of the later idea that Christianity was the religion of the Empire. We trace the rise of this idea from the time when Paul went from Perga into the province Galatia "to the work" (Acts xiii. 14, xv. 38.)

The discussion which is here given of the missionary journeys of St. Paul in Asia Minor is not intended to be complete. It is unnecessary to repeat what has already been well stated by others. The writer presupposes throughout the discussion a general familiarity with the previous descriptions of the journeys. His intention has been to avoid saying again what has been rightly said in the works of Conybeare and Howson, of Lewin, of Farrar, etc. ; and merely to bring together the ideas which have been suggested to him by long familiarity with the localities, and which seemed to correct, or to advance beyond, the views stated in the modern biographies of St. Paul, and in the Commentaries on the Acts and the Epistles.*

The notes which follow may perhaps seem to be unnecessarily minute ; but the reason for their existence lies in the fact that it is important to weigh accurately and minutely minute details. Fidelity to the character and circumstances of the country and people is an important criterion in estimating the narrative of St. Paul's journeys ; and such fidelity is most apparent in slight details, many of which have, so far as I can discover, hitherto escaped notice. The writer's subject is restricted to the country with which he has had the opportunity of acquiring unusual familiarity,

---

* Considerable parts of Chapters I., II., III. appeared in the *Expositor*, January, September, October, and November, 1892.

and about which many false opinions have become part of
the stock of knowledge handed down through a succession
of commentators. Even that most accurate of writers, the
late Bishop Lightfoot, had not in his earlier works succeeded in emancipating himself from the traditional miscon-
ceptions ; we observe in his successive writings a continuous
progress towards the accurate knowledge of Asia Minor
which is conspicuous in his work on Ignatius and Polycarp.
But in his early work, the edition of the *Epistle to the
Galatians*, there is shown, so far as Asia Minor is concerned,
little or no superiority to the settled erroneousness of view
and of statement which still characterises the recent commentaries of Wendt and Lipsius ; * and only a few signs
appear of his later fixed habit of recurring to original
authorities about the country, and setting the words of St.
Paul in their local and historical surroundings, a habit
which contrasts strongly with the satisfied acquiescence of
Lipsius and Wendt in the hereditary circle of knowledge
or error. The present writer is under great obligations to
both of them, and desires to acknowledge his debt fully ;
but the vice of many modern German discussions of
the early history of Christianity—viz., falseness to the facts

---

* Wendt's sixth (seventh) edition of Meyer's *Handbuch über die
Apostelgeschichte*, Göttingen, 1888 ; Lipsius' edition of *Epistle to
the Galatians* in Holtzmann's *Handcommentar zum N.T.*, ii. 2,
Freiburg, 1891. These works are referred to throughout the eight
opening chapters simply as Wendt and Lipsius. I am sorry to
speak unfavourably of Lipsius so soon after his lamented death ; but
my criticism refers only to his statements about the antiquities of
Asia Minor. The obscurity of this subject does not justify wrong
statements, and inferences founded on them. Harnack's excellent
edition of *Acta Carpi* shows how a judicious reticence may be
observed in cases where certainty is unattainable.

of contemporary life and the general history of the period—
is becoming stereotyped and intensified by long repetition
in the most recent commentators, and some criticism and
protest against their treatment of the subject are required.*

I regret to be compelled in these earlier chapters to
disagree so much with Lightfoot's views as stated in his
edition of *Galatians* : perhaps therefore I may be allowed
to say that the study of that work, sixteen years ago,
marks an epoch in my thoughts and the beginning of my
admiration for St. Paul and for him.†

2. THE " TRAVEL-DOCUMENT."

In order to put the reader on his guard, it is only fair to
state at the outset that the writer has a definite aim—viz., by
minutely examining the journeys in Asia Minor to show
that the account given in Acts of St. Paul's journeys is
founded on, or perhaps actually incorporates, an account
written down under the immediate influence of Paul him-

---

* It is hardly necessary to say that my criticism is directed
against one single aspect of modern German work in early Christian
history. Of the value, suggestiveness, and originality of that work
no one can have a higher opinion than I ; but I cannot agree with
certain widely accepted views as to the relation of the early Christians
to the society and the government of Asia Minor and of the Empire
generally.

† The Epistle to the Galatians formed part of the Pass Divinity
Examination in the Final Schools at Oxford. It is only fair to
acknowledge how much I gained from an examination which I sub-
mitted to with great reluctance. Immersed as I was at the time in
Greek Philosophy, it appeared to me that Paul was the first true
successor of Aristotle, and his work a great relief after the unen-
durable dreariness of the Greek Stoics and the dulness of the
Epicureans.

self. This original account was characterised by a system
of nomenclature different from that which is employed by
the author of some of the earlier chapters of Acts: it used
territorial names in the Roman sense, like Paul's Epistles,
whereas the author of chap. ii., ver. 9, uses them in the
popular Greek sense ; and it showed a degree of accuracy
which the latter was not able to attain.* In carrying out
this aim, it will be necessary to differ in some passages of
Acts from the usual interpretation, and the reasons for this
divergence can be appreciated only by careful attention to
rather minute details. For the sake of brevity, I shall, so
far as regard for clearness permits, venture to refer for some
details to a larger work,† whose results are here applied to
the special purpose of illustrating this part of the Acts ;
but I hope to make the exposition and arguments complete
in themselves.

As this idea, that the narrative of St. Paul's journeys,
or at least parts of it, had an independent existence
before it was utilised or incorporated in Acts, must be
frequently referred to in the following pages, the supposed
original document will be alluded to as the " Travel-Document." The exact relation of this document to the form
which appears in Acts is difficult to determine. It may
have been modified or enlarged ; but I cannot enter on
this subject. My aim is only to investigate the traces of

---

* The general agreement of this view with that stated by Wendt,
pp. 23 and 278, is obvious ; and certain differences also are not
difficult to detect. He dates the composition of Acts between 75
and 100 A.D., and holds that the original document alone was the
work of Luke.

† *Historical Geography of Asia Minor*, where I have discussed
the points more fully.

minute fidelity to the actual facts of contemporary society
and life, which stamp this part of Acts as, in part or in
whole, a trustworthy historical authority, dating from
62–4 A.D.

I hope to show that, when once we place ourselves at the
proper point of view, the interpretation of the " Travel-
Document" as a simple, straightforward, historical testimony
offers itself with perfect ease, and that it confirms and
completes our knowledge of the country acquired from
other sources in a way which proves its ultimate origin
from a person acquainted with the actual circumstances.
If this attempt be successful, it follows that the original
document was composed under St. Paul's own influence,*
for only he was present on all the occasions which are
described with conspicuous vividness.

3. THE CHURCHES OF GALATIA.

For a long time I failed to appreciate the accuracy of
the narrative in Acts.†   It has cost me much time,
thought, and labour to understand it ; ‡ and it was impossible to understand it so long as I was prepossessed with
the idea adopted from my chief master and guide, Bishop

---

* I wish to express his influence in the most general terms, and to
avoid any theorising about the way in which it was exercised,
whether by mere verbal report or otherwise.

† My earlier views were expressed in the *Expositor*, January
1892, p. 30. Compare also the paragraph which I wrote in *Expositor*, July 1890, p. 20.

‡ Among other things I have been obliged to rewrite the sketch
of the history of Lycaonia and Cilicia Tracheia in *Hist. Geogr.*,
p. 371, where I wrongly followed M. Waddington against Professor
Mommsen in regard to the coins of M. Antonius Polemo. This error
vitiated my whole theory.

Lightfoot, that in St. Paul's Epistle the term Galatians denotes the Celtic people of the district popularly and generally known as Galatia. To maintain this idea I had to reject the plain and natural interpretation of some passages ; but when at last I found myself compelled to abandon it, and to understand Galatians as inhabitants of Roman Galatia, much that had been dark became clear, and some things that had seemed loose and vague became precise and definite. As the two opposing theories must frequently be referred to, it will prove convenient to designate them as the North-Galatian and the South-Galatian theories ; and the term North Galatia will be used to denote the country of the Asiatic Gauls, South Galatia to denote the parts of Phrygia, Lycaonia, and Pisidia, which were by the Romans incorporated in the vast province of Galatia.*

The question as to what churches were addressed by St. Paul in his Epistle to the Galatians is really of the first importance for the right understanding of the growth of the Christian Church during the period between 70 and 150 A. D. ; and the prevalent view, against which we argue, leads necessarily to a misapprehension of the position of the Church in the Empire. The diffusion of Christianity was, as I hope to bring out more clearly in the following pages, closely connected with the great lines of communication across the Roman Empire, with the maintenance of intercourse, and with the development of education and

---

* I did not expect to be obliged to argue that this great province was called Galatia; but even this simple fact, which had been assumed by every writer since Tacitus, has recently been contested by Dr. Schürer, and I have appended a note on the subject at the end of this chapter.

the feeling of unity throughout the Empire. The spread of Christianity had a political side. The Church may be, roughly speaking, described as a political party advocating certain ideas which, in their growth, would have resulted necessarily in social and political reform.* All that fostered the idea of universal citizenship and a wider Roman policy —as distinguished from the narrow Roman view that looked on Rome, or even on Italy, as mistress of a subject empire, instead of head and capital of a co-ordinate empire —made for Christianity unconsciously and insensibly ; and the Christian religion alone was able to develop fully this idea and policy.

The chief line along which the new religion developed was that which led from Syrian Antioch through the Cilician Gates, across Lycaonia to Ephesus, Corinth, and Rome.† One subsidiary line followed the land route by Philadelphia, Troas, Philippi, and the Egnatian Way‡ to Brindisi and Rome ; and another went north from the Gates by Tyana and Cæsareia of Cappadocia to Amisos in Pontus, § the great harbour of the Black Sea, by which the trade of Central Asia was carried to Rome. The main-

---

* In the writer's opinion the Church proved unfaithful to its trust, ceased to adhere to the principles with which it started, and failed, in consequence, to carry out the reform, or rather revolution, which would have naturally resulted from them. But that chapter of history is later than the scope of the present volume.

† This line is referred to in several passages which have never yet been properly understood, *e. g.*, Ignatius, *Ephes.*, § 12, Clement *Ep*. i., *ad Corinth.*, § 1.

‡ Cp. Rom. xv. 19. This route was taken by Ignatius' guards.

§ The early foundation of churches in Cappadocia (1 Peter i. 1) and in Pontus (1 Peter i. 1 ; Pliny *ad Traj.*, 96) was due to this line of communication.

tenance of close and constant communication between the scattered congregations must be presupposed, as necessary to explain the growth of the Church and the attitude which the State assumed towards it. Such communication was, on the view advocated in the present work, maintained along the same lines on which the general development of the Empire took place; and politics, education, religion, grew side by side. But the prevalent view as to the Galatian churches separates the line of religious growth from the line of the general development of the Empire, and introduces into a history that claims to belong to the first century, the circumstances that characterised a much later period. The necessary inference from the prevalent view is, either that this history really belongs to a much later period than it claims to belong to (an inference drawn with strict and logical consistency by a considerable body of German scholars), or that the connexion between the religious and the general history of the Empire must be abandoned. If the arguments for the prevalent view are conclusive, we must accept the choice thus offered; but I hope to show that the prevalent view is not in accordance with the evidence.

4. SOCIAL CONDITION OF ASIA MINOR, A.D. 50-60.

The discussion of St. Paul's experiences in Asia Minor is beset with one serious difficulty. The attempt must be made to indicate the character of the society into which the Apostle introduced the new doctrine of religion and of life. In the case of Greece and Rome much may be assumed as familiar to the reader. In the case of Asia Minor very little can be safely assumed; and the analogy of Greece and Rome is apt to introduce confusion and misconception. Conybeare and Howson have attempted, in a most scholarly way, to set forth a picture of the situation in which St. Paul found himself placed in the cities of Asia and of Galatia. But the necessary materials for their purpose did not exist, the country was unknown, the maps were either a blank or positively wrong in regard to all but a very few points ; and, moreover, they were often deceived by Greek and Roman analogies. The only existing sketch of the country that is not positively misleading is given by Mommsen in his *Provinces of the Roman Empire* ; and that is only a very brief description, which extends over a period of several centuries. Now the dislike entertained for the new religion was at first founded on the disturbance it caused in the existing relations of society. Toleration of new religions as such was far greater under the Román Empire than it has been in modern times : in the multiplicity of religions and gods that existed in the same city, a single new addition was a matter of almost perfect indifference. But the aggressiveness of Christianity, the change in social habits and every-day life which it introduced, and the injurious effect that it sometimes exercised on trades which were encouraged by paganism, combined with the intolerance that it showed for other religions, made it detested among people who regarded with equanimity, or even welcomed, the introduction into their cities of the gods of Greece, of Rome, of Egypt, of Syria. Hence every slight fact which is recorded of St. Paul's experiences has a close relation to the social system that prevailed in the country, and cannot be properly understood without some idea of the general character of society and the tendencies which moulded it

The attempt must be made in the following pages to bring out the general principles which were at work in each individual incident; and such an attempt involves minuteness in scrutinising the details of each incident and lengthens the exposition. It will be necessary to express dissent from predecessors oftener than I could wish; but if one does not formally dissent from the views advocated by others, the impression is apt to be caused that they have not been duly weighed.

NOTE ON THE NAME OF THE PROVINCE GALATIA.

IT is not easy to find a more absolute contradiction than there is between the view adopted in the text and that of Dr. E. Schürer in *Theologische Literaturzeitung*, 1892, p. 468: "An official usage, which embraced all three districts (Galatia, Pisidia, and Lycaonia) under the single conception *Galatia*, has never existed." This extraordinary statement is made with equal positiveness by Dr. Schürer in *Jahrbücher für protestantische Theologie*, 1892, p. 471, where he affirms that "the name Galatia is only *a parte potiori*, being taken from the biggest of the various districts which were included in the provinces, and is not an official designation: the name and the conception Galatia did not embrace more than the special district of this name." When I read such a statement I fall into despair.* I have stated the facts with some care in my *Histor. Geogr.*, pp. 253 and 453; and Dr. Schürer devotes considerable space to restating them in a less complete, and, as I venture to think, less accurate way, treating a small selection of inscriptions as if they represented the official usage, while the overwhelming majority of passages, which describe the entire province by the name Galatia, are entirely disregarded by him. Dr. Schürer twice refers to my work at the end of footnotes, but does not think it worthy of a place in his list of recent authorities. The history which I have given in it of the development of the province Galatia is inconsistent with his

---

* Some of my German critics consider that I have spoken too strongly in my *Histor. Geogr.* regarding the erroneous ideas about the country held by some German scholars.

view, and I see no reason to alter what I have said on any important point: a Roman province must have had a name, and the name of the province in question was Galatia. I shall not spend time in arguing the point, but shall lay down the following series of propositions, which I believe to be correct and founded on the ancient authorities :—

1. The province in question was, in its origin, the kingdom left by Amyntas at his death in B.C. 25.

2. Amyntas was, in the estimation of the Romans, primarily and characteristically, king of Galatia. Galatia proper was the nucleus and the mainstay of his kingdom.

3. The first governor appointed is called " Governor of Galatia."

4. Inscriptions found in the extreme parts of Galatic Pisidia and Galatic Lycaonia mention the governor of the district as governor of Galatia. A striking case is the following :—A Latin official document of the most formal type, recording a demarcation of boundaries in the western part of Galatic Pisidia, and dating in A.D. 54, or immediately after, defines the Roman officer who carried out the delimitation as procurator, and an inscription of Iconium describes the same person as procurator of the Galatic province (C.I.G., 3991).*

5. Honorary inscriptions, in which it is an object to accumulate titles, speak of the official as governor of Galatia, Pontus, Paphlagonia, Pisidia, Phrygia, Lycaonia, etc.; but we possess the actual text of the inscription in which the people of Iconium expressed their gratitude to the procurator of the Galatic province, who had been charged by the Emperor Claudius with the duty of reorganising the city; hence they call him " Founder." The city takes its new name of Claudiconium in this inscription, and the date must be about the year 54.† Here Iconium formally reckons itself as Galatic.

6. When a large part of Pontus was incorporated in the province about A.D. 2—35 it was named Galaticus, *i.e.*, the part of Pontus attached to the province Galatia, as distinguished from Pontus Polemoniacus, *i.e.*, the part of Pontus governed by King Polemon.

---

* I have published it in *American Journal of Archæology*, 1886, p. 129, 1888, p. 267.

† C. I. G. 3991. The date is shown by the fact that the procurator was appointed by Claudius, who died October 13th, 54; and the inscription was composed under his successor Nero.

The term Galaticus implies that Galatia was recognised as the official name of the province. Precisely the same distinction exists between Lycaonia Galatica and Lycaonia Antiochiana (C. I. L., V., 8860).

7. There are cases in which the Roman official title of a province was a compound name, *e.g.*, Bithynia Pontus, Lycia Pamphylia, the three Eparchiæ, Cilicia, Lycaonia, Isauria. But in all these cases there was a permanent distinction between the component parts : each retained a certain individuality of constitution, which is well marked in our authorities. In the case of Galatia there is no trace * that such distinction between its constituent parts existed ; but all the evidence points to the conclusion that the parts were as much merged in the unity of the province as Phrygia was in Asia. The name Phrygia retained its geographical existence as a district of Asia ; but the official name of the province was Asia.

8. Under Vespasian the province Cappadocia was added to Galatia, but continued to enjoy a separate constitution. The governor presided over united, yet distinct, provinces ; and this novelty is clearly marked in the inscriptions, which henceforward use the plural term " provinciarum," or ἐπαρχειῶν.

9. After Cappadocia was separated from Galatia by Trajan, the plural usage persisted, at least in some cases, as is clear from the inscription given in C. I. L., III., Suppl., No. 6813. This is contrary to the old usage. The plural gave more dignity to the title ; and, moreover, it was in accordance with the spirit of individuality which was stimulated in these oriental districts by western education and feeling under the Empire. It is possible that the Koinon of the Lycaonians was founded under the Flavian Emperors, but I still think that it was instituted later (see *Hist. Geogr.*, p. 378). It is, however, not improbable that a distinction in constitution between Lycaonia and Galatia proper began in the Flavian period, and culminated in their separation between 137 and 161 A.D., when Lycaonia became one of the three southern Eparchiæ under a single governor.

---

* One exception, dating from the second century, is alluded to below (9). Consideration of space prevents me from discussing more fully the evidence in favour of identity in constitution among the various parts of Galatia Provincia.

CHAPTER II.

LOCALITIES OF THE FIRST JOURNEY.

I. PAMPHYLIA.

I T was about the year 48 or 49, probably, that Paul,
Barnabas, and Mark landed at Perga. They had sailed
some miles up the Cestrus in the ship which had brought
them from Paphos in Cyprus. The feat seems so remarkable in view of the present character of the river, even duly
considering the small size of the ship, as to show that much
attention must have been paid in ancient times to keeping
the channel of the river navigable. Similarly it is a well-
attested fact that Ephesus was formerly accessible to sea-
borne traffic, and the large works constructed along the
lower course of the Caystros to keep its channel open as
far as Ephesus, can still be seen as one rides from the city
down to the coast.

The only incident recorded as having occurred during
their stay, obviously a brief one, at Perga, has no relation
to the state of the country, and therefore we need not spend
time on it at present. At a later point in our investigation
it will be possible to acquire a better idea of the relations
among the three travellers and their separation, which took
place at Perga. At present we cannot gain from the
narrative any idea even of the time of year when they were
at that city.

Conybeare and Howson indeed in their *Life and Epistles*

*of St. Paul** argue that Paul and Barnabas came to Perga about May, and found the population removing *en masse* to the upper country, to live in the cooler glens amid the mountains of Taurus. In this way they explain why the apostles are not said to have preached in Perga ; they went on to the inner country, because no population remained in Perga to whom they could address themselves. But C. H. can hardly be right in supposing that a general migration of the ancient population took place annually in the spring or early summer. The modern custom which they mention, and which they suppose to be retained from old time, is due to the semi-nomadic character of the Turkish tribes that have come into the country at various times after the twelfth century. Even at the present day it is not the custom for the population of the coast towns, who have not been much affected by the mixture of Turkish blood, to move away in a body to the interior.† The migrations which take place are almost entirely confined to certain wandering tribes, chiefly Yuruks. A small number of the townsmen go up to the higher ground for reasons of health and comfort ; and this custom has in recent years become more common among the wealthier classes in the towns, who, however,

---

* I need not quote the pages of this excellent and scholarly work, partly because it is published in editions of various form, partly because any one who desires to verify my references to it can easily do so. As I shall often have occasion to refer to the book, I shall, for the sake of brevity, do so by the authors' initials C. H. In this particular point C. H. are followed by Canon Farrar.

† The rule is universal : such migrations occur only where the Turkish element in the population is supreme, and where therefore the nomadic habit has persisted. *Yaila* and *Kishla* denote the summer and the winter quarters respectively.

2

do not go away from the cities till the end of June or July. But a migration *en masse* is contrary to all that we know about the ancient population. The custom of living in the country within the territory of the city is a very different thing; and this was certainly practised by many of the people of Perga. But it is practically certain that the territory of Perga did not include any part of the upper highlands of Taurus; and there can be no doubt that the festivals and the ceremonial of the Pergæan Artemis went on throughout the summer, and were celebrated by the entire population. The government was kept up during summer in the same way as during winter.

2. Pisidia and Ayo Pavlo.

The apostles, starting from Perga, apparently after only a very brief stay, directed their steps to Antioch, the chief city of inner Pisidia, a Roman colony, a strong fortress, the centre of military and civil administration in the southern parts of the vast province called by the Romans Galatia. There can be no doubt that there existed close commercial relations between this metropolis on the north side of Taurus and the Pamphylian harbours, especially Side, Perga, and Attalia. The roads from Antioch to Perga and to Attalia coincide ; that which leads to Side is quite different. There can also be no doubt that in Antioch, as in many of the cities founded by the Seleucid kings of Syria, there was a considerable Jewish population. Josephus mentions that, when the fidelity of Asia Minor to the Seleucid kings was doubtful, 2,000 Jewish families were transported by one edict to the fortified towns of Lydia and Phrygia.* Being strangers to their neighbours in their new home, they were likely to be faithful to the Syrian kings; and special privileges were granted them in order to insure their fidelity. These privileges were confirmed by the Roman emperors; for the imperial policy was, from the time of Julius Cæsar onwards, almost invariably favourable to the Jews. The commerce of Antioch would in part come to Perga and Attalia; and in all probability the Jews of Antioch had an important share in this trade.

Paul therefore resolved to go to Antioch; and the immediate result was that one of his companions, for some reason about which we shall offer some suggestions later, abandoned the expedition, and returned to Jerusalem.

The commerce between Antioch and Perga or Attalia must of course have followed one definite route; and Paul and Barnabas would naturally choose this road. C. H. seem to me to select a very improbable path : they incline to the supposition that the Apostles went by the steep pass leading from Attalia to the Buldur Lake, the ancient Lake Ascania. Professor Kiepert, who has drawn the map attached to Renan's *Saint Paul*, makes the Apostles ascend the Cestrus for great part of its course, and then diverge towards Egerdir. C. H. also state unhesitatingly that the path led along the coast of the Egerdir double lakes, the ancient Limnai, the most picturesque sheet of water in Asia Minor. But the natural, easy, and direct course is along one of the eastern tributaries of the Cestrus to Adada ; and we must suppose

---

* Joseph., *Antiq. Jud.* xii. 3. It must be remembered that, though Antioch is generally called of "Pisidia," yet the bounds were very doubtful, and Strabo reckons Antioch to be in Phrygia. It was doubtless one of the fortresses here meant by Strabo.

that this commercial route was the one by which the strangers were directed.

Adada now bears the name of Kara Bavlo. Bavlo is exactly the modern pronunciation of the Apostle's name. In visiting the district I paid the closest attention to the name, in order to observe whether Baghlu might not be the real form, and Bavlo an invention of the Greeks, who often modify a Turkish name to a form that has a meaning in Greek.* But I found that the Turks certainly use the form Bavlo, not Baghlu. The analogy of many other modern Turkish names for cities makes it highly probable that the name Bavlo has arisen from the fact that Paul was the patron saint of the city, and the great church of the city was dedicated to him. It was very common in Byzantine times that the name of the saint to whom the church of a city was dedicated should come to be popularly used in place of the older city name. In this way apparently Adada became Ayo Pavlo. Now such religious names were specially a creation of the popular language, and accordingly they were taken up by the Turkish conquerors, and have in numerous cases persisted to the present day.†

It is impossible not to connect the fact that Adada

---

* For example, they have transformed Baluk hissar, "Town of the Castle," into Bali-kesri, "Old Cæsareia." Baluk, as I am informed by Kiepert, is an old Turkish word, not now used in the spoken language, meaning "town"; it is a very common element in Turkish names, and being now obsolete is commonly confused with other words. C. H. quote a report heard by Arundel about the existence of Bavlo (or Paoli, as he gives it); but they suppose it to be on the Eurymedon, and far away east of the road which they select.

† Various examples are given in *Hist. Geogr.*, p. 227 note; *e.g.*, Aitamas (*i.e.*, Ayi Thomas), Elias, Tefenni (*i.e.*, [εἰς Σ]τεφάνου), etc.

looked to St. Paul as its patron with its situation on the natural route between Antioch and Perga ; the church dedicated to Paul probably originated in the belief that the Apostle had visited Adada on his way to Antioch. There is no evidence to show whether this belief was founded on a genuine ancient tradition, or was only an inference, drawn after Adada was christianised, from the situation of the city ; but the latter alternative appears more probable. It is obvious from the narrative in Acts xiii. that Paul did not stop at Adada ; and it is not likely that there was a colony of Jews there, through whom he might make a beginning of his work, and who might retain the memory of his visit.

It is possible that some reference may yet be found in Eastern hagiological literature to the supposed visit of Paul to Adada, and to the church from which the modern name is derived. If the belief existed, there would almost certainly arise legends of incidents connected with the visit ; and though the local legends of this remote and obscure Pisidian city had little chance of penetrating into literature, there is a possibility that some memorial of them may still survive in manuscript.

Rather more than a mile south of the remains of Adada, on the west side of the road that leads to Perga, stand the ruins of a church of early date, built of fine masonry, but not of very great size. The solitary situation of this church by the roadside suggests to the spectator that there was connected with it some legend about an apostle or martyr of Adada. It stands in the forest, with trees growing in and around it ; and its walls rise to the height of five to eight feet above the present level of the soil. One single hut stands about half a mile away in the forest ; no other habitation is near. Adada itself is a solitary and deserted heap of ruins ; there is a small village with a fine spring of water about a mile north-east from it. So lonely is the country, that, as we approached it from the north our guide failed to find the ruins ; and, when he left us alone in the forest, we were obliged to go on for six miles to the nearest town before we could find a more trustworthy guide. After all, we found that we had passed within three or four hundred yards of the ruins, which lay on a hill above our path.

The ruins of Adada are very imposing from their extent, from the perfection of several small temples, and from their comparative immunity from spoliation. No one has used them as a quarry, which is the usual fate of ancient cities. The buildings are rather rude and provincial in type, show-ing that the town retained more of the native character, and was less completely affected by the general Græco-Roman civilisation of the empire. I may here quote a few sentences which I wrote immediately after visiting the ruins.*

" With little trouble, and at no great expense, the mass of ruins might be sorted and thoroughly examined, the whole plan of the city discovered, and a great deal of information obtained about its condition under the empire. Nothing can be expected from the ruins to adorn a museum ; for it is improbable than any fine works of art ever came to Adada, and certain that any accessible fragment of marble which ever was there has been carried

---

* *Athenæum,* July 1890, p. 136, in a letter written in part by my friend and fellow-traveller Mr. Hogarth ; the description of Adada was assigned to me.

away long ago. But for a picture of society as it was formed by Græco-Roman civilisation in an Asiatic people, there is perhaps no place where the expenditure of a few hundreds would produce such results. The opinion will not be universally accepted that the most important and interesting part of ancient history is the study of the evolution of society during the long conflict between Christianity and paganism; but those who hold this opinion will not easily find a work more interesting and fruitful at the price than the excavation of Adada."

C. H. are right in emphasizing the dangers to which travellers were exposed in this part of their journey: "perils of rivers, perils of robbers." The following instances, not known to C. H., may be here quoted. They all belong to the Pisidian highlands, not far from the road traversed by the Apostles,* and, considering how ignorant we are of the character of the country and the population, it is remarkable that such a large proportion of our scanty information relates to scenes of danger and precautions against violence.

1. A dedication and thank-offering by Menis son of Daos to Jupiter, Neptune, Minerva, and all the gods, and also to the river Eurus, after he had been in danger and had been saved.† This inscription records an escape from drowning in a torrent swollen by rain. There is no river in the neighbourhood which could cause danger to a man, except when swollen by rain.

---

* If the road was frequented by commerce, it would of course be more dangerous. Brigands must make a living, and go where most money is to be found.

† Abbé Duchesne in *Bulletin de Corresp. Hellen.*, vol. iii., p. 479. The name of the river is uncertain, Eurus or Syrus; I tried in vain to find the stone in 1886, in order to verify the text.

2. An epitaph erected by Patrokles and Douda over the grave of their son, Sousou, a policeman, who was slain by robbers.*

3. References to *gens d'armes* of various classes (ὁρο-φύλακες, παραφυλακῖται) occur with unusual frequency in this district. Very few soldiers were stationed in Pisidia ; and armed policemen were a necessity in such an unruly country.†

4. A *stationarius*, part of whose duty was to assist in the capture of runaway slaves (often the most dangerous of brigands), is also mentioned in an inscription.‡

The roads all over the Roman Empire were apt to be unsafe, for the arrangements for insuring public safety were exceedingly defective ; but probably the part of his life which St. Paul had most in mind when he wrote about the perils of rivers and of robbers, which he had faced in his journeys, was the journey from Perga across Taurus to Antioch and back again.

Between Adada and Antioch the road is uncertain. One of the paths leads along the south-east end of Egerdir Lake, traversing the difficult pass now called Demir Kapu, "the Iron Gate." But I believe there is a more direct and easy road, turning from Adada towards the north-east, though further exploration is needed before it is possible to speak confidently.

* Professor Sterrett in *Epigraphic Journey in Asia Minor*, p. 166.

† *Historical Geography of Asia Minor*, pp. 177 ff.

‡ *Mittheilungen des Instituts zu Athen*, 1885, p. 77. Examples might be multiplied by including the parts of Taurus farther removed from the road. On the whole subject see the paper of Professor O. Hirschfeld in *Berlin. Sitzungsber.*, 1891, pp. 845 ff., on "Die Sicherheitspolizei im römischen Kaiserreich."

3. PISIDIAN ANTIOCH.

The city of Antioch was the governing and military centre of the southern half of the vast province of Galatia, which at this time extended from north to south right across the plateau of Asia Minor, nearly reaching the Mediterranean on the south and the Black Sea on the north. Under the early emperors it possessed a rank and importance far beyond what belonged to it in later times. This was due to the fact that between 10 B.C. and 72 A.D. the "pacification"—*i.e.*, the completion of the conquest and organisation—of southern Galatia was in active progress, and was conducted from Antioch as centre. Under Claudius, 41-54 A.D., the process of pacification was in especially active progress, and Antioch was at the acme of its importance.

In the Roman style, then, Antioch belonged to Galatia, but, in popular language and according to geographical situation, it was said to be a city of Phrygia. Even a Roman might speak of Antioch as a city of Phrygia, if he were laying stress on geographical or ethnological considerations ; for the province of Galatia was so large that the Romans themselves subdivided it into districts (which are enumerated in many Latin inscriptions), *e.g.*, Paphlagonia, Phrygia, Isauria, Lycaonia, Pisidia, etc.* It is commonly said that Antioch belonged to Pisidia, but, for the time with which we are dealing, this is erroneous. Strabo is quite clear on the point.† But after the time of Strabo there took

---

* See note appended to Chap. i.

† See pages 557, 569, 577. Ptolemy mentions Antioch twice, v. 4. 11, and v. 5. 4; in one case he assigns it to the district Pisidia and the province Galatia, in the other to the district Pisidian Phrygia (*i.e.* the part of Phrygia which had come to be included in

place a gradual widening of the term Pisidia to include all
the country that lay between the bounds of the province of
Asia and Pisidia proper. It is important to observe this
and similar cases in which the denotation of geographical
names in Asia Minor gradually changes, as the use of a
name sometimes gives a valuable indication of the date
of the document in which it occurs.

The accurate and full geographical description of Antioch
about 45-50 A.D. was "a Phrygian city on the side of
Pisidia" (Φρυγία πόλις πρὸς Πισιδίᾳ). The latter addition
was used in Asia Minor to distinguish it from Antioch on
the Mæander, on the borders of Caria and Phrygia. But
the world in general wished to distinguish Antioch from
the great Syrian city, not from the small Carian city ;
hence the shorter expression " Pisidian Antioch " (Ἀντιόχεια
ἡ Πισιδία),* came into use, and finally, as the term Pisidia
was widened, "Antioch of Pisidia" became almost universal. The latter term is used by Ptolemy, v. 4. 11, and
occurs in some inferior MSS. in Acts xiii. 14. " Pisidian
Antioch," however, is admittedly the proper reading in the
latter passage.†

Pisidia) and the province Pamphylia. This error arises from his
using two authorities belonging to different periods, and not understanding the relation between them. He makes the same mistake
about several other places : *e.g.*, Olba, Claudiopolis, etc. (*Hist.
Geogr.*, pp. 336, 363, 405, 447).

* Compare Ptolemy's " Pisidian Phrygia," quoted in the preceding
note.

† *Codex Bezæ* reads " Antioch of Pisidia," which is one of many
proofs that it is founded on a modernisation of the text made not
earlier than the second century by an intelligent and well-informed
editor. This editor introduced various changes which betray the
topography of the second century.

From these facts we can infer that it would have been an insult to an Antiochian audience, the people of a Roman Colonia, to address them as Pisidians. Pisidia was the " barbarian " mountain country that lay between them and Pamphylia ; it was a country almost wholly destitute of Greek culture, ignorant of Greek games and arts, and barely subjugated by Roman arms. Antioch was the guard set upon these Pisidian robbers, the trusted agent of the imperial authority, the centre of the military system designed to protect the subjects of Rome. " Men of Galatia " is the only possible address in cases where " Men of Antioch " is not suitable ; * and " a city of Phrygia " is the geographical designation which a person familiar with the city would use if the honorific title " a city of Galatia " was not suitable. These accurate terms were used by the Roman Paul, and they are used in the original document employed by the author of Acts, though in one case the looser but commoner phrase, " Pisidian Antioch," is used to distinguish it from Syrian Antioch.

4. ROUTE FROM ANTIOCH TO ICONIUM.

As to the route by which Paul and Barnabas travelled from Antioch to Iconium, widely varying opinions have been entertained by recent authorities. Professor Kiepert, the greatest perhaps of living geographers, who has paid special attention to the difficult problems of the topography of Asia Minor, has, in the map attached to Renan's *Saint Paul*, represented that in all his three journeys Paul travelled between the two cities along the great Eastern

---

* " Phrygians " was also an impossible address, for Phrygian had in Greek and Latin become practically equivalent to slave.

Trade Route,* a section of which connected Philomelium and Laodicea Katakekaumene : according to Kiepert, Paul crossed the Sultan Dagh to join this route at Philomelium, and left it again at Laodicea to go south to Iconium. C. H. indicate his route along the western side of Sultan Dagh, until that lofty ridge breaks down into hilly country on the south, across which the route goes in as direct a line as possible to Iconium. The map attached to Canon Farrar's *Saint Paul* indicates a route midway between these two, passing pretty exactly along the highest ridge of the Sultan Dagh.

The line marked out by C. H., though not exactly correct, approximates much more closely than either of the others to that which we may unhesitatingly pronounce to be the natural and probable one. But, partly in deference to Professor Kiepert's well-deserved and universally acknowledged authority, and partly on account of an interesting problem of Christian antiquities which in part hinges on this question, it is necessary to state as briefly as possible the main facts.

According to Kiepert, Paul in going and in returning crossed the lofty Sultan Dagh. There is no actual pass across that lofty ridge. The path climbs a steep and rugged glen on one side, crosses the summit of the ridge fully 4,000 feet above the town of Antioch, and descends a similar glen on the other side.† On the map Antioch seems very near Philomelium ; but six hours of very toilsome travelling lie between them. Then follows a

---

* Of this road, which came into use during the later centuries B.C., and which was the main artery of communication and government in Asia Minor under the Roman Empire, a full account is given *Hist. Geogr.*, chaps. iii., iv.

† See the description given of the crossing by my friend, Professor Sterrett, in his *Epigraphic Journey in Asia Minor*, p. 164.

peculiarly unpleasant road, twenty-eight hours * in length,
by Laodicea to Iconium. Except in the towns that lie on
the road, there is hardly any shade and little water along
its course. It is exposed to the sun from its rising to its
setting : and, if my memory is correct, there are only two
places where a tree or two by the roadside afford a little
shadow and a rest for the traveller. This road makes a
circuit, keeping to the level plain throughout ; but it would
not be used by pedestrians like Paul and Barnabas. If
they went to Philomelium, they would naturally prefer the
direct road thence to Iconium through the hill country by
Kaballa. This path is nowhere very steep or difficult, is
often shady and pleasant, and is shorter by an hour or two
than the road through Laodicea ; it is in all probability
older than the great Trade Route, and was undoubtedly
used at all periods for direct communication by horse or
foot passengers between Philomelium and Iconium.

But there is no reason to think that Paul ever crossed the
Sultan Dagh. The natural path from Antioch to Iconium
went nearly due south for six hours by the new Roman
road to Neapolis, the new city which was just growing up
at the time.† Thence it went to Misthia on the north-

---

* The " hour " indicates a distance of about three miles, or slightly
over. The exact distances, as measured for the proposed extension
of the Ottoman Railway, are,—

    Philomelium to Arkut Khan . . 18 miles (6 hours).
    Arkut Khan to Tyriaion (Ilghin) . $10\frac{1}{2}$,, ($3\frac{1}{2}$,,).
    Ilghin to Kadin Khan . . . $16\frac{1}{2}$,, ($5\frac{1}{2}$,,).
    Kadin Khan to Laodicea . . . 13 ,, (4 ,,).

From Laodicea (Ladik) to Iconium the distance (43 miles) is
measured by a circuitous route to avoid a ridge : the distance by
road cannot be much over 27 miles (9 hours). I am indebted for
these figures to Mr. Purser and Mr. Cook.

† On the history of Neapolis, see *Hist. Geogr.*, pp. 396-7

eastern shores of the great lake Caralis.   A little way beyond
Misthia it diverged from the Roman road, and crossed the
hilly country by a very easy route to Iconium.   The total
distance from Antioch to Iconium by this route is about
twenty-seven hours,* as compared with thirty-two or thirty-
four by way of Philomelium.   This route is still in regular
use at the present day.

The line indicated in the map of C. H. is straighter, and
I believe that it is actually practicable ; but it has never
been traversed by any explorer, and I know only part of
the country through which it runs.   It would pass east
of Neapolis, and may possibly have been a track of communication in older time.   But in B.C. 6 Augustus formed
a series of roads to connect the Roman colonies which
he founded as fortresses of defence against the Pisidian
mountain tribes.†   Hence we might feel some confidence
in assuming that Paul and Barnabas would walk as far as
possible along the Roman road.   This road indeed was not
the shortest line between Antioch and Iconium, because
its purpose was to connect Antioch, the military centre of
defence, with the two eastern colonies, Lystra and Parlais ;
and it did not touch Iconium.   But communication would
be so organised as to use the well-made road to the utmost ;
all trade undoubtedly followed this track, entertainment
for travellers was naturally provided along it, and the direct
path, though a little shorter, would be less convenient
and would no longer be thought of or used.   We are

* Arundel, *Asia Minor*, ii., p. 8., gives the distance as twenty-
eight hours by report ; neither he nor Hamilton traversed this route.
No description of the road is published, so far as I remember.

† The existence of a system of military roads may always be
assumed, according to the Roman custom, connecting a system of
fortresses (*coloniæ*) on these roads.   See pages 32, 34.

not, however, left in this case to mere probabilities. We have the express testimony of an ancient document that Paul used this Roman road; and my object in giving this minute and perhaps tedious description of the road and of its origin has been to bring home to the reader the exactness with which this document describes the actual facts.

The document in question is one of the apocryphal Apostle-legends, the *Acts of Paul and Thekla*. The general opinion of recent scholars * is that this tale was composed about the latter part of the second century; and in that case it would have no historical value, except in so far as it quoted older documents. Reserving for another place the whole question of the date and character of these Acta, we are at present concerned only with one passage, in which the road from Antioch to Iconium is described.

In the opening of the Acta a certain Onesiphorus, resident at Iconium, heard that Paul was intending to come thither from Antioch. Accordingly he went forth from the city to meet him, and to invite him to his house. And he proceeded as far as the Royal Road that leads to Lystra, and there he stood waiting for Paul; and he scanned the features of the passers-by.† And he saw Paul coming, a

---

* There are some exceptions.

† The Greek text is usually and naturally translated, "he proceeded along the Royal Road," but the following εἱστήκει implies that the first clause indicates the point to which Onesiphorus went and where he stood. The Syriac translation makes the sense quite clear: "he went and stood where the roads meet, on the highway which goes to Lystra." Lipsius, in his recent critical edition, omits this Syriac passage, which is of cardinal importance. In several cases he shows a preference for the easiest, the least characteristic, and therefore the worst reading; *e.g.*, he here prefers ἐρχομένους to διερχομένους.

man small in size, with meeting eyebrows, with a rather large nose, baldheaded, bowlegged, strongly built, full of grace, for at times he looked like a man, and at times he had the face of an angel. This plain and unflattering account of the Apostle's personal appearance seems to embody a very early tradition.

The "Royal Road" (βασιλικὴ ὁδός, *via regalis*) that leads to Lystra is obviously the Roman road built by Augustus from Antioch to Lystra. The epithet is a remarkable one, and very difficult to explain. The first impression that any one would receive from it is that it denotes the Roman road built by the Basileis, as the emperors were commonly called in the second century, and that it points to a second century date more naturally than to any earlier period.

So far as I can judge, this argument as to date would be unanswerable, were it not for an inscription discovered in 1884 at Comama, the most western of Augustus' Pisidian colonies, a city whose name had entirely disappeared from human knowledge until this and other Latin inscriptions were found on the site. It was then observed that numerous coins of the city existed, but had been misread and attributed to Comana in Cappadocia ; it also appeared that the city was mentioned by Ptolemy and other authorities, but that the name was always corrupted.

In the ruins of Comama there still lies a milestone, with the inscription—

> "The Emperor Cæsar Augustus, son of a god, Pontifex Maximus, etc., constructed the Royal Road by the care of his lieutenant, Cornelius Aquila."*

---

* C. I. L. III., Supplem., No. 6,974. Regalem, suggested tentatively by Mommsen, suits the copy in my note-book even better than appears from the printed text, and may safely be accepted.

The roads built by Augustus to connect his Pisidian colonies* were doubtless built with a solidity unusual in the country. They are two in number, one leading to Olbasa Comama and Cremna, the other to Parlais and Lystra. The former is called Via Regalis on the milestone, the latter in the *Acta*.

The original *Acta* then described the scene with a minute fidelity possible only to a person who knew the localities. Onesiphorus went out from Iconium till he came to the point a few miles south of Misthia, where the path to Iconium diverged from the built Roman road that led from Antioch to Lystra ; and here he waited till he observed Paul coming towards him. I am far from assuming that the facts here narrated are historical ; but I do hold that the tale was written down by a person familiar with the localities, and that the route now employed for traffic between Iconium and Antioch was used to the exclusion of any other at the time when he wrote.

It is therefore proved that the term Royal Road in the Acta furnishes no proof of a second century date. It may even be proved that the term is not consistent with an origin later than the first century, because the very name Via Regalis, denoting the road from Antioch to Lystra, was soon disused. The sentence where it occurs was written†

---

* The name " Pisidian " is convenient, though they were not all in Pisidia. Augustus in enumerating his colonies seems to sum them all up as in Pisidia. (Mommsen, *Monumentum Ancyranum*, p. 119.) But colonies on the Pisidian frontier to keep under control the Pisidian mountain tribes are readily called Pisidian. Thus we have above explained the term " Pisidian Antioch."

† No mere tradition can be so strong as to fix in the memory of posterity verbal peculiarities which no longer correspond to actual facts. It will appear in the following paragraphs that the name Via Regalis was retained in the text long after it had ceased to be understood.

3

before the name passed out of use. Can we fix approximately the date when the name ceased to exist, and before which some written authority for the tale must have come into existence? Several arguments point decisively to the conclusion that the name did not survive the first century, but belonged to a state of the country which characterised the first half of the first century and then ceased to exist. As this subject is of great consequence in our attempt to realise the circumstances in which Paul's journey was made, and has never been properly described or understood, I shall try to state briefly the main facts.

The purpose of Augustus's roads was to keep in order the recently subdued Pisidian mountaineers. When the pacification of Pisidia, and the naturalisation of the imperial rule and the Græco-Roman civilisation in the country had been completed, the need for these roads disappeared ; they were no longer maintained by the imperial government with the care that was applied to roads of military importance, and they were merged in the general system of communication across Asia Minor.*

The period when this pacification of Pisidia was taking place can be determined precisely from the evidence of coins, of inscriptions, and of authors, and from the dates at which the constitutions of cities on the northern frontiers were fixed. I need not weary the reader by enumerating here the long lists of facts, which show that the earlier emperors from Augustus to Nero directed close and continuous attention to this district of Asia Minor, and that in the reign of Claudius the process of organisation

---

* This opinion was arrived at as the natural explanation of the known facts, and published before its application to the present case had become apparent. (See *Hist. Geogr.*, pp. 57–8.)

was in specially active progress. Vespasian in A.D. 74 remodelled the government, separated great part of Pisidia from the province of Galatia, and attached it to Pamphylia,* This marks the end of the Pisidian colonial system and military roads. Antioch, the centre of the system, was now entirely separated from at least three of the colonies.† which were transferred to a different province. Moreover there were no soldiers in the province Lycia-Pamphylia, as there were in Galatia ; great part of Pisidia would not have been united to the unarmed province, unless all possible need for soldiers and garrisons had been considered to be at an end.

Lystra, the most easterly point of the colonial system, must have been a place of great importance under the early emperors ; but after 74 it sank back into the insignificance of a small provincial town with nothing to distinguish it. Direct communication between Antioch and Lystra had previously been maintained only for military and political reasons ; no commerce could ever have existed between them. After A.D. 74 therefore the road from Antioch to Lystra ceased to be thought of as a highway, and must have disappeared from popular language. Iconium, not Lystra, was the natural commercial centre, and has maintained that rank from the earliest time to the present day. Thus the road from Antioch to Iconium was, after the year 74, the only one present to the popular mind ; and it ceased to be possible that a traveller from Antioch to Iconium should be described as going along the road to Lystra for a certain distance and then diverging from it.

---

* He made Lycia and Pamphylia a single province.

† Comama, Cremna, and Olbasa were henceforth attached to Pamphylia.

It is characteristic of the way in which the figure of Paul dwarfed that of Barnabas in the memory of later generations that no reference to the latter occurs in these *Acta.* The companions of Paul are only the treacherous Hermogenes and Demas.   An example of the same feeling is observable in the text of *Codex Bezæ*, xiv., 1.   The reviser has there substituted "he" for "they."*   The change is entirely out of accord with the tone of the "Travel-Document," but in perfect agreement with later tradition in the district, as attested in the *Acta* of Paul and Thekla. Such a change would not naturally be made except in a country where the memory and influence of St. Paul was especially strong.   That this was the case in Phrygia during the second century is proved by the Testament of Avircius Marcellus, dating about 190–200 A D. ; † and we may safely assume that the same feeling would remain in the Galatian churches.

5. ICONIUM.

According to the route described, Paul and Barnabas entered Iconium from the west, having a good view of the extensive gardens and orchards, which form such a charming feature of the suburbs.   C. H. give a very fair account of Iconium,‡ of the great part that it played in later history, and of the natural features amid which it is placed,

---

* εἰσελθεῖν αὐτὸν εἰς τὴν συναγωγήν.   On the reviser, his character and date, see Chapter VIII.

† See *Expositor*, April 1889, p. 265.

‡ But they ought not to quote Leake's incorrect statement that Mount Argæus in Cappadocia is visible from the outskirts of the city.   Hamilton has rightly expressed his disbelief in this statement.   The two snowy peaks which Leake saw are the peaks of the Hassan Dagh, a lofty mountain north-west of Tyana, which I

at the western extremity of the vast plains of Lycaonia, with a mountainous country beginning to the west about six miles away, and hills on the north and south at a distance of about ten or twelve miles.

Iconium was in early times a city of Phrygia, situated on the eastern frontier, where Phrygia borders on Lycaonia ; but in later times it was called a city of Lycaonia. It is important for our purposes to discover at what period it began to be called a city of Lycaonia and ceâsed to be Phrygian. Modern geographers all state that no writer later than Xenophon calls Iconium Phrygian ; but this is erroneous. In Acts xiv. 6 the apostles, being in danger at Iconium, are said to "have fled to the cities of Lycaonia, Lystra, and Derbe, and the surrounding country." The writer obviously considered that in their flight from Iconium to a town eighteen miles distant they crossed the Lycaonian frontier, and his view is precisely that of Xenophon, who also entered Lycaonia immediately on leaving Iconium.

The coincidence is perfect. The phrase is a striking instance of local accuracy, and at the same time a strong proof that even in the first century after Christ Iconium was by the natives reckoned as Phrygian. It is true that Cicero, Strabo, and Pliny make Iconium a Lycaonian city. This constitutes a perfectly satisfactory proof that such was the general usage between at least 100 B.C. and 100 A.D., founded on the fact that for administrative purposes Iconium was united with Lycaonia ; but it is quite con-

---

have seen from a still greater distance. The summit of Argæus is single, and though it is higher than Hassan Dagh, being about 13,000 feet, it could not possibly be visible from such a distance as Iconium ; moreover, Hassan Dagh lies right in the way.

sistent with the view that the Iconians continued to count themselves Phrygian, and to distinguish themselves from their Lycaonian neighbours even after they were united with them in one governmental district. The witness to this view actually visited Iconium, came into intimate relations with the people, and spoke according to the native fashion.

In the third century another visitor's testimony assigns Iconium to Phrygia. The witness is Firmilian, Bishop of Cæsarea in Cappadocia. It is certain that he had visited the city, for he implies that he was present at the council held there about 215 A.D.*

The supposition that the Iconians clung to their old nationality, after it had become a mere historical memory devoid of political reality, may appear rather hazardous, as the ancients are certainly rather loose in using geographical terms. But one who has studied the history of Asia Minor realises how persistently ethnical and national distinctions were maintained, and how strong were the prejudice and even antipathy felt by each tribe or nation against its neighbours. The Iconians cherished their pride of birth ; and in all probability difference of language originally emphasised their diversity from their Lycaonian neighbours. It is inconsistent with the whole character of these races to suppose that the Phrygians of Iconium could be brought to call themselves Lycaonians, and to give up the old tribal hatred against their nearest neighbours. It was precisely the nearness which accentuated the hatred.

---

* See Cyprian, Epist. lxxv. 7. On the other hand, Ammianus speaks of it as a town of Pisidia ; the rearrangement of the provinces about A.D. 297 led to this temporary connection, which does not concern us. (See *Hist. Geogr.*, p. 393.)

This tribal jealousy is characteristic of Asia Minor still. The traveller frequently finds the people of two neighbouring villages differing from each other in manners and in dress ; they speak the same language, profess the same religion, but have little intercourse with each other and no intermarriage, and each village regards the other as hateful and alien.*

But I should hardly have ventured to state this supposition publicly, were I not able to prove it by the testimony of the only native of Iconium whose evidence is preserved to us. In the year 163 A.D. Hierax, one of the Christians associated with Justin Martyr in his trial before the Prefect of Rome, Junius Rusticus, was asked by the judge who his parents were. He replied, " My earthly parents are dead ; and I have come hither (*i.e.*, as a slave), torn away from Iconium of Phrygia."†

By this single testimony of a native, preserved in such an accidental way, we are enabled to realise that the expression in Acts xiv. 6 was contrary to general usage and peculiar to Iconium, and that it could hardly have occurred except to one who had actually lived in the city and caught the tone of its population. It is perhaps unnecessary for

---

* After the " Union of the Lycaonians " was established towards the middle of the second century after Christ, Iconium was not a member ; but we are precluded from using this fact as evidence that Iconium still held aloof in social matters from the Lycaonians, for it had been made a Roman colony by Hadrian, and as such it was raised far above the level of the " Union "; the colony Lystra, also, though originally a Lycaonian city, did not condescend to join it.

† Rusticus was prefect in A.D. 163, as Borghesi has shown. Hierax was in all probability a slave of the Emperor. It is noteworthy that Ruinart proposed to change Phrygia in the text to Lycaonia, not recognising the importance of this testimony. (See *Acta Justini*, 3.)

me to reply to the possible objection that Cicero also
visited Iconium, and yet he calls it part of Lycaonia ; no
one who has comprehended the reasoning would make this
objection.   Cicero was a Roman governor, who looked on
Iconium merely as the chief city of the government district.
He did not mix with the people or catch their expressions.
He was devoid of interest in the people, the country, the
scenery, and the antiquities ; the smallest scrap of political
gossip or social scandal from Rome bulked more largely in
his mind than the entire interests of Lycaonia.   A complete
change of feeling towards the provincials was produced
by the Imperial government; and no better proof of the
change can be found than the contrast between Pliny's and
Cicero's letters written from their respective provinces.

The two instances which have been mentioned in this
chapter show how accidental is the preservation of the
knowledge which enables us to refute negative arguments.
But for the answer given in the Roman trial by a native of
Iconium in 163 A.D., we should be unable to reply to the
argument that the phrase in Acts is inaccurate, because
Iconium was universally entitled Lycaonian in the centuries
immediately before and after Christ ; and but for the accident that in 1884 the present writer persevered in minutely
examining a hillock in the plain, which had previously
been passed by other travellers unnoticed, we should be
unable to answer the presumption that the term " Royal
Road," as applied to a Roman Imperial road, indicated
rather a second than a first century date.

Iconium was, under the Persian Empire, a part of
Phrygia.   Afterwards geographical situation prevailed over
tribal character, and it came to be recognised by the world
in general as the chief city of Lycaonia.   This may pro-

bably have taken place during the third century B.C., when it was part of the vast kingdom ruled by the Seleucidæ of Syria. It was perhaps in 63 B.C. that a tetrarchy of Lycaonia, containing fourteen cities, with Iconium as capital, was formed. This tetrarchy was given to King Polemo in 39 B.C. by Mark Antony ; but soon afterwards it passed into the hands of King Amyntas, and on his death it became a Roman province in 25 B.C. The tetrarchy included Derbe, which was the frontier city of the Roman Empire in this quarter down to the year 72 A.D.

Under the Roman Empire one of the most prominent features in the development of society in Asia Minor was the way in which it was affected, first by the Greek, and afterwards by the Græco-Roman civilisation. The Greek civilisation was dominant in a few great cities, which had been founded or reorganised by the Greek kings, and into which many foreigners—Greeks, Syrians, and Jews—had been introduced. But it never affected the country very strongly until Roman organisation began to spread abroad that mixture of Greek and Roman ideas which we may style the Græco-Roman civilisation. Few questions relating to Asia Minor during the first two centuries of the Empire can be understood properly unless we appreciate the true character of this movement, which took the form of a conflict between the native, primitive, Oriental, " barbarian " * manners of the country and the new European fashion. The western civilisation and spirit spread first through the towns, and at a later time very slowly through the country districts. All who got any education learned the Greek

---

* The term "barbarian" is, of course, used here to indicate all that is opposed in character to "Græco-Roman."

language, adopted Greek manners, and no doubt Greek dress also, called themselves, their children, and their gods by Greek names, and affected to identify their religion with that of Greece and Rome. All this class of persons despised the native language and the native ways ; and just as they adopted Greek mythology and Greek anthropomorphic spirit in religion, so they often professed to be connected with, or descended from, the Greeks.*

In Iconium especially, the metropolis of the tetrarchy, the population, we may be sure, prided themselves on their modern spirit and their high civilisation ; and they naturally distinguished themselves both from the rustics of the villages, and from the people of the non-Roman part of Lycaonia. Now it is a fact that the latter were called at this time Lycaones ; the name appears on the coins of Antiochus IV., who was their king from A.D. 38 to 72.† In contrast to them, the Iconians prided themselves on belonging to the Roman province ; for the loyalty of the Asian provinces to the empire was extraordinarily strong. But, if they contrasted themselves with the Lycaonian subjects of a barbarian king, by what ethnic or geographical name could they designate themselves ? "Phrygian" was equivalent in popular usage to "slave." There was no

---

* It is characteristic of the inconsistencies and curiosities of "patriotism," that the same persons who stubbornly maintained that they were Phrygians in contrast with their Lycaonian neighbours, were flattered by any suggestion that they were of the Greek style and kindred. Myths of the Greek origin of Phrygian cities are common (see, *e.g.*, Synnada, *Hist. Geogr.*, p. 14). It would have been, of course, treasonable to coquet in any way with the name "Roman."

† With a brief interval, 39–41, during which he was deprived of his kingdom by Caligula.

possible name for them except that which was derived from the Roman province to which they belonged. I can entertain no doubt that about 50 A.D. the address by which an orator would most please the Iconians, in situations where the term "Iconians" was unsuitable, was ἄνδρες Γαλάται, "gentlemen of the Galatic province." This general term was still more necessary in addressing a mixed audience drawn from various towns of the Roman part of Lycaonia.* Some term applicable to all, yet not calculated to grate on the ethnic prejudices of any, was needed for purposes of courtesy. Besides using this generic term, the skilful orator would also introduce allusions to the Greek feeling and culture of his audience, assuming that they belonged to the more advanced and intelligent part of the population.

This tone of courtesy and solicitude for the feelings of his audience, which we attribute to the supposed orator of the period, is precisely the tone in which Paul addresses the "Galatians"; and he introduces in iii. 28 an allusion to them as Greeks, when he contrasts them with the Jews.

The most instructive commentary on St. Paul's way of addressing the Galatians is to be found in the orations of Dio Chrysostom half a century later, addressed to the people of Nicomedeia, of Nicæa, of Apameia in Bithynia, and of Apameia in Phrygia. In the latter case he pointedly avoids an ethnic term: "Phrygians" had a bad connotation, "Asians" was too general; and he styles them simply

---

* But when we take into account that Antioch also was one of the churches addressed, the term "Galatians" becomes still more necessary. In the apostrophe, "Ye foolish Galatians," the adjective is softened by the polite and general ethnic appellation: it would have been personal and rude to say, "Ye foolish Antiochians and Iconians," etc.

"Gentlemen." But he uses the old historic name Kelainai, not the modern name Apameia, ·and he speaks of their country sometimes as Asia, sometimes by the more precise geographical term Phrygia.

An objection may be urged that Christianity was opposed to such a tone as is here implied in the civilised towns-people towards the ruder population of the uncivilised extra-Roman districts. But this objection seems to be out of keeping with the facts. The Christian Church in Asia Minor was always opposed to the primitive native cha-racter. It was Christianity, and not the Imperial govern-ment, which finally destroyed the native languages, and made Greek the universal language of Asia Minor. The new religion was strong in the towns before it had any hold of the country parts. The ruder and the less civilised any district was, the slower was Christianity in permeating it. Christianity in the early centuries was the religion of the more advanced, not of the "barbarian," peoples; and in fact it seems to be nearly confined within the limits of the Roman world, and practically to take little thought of any people beyond, though in theory "Barbarian and Scythian" are included in it.

Why then, it may be asked, does St. Paul counte-nance the expression, "the cities of Lycaonia, Lystra and Derbe"? Simply because in the narrative he is expressing himself geographically, and is using the precise words in which his advisers and informants might have described his route to him when he was arranging his flight from Iconium, whereas in the epistle he is using the language of polite address. Lystra and Derbe were cities of Lycaonia Galatica, *i.e.*, the part of Lycaonia which was attached to the province Galatia, while Iconium reckoned itself as a city of Phrygia Galatica, *i.e.*, the part of Phrygia which was attached to the province Galatia.

The account of Iconium given by Mr. Lewin and by Canon Farrar (who is in perfect agreement with him) differs greatly from that which has just been given. The latter calls it " the capital city of an independent tetrarchy," says that it was not in the province Galatia, * and that " the diversity of political governments which at this time prevailed in Asia Minor was so far an advantage to the apostles that it rendered them more able to escape from one jurisdiction to another." In so far as it concerns antiquities, this view is against the evidence ; † and, when a correct map is before us, we see that Paul did not use the frontier, like the modern brigands in Turkish Macedonia, to " dodge the law." He did not go out of the Roman province, but found safety through the self-government of the various cities. He never came into collision with the Roman administration on this first journey, but only with the city officials ; and the action of the magistrates of Antioch had no force beyond the territory that belonged to the city.

There is an interesting reading in *Codex Bezæ*, xiv. 2. " The archisynagogoi of the Jews and the rulers of the synagogue brought persecution against them κατὰ τῶν

---

* I find that this error is widespread. Dr. Salmon, *Introduction to the New Testament*, 1891, Chap. XVIII., p. 323, even employs it to get a proof of the historical accuracy of Acts. Coins are extant struck by Iconium as a Roman city from the time of Claudius onwards; and it was certainly Roman from B.C. 25.

† It would be tedious and unsuitable for the present occasion to discuss the evidence ; but the allusion to evidence against him made by Canon Farrar in note 1, p. 378, is sufficient to disprove his own case.

δικαίων, and stirred up the souls of the Gentiles against the brethren. And the Lord quickly gave peace." *

The officials of the synagogue are here clearly distinguished from the archisynagogoi. The distinction is perfectly correct, and makes an important addition to our knowledge of the administration of the Jewish synagogues in Asia Minor.† The carefulness with which the different classes of Jews are enumerated seems hardly explicable except on the supposition that actual popular tradition is here preserved. Such minuteness is not consistent with mere expansion of the text by a scholiast or composer of glosses. The reviser had something definite to relate.

The words κατὰ τῶν δικαίων, " against the just ones," are perhaps a gloss on αὐτοῖς ; and they are so rendered in the Latin version. But I cannot help suspecting that they are used in a different and unusual sense, *viz.*, " in respect of legal proceedings," and that they embody a tradition which survived in Iconium to the effect that Paul was prosecuted before the city magistrates. In the *Acta* of Paul and Thekla, the same tradition is preserved in a later and more corrupt form. In the latter place, the legal proceedings take place in the most absurd and impossible way before a Roman governor and proconsul.‡ Here the term is consistent with, and even suggests, proceedings before the magistrates of the city ; and only such a trial is possible in this case, for Iconium was not the residence of the

---

* [οἱ δὲ ἀρχισυνάγωγοι τῶν Ἰουδαίων καὶ οἱ ἄρχοντες τῆς συναγωγῆς ἐπήγαγον αὐτοῖς διωγμὸν κατὰ τῶν δικαίων, καὶ] ἐκάκωσαν τὰς ψυχὰς τῶν ἐθνῶν κατὰ τῶν ἀδελφῶν· [ὁ δὲ κύριος ἔδωκεν ταχὺ εἰρήνην].

† See Reinach, *Revue des Études Juives,* vii., 161 ff.; and below, p. 480.

‡ The governor of Galatia was not a proconsul, but a legatus pro prætore

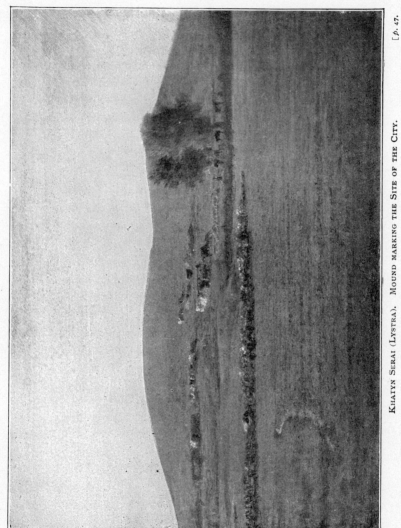

KHAIYN SERAI (LYSTRA). MOUND MARKING THE SITE OF THE CITY.

[*p.* 47.

Roman governor. At the end of the verse the reviser added a phrase showing how the proceedings ended, in order to explain the statement in the following verse that " they remained therefore a long time."

6. LYSTRA.

Lystra is about six hours S.S.W. from Iconium. The road passes for a mile or more through the luxuriant gardens of the suburbs, and then across the level plain. It ascends for the first fourteen miles so slightly that it needs a barometer to make the fact perceptible. Then it reaches a range of hills, which stretch outwards in a south-easterly direction from the mountainous country that bounds the vast Lycaonian plains on the west and separates them from the great depression in which are situated the two connected lakes Karalis and Trogitis, now called Bey Sheher and Seidi Sheher lakes (the former the largest in Asia Minor). This range of hills, which entails a further ascent of about 500 feet, gradually diminishes in height as it stretches further away towards the east, and finally sinks down into the plain about ten miles away. After crossing these hills, the road descends into a valley, in breadth about a mile, down the centre of which flows a river * towards the south-cast ; and on the southern bank of the river about a mile from the place where the road leaves the hills, stands

---

* This river is wrongly represented in every published map. It has had a considerable course before it reaches Khatyn Serai, draining a large part of the mountain district, in which Kiepert's latest maps represent the water as flowing westwards to Bey Sheher Lake. My friend, Professor Sterrett, has erred in this point in his *Wolfe Expedition*, pp. 159 and 190. The map in my *Hist. Geogr.* is also wrong. I examined this point in 1891, but the map was complete before that time.

the village of Khatyn Serai, "The Lady's Mansion." The name dates no doubt from the time of the Seljuk Sultans of Roum, when the village was an estate and country residence of some sultana from Konia (as Iconium is now called). Its elevation, about 3777 feet above the sea and 427 above Iconium, fits it for a summer residence.*

This situation for Lystra was guessed in 1820 by Colonel Leake with his wonderful instinct, and was rejected by succeeding geographers. To Professor Sterrett belongs the credit of having solved this most important problem by discovering epigraphic proof that Lystra was situated beside Khatyn Serai.

A little personal reminiscence, concerning the greatest disappointment of my exploring experiences, may perhaps be pardoned. It gives some idea of the chances of travel, and puts in a stronger relief Professor Sterrett's patience and skill in exploration, to which we owe the discovery of the site of Lystra and all the results that follow from it. When I was travelling in 1882 in the company of Sir Charles Wilson, we had set our hearts on discovering Lystra. Leake's conjecture, confirmed by the fact that Hierocles implies Lystra to be near Iconium, turned our minds to Khatyn Serai; and when we heard that it was reported to contain great remains, we left Iconium with the full expectation of finding Lystra there. But in the village six inscriptions were discovered, four of which were Latin. This preponderance of Latin inscriptions made me certain that a Roman colony must have been situated there; and as Lystra was not a colony, it must be

---

* The height of Iconium, 3350, is given by the Ottoman Railway Survey; that of Lystra is calculated from my friend Mr. Headlam's aneroid observations.

looked for elsewhere. Sir C. Wilson did not admit my reasoning, and maintained his own opinion that Lystra might be there. On the morrow we rode up the water two hours' distance to Kilisra, and spent great part of the day examining the interesting and really beautiful series of churches, cut in the rock, which prove that an ancient monastery (rather than a town) was situated there. As we returned in the afternoon, our road passed near the ancient site beside Khatyn Serai, and we thought of crossing the river to examine it. But the day was far spent, and the camp had been sent to a village four hours beyond Khatyn Serai, so that time was short. Had we gone over * to the small hill, to a considerable extent artificial, on which the ancient city was built, we should have discovered the large inscribed pedestal on which the colony Lystra recorded the honour which it paid to its founder, the Emperor Augustus, and we should have found that both our opinions were right—Sir C. Wilson's that Lystra was situated at Khatyn Serai, and mine that a Roman colony was situated there. But at that time no evidence was known, no coin of Lystra had been preserved to prove that it was a colony; and the fact remained unknown till 1885, when Professor Sterrett's exploring instinct guided him to the marble pedestal. Then other evidence came to light : M. Waddington possessed a coin of the colony Lystra, Dr. Imhoof-Blumer another, and the British Museum has recently acquired a third.

The exact site of Lystra is on a hill in the centre of the valley, a mile north of the modern village, and on the opposite side of the river. The hill rises about 100 to 150

---

* I must bear the blame for this omission. I had had fever, and was suffering greatly during that part of the journey, and I was ready to take any excuse to get to camp an hour earlier.

feet above the plain, and the sides are steep. Few traces of ancient buildings remain above the surface. A small ruined church of no great antiquity stands in the low ground beneath the hill on the south-west; and beside it a fountain gushes forth from beneath a low arch. This fountain is still counted sacred, and is called Ayasma (*i.e.*, ἀγίασμα), a generic name in Asia Minor for fountains visited as sacred by the Christians. As Khatyn Serai io a purely Turkish village, this fountain, which has retained its character among the Christians of Iconium, must mark a spot which was peculiarly sacred in ancient Lystra.

Situated on this bold hill, Lystra could easily be made a very strong fortress, and must have been well suited for its purpose of keeping in check the tribes of the mountain districts that lie west and south of it. It was the furthest east of the fortified cities, which Augustus constructed to facilitate the pacification of Pisidia and Isauria; * and for seventy years after its foundation it must have been a town of considerable consequence, proud of its Roman character and its superior rank. As a Lycaonian town Lystra had been quite undistinguished; as a Roman garrison town it was a bulwark of the province Galatia, and a sister city to the great Roman centre at Antioch. A contemporary memorial of this pride of relationship is preserved in the following inscription found in Antioch† on a pedestal which once supported a statue of Concord :—

> " To the very brilliant colony of Antioch her sister the very brilliant colony of Lystra did honour by presenting the statue of Concord."

* They were really old cities, which Augustus remodelled and reconstituted.

† Discovered by Professor Sterrett in 1885; recopied by me in 1886.

When we consider these facts we can hardly hesitate to admit that St. Paul might in a letter address the church at Lystra by the Roman provincial title, Galatians.

Much may yet be discovered at Lystra. We should be especially glad to find some independent proof that a temple of Jupiter before the city (Διὸς Προπόλεως) existed there. From the many examples of such temples quoted by the commentators on Acts, it seems highly probable that there was one at Lystra. The nearest and best analogy, which is still unpublished, may be mentioned here. At Claudiopolis of Isauria, a town in the mountains south-east from Lystra, an inscription in the wall of the mediæval castle records a dedication to *Jupiter-before-the-town* (Διὶ Προαστίῳ). In 1890 Mr. Hogarth and Mr. Headlam visited Lystra along with me ; and our hope was to fix the probable position of the temple and perhaps to discover a dedication to the god. In the latter we were disappointed ; but there is every probability that some great building once stood beside the pedestal dedicated to Augustus. This pedestal stands near the hill on the south-east side ; and looking from the hill down the valley towards the open plain, one cannot fail to see it in front of the city, and the signs of concealed ruins beside it.

The pedestal of Augustus seems to be in its original place, and there is every probability that the worship of the Imperial founder was connected with the chief temple, and that the pedestal was placed in the sacred precinct of Zeus, as at Ephesus the Augusteum was built within the sacred precinct of Artemis. The other possibility, that the Ayasma marks the *peribolos* of Zeus and retains the sacred character attaching to the spot in pre-Christian and Christian times alike, is not so probable.

Very little excavation would be needed to verify this identification, and probably to disclose the remains of the temple, in front of whose gates the sacrifice was prepared for the Apostles.

The text of the *Codex Bezæ* is specially remarkable in the case of Lystra. In xiv. 13, it preserves a more accurate form than the majority of MSS. It has τοῦ ὄντος Διὸς πρὸ πόλεως,* whereas the character of the epithet is lost in τοῦ Διὸς τοῦ ὄντος πρὸ τῆς πόλεως. The participle in the phrase τοῦ ὄντος Διὸς Προπόλεως is, as Mr. Armitage Robinson points out to me, used in a way characteristic of Acts : it introduces some technical phrase, or some term which it marks out as having a technical sense (compare v. 17, xiii. 1, xxviii. 17), and is almost equivalent to τοῦ ὀνομαζομένου. This use has been mistaken in the accepted text, and ὄντος has been transposed, and the character of the whole phrase lost. The regular usage of πρὸ πόλεως or Προπόλεως is immediately before or after either the name of the god, or the word θεός.

It seems also quite probable that *Codex Bezæ* is more true to actual facts in using the plural ἱερεῖς. In such a sacrifice it would not be the priest of Zeus who brought the oxen and the garlands ; these operations would be performed by *ministri*. The strictly correct expression is that the priests brought the victims and the garlands ; for all the inferior officials of the cultus are included in the generic term priests. Our theory of the accuracy of the "Travel-Document" inclines us once more to prefer the

---

* It is difficult to determine whether this last word is to be taken as two words or one ; probably it was felt to be a single word. In an unpublished inscription of Smyrna the phrase ἱέρεια πρὸ πόλεως or Προπόλεως occurs.

text of *Codex Bezæ.** It is of course quite true that the chief priest may be conceived as ordering and guiding the whole scene, and therefore the subordinate ministers may be left unnoticed. But that is the historian's point of view; whereas the eye-witness, describing a picture clear in his memory, sees the subordinates playing a part quite as prominent to the eye as the chief priest, and uses the plural.

But in addition to these two points, the abundance of minute and yet quite suitable details in this episode is a notable feature in *Codex Bezæ*. In xiv, 7, it adds, " And the whole multitude was moved at their teaching : and Paul and Barnabas abode in Lystra." The reviser who added this (for we cannot accept it as original, as we did the two variants in xiv. 13) felt that something was wanting here to make the narrative run on clearly ; but his addition is not successful, and does not render the sequence of thought perfect. I have (pp. 68–9) remarked that I do not clearly comprehend the received text in this place.† If I were required to advance a theory about the passage, it would be that the author of Acts, reproducing the account given by Paul, had not clearly caught the sense and sequence of his narrative ; and that we have here a trace of the imperfect medium through which a report substantially

---

* If, on the other hand, it be considered more probable that the reviser, whose work has been preserved to us in *Codex Bezæ*, has here restored accuracy and individuality to a story that he found badly related in the text before him, this will only strengthen the argument which is urged in Chap. VIII., that he was intimately acquainted with the antiquities of Asia Minor, and probably a native of the country.

† My remark was actually in print a month before I looked into the text of *Codex Bezæ*.

emanating from Paul himself has reached us. The variant given by *Codex Bezæ* in xiv. 19 * is distinctly an alteration made by a person who worked up the text with minute care, and was offended by the order of the two city names. The order of the original text suited the circumstances of A.D. 45, but not those of the second century, which alone were familiar to the reviser. The reviser was offended by the strange order, and made what he thought an improvement.

Such an alteration could only have been made by a person to whom the topography was so familiar, that even the slightest deviation from the natural order offended him : in that case the revision must have been made in Asia Minor by a native of the country.

7. DERBE.

The site of Derbe is not established on such certain evidence as that of Lystra. The credit of reaching approximate accuracy about its situation belongs again to Professor Sterrett. His argument was that " in reading the account [in Acts xiv.], one is impressed with the idea that Derbe cannot be far from Lystra." † He therefore placed Derbe between the villages Bossola and Zosta, which are only about two miles distant from each other, and "the ruins of which, being so near together, represent one and the same ancient city." But after visiting the district in 1890, I should say that Bossola is only a Seljuk khan and halting-place on a great road, and that the remains at Zosta are not *in situ*, but have all been carried. The great site

---

* "Iconium and Antioch" in place of "Antioch and Iconium."
† *Wolfe Expedition*, p. 23.

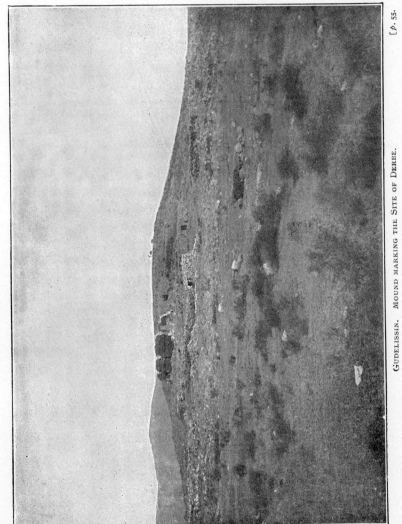

GUDELISSIN. MOUND MARKING THE SITE OF DERBE.

[p. 55.

of this district is at Gudelissin, three miles W.N.W. from Zosta. Professor Sterrett rightly observes that " here a large mound, in every way similar to the Assyrian Tels, shows many traces of an ancient village or town." But after thus correctly estimating the antiquity of the site, he proceeds to say with less accuracy that " most of the remains must be referred to Christian influence."*

Gudelissin is the only site in this district where a city of the style of Derbe, the stronghold of " the robber Antipater," could be situated. The remains at Zosta have been taken from it, so that it now presents a bare and poor appearance ; but excavation in the mound, which is obviously to a great extent artificial, would certainly reveal many traces of a very old city, of the style of Tyana or Zela. The mound belongs to that class which Strabo entitles " mounds of Semiramis," and which are a sure sign of ancient origin and Oriental character. On this deserted site excavation would be comparatively inexpensive, the ground could be had for a few pounds, labour in those remote parts costs little, and no difficulty would be experienced with the excavated soil.

Derbe was the frontier city of the Roman province on the south-east, and on this account a certain importance attached to it, which led Claudius to remodel its constitution and to honour it with the name Claudio-Derbe. Probably this took place in the earlier part of his reign ; and the hypothesis may be hazarded that Iconium was made jealous by such an honour to another city of the Tetrarchy,

---

* The site must have been inhabited till a comparatively recent time, as there is a large ruined building of no very ancient date on the upper part of the mound. This building is prominent in the photograph which Mr. Hogarth took of the site

and by representations at Rome succeeded in obtaining the same honour towards the end of Claudius' reign, A.D. 50–54.[*]

8. CHARACTER OF LYCAONIA IN THE FIRST CENTURY.

The preceding description of the political situation in Lycaonia in the first half of the first century shows how mistaken are some of the statements which are commonly made about St. Paul's action on this journey. C. H. consider that " after the cruel treatment they had experienced in the greater towns on a frequented route," the Apostles retired to a wilder region, " into which the civilisation of the conquering and governing people had hardly penetrated," viz., to Lystra and Derbe. We now see that Lystra was a town of precisely the opposite character, a centre and stronghold for the " civilisation of the governing people." Paul's procedure was very different from that suggested by C. H. So far from going to the less civilised parts, he always sought out the great civilised centres. The towns which he visited for the sake of preaching were, as a rule, the centres of civilisation and government in their respective districts—Ephesus, Athens, Corinth, Thessalonica, Philippi. He must have passed through several uncivilised Pisidian

---

[*] The approximate date is assured by C. I. G., 3991, if we may assume that the title *ktistes* there applied to Pupius Præsens, procurator of Galatia about 53-55, implies that the remodelling of Iconium was conducted by him. The governor of Galatia about this time was Afrinus. A coin of Claudiconium bearing his portrait and that of Claudius is preserved at Paris in the national collection, and has been published by M. Babelon (*Mélanges Num.*, p. 57). Governors and procurators regularly held office for a number of years at this time. Afrinus was succeeded by Petronius Umber in 54.

towns, such as Adada and Misthia and Vasada ; but nothing is recorded about them. He preached, so far as we are informed, only in the centres of commerce and of Roman life, and among these ranked Lystra Colonia and Claudio-Derbe.

This point is one of peculiar importance in studying the effect produced by the Christian religion on the Roman world. It spread at first among the educated more rapidly than among the uneducated ; nowhere had it a stronger hold (as Mommsen observes) than in the household and at the court of the emperors. Where Roman organisation and Greek thought have gone, there Paul by preference goes.

Moreover it must be mentioned that in the ruder parts of Lycaonia Paul could not have made himself understood. He had to go where Greek was known ; and it is pretty certain that at this time Greek was known only in the more important cities, and that there the people were probably for the most part bilingual. In Lystra the Roman settlers no doubt knew Latin as well as Greek, while the native inhabitants, who were much more numerous, spoke both Greek and their native language. Greek then, and not Latin or Lycaonian, would be the common language of these two classes of the population.

In reference to the sacrifice and worship which were tendered to Paul as Hermes and Barnabas as Zeus,* it would be quite a misconception to suppose that faith in the old native religion was stronger in Lystra than in more civilised towns, as is implied by C. H. and by Canon Farrar.

---

* True to the Oriental character, the Lycaonians regarded the active and energetic preacher as the inferior and the more silent and statuesque figure as the leader and principal.

Where the Græco-Roman civilisation had established itself, the old religion survived as strongly as ever, but the deities were spoken of by Greek, or sometimes by Roman, names, and were identified with the gods of the more civilised races. This is precisely what we find at Lystra : Zeus and Hermes are the names of the deities as translated into Greek, but the old Lycaonian gods are meant and the Lycaonian language was used, apparently because, in a moment of excitement, it rose more naturally to the lips of the people than the cultured Greek language. It is noteworthy that those to whose lips Lycaonian rose so readily were not converts, but the common city mob.

The commentators aptly compare the pretty tale, localised in these plains, of the visit paid by the same two gods to the old couple, Philemon and Baucis.* For the right understanding of the story, we must remember that in this Asian religion Zeus and Hermes are the embodiment of two different aspects of the ultimate divinity, " the god," who was represented sometimes as Zeus, sometimes as Hermes, sometimes as Apollo, according to the special aspect which was for the moment prominent.

The attitude of the native priests towards the Christian missionaries is described in connection with the attitude of the Ephesian priesthood. (See below, p. 144.)

---

* Philemon and Baucis alone received the two gods into their hut, when their Phrygian neighbours denied shelter to the strangers. The gods afflicted the country with a flood, and saved only Philemon and Baucis, whom they led up to a hill. On this hill a temple was built to Zeus, and Philemon and Baucis became its guardians : finally, they died at the same moment, and their spirits passed into trees. The reading of Ovid, *Metam.* VIII., 719, which puts the scene at Tyana, is not certain.

CHAPTER III.

ST. PAUL'S FIRST JOURNEY AS A NARRATIVE OF TRAVEL.

AFTER these topographical and historical details, it is proposed, as the next part of our task, to go over the first missionary journey as a plain narrative of travel and adventure, and to show how the references, which St. Paul in his letter to the Galatian churches makes to his experiences when he first preached to them, work in with the narrative in Acts xiii. and xiv. to produce a consistent picture. On the theory (which the present writer is concerned to maintain) that Acts xiii., xiv. are founded on, or even embody, with some slight modifications and additions, a document written under the immediate influence of Paul himself, it is absolutely necessary that the epistle should agree with and complete the narrative in Acts. Herein lies what is generally counted one of the strong points of the North-Galatian view: it is contended that the details of the visit to the Galatians mentioned in the epistle are inconsistent with the account of the journey in South Galatia given in Acts xiii., xiv. If that be the case, I fully acknowledge that the North-Galatian view must be adopted, in spite of the numerous difficulties attending it; but then, as I hope to show, it must be admitted that the account of the second journey in Acts xvi. is inaccurate in itself, and written by one who had not access to a trustworthy account of the facts.

Let us try to realise the facts of the journey and the situation of the Apostles. How were they guided on this particular route? At certain points in this and in other journeys we are told what was the guiding impulse; a vision led Paul from Asia into Europe; the Spirit ordered him not to preach in Asia, and not even to enter Bithynia. In the first journey they were sent forth by the Holy Spirit "for the work whereunto I have called them"; and Paul explains in Galatians that the work was to preach among the Gentiles (i. 16 ff.). There can be no doubt that the expression in Gal. i. 15, 16 tallies exactly with that in Acts xiii. 1, and that it would be appropriate for Paul to address to the churches which he founded on his first missionary journey an elaborate argument in favour of his special call to Gentile work.*

It is not stated that the Holy Spirit prescribed the details of the route. How then should Paul and Barnabas proceed? To leave Syria they must go first to Seleuceia, the harbour of Antioch, where they would find ships going south to the Syrian coast and Egypt, and west either by way of Cyprus or along the coast of Asia Minor. The western route led towards the Roman world, to which all Paul's subsequent history proves that he considered himself called by the Spirit. The Apostles embarked in a ship for Cyprus, which was very closely connected by commerce and general intercourse with the Syrian coast. After traversing the island from east to west, they must go onward. Ships going westward naturally went across to

---

* I do not argue that it would be less appropriate in writing to other churches. I am only concerned to show that it is appropriate on the South-Galatian theory.

the coast of Pamphylia, and the Apostles, after reaching Paphos, near the west end of Cyprus, sailed in one of these ships, and landed at Attalia in Pamphylia.

In the east a man with a day's journey before him always rises early in the morning; and similarly we may feel fairly confident that in view of this great expedition the Apostles started early in the year, in April, when the season for navigation began.* It is not possible to allow less than two months in Cyprus, where they preached in the Jewish synagogues along their route. We must allow a certain time in each of the Jewish settlements to enable the Apostles to test the feeling of the town before they proceeded on their way in search of a favourable opening; and yet, if the document possesses vividness and direct accuracy, it is hardly consistent with the language to suppose that they stayed very long at any place. Nothing of permanent interest occurred until they reached Paphos; and even there the words describing their experience do not suggest any prolonged stay. It seems then a fair and natural interpretation of the document to place their arrival in Pamphylia in the latter part of June. Some slight stay at Perga is implied by the dissension which was caused by the proposal to cross Taurus to the upper country; then they proceeded to the interior without preaching at Perga or in Pamphylia.

We can hardly suppose that this was part of the original scheme, for John Mark was willing to come into Pamphylia with them, but not willing to go on into the country north of Taurus, and therefore he evidently considered that the latter proposal was a departure from the original

---

* C. H. adopt this view.

scheme.   Cyprus and Pamphylia were countries of similar
situation to Cilicia and Syria, and in the closest possible
relations with them, whereas it was a serious and novel
step to go into the country north of Taurus.   We need not
therefore suppose that John Mark was actuated solely or
mainly by cowardice ; the facts of the situation show that
he could advance perfectly plausible arguments against the
change of plan, which was to carry their work into a region
new in character and not hitherto contemplated by the
church.   It seems no unwarrantable addition, but a plain
inference from the facts, to picture the dissension as proceeding on lines like these ; and it relieves John Mark
from a serious charge, which is not quite in keeping with
his boldness in orginally starting on this first of missionary
journeys.   What then was the motive of Paul and Barnabas
in taking this new step?   Evidently the Spirit did not
order them, for we are precluded from supposing that John
Mark actually disobeyed the Divine injunction which he
had already obeyed in coming to Cyprus and Pamphylia ;
and moreover we are not justified in interpolating such
Divine action in the narrative without express warrant in
its own words.   Was it that circumstances independent of
their own will dictated this change?   To this question
Paul himself gives the answer.   " Ye know," he says to the
Galatians, " that because of an infirmity of the flesh I
preached the gospel to you the first time " (iv. 13).

Every one who has travelled in Pamphylia knows how
relaxing and enervating the climate is.   In these low-lying
plains fever is endemic ; the land is so moist as to be
extraordinarily fertile and most dangerous to strangers.
Confined by the vast ridges of Taurus, 5,000 to 9,000 feet
high, the atmosphere is like the steam of a kettle, hot,

moist, and swept by no strong winds. Coming down in July 1890 from the north side of Taurus for a few days to the coast east of Pamphylia, I seemed to feel my physical and mental powers melting rapidly away. I might spend a page in quoting examples,* but the following fact bears so closely on our present purpose that it must be mentioned. In August 1890 I met on the Cilician coast an English officer on his way home from three years' duty in Cyprus : previously he had spent some years in Eastern service. He said that the climate of the Cilician coast (which is very similar to that of Pamphylia, and has not any worse reputation for unhealthiness) reminded him of Singapore or Hong-kong, while that of Cyprus was infinitely fresher and more invigorating.

We suppose then that Paul caught fever on reaching Perga. Here it may be objected by those who have no experience of such a situation that Paul was used to the climate of Cilicia and Syria ; why should he suffer in Pamphylia ? In the first place, no one can count on immunity from fever, which attacks people in the most capricious way. In the second place, it was precisely after fatigue and hardship, travelling on foot through Cyprus amid great excitement and mental strain, that one was peculiarly liable to be affected by the sudden plunge into the enervating atmosphere of Pamphylia. The circumstances implied in the epistle are therefore in perfect keeping with the narrative in Acts ; each of the authorities lends additional emphasis and meaning to the other.

A bad attack of malarial fever, such as we suppose to

---

* The Rev. Mr. Daniell, who travelled with Spratt and Forbes, died of fever at Attalia, a few miles from Perga.

have befallen St. Paul in Pamphylia, could not be described better than in the words in which Lightfoot (an advocate of the North-Galatian theory) sums up the physical infirmity implied in the *Epistle* iv. 13–15 : " A return of his old malady, ' the thorn in the flesh, the messenger of Satan sent to buffet him,' some sharp and violent attack it would appear, which humiliated him and prostrated his physical strength." I appeal to all who have experience, whether this is not a singularly apt description of that fever, which has such an annoying and tormenting habit of catching one by the heel just in the most inconvenient moments, in the midst of some great effort, and on the eve of some serious crisis, when all one's energies are specially needed.*

The treatment for such an illness would be prescribed by universal consent as either the sea or the high lands of the interior. Thus the remarks which have been made above, page 17, acquire much pertinence, now that we have succeeded in eliciting the probable character of the case. In this way Paul and Barnabas were led to visit the Jewish settlement of Antioch, and the evangelisation of the Galatian churches was due to " an infirmity of the flesh."

On the North-Galatian theory, I fail to comprehend what can be the situation. It is a remarkable fact, that the long toilsome journey, involving great physical and mental

---

* I have not in the slightest word or detail altered my description to suit the case. The sentence in the text has been often in my mouth in describing what I have seen ; and the words " catching by the heel " have become with me a stock phrase to describe the behaviour of this fever, when chronic. Lightfoot's quotation from 2 Cor. xii. 7 has no certain connection with the present case ; but the connection is generally admitted.

effort, and yet voluntarily undertaken, should be described as the result of a severe illness ; such a result from such a cause is explicable only in certain rare circumstances. We have seen that the result naturally follows from a Pamphylian illness. On the other hand, I cannot see any possible circumstances in which a preaching tour in North Galatia could be due to an illness during the second journey. Let those who advocate that theory suggest some actual facts and details which are in accordance with the situation and the record. But this is a point to which I shall return in Chapter IV., p. 86.

It may be suggested in objection to our theory, that if so much importance attaches to this illness, a document composed under St. Paul's influence would make some reference to it. In answer, it might be sufficient to ask whether St. Paul's character would make us expect from him a formal reference to his illness.* But suppose the reference made, what is the result? It would be hardly possible in such a brief account to speak of the illness without giving a worse tone to the action of Mark than it· fairly deserved ; and the silence preserved in regard to it is perhaps not unconnected with this fact.

The attack described in the letter to the Galatians need not be understood as lasting long ; that is not the character of such attacks. But the journey to Antioch could not be made rapidly. At the ordinary rate of twenty miles per day it would need eight days ; but we must allow a slower progress in this case. The latter part of July, on the conception we have formed of the journey, is the earliest date

---

* Compare the experiences which become known to us only incidentally through the passage 2 Cor. xi. 23 ff.

when the Apostle can have reached Antioch ; and the beginning of August is more probable. About that time the journey to the upper country would be most imperatively required for a fever-struck patient ; whereas after the middle of September a journey to the plateau would no longer be recommended.

The motives which might lead the Jewish strangers to select Antioch have been already described. (See p. 19.) We suppose Paul and Barnabas to have arrived there. After some days' stay they turned from the Jews to the Gentiles. Among them it is clear from Acts xiii. 48–9, and Gal. iv. 13–15, that Paul was welcomed gladly, was treated with extraordinary affection, with kindly solicitude as an invalid, and with admiration as a teacher. These two passages fit into each other perfectly. It may also be noticed that the hospitality with which Onesiphorus went out to meet and invite Paul to his house, in the romance of St. Thekla,* may be treated as implying some tradition with regard to the hearty welcome extended to the Apostles in the whole of this region.

They resided in Antioch for some time. A certain interval is required for the recorded effect,—" the word of the Lord was spread abroad throughout all the region " Two months is the minimum that can be allowed for such widespread effect. On the other hand, the stay in Antioch is not said to be " long," as is that in Iconium. We may estimate a " long time " (ἱκανὸν χρόνον) by comparison with Paul's later journeys. He stayed " a long time " (ἱκανὰς ἡμέρας, xviii. 18) at Corinth after the trial before Gallio, and as we know that the whole duration of his residence

---

* See above, p. 31.

there was eighteen months, this phrase must denote some
period like six to ten months. We may fairly suppose a
similar time to have been spent at Iconium, let us say
eight months; whereas at Antioch he resided less than
six months, and not less than two. Moreover if we may
assume that the new magistrates at Antioch came into
office, according to the general Asian fashion,* on September 23rd, it is probable that any machinations against the
Apostles, would be directed to influence not the retiring, but
the incoming, magistrates. After entering on office, the
new magistrates would be occupied with pressing official
duties in their first days; and the middle or end of October
is likely to have been the earliest time at which they could
attend to the complaints made by the influential classes
against Paul. All this leads us to the conclusion that the
three or four days' journey to Iconium falls in the latter
part of October, or in November, and that the whole winter
was spent in Iconium.

A point which illustrates and is illustrated by the
state of society in Asia Minor, is the influence exerted on
the Apostles' fortunes in Antioch by the women. The
honours and influence which belonged to women in the
cities of Asia Minor form one of the most remarkable
features in the history of the country. In all periods the
evidence runs on the same lines. On the border between
fable and history we find the Amazons. The best authenti-
cated cases of *Mutterrecht* belong to Asia Minor. Under
the Roman Empire we find women magistrates, presidents

---

* It is, however, quite possible that the Roman year was used in
the colony, and that the magistrates entered on office, according to
the Roman fashion, on January 1st.

at games, and loaded with honours.* The custom of the
country influenced even the Jews, who in at least one case
appointed a woman at Smyrna to the position of archi-
synagogos.† It would be strange if the women had not
exercised some influence over St. Paul's fortunes.

The journey to Iconium was probably performed in
greater ease and comfort, perhaps in a carriage. The
Apostles had now many friends, and Paul lays special stress
on their extraordinary anxiety to give him anything in
their power that could be of service to him ‡ (Gal. iv. 15);
this implies a liberal and overflowing hospitality, and quite
naturally includes help in his actual journey, recommenda-
tions to residents at Neapolis, Misthia, and other towns on
the way, and the use of horses for the journey.

The hurried flight from Iconium to Lystra, according to
our reckoning, took place about June. It is difficult to find
an indication of time in the following part of the narrative.
It seems to be implied (xiv. 6) that the Apostles' residence
in this district was not confined to a certain time in Lystra,
and then a certain time in Derbe, but that they made
some excursions, and remained in the district engaged
in missionary work. I must, however, confess that the
language here is vague, and I do not comprehend it

---

* Examples have been collected with much diligence by M. Paris
in his treatise, *Quatenus feminæ in Asia Minore res publicas
attigerint;* but the conclusions which he draws appear to me
unsatisfactory, and the tone of the writer is rather flippant and
unpleasant.

† See Neubauer in *Studia Biblica,* i., p. 70; Reinach in *Revue
des Études Juives,* vii., p. 161.

‡ Mere attention to Paul in sickness is not enough to explain the
words in Gal. iv. 15; the actual giving or offering of their own valued
possessions is necessarily included.

clearly.* During the heat of summer this country district would be much cooler and pleasanter than the city of Iconium, though even there the heat is not excessive, and the suburban gardens are agreeable.

During this residence in the Isaurian hill country, certain Jews came to Lystra from Antioch and Iconium. If we may judge from modern experience, these Jews were traders of the class of brokers or middle-men, who were speculating in the approaching harvest, and came to look after their business. Greeks and Armenians play among the primitive natives at the present day exactly the part which I attribute to the Jews in the first century, buying up the grain and other produce from the agricultural population, and exporting it to harbours on the south coast, or selling it in retail trade in the cities.† If this supposition is correct, August is a very likely month for their coming to Lystra, and the stoning of Paul would come some weeks later. The two days' journey to Derbe ‡ would then fall perhaps as late as September. Three months is no exaggerated allowance for the effect produced at Derbe, "making many disciples." That brings us at least to the end of November. After that season the passes over Taurus are liable to be blocked by snow, and are at best very trying and difficult to cross. What, then, were the Apostles to do? The journey across

---

* In the country round about, among the Isaurian hills, it is highly improbable that the Apostles could speak to the rustic population, who were, it is practically certain, ignorant of Greek till a far later date.

† The tithes were no doubt also farmed by speculators, as at present in some districts. Some of these visitors might be agents of the company of speculators.

‡ The distance is about ten or eleven hours, and might be done in one day with an early start.

Taurus was described to them as impossible. They were at the extremest limit of Roman territory, and could not go further forward to preach, except by entering the kingdom of Antiochus. Now it is not a too fanciful idea that St. Paul may already have begun to realise the great conception (which he certainly realised afterwards) of Christianity as the religion of the Roman Empire, and was already confirmed in his preference for centres of Roman life and influence. In this situation the Apostles resolved to return by the way they had come, and to take the opportunity of organising the administration of the newly founded communities, all of which they had been obliged to leave quite suddenly.

The Apostles had been expelled, or had fled in danger of their lives, from Antioch, Iconium, and Lystra; and it is clear that the riotous action of the populace had been connived at, or even encouraged, by the magistrates. How then could they venture to re-enter the cities against the authority of the magistrates?

The question touches on a branch of ancient law—viz., the powers and rights of the magistrates in such provincial cities—which is so obscure that we cannot answer it with certainty or confidence, but can only indicate some probabilities. It is worth notice that the magistrates of Antioch seem to have taken a more decided action than those of Iconium or Lystra. Antioch was a Roman colony and an administrative centre; and it is quite natural that its magistrates should be of higher rank, and should venture on bolder action.

We may take it for granted that Roman law and custom prevailed in the Roman colonies, Antioch and Lystra; and in all probability they exercised great influence even in

Iconium. We may then understand that the magistrates could not permanently banish any person from the city; but that, in the exercise of their powers for the preservation of peace and order, they could go to very great lengths in the way of summary punishment against any individuals whose action or presence was inconsistent with peace and order. They could turn them out of the city (though not permanently exile them), they could tear their clothes, inflict personal indignities on them, or beat them (unless they were Roman citizens). But the punishments which they inflicted caused no permanent disability, except in so far as the mere physical effect might be indelible; they could not pass sentence of death or of exile. The person who was turned out of the city might return after a little; but of course he would be wise not to return so long as the magistrate who ejected him remained in office.

But though the magistrates could not punish a culprit with death, "a regrettable incident," such as a popular riot, might occasionally occur, leading to the death of an obnoxious individual, and mildly blamed in public by the magistrates, who privately rejoiced at it. Hence in Iconium and Lystra we may be pretty sure that the magistrates connived at the stoning intended in the one case, and effected in the other; but it was only by such irregular proceedings that the death of the missionaries could be compassed. The magistrates could take no overt action.

It would appear then that Paul and Barnabas had been brought before the magistrates of Antioch, but not of Iconium or of Lystra. But even in Antioch the orders of the magistrates inflicted on them no permanent disability, and in Lystra they had been the victims of illegal conduct so extreme that they had acquired a strong legal position.

They were legally free also to return to Iconium and
Antioch, but in common prudence they would hardly return until new magistrates came into office. Now, according
to the account of the journey which has just been given, it
appears that new magistrates had already been appointed
in all three towns.*

The rest of the winter then was spent in Lystra, Iconium,
and Antioch. The magistrates and the Jews are not
again referred to ; it is probable that the Apostles' freedom
from interference was gained by their refraining from such
open preaching as before, while they devoted themselves to
organising some kind of self-government in the congregations. Some years later, we know that Paul could direct
the Galatian churches to make weekly contributions for the
benefit of the poor at Jerusalem ; and this implies officials
and a system of administration. It was not before the
middle of May in the following year that the Apostles could
venture to cross the Pisidian mountains. They perhaps
spent June in Perga, and in July, after an absence of two
years and four months, they may have reached the Syrian
Antioch once more.

It will strike every reader that the estimates of time
given in the preceding sketch of the Apostle's journeys are
the lowest possible in view of the effects produced. A
certain amount of time is necessary in order that two
unknown strangers should first gain a hearing, and then
make many converts and establish a permanent congrega-

---

* Unless the magistrates in the colony of Lystra entered office on
January 1st. But Lystra was the town in which St. Paul's legal
position was strongest. A Roman citizen, violently assaulted by the
populace, had a very strong case.

tion in a city where the established religion was so opposite in character to that which they preached. Many may think that our estimates err by being too short; and it is quite possible that they ought to be lengthened. Probably hardly any one will consider that they are too long.

CHAPTER IV.

THE SECOND JOURNEY.

ST. PAUL'S second journey took place some years later
than the first. The intermediate period he had spent
chiefly in Antioch, but partly in a journey to Jerusalem.*
He had now old friends in South Galatia to visit, and he
went in the first place straight to them. Accompanied by
Silas, he passed through Cilicia, crossed Taurus no doubt
by the Cilician Gates, and came first to Derbe, and then
to Lystra, where he found a disciple named Timothy, son
of a Jewess by a Greek father. He resolved to take
Timothy with him, and in order to conciliate the prejudices of the Jews, who were numerous in these regions,

---

* It was probably not less than a year after the Apostles had
returned when they started for Jerusalem ; the expression χρόνον
οὐκ ὀλίγον is an emphatic expression, which may quite well denote
an even longer period. Mr. Lewin, in his singularly useful work,
Fasti Sacri, p. 288, No. 1722, argues from the fact that "Paul
and Barnabas related the conversion of the Gentiles" during their
journey to Jerusalem, that no very long interval had elapsed since
their return from their journey in Asia Minor, "as otherwise their
success among the Gentiles would have been sufficiently well
known." This argument is incorrect. They are not said to give
the first news ; it is rather implied by the word selected (ἐκδιηγούμενοι)
that the communities on their way had already heard of the fact
generally, and took the opportunity of learning the full details from
the missionaries. After they returned from Jerusalem, a considerable stay in Antioch is again implied.

74

he performed on him that operation which the Hebrew religion required in the case of all males. This can hardly have been done merely for the sake of the Jews in Lystra, Iconium, and Antioch, whom Paul already knew to be hostile to him. It implies that he had the intention of preaching in other towns where Jews lived, through whom he would as usual make a beginning. As we shall see, he was evidently thinking of going on westward into the province Asia.

The passage xvi. 4–6 is one of extreme obscurity; but it must be examined, for the decision of the controversy as to the signification of the term Galatia depends on the meaning to be taken out of it. It appears that Paul, after leaving Lystra with Silas and Timothy, spent some time in the country, for it is clearly implied in verses 4 and 5, that they taught and preached in "the cities" on their route. We may then conclude that they visited those cities of the district where Paul had so many friends and converts, Iconium and Antioch; and it was in all probability while they were in Antioch that they were "forbidden of the Holy Ghost to speak the word in Asia." The prohibition implies a previous intention on their part, by which Paul's action hitherto had been guided.

When their first plan was thus altered, they turned northwards, with the intention of entering Bithynia, presuming that they would be allowed to preach there. But when they came opposite Mysia,* and tried to continue

---

* I understand κατὰ here in the sense which it has, *e.g.*, in Acts xxvii. 7, κατὰ Κνίδον, or in Herodotus I. 76, κατὰ Σινώπην—" when they reached such a point that a line drawn across the country at right angles to the general line of their route would touch Mysia."

their northward route into Bithynia, "the Spirit of Jesus suffered them not." They were compelled to turn westwards ; and keeping along the southern frontier of Mysia, they reached Troas, whence they sailed to Macedonia.

The language of this passage clearly implies that they were forbidden to preach, but not to travel in Asia ; whereas they were forbidden even to set foot in Bithynia. Accordingly, when they found about Antioch that they must not preach in Asia, they went straight north through the Phrygian parts of Asia, intending to preach as soon as they reached Bithynia ; but of course they understood that the Phrygian country which they crossed was part of Asia, and forbidden to them for preaching.*

This interpretation gives a definite picture of a probable route, which lies fairly in the words. I can find no such picture in any of the other interpretations that have been advanced, and I do not see any other satisfactory possibility. There are two difficulties in the interpretation. First, we have to take certain terms in the Roman sense,

---

In the passage of Herodotus this implies a line from north to south ; here it implies a line from east to west. Wendt understands " to the border of Mysia." This would come to nearly the same result, taking Mysia in the wide sense which it has in Ptolemy and which is mentioned in Strabo as common. I should suppose that about Nakoleia they found that their northward route was prevented ; Wendt's view would involve that they realised this somewhere near Kotiaion. They had two roads possible from Antioch into Bithynia, one by Nakoleia and Dorylaion, which is the shortest and was by far the most important at that time, the other by Kotiaion.

* Lewin, *St. Paul*, p. 193, not observing that Phrygia is a part of Asia, supposes that they went at this time to Colossæ and preached there. Such a route to Bithynia is impossible except with the wrong conception Mr. Lewin has of the topography of the country ; and Colossæ was a city of Asia, and forbidden to them.

and not in the popular sense which is certainly found in the early chapters of Acts. Our fundamental hypothesis of the "Travel-Document" is intended to meet this difficulty; and we have found that hypothesis confirmed by the signs of first-hand acquaintance with the country which appear in chapters xiii. and xiv. The writer retains the precise words of his authority in xvi. 6 and 7, and this authority was a document written, whether by himself at an earlier time or by some other person, under the immediate influence of St. Paul himself.*

Then the second difficulty, which lies in the relation of verse 6 to 4 and 5, finds an easy solution. "They passed through the Phrygian and Galatic country" is a geographical recapitulation of the journey which is implied in verses 4, 5. These two verses describe the conduct and action that characterised the entire journey through South Galatia, both the journey to Lystra and Derbe, already mentioned from the geographical point of view in verse 1, and that to Iconium and Antioch. Verse 6 then continues the geographical description from verse 1, and describes the journey from Lystra onwards; † it led through "the country which is Phrygian and

region

---

* It was at this point that the idea which is worked out in the first four chapters of this work was first conceived—viz., that great part of Acts xiii. ff. was composed under Paul's immediate influence.

† There is much to be said in favour of Wendt's view, that verses 4 and 5 are an addition made to the original document by the author of Acts, who incorporated in his work the original document. The preceding exposition might have been made clearer by assuming this view; but I have preferred throughout these chapters to start from the received text, though I feel confident that there has been a good deal of editing and contamination in the text as we have it.

Galatic," a single district to which both adjectives apply.
Lightfoot has correctly seen that this is the only possible
sense of the Greek words as they are now read.* The
description applies to the country round Iconium and
Antioch ; to make quite clear in brief terms what country
he meant, the writer of the original document said "the
country which according to one way of speaking is
Phrygian, but which is also called Galatic." The preceding account of the country about Iconium and Antioch
has shown how strictly true the description is, and how
perfectly it agrees with the expression used in Acts xiv. 6,
which puts the boundary of the Phrygian land between
Iconium and Lystra.

Lightfoot, on the other hand, considers that "the Phrygian
and Galatic country" is Galatia in the narrow sense, the
land occupied by the Gaulish settlers during the third
century before Christ, which previously had been part of
Phrygia.   It seems to me inconceivable and contrary to the
evidence, either that the name Phrygia should have remained in popular use to denote the country of the Asiatic
Gauls till the time when Acts was written,† or that the

---

* Τὴν Φρυγίαν καὶ Γαλατικὴν χώραν, so Tischendorf, Westcott and
Hort, Wendt, and almost all modern critics.   But Wendt, though
he accepts the text, gives a translation which results naturally from
the old text, but which cannot be got from the text which he approves
of.   His rendering is *Phrygien und das galatische Land.*   Lipsius,
in Holtzmann's *Hand-Kommentar*, II. ii. 2, is the only modern
critic known to me who quotes the text as τὴν Γαλατικήν ; this is
probably only an inaccuracy in quotation, and does not indicate a
difference of judgment as to the text, which is determined by the
manuscripts.

† Lipsius regularly speaks of North Galatia as *der Galaticus.*
This name has no authority, and is a mere fiction founded on his
misunderstanding of τὴν Γαλατικὴν χώραν ; but it might suggest to the

author should indulge in a display of pedantic antiquarianism, suitable for Strabo's learned work, but utterly incongruous here. To make possible the reference to North Galatia which Lightfoot and most commentators seek to derive from this passage, it is necessary to go back to the discarded reading τὴν Φρυγίαν καὶ τὴν Γαλατικὴν χώραν, and it is noteworthy that, as we have seen, Wendt translates this text in his commentary, though he rejects it in his critical notes.

The objection may be made that I am inconsistent in refusing to admit the possibility that North Galatia could retain in popular language in the first century after Christ the ancient name of Phrygia, whereas I have argued * that Iconium continued to be counted Phrygian by its inhabitants at least as late as the second century. But the cases are quite different. In Iconium the old Phrygian population continued to call themselves Phrygian, and probably in part retained the use of the Phrygian language alongside of Greek. But in Galatia the population had changed; the Galatai had conquered the country, and so far from wishing to retain the name Phrygian, they would have treated it as an insult to be called Phrygians. General popular usage throughout Asia Minor had long ago ceased to apply the name Phrygia either to Iconium or to Galatia, though antiquaries and historians recognised that North Galatia was originally part of Phrygia.

There can, I believe, be no doubt what country was denoted by these words, which may in English be most

---

unwary reader that his translation agrees with ancient usage. Paul heard the term *Galaticus* in Iconium, where it was in use at the time to denote the province (p. 14, and C. I. G. 3991). Later, the word changed its meaning (p. 95).

* See above, pp. 37-9.

idiomatically rendered "the Phrygo-Galatic territory." Abundant analogy may be quoted to show that this phrase was natural and common in the first century, and that it was the most clear and complete and precise description which a writer who was striving after accuracy could select. As this point is a decisive one, and is independent of any theory as to the composition of Acts,* it deserves closer examination.

The district is not called Galatia, but ἡ Γαλατικὴ χώρα, *i.e.*, a district which was connected with Galatia or included in Galatia, but which the writer for some reason or other does not choose to designate by the term Galatia. The adjective Galaticus is actually employed elsewhere as a geographical term. The term Pontus Galaticus † was already in use during the first century after Christ to denote a large district of Pontus which was added to the province of Galatia a few years B.C. The natural sense of the Greek words, confirmed by this analogy, is decisive as to the sense of Γαλατικὴ χώρα. Now let us turn to the Roman documents of the first century, describing the extent of the authority exercised by the governor of Galatia. In some inscriptions he is called simply the governor of Galatia, while in others he is styled governor of Galatia, Pisidia, Phrygia, Lycaonia, Isauria, Pontus Galaticus, etc.

---

* It is the argument which first led me definitely to abandon my earlier belief that the Epistle was addressed to the North Galatians. Arrian, *An.* 2, 4, 1, uses Galaticus in its natural and strict sense.

† The origin of the term is discussed in *Hist. Geogr.*, p. 253. In literature it is used only by Ptolemy but must be older, for it had ceased to be true in his time. It is employed in inscriptions of the first century, *e.g.* C.I.L., III., Suppl., no. 6818, which belongs to the years 73-78.

The district here denominated Phrygia is that which includes Iconium, Antioch, and Apollonia,* and which might, during the first century, in perfect accordance with analogy, be called by such names as Phrygia Galatica, or ἡ Φρυγία καὶ Γαλατικὴ χώρα.† This statement of actual facts, as recorded in contemporary documents, seems to be in itself a conclusive and sufficient proof of the meaning of the phrase used in Acts xvi. 6; and this interpretation proves that the route described in Acts xvi. did not touch North Galatia at any point. But as the theory that the route passed through North Galatia is rested on the necessity of accommodating Acts to the Epistle, we must examine this point.

Let us admit for the moment the possibility that, either by recurring to the now discarded reading in xvi. 6, or by some other means, a passage through North Galatia could be made consistent with the narrative in Acts. The question has then to be met, how did St. Paul come to be in North Galatia? What theory can be suggested to explain his route and his plans consistently with the rest of the narrative? Lightfoot and most others do not suggest any reason, nor do anything to introduce coherence into the journey. C. H. say: " The obvious inference is that he was passing through Galatia to some other district (possibly Pontus)." The inference, whether "obvious" or not, is rather a bold one, when we consider how utterly unjustified it is by anything that is related in this or any other part of

---

* See *Hist. Geogr.*, p. 253.

† Phrygia Galatica on the analogy of Pontus Galaticus or of Ptolemy's Phrygia Pisidia—*i.e.*, Pisidian Phrygia, the part of Phrygia reckoned along with Pisidia—(compare Antiochia Pisidia).

the Acts about Paul's travels or his aims.   The idea of a
proposed visit to Pontus must be rejected.   But another
account might be suggested as in better agreement with the
record.   We may suppose that Paul, after leaving Lystra,
went on through Iconium to Antioch.   There he was forbidden to preach in Asia.   He then went across the continent
toward the north with the intention of preaching in the
extreme eastern parts of Bithynia, Amastris and the surrounding districts.   The direct road to Amastris went by way
of Ancyra, the capital of North Galatia.   Here or at some
other point in his journey he was detained by illness.   He
postponed his journey to Bithynia, and proceeded to preach
in Galatia.   Lightfoot names Ancyra, Juliopolis,* Tavium,
and Pessinus as probably the earliest Galatian churches
in this district.†   Thereafter he proceeded on his way to
Bithynia, and when he came "over against Mysia" (or,
according to Wendt, "to the frontier of Mysia"), he was
forbidden to enter Bithynia, and passing along the southern
boundary of Mysia he reached Troas.

In the first place we have to object to this account that
it does not suit the text.   From North Galatia no possible
route to Bithynia could be said to bring a traveller to a
point "over against Mysia," still less "to the frontier of

---

* Juliopolis, however, was at this time a city of Bithynia, not of
Galatia (*Hist. Geogr.*, p. 196).

† We may confidently say that no other towns (except Colonia
Germa) in North Galatia possessed a Greek-speaking population to
which St. Paul could preach ; in fact, it is exceedingly doubtful if
Tavium could have contained many people who were familiar with
Greek at this period.   In the rest of the country it seems certain
that only a few words of broken Greek were known to the population,
whose familiar tongue was Celtic.   According to Jerome they
retained their native language as late as the fourth century.

Mysia." A glance at a map (preferably a large map) of the country will make this clear to all. Moreover the phrase "They went through Phrygia, etc., and when they came opposite Mysia," implies a single definite journey reaching a definite point and there suddenly checked. But on the above interpretation, we have to interpose between the two verbs a tale of months of wandering over Galatia. No person who possessed any literary faculty could write like this. Either the writer of Acts misunderstood the facts entirely, and wrote something which is not correct, and which we must alter in order to introduce the above interpretation ; or else his words definitely exclude the supposition that Paul on this occasion travelled in North Galatia. If we cling to the North-Galatian theory, we must abandon the view that this part of Acts possesses the characteristics of an original, genuine, and valuable historical document. But if we adopt the South-Galatian theory, we merely follow the text of all modern critics and translate it according to the meaning which was common in documents of the time.

Secondly, Amastris, in Roman and in common usage, was a city of Pontus, and not of Bithynia. Though it is true that both districts were included in one province, yet the province was always called Bithynia-Pontus or Bithynia et Pontus.

The supposition that Amastris was the object of St. Paul's route from Pisidian Antioch is inconsistent with natural probability ; Western Bithynia about Nikomedeia and Nikaia was the district which would be naturally inferred from the expression "to go into Bithynia." The wealth and the civilisation and the administration of Bithynia had their centre there. A connection with Syria and a Jewish population are more probable in Western Bithynia.* Amastris itself was a civilised city with a considerable Greek-speaking population, but the surrounding country was barbarous and uncivilised and in the last degree unlikely to have attracted Paul. Moreover a very difficult and mountainous country lies south of Amastris, and intercourse between it and the civilised world was maintained almost entirely by sea.

When the design of preaching in Asia was frustrated, it seems to have occurred to St. Paul to go on to the country immediately beyond—viz., Bithynia ; and the road by Dorylaion to Nikaia and Nikomedeia was a great route. But the design of going from Antioch or from Iconium to Amastris, without any thought of preaching in the inter-mediate districts, is in itself utterly improbable, and puts an end to all naturalness and consistency in the narrative.

Thirdly, chronology is opposed to this view. The process of preaching in the great cities of Galatia needed in any case a considerable time ; an invalid, as St. Paul is supposed on the North-Galatian theory to have been, would require a long time in that vast and bare country. But the period allotted on any of the proposed systems of chronology to this journey, leaves no room for such a great work as the evangelisation of Galatia. We may safely assume that Paul left Antioch on his second journey in the spring. No one who knows the Taurus † will suppose that he crossed it before the middle of May ;

---

* Amisos was the only city of Pontus which might naturally have close relations with Syria (see p. 10) ; but it is unnecessary to argue that Paul could not think of Amisos as in Bithynia.

† See above, pp. 69–70.

June is a more probable time. Say he passed the Cilician Gates on the first of June. If we calculate his journey by the shortest route, allowing no detention for unforeseen contingencies,* but making him rest always on Sabbaths, and supposing a stay of two Sundays each at Derbe, Iconium, and Antioch, and of at least five weeks at Lystra (which is required to select Timothy as comrade, to perform the operation on him, and to wait his recovery), we find that, even if he did not touch North Galatia, October would be begun before he reached Philippi.† Eleven months may fairly be allotted to the events recorded at Philippi, Thessalonica,‡ Berœa, and Athens ; and then Paul went to Corinth, where he resided a year and a half. He would then sail for Jerusalem in the spring. Thus, three entire years are required as the smallest allowance for this journey, even if it was done in the direct way which our theory supposes. Among the commentators, some assign two years for these

---

* But such contingencies always happen and cause some delay.

† For mere walking, we may allow eight days to Derbe, two to Lystra, one to Iconium, four to Antioch, seventeen to Troas ; besides a stay of some days in Troas. The shipping season had not come to an end, so that winter was not yet set in when he reached Troas.

‡ The three weeks at Thessalonica (Acts xvii. 2) must not be pressed : the time is insufficient ; but I need not repeat the reasons which are well stated in the *Speaker's Commentary* on Thessalonians, p. 711. But the argument there used that Paul could only have had the Sundays for preaching in Thessalonica, because he worked with his hands "night and day " (1 Thess. ii. 9), depends on a misconception. Paul means by the phrase "night and day " only that he started work before dawn : the usage is regular and frequent. He no doubt began so early in order to be able to devote some part of the day to preaching.

events, some three, hardly any one allows four. The
usual systems of chronology must therefore be modified
greatly, if the evangelisation of North Galatia is to be
interpolated in this journey.

Finally, it is required by the North-Galatian theory that
St. Paul, stricken at Ancyra by the severe illness already
described in the words of Lightfoot, took that opportunity
to make the long, fatiguing journeys needed in order to
preach in Tavium and Pessinus. Those who know the
bare, bleak uplands of Galatia, hot and dusty in summer,
covered with snow in winter, will appreciate the improbability and the want of truth to nature which are involved
in the words, "because of an infirmity of the flesh I
preached unto you."

The truth is that no suggestion ever has been offered,
and in view of the geography no suggestion can be offered,
which will introduce rational coherence into the narrative
in Acts on the supposition that on this journey St. Paul
evangelised in Northern Galatia. If that be the case, the
narrative in Acts is so confused, so self-contradictory, and
so unintelligible, that it cannot be written by one who had
access to good authorities or who had any opportunity of
acquiring knowledge of the facts. The most charitable
account of the writer would be that he had no exact
record about the first journey made by Paul into Galatia ;
but he inferred from the Epistle that two such journeys
had been made, and mentioned the first in a rather
incoherent way at this point in his narrative. In some
way or other all particulars of the first Galatian journey
had disappeared, and the author of Acts had to dismiss
it with a word. How inconsistent is this supposition
with the life-like narration in other parts of St. Paul's

journeys! How should the same writer be so well
informed about the other journeys in Asia Minor, Greece,
and Italy, while this one was as unknown to him as the
Arabian journey? *

On the South Galatian theory, however, I hope that the
preceding discussion has shown in detail the perfect
coherence of the narrative throughout the first and second
journeys, and its agreement with the allusions in the epistle,
and has proved that the combination of Acts and the
epistle produces a complete, natural, harmonious, and
intrinsically probable picture.

In *Codex Bezæ* the various readings in the description
of the second journey, though not of very striking character, are not devoid of interest. The addition to
xv. 41 † is derived from xvi. 4; it brings out clearly (what
is certainly implied in the received text) that the delivery
of the decrees to the churches, which is described in xvi. 4,
and the confirmation of the churches in xv. 41, are both
intended to apply to all the churches visited. The clause
inserted at the beginning of xvi.‡ makes the geographical
description clearer and more precise, but does not make any
material addition to the sense. It is, however, important
in its bearing on a later verse, xvi. 6, to the opening
words of which it is obviously parallel. It sums up the
description of the visit to Syria and Cilicia given in
the preceding verse. Several other additions belong to

---

* Most writers who hold the North-Galatian theory speak in very
strong terms of the incompleteness of the narrative in Acts. Much
of the justification for their criticism disappears when the narrative
is properly interpreted.

† παραδιδοὺς τὰς ἐντολὰς τῶν πρεσβυτέρων.

‡ διελθὼν δὲ τὰ ἔθνη ταῦτα.

classes of variants described by Professor Rendel Harris,* and need not be enumerated.

The substitution of γενόμενοι for ἐλθόντες in xvi. 7 is more significant than any other of the variants in this passage. The verb used brings out even more clearly the continuity of the action described in ver. 7 with that described in ver. 6, and the impossibility of supposing that a long residence and evangelisation in North Galatia is to be interposed between the verb διῆλθον and the verb ἐπείραζον (ἤθελαν in *Codex Bezæ*). No one can read the sentence contained in verses 6 and 7 without being struck with the obvious ignorance of the reviser that any process of evangelisation in a new land, hitherto untrodden by the Apostle and unmentioned in the previous chapters, is described in the opening clause of ver. 6. His addition to xvi. 1 brings out into marked prominence his conception that the clause in xvi. 6, " they passed through the Phrygo-Galatic country," is a mere geographical recapitulation of the more general description in verses 4 and 5. In xvi. 1 the clause διελθὼν, etc., sums up the description introduced by διήρχετο, and in xvi. 6 the clause διῆλθον, etc., sums up the description introduced by διερχόμενοι. We have here a complete proof that the reviser whose work has been preserved to us in *Codex Bezæ*† understood the passage as we have interpreted it. If the other points about this revision which we attempt in these chapters to establish are satisfactorily proved, the con-

---

* *A Study of Codex Bezæ*, p. 222.

† The question whether the text of *Codex Bezæ* is due entirely to this reviser or is complicated by other influences lies apart from our subject. My remarks about it are confined, like my knowledge, to Acts xiii.—-xxi.

clusion must be accepted that in the first half of the second century, by a skilful, well-informed, careful, and clear-headed reviser, who was familiar with an independent tradition preserved in Asia Minor, the passage in Acts xvi. 1–6 was interpreted precisely in the same way that we have interpreted the received text.*

It is advisable to notice an argument derived from the syntax of xvi. 6. It has been contended that the participle κωλυθέντες gives the reason for the finite verb διῆλθον, and is therefore preliminary to it in the sequence of time. We reply that the participial construction cannot, in this author, be pressed in that way. He is often loose in the framing of his sentences, and in the long sentence in verses 6 and 7 he varies the succession of verbs by making some of them participles. The sequence of the verbs is also the sequence of time: (1) they went through the Phrygo-Galatic land; (2) they were forbidden to speak in Asia; (3) they came over against Mysia; (4) they assayed to go into Bithynia; (5) the Spirit suffered them not; (6) they passed through Mysia; (7) they came to Troas.

---

* The account of the journeys which is here given was printed before I had looked into *Codex Bezæ*. Working at the Thekla-legend for a later chapter of this work, I was struck with the fact that the legend presupposes the reading of *Codex Bezæ* in xxi. 1; and a letter from Professor Rendel Harris, in answer to an inquiry on this point, turned my attention to the wider question. The character of *Codex Bezæ* is so plainly marked in these chapters that a few hours' work at it convinced me of its origin and date. The character of this *Codex* is discussed more fully in Chapter VIII., §§ 3–5.

CHAPTER V.

THE THIRD JOURNEY.

IN St. Paul's third journey it seems clear that his original object was the province of Asia, and the visit to the churches of the Galatian country was a mere episode by the way. The aim which he had when he started on the second journey, and which he was forbidden by the Spirit when he reached Antioch to carry into effect, was realised in his third journey. The terms in which the country traversed by him before reaching Asia is described are unfortunately very obscure; he "went through the Galatic region and Phrygian" (or perhaps "and Phrygia") "in order stablishing all the disciples" ($\delta\iota\epsilon\rho\chi\acute{o}\mu\epsilon\nu\sigma\varsigma$ $\kappa\alpha\theta\epsilon\xi\hat{\eta}\varsigma$ $\tau\grave{\eta}\nu$ $\Gamma\alpha\lambda\alpha\tau\iota\kappa\grave{\eta}\nu$ $\chi\acute{\omega}\rho\alpha\nu$ $\kappa\alpha\grave{\iota}$ $\Phi\rho\nu\gamma\acute{\iota}\alpha\nu$, xviii. 23).

The difficulty is whether we are to understand $\Phi\rho\nu\gamma\acute{\iota}\alpha\nu$ as adjective or as noun: if the former, the expression is to be understood in the same way as xvi. 6, "the territory which in one way is called Galatic and in another Phrygian"; if the latter, the expression means "the Galatic territory and Phrygia." If the former interpretation is correct, the reversed order of the adjectives must be explained as merely accidental, and due to the perfect indifference as to which should come first, the meaning being precisely the same in either case. When we follow that interpretation, the passage must be understood on the analogy of xvi. 6, and affords no new evidence.

But if, on the other hand, we follow the second interpretation, the meaning is not quite clear; for Paul must traverse Phrygia before reaching Asia, by whatever route he travelled. He came from Antioch of Syria through the Syrian and the Cilician Gates; but the line of his route is not indicated until he reached districts which he had previously visited and where he had converts. He traversed this country, systematically visiting every place where there were disciples. Besides being called in xviii. 23, "the region of Galatia and Phrygia," the district is briefly described by another expression in xix. 1, "Paul, having passed through the upper country" (διελθόντα τὰ ἀνωτερικὰ μέρη), "came to Ephesus,"—*i.e.*, he traversed the country from Cilicia to Ephesus, crossing the great central plateau, and descending to the sea again. He had a choice of two routes, one direct, passing through the churches which he visited on his first and second journeys, Derbe, Lystra, etc., and the other making an enormous circuit through Cappadocia and North Galatia, and omitting all the churches which are known to us by name. Can we, in the face of the word καθεξῆς, suppose that he left unvisited every church known to us, and visited only others which are never elsewhere mentioned in this book,* and whose existence is only assumed in order to explain the Epistle to the Galatians? Certainly the writer could not easily have described the journey in a way more calculated

---

* On any interpretation of the words of Acts xvi. 6, the foundation of North-Galatian churches is not there actually alluded to; St. Paul is merely said to have traversed the Galatian country, but no hint is given that he founded churches. But the churches mentioned in xviii. 23 are spoken of by the author as if they were already familiar to his readers.

to mislead, if his meaning is that Paul chose the northern route through Cappadocia and North Galatia.

Why should the narrator, who in other cases describes St. Paul's route with accuracy, leave it entirely doubtful whether he took the northern or the southern route? The reason is that the northern route never occurred to him as a possibility. The route from Syria by the Cilician Gates to the Ægean coast was a familiar and much frequented one; and unless another route was expressly mentioned, every one would understand that Paul passed through Lycaonia, and not through North Galatia. Moreover, on our theory, the reference to the disciples who were visited in their several places by the way is left in no doubt. After our explanation of the two previous journeys, the third is perfectly clear; it is only on the North-Galatian theory that any doubt about it can exist.

Further, the North-Galatian theory does not explain the words "all the disciples." If the journey passed through North Galatia, Paul could not visit the South-Galatian churches: why then should the writer be so careful to mention that he visited "all the disciples"?* On the South-Galatian theory he would naturally visit them all, for no congregations existed except those which lay along his route.

The account of the third journey is, therefore, not expressed in language which, taken by itself, gives any conclusive argument as to the route followed; but it gives a much clearer and more satisfactory picture, when interpreted according to the South-Galatian theory.

---

* Moreover καθεξῆς implies " in order from the first to the last, from east to west."

We must therefore interpret the phrase τὴν Γαλατικὴν χώραν καὶ Φρυγίαν, as corresponding on the whole to the similar phrase τὴν Φρυγίαν καὶ Γαλατικὴν χώραν in xvi. 6. Why, then, did the author of the "Travel-Document" change his expression? He did so because the phrase in xvi. 6 would be incorrect in xviii. 23. The country denoted by the phrase in xvi. 6 is that which was traversed by Paul after leaving Lystra : it is therefore the territory about Iconium and Antioch, and is rightly called Phrygo-Galatic, "the part of Phrygia that was attached to Galatia." But the country which is meant in xviii. 23 includes Derbe, Lystra, Iconium, and Antioch, and could not rightly be called "Phrygo-Galatic." If the writer wished to carry out this complicated phraseology, he would have had to say "Lycaono-Galatic and Phrygo-Galatic." He avoids the difficulty by using the simple phrase "the Galatic country." The sense of Φρυγίαν still remains doubtful : it may denote either Phrygia Galatica, or Phrygia Magna (which Paul would traverse after leaving the Galatic territory), or both.

It must be acknowledged that there is in this journey one difficulty from which the North-Galatian theory is free. St. Paul's object was the west coast of Asia, and Ephesus was the point at which he arrived. The ordinary and frequented route for trade between Antioch and the west coast passed through Apameia and Colossæ and Laodiceia. But it would appear from the Epistle to the Colossians (ii. 1) that the Christians at Colossæ and at Laodiceia had not seen his face. On the other hand, his natural route, according to the North-Galatian theory, would not lead him through Colossæ and Laodiceia, but would pass more to the north through Philadelpheia.

We may remark on this that, in the first place, the journey, so far as it traversed new country, was evidently rapid and unbroken; for there is no allusion to preaching in new places, but only to the confirming of old converts, until Ephesus was reached. It is therefore quite possible that St. Paul might have spent a night either at Colossæ or at Laodiceia,* and yet that he might several years afterwards write to the Christians there as persons who had never seen his face. Moreover, though trade and vehicles regularly took the road through Apameia and Laodiceia, foot-passengers might quite possibly prefer the shorter hill road by the plain of Metropolis and the Tchyvritzi Kleisoura, in which, many centuries later, the last serious attempt of the Byzantine Emperors to break the rising power of the Seljuk Turks failed through the headstrong folly of the brave but rash Manuel Comnenus. This path would take them by way of Eumeneia and the Cayster valley, and would save a day's journey.†

The text of *Codex Bezæ* in this passage is remarkable. It reads in xix. 1, "And when Paul was minded according to his own plan to go to Jerusalem, the Spirit bade him turn back into Asia; and having passed through the upper country he came unto Ephesus."

---

* If he was going at even a moderate rate, he would not pass a night in each, for the distance between them is only about ten miles. We observe here, as always, that Paul hurries on to the great centres of civilisation and education (in this case to Ephesus).

† The inference from Col. ii. 1 that St. Paul's face had never been seen by the Christians at Colossæ and Laodiceia is by no means universally accepted. For example, Lewin, *St. Paul*, p. 196, understands from the verse that Paul had been at Colossæ, but not at Laodiceia. I cannot, however, doubt that the inference in the preceding paragraph is right.

The reviser understood that Paul, after having traversed the Phrygo-Galatic country and stablished all the disciples, began to return with the intention of proceeding to Jerusalem; but thereupon the Spirit ordered him to turn back and go into Asia. The reviser obviously considered, therefore, that Paul, when he began to return towards Jerusalem, had not entered Asia; and, if so, he did not understand $\Phi\rho\nu\gamma\ell\alpha\nu$ in the sense ordinarily given to it, for Phrygia, as distinguished from the Galatic territory, belongs to the province Asia, and both North and South-Galatian theories have to start from that fact.

The readings described here and on pp. 87 ff. are peculiarly valuable; for they give us a slight but yet sufficiently trustworthy indication of the date when the reviser did his work. Previous indications have shown that he worked later than the first century; now we shall see that he worked before the middle of the second century. The reviser, as we saw in the preceding chapter, had no thought that Paul travelled in North Galatia, and understood $\Gamma\alpha\lambda\alpha\tau\iota\kappa\dot{\eta}\ \chi\omega\rho\alpha$ in the sense which we have proved to be common and usual in the first and early second century. He therefore considered that this third journey also led through Derbe, Lystra, Iconium, and Antioch; and that Paul, after visiting and stablishing all his converts, was returning to Jerusalem, when he was ordered to go into Asia. We have also seen that the reviser adapted the topography of the document to the facts of his own time. It is therefore clear that the cities visited by Paul were still considered by the reviser to be in the Galatic country when he worked over the text. Now great part of Lycaonia was separated from Galatia in the reign of

Antoninus Pius, between 138 and 161 A.D. ;* and we may feel confident that, if the reviser had worked after the change of system had become familiar and had produced a new nomenclature, he would have remodelled the text accordingly. The revision therefore took place before A.D. 161, and probably not later than A.D. 150.

The reference to the bidding of the Spirit marks the addition at the beginning of xix. 1 as one of a class of insertions in this *Codex*, with which we are not directly concerned here.† But this passage goes beyond its class in asserting that Paul actually intended to act differently, and that his intention to go to Jerusalem was checked by the Spirit. It seems hardly possible to reconcile this positive statement with the reverence for the text which the reviser certainly felt, except on the assumption that he was acquainted with an independent tradition on the point which he believed to be true, and considered himself justified by its truth in adding to the text.

---

* See *Hist. Geogr.*, pp. 253, 376. The probability is that the change took place in an early part of the reign (*Ib.*, p. 376, note), and A.D. 150 may fairly be taken as the latest date.

† Rendel Harris, *Study of Codex Bezæ*, p. 221.

CHAPTER VI.

THE EPISTLE TO THE GALATIANS.

1. ARGUMENTS FOUNDED ON THE EPISTLE.

I HAVE intentionally refrained from mentioning any of the general arguments which have been advanced by previous advocates of the South-Galatian theory. They vary in value. Some have very little value, while others at least corroborate the theory. The real proof must depend on the interpretation of Acts, and the theory stands or falls thereby; but a brief summary of these arguments, as they are given by Lipsius, may properly find a place here, and his counter-arguments may be noticed, where they seem to require it.

1. St. Paul habitually uses district names in the Roman sense; and Lycaonia was in Roman Galatia. This we have already discussed and put more accurately.

2. St. Paul uses the Greek language to the Christians whom he addresses, and apparently calls them Greeks; whereas the North-Galatians spoke Celtic. This argument, put in this bare way, has no real value; its proper character has already been discussed. (See p. 82.)

3. He mentions (Gal. ii. 13) Barnabas as a person known to his readers; Barnabas was not personally known to the North-Galatians. I can see no great value in this argument. Barnabas is alluded to, and his views on the question of evangelising the Gentiles are assumed to be

familiar to the readers; but the same assumption is made about Peter and some of the other apostles. It is, however, true that Barnabas was not such a prominent figure, and acquaintance with his views is more remarkable than knowledge of what Peter thought.

4. Paul's companions, when he was returning from Corinth to Jerusalem, seem to represent the different churches, and bear their contributions. Among them are Gaius of Derbe and Timothy of Lystra, but none from North Galatia. This argument has very little value; Timothy at least might be with Paul as his travelling companion, and several other churches have no representatives.

5. There is no record in Acts of the foundation of churches in North Galatia. This depends entirely on the interpretation of the narrative in Acts xvi. and xviii.

6. The presence of Jewish emissaries, which is presupposed in the epistle, is natural in South Galatia and improbable in North Galatia. This is an important piece of corroborative evidence, and requires more careful attention, as it is connected with a general law observable in the development of the country.

The change in the feeling of the Galatians was due to the action of a definite individual, a person of some consequence and standing, who had beguiled them into an exaggerated devotion to the Jewish law and practices.* St. Paul knows him, but does not name him in writing to the Galatians. This visit of several strangers (the great man and his companions), taken in connection with St. Paul's two passages across the Galatian territory, makes it pro-

---

* See Gal. v. 7 and 10, with the notes of Lipsius. I accept his interpretation in preference to other views.

bable that a frequented and common route from Syria led through it.* It is hardly probable that they went forth for the express purpose of counteracting Paul; rather they would be travelling with the general intention of preaching in the most populous and frequented districts of Asia, along a familiar and important road. This consideration suits the South-Galatian, but not the North-Galatian territory. Elsewhere I have shown at length † that the development and the importance of the territory on the northern side of the plateau—*i.e.*, Northern Galatia and Northern Phrygia—belong to the period following after 292, and result from the transference of the centre of government first to Nicomedeia and afterwards to Constantinople. Under the earlier Roman Empire, the southern side of the plateau was far more important than the northern side. It would be easy, but is here unnecessary and unsuitable, to strengthen this proof by quoting many facts which confirm the view that North Galatia as a whole was slow in adopting the Græco-Roman civilisation,‡ that it was not as a country so familiar to strangers from Syria as South Galatia, that except in Ancyra and Pessinus and Germa § there was probably no

---

* Lipsius replies by quoting proof that Ancyra and Tavium (the latter he identifies with Gordium, which was 100 miles distant) were on an important trade route, but he does not prove (and could not prove) that they were on a route of Syrian trade. His remarks about the situation of Iconium, etc., show such erroneous views of the country and its antiquities that I need not mention them. (See *Hand Kommentar*, II. 2, p. 3.)

† *Hist. Geogr.*, chaps. G, H, J, K.

‡ See one fact mentioned on pp. 146–7.

§ Germa was a colony, though not one of much importance. It struck coins. See p. 82.

Greek-speaking population in North Galatia to which St. Paul could address himself, and no Jewish congregations with which he could make a beginning.

Why then did the Roman governor reside at Ancyra, and not in Southern Galatia? Ancyra was the capital of the province, because it was a city of great importance and wealth (beyond Iconium or Antioch), commanding a fertile country; and because the problems of Roman policy in the north of Asia Minor were very serious, and required an official of high rank there. The absorption of the neighbouring countries into the Empire was going on in that quarter with great rapidity during the first century, and each new addition to the Empire was incorporated in the province Galatia.

7. St. Paul had been twice in Galatia before he wrote the epistle; if North Galatia is the country in question, he had visited Jerusalem at least three times before he wrote, whereas in the epistle he speaks only of two visits to Jerusalem. This is an important subject; but it is so difficult, and opens up so many disputed points, that it has no value as a piece of corroborative evidence. It is, of course, in any case difficult to reconcile the two visits of the epistle with the account given in the earlier part of Acts, which seems to necessitate the recognition of more visits; and the difficulty is greatly increased if the epistle is placed after the third journey, when an additional visit to Jerusalem has to be reckoned with. On the South-Galatian theory, the epistle might have been written soon after St. Paul crossed into Europe. It would thus be one of the earliest of the extant epistles; and the oldest authority on the subject, Marcion, about a century later, placed it actually first in his edition of the epistles. This

fact is far from conclusive, for it is not proved that Marcion arranged his collection according to what he believed to be chronological order ; but his order must be allowed to have a certain value * in regard to the opening epistle.

There is, however, no doubt that the Epistle to the Galatians has far closer analogies with 1 and 2 Corinthians and Romans (which were composed on the third journey), than with 1 and 2 Thessalonians (which were written during the second journey). But it is a question whether the difference of tone in the latter may not be quite explicable by the peculiar circumstances of the church at Thessalonica ; and, even if Paul wrote to the Galatians from Corinth, there seems no reason why his views and thoughts should not be very similar to those he expressed to the Romans and Corinthians on his third journey a little later.

There can be no doubt that a date during the second journey would suit several passages in Galatians well ; and this date is consistent with the South-Galatian, but not with the North-Galatian, theory. But so long as the well-known problem connected with St. Paul's visits to Jerusalem remains unsolved, nothing final can be said on this point.

8. The dispute which took place during St. Paul's visit to Jerusalem (Gal. ii. 5) concerned those whom Paul addresses ($\hat{v}\mu\hat{a}s$); but the visit took place before the second journey, and he is not supposed by any one to have visited North Galatia on his first journey. This is not an important point.

9. Another argument is mentioned by Lightfoot as strong but not convincing. At Lystra St. Paul was taken for an impersonation of the Divine power, and

---

* Wieseler argues that his order was in a rough way chronological.

similarly the Galatians of the epistle received him as an angel of God (iv. 14) ; and this idea dwells in the writer's mind, and suggests his expression in i. 8, "though we, or an angel from heaven, should preach unto you any gospel." The extraordinary effect produced by Paul in Antioch, etc., is shown in Acts xiii., xiv. ; we cannot say that anything quite similar to it is related of any other part of his missionary work. Precisely such extraordinary effect is implied in the epistle ; and the coincidence between the two documents is acknowledged by Lightfoot to be striking.

10. It is implied that the opponents of St. Paul quoted his own action and misrepresented him as preaching circumcision (v. 11).* The reference to his action in the case of Timothy is here unmistakable, and is fully admitted by Lightfoot in his commentary on the verse. Such an argument would appeal with peculiarly strong effect to the South-Galatian churches after what is related in Acts xvi. 3.

2. ST. PAUL'S FEELINGS TOWARDS THE GALATIAN CHURCHES.

The churches of Antioch, etc., were the firstfruits of St. Paul's wider activity, and the narrative in Acts shows that his experiences among them on his first journey were most encouraging for the initiator of a new departure in the guidance of missionary effort. Moreover, they gave him his most faithful and devoted companion throughout his subsequent life, Timothy. We should certainly suppose

---

* *Die eingedrungenen Sendlinge . . . vorwerfen dem Paulus, er predige ja selbst die Beschneidung.*

from his general character, and from the personal affection which he often shows for his converts, that he would retain a warm interest in his earliest Gentile churches. The Philippians, the first of his European hearers, were regarded by himself with special love. He refers to his earliest converts in Greece and in Asia as the firstfruits of Achaia and of Asia. Surely we should find in his epistles some proof of interest in Antioch, Iconium, Derbe, and Lystra.

The narrative in Acts proves that he did retain such an interest in this South-Galatian group of churches, for he visited Derbe at least twice, Lystra and Iconium and Antioch at least three times; while, on our theory, he visited them all once more on his third missionary journey. Yet, on the usual theory, we find throughout St. Paul's writings no single word to show that he retained a kindly recollection of them or an interest in them. Once he does refer to them, but only to recall his sufferings and persecution among them (2 Tim. iii. 11); in no other way, at no other time, does he make any allusion to them. Even when he orders a contribution for the sufferers by the famine in Palestine (1 Cor. xvi. 1), he thinks of the Galatian churches, but not (according to the dominant theory) about the churches of Antioch, Iconium, Derbe, and Lystra. It would be impossible to conceive a more direct contradiction in tone and emotional feeling than exists, on this theory, between Acts and Galatians, as regards St. Paul's attitude to the South-Galatian churches. Such a contradiction is inexplicable, except on the supposition that Acts belongs to a different period and to different surroundings from the Epistles; the Epistles give the real tone and feeling that ruled in the actual circumstances, Acts gives the later memory that survived among

the Christians of the second century, and its composition
would have to be dated in that period. I can see no escape
from this conclusion, if we admit that the contradiction
exists; and in opposition to it my aim is to show that
both accounts belong to the same period, and are instinct
with the same emotion.

Moreover, we might ask how a later age, to which the
composition of Acts is relegated on this supposition, came
to attach so much more importance to these churches than
Paul himself did? It is certain that the South-Galatian
churches did not in later time play a very prominent part
in Christian history; they had for a short time, during
St. Paul's own life, the interest naturally attaching to the
first Gentile churches, and they never again held the same
position. The account given in Acts is historically true
to the period 48–64 A.D., and not to later time.

Thus, on every ground, the inconsistency and self-contra-
diction involved in the dominant North-Galatian theory
become clear. The conclusion is plain. That theory is
wrong; and the interpretation which restores consistency
to the documents, and reality to the history contained in
them, must be accepted.

As to the discrepancy which exists, on the North-Galatian
theory, between the silence of Acts about the North-
Galatian churches, and the importance which the epistle
implies them to possess, it is no defence to quote the fact
that St. Paul wrote to the Colossians, yet they are never
mentioned in Acts. In the letter he expressly says that
they had never seen him, and hence in Acts there was no
opportunity of mentioning them; but yet a clear and
admitted allusion to Colossæ and Laodiceia occurs in
xix. 10, "all they which dwelt in Asia heard the word."

3. ARGUMENTS FOR THE NORTH-GALATIAN THEORY.

If we ask for positive arguments in favour of the North-Galatian theory, none are offered. All arguments in its favour take the form of pointing out difficulties in the other theory. There are undoubtedly difficulties in the other theory; but the history of the Apostolic period is full of difficulties, in comparison to which those involved in the South-Galatian theory are trifles. The North-Galatian theory avoids the difficulties by creating an unknown set of churches, to which the epistle was addressed, as the Greek mythologists explained the contradictions in their fables by creating two or five or ten persons bearing the same name ; but in one case alone did we find that it solved a difficulty in which the South-Galatian theory was involved. Hence no positive argument can be brought forward in its favour, for the North-Galatian churches are an unknown factor ; and it cannot be either proved or disproved that the facts alluded to in the epistle suit them. One single argument which looks like a positive reason may detain our attention for a moment.

The North Galatians were a Celtic race who had invaded Asia Minor in the third century B.C. It has been argued with much unanimity and strength of assertion that the character, conduct, and emotions of the Galatians to whom the epistle is addressed are those of a Celtic people. It is certainly a sound principle to compare the qualities implied in St. Paul's epistles with the national character of the persons addressed ; but national character is a very delicate subject to deal with, and the Celtic faults and qualities are certainly overstated by some of the commentators. The climax of imaginative insight into national character is reached by some Germans, who consider the population of North Galatia to be not Celtic but Germanic, and discover in the Galatians of the epistle the qualities of their own nation.

Much might be said in the way of arguing that the action of the Galatians was due, not to the peculiarities of Celts, but to the nature of an Oriental people like the Phrygians and Lycaonians, who had a strong natural affinity for the Hebraic type of Christianity (*v.* p. 57 *n.*).   But it will be readily granted that this line of argument has no force in the decision of the question ; the nationality of the persons addressed must be settled on other considerations, and then it will be time to search for indications of their national character in the traits and acts recorded of them.

Wendt, in his last edition of " Meyer's Commentary," appears to take a sort of middle view, if I rightly understand him.   He expressly admits that St. Paul uses the term Galatia, like all provincial names, in the Roman sense, and that it would be quite in accordance with his style to use the expression "churches of Galatia," indicating the churches of Antioch, Iconium, etc.*   He quotes the reference to Galatia, 1 Cor. xvi. 1, as an example of St. Paul's custom of using such terms in the Roman sense.†   He therefore considers that in 1 Cor. xvi. 1 " the churches of Galatia " includes the South Galatian churches.   Yet he proceeds to deny that the Epistle to the Galatians could possibly be written to the South-Galatians, and asserts that it must be written to the North-Galatian churches alone. This view appears to imply utter confusion of thought in

---

* Commentary on xvi. 6-10, footnote to pp. 353, 354.
† Commentary on xiii. 9.

Paul, and to attribute to him a carelessness in the use of terms which no accurate writer could be guilty of. To justify this view Wendt adduces one single argument, which he considers decisive. It is as follows. In Gal. i. 21 St. Paul says that he spent in Syria and Cilicia the interval of fourteen years between his first and second visits* to Jerusalem, and does not mention that he was in Galatia during that time. It was unnecessary for him to mention to North-Galatian Christians that he had been in South Galatia during the interval; but it appears to Wendt "psychologically impossible" that Paul should not have mentioned the visit to South Galatia, if he had been writing to the South-Galatian Christians.

It might be a sufficient answer that the reconciliation of the account given in the epistle of St. Paul's visits to Jerusalem with the narrative in Acts is the greatest historical problem in his life; and that no argument founded on that account has any great value until the whole problem is solved. But, further, I think that Wendt's argument does not take the simplest way of treating the difficulty which he has touched. The view which I shall suggest seems easier; and for that reason I mention it, though I feel that it does not solve the difficulty fully.

The best way to test this argument is to carry into effect the "psychological" necessity. Let us still suppose that the letter was addressed to the South Galatians, and let us add the words which, according to Wendt, would in that case

---

* I do not intend to prejudge the question whether the interval is between the first and second visits, or between the conversion and the second visit. Both interpretations are possible in the Greek, and only a complete chronological system can determine which of the two is meant.

be so necessary. Let any one read over Gal. i. 18—ii. 1, making verse 21 into " Then I came into the regions of Syria and Cilicia, and, as you are aware, I preached among you," (who dwell in the Roman province adjoining Cilicia). Does this add to the effect of the narrative as a piece of impassioned argument ? Is it inconceivable or inconsistent with Paul's style, rapid, disjointed, leaving much to the intelligence of his readers, that he should assume that the churches of Iconium, etc., knew his history during those years well enough to fill in for themselves the details which, as we know, are concealed in the expression " the regions of Syria and Cilicia "? It is precisely because he was writing to persons among whom he had spent a long time, during the interval of fourteen years about which he is writing, precisely because he can assume that they had the knowledge needed to fill in the details, that he contents himself with the hurried words, " the regions of Syria and Cilicia." During those years he had always been in Syria, or in Cilicia, or near the Cilician frontier and in regions closely connected with Cilicia.* This was familiar at Iconium, but we have no reason to think that Paul could have presumed upon its being familiar at Ancyra and Pessinus, which he is not supposed to have seen until after the fourteen years had expired.

Another objection may be noticed. It has been stated

---

* The road through the Cilician Gates by Iconium to the west was one of the great routes of history ; and a considerable connection between Iconium and Tarsus is certain, though not so close as that between Syria and Cyprus or Pamphylia. Cilicia Tracheia reached nearly to Derbe ; and the name Cilicia is several times used by Appian in a very wide sense to include the southern parts of Lycaonia.

by some commentators that at Apollonia, a town which in many respects occupied a similar position to Antioch (for it was originally Phrygian and afterwards Pisidian, and moreover was included in the province Galatia from 25 B.C. onwards), the Lydo-Phrygian era of the organisation by Sulla 85-4 B.C. was employed.* The use of this era implies that the people of Apollonia did not set great store by their connexion with the province Galatia ; otherwise they would have reckoned their chronology from the incorporation of that province. When it has been proved that the Lydo-Phrygian era was employed in Apollonia, some historical inferences of a different character will be deducible ; but up to the present it has not been proved. The commentators refer to an inscription dated in the year 247 ; but it is quite uncertain from what era this number is reckoned. M. Waddington indeed, who is perhaps the highest authority on the antiquities of Asia Minor, says in his commentary that the date ought *perhaps* to be reckoned according to the Lydo-Phrygian era ; but it is just as easily reckoned from the Galatian era, and, until other dated inscriptions are found to decide, nothing can be inferred from this one.†

A *via media*, which perhaps might be thought to reconcile the two opposite theories,—viz., that the epistle is written to both North and South Galatian churches,—is decisively to be rejected. The churches addressed in the epistle were converted at one time (iv. 13), whereas the South-Galatians were converted on the first journey, and the North-Gala-tians were, according to the theory, converted on the second

---

* *Corpus Inscript. Græc.*, No. 3973 ; Le Bas and Waddington, No. 1192.

† Franz on C.I.G. 3973 suggests the era 49 B.C. The suggestion has no antecedent probability, but cannot be proved to be false.

journey. Moreover, if these chapters have succeeded in proving anything, they have proved that the narrative in Acts is inconsistent with the theory that St. Paul was thought by the writer to have ever been in North Galatia.

4. ANALOGY OF FIRST PETER.

Another objection may be urged: why is it that these churches are called Galatian only in the epistle, and nowhere else? But they are elsewhere referred to as Galatian. The superscription of I. Peter to the elect who are sojourners of the Dispersion in Pontus, Galatia, Cappadocia, Asia, and Bithynia, beyond a doubt employs these terms in the Roman sense. It sums up the whole of Asia Minor north of the Taurus range. The fringe of coast-land south of Taurus is excluded; but Cilicia goes with Syria, not with Asia Minor,* and Pamphylia and Lycia seem not to have had important Christian communities in early times. If, on the other hand, we take these terms in the popular sense in which they were employed by some writers, what an amorphous and haphazard enumeration it is! Mysia, Phrygia, Pisidia, Lycaonia, are omitted, some of the most important and many of the earliest Christian churches are excluded, and precisely the countries where evidence of the strength and numbers of the Jews is strongest are left out.

Why then did this writer use the Roman nomenclature? For much the same reason as Paul. He was writing from Rome, and he also had the mind of an organiser, and had caught a glimpse of the great con-

---

* The governor of Syria had a certain military charge over Cilicia, and Marquardt thinks he even governed it. In the system of the Christian Empire the Cilician churches were subject to Antioch.

ception of Christianity as the religion of the Roman Empire. He saw the immense importance of the churches of Asia Minor, he foresaw the situation in which they were about to be placed, and hence he writes to them as a body.

Lightfoot fully admits this interpretation in the case of I. Peter ; but explains it as " not unnatural in one who was writing from a distance and perhaps had never visited the district." This seems to me to explain nothing : Paul also, according to Lightfoot, wrote from a distance—viz., from Macedonia. But why a person writing from a distance should prefer the Roman term, he has not explained. As we contemplate the facts, the reason lies in the writer's habit of thought.

5. CHANGE IN THE MEANING OF THE NAME GALATIA.

Why, then, was an interpretation, which is so natural and so necessary, lost for so many centuries and recovered only in the beginning of the present century? It was lost because, during the second century, the term Galatia ceased to bear the sense which it had to a Roman in the first century. The whole of central and southern Lycaonia was, before the middle of the second century, separated from Galatia, and formed into a province Lycaonia, which was united with Isauria and Cilicia under the title of " the three Eparchies," and put under the command of a governor of the highest rank. From this time onwards the true sense of the term Galatia in St. Paul's time was lost ; and the misconception has lasted unchallenged till this century and dominant to the present day. Among French scholars alone * is the true view generally accepted.

---

* See, *e.g.*, Renan, or Perrot in his treatise *de Galatia Provincia Romana.* In Germany Weizsäcker rejects the dominant view.

CHAPTER VII.

ST. PAUL AT EPHESUS.

EXPLANATORY NOTE.

THE following chapter was originally written in reply
to a paper entitled "Demetrius the Silversmith:
an Ephesian Study," which was contributed by the Rev.
Canon Hicks to the *Expositor* for June 1890, pp. 401–422.
My reply was composed on the spur of the moment,
immediately on reading the paper.* Still it appears better
to republish it substantially as it was written, merely
adding some new evidence. A paper which fully corresponded to the title "St. Paul at Ephesus," would be very
long, and would have to repeat much that has been well
said by others, and particularly by Bishop Lightfoot in the
Contemporary Review, May 1878.

Mr Hicks' paper was suggested by an inscription found
at Ephesus by Mr. Wood. It was published as a fragment
by the latter; but Mr. Hicks was able to render it nearly
complete by the acute observation that a small scrap of
marble with a few letters on it, which had not been noticed
by Mr. Wood, fitted on to the larger piece which the latter
had published. I regret to have found myself obliged to
differ *toto cælo* from the theory which Mr. Hicks based
on the inscription. Considering how much we are agreed
on in regard to Ephesus, and how much I have since

---

* It was published in the *Expositor*, July 1890.

learned from his scholarly publication of the Ephesian inscriptions (in the *Ancient Greek Inscriptions of the British Museum*, vol. iii.), it is almost unfortunate that we should present in this point (the only one that comes before the public) the appearance of disagreement. Before reprinting this paper, I wrote to Canon Hicks, asking whether he had any further evidence to confirm any points in his case. I hoped that we might settle some of our differences out of court. I understand from his kind and scholarly reply that his view is, like mine, that the arguments on the two sides should be fully and frankly stated, and that nothing but good will come of active discussion and criticism.

1. DEMETRIUS THE NEOPOIOS.

The inscription of Ephesus that suggested Canon Hicks' paper and the following reply is translated * as follows :—

"The Senate [and the People do public honour] to them that served as N[eopoioi, *i.e.*, Temple-wardens] during the prytany of ——, in the year of Demetrius : viz.,

"Of the Ephesine Tribe : Demetrius, son of Menophilos, the son of Tryphon, of the thousand Boreis : Thoas, son of Drakontomenes, of the thousand Oinopes.

"Of the Augustan Tribe : Alexander, etc ; Pythion, etc.

"Of the Teian Tribe : [Herm]as † ; Pythodorus.

"Of the Karenaean Tribe : Eusebes : Tryphon.

"Of the Tribe Euonymoi : Heraklitus ; Apellas.

"Of the Bembinaean Tribe : [Pr]esbon ; [another name lost]."‡

---

* I modify very slightly the words and arrangements of the translation given by H. To save space, and to avoid the personal reference as far as possible, I shall in the rest of the paper use the letter H. to denote Canon Hicks' paper. The inscription is now published as number DLXXVIII in his volume of Ephesian inscriptions.

† I omit the description of this and the following officials.

‡ A second inscription, unconnected with this one, was engraved at a later time on another side of the same stone.

The words or letters enclosed in square brackets are restored in places where the inscription is mutilated. It is to be observed that the crucial word is a restoration ; only the first letter of it remains. It must be admitted that the restoration given by H. is in the highest degree probable, but it cannot be pronounced certain. There were other officials whose name began with N. : *e.g.*, *Nomothetæ*, *Nomophvlakes.* I attach, however, no importance to these possibilities ; the reasons excellently stated by H. show that his restoration approximates towards certainty. But, in the dearth of knowledge about the officials of the Asian cities, nothing can be pronounced certain about them, unless it is expressly guaranteed by exact evidence. It is as nearly certain as any inference on the subject can be that we do not know the names of all the various boards of magistrates at Ephesus. Hence, even though the inferences drawn by H. were more probable than they are, the doubt always remains whether the Neopoioi were really mentioned in the inscription. But in this chapter H.'s restoration is accepted, and the theory which he founds on it is tested on its own merits.*

2. ACTS XIX. 23–41.

It is impossible for any one to invent a tale whose scene lies in a foreign land without betraying in slight details his ignorance of the scenery and circumstances amid which the event is described as taking place. Unless the writer studiously avoids details, and confines himself to names

---

* The paper originally began with the following paragraph. Additions are here made to it, and some slight modifications are introduced. It seems unnecessary to indicate the changes, which merely make more emphatic the views originally stated.

and generalities, he is certain to commit numerous errors. Even the most laborious and minute study of the circumstances of the country in which he is to lay his scene, will not preserve him from such errors. He must live long and observe carefully in the country, if he wishes to invent a tale which will not betray his ignorance in numberless details. Allusions of French or German authors to English life supply the readiest illustration of this principle. Even after all the study that has been expended on classical writers, I will engage to prove it in detail from almost any commentary on a Greek or Roman author, where the commentator ventures beyond mere linguistic exposition of his text.

Even to relate with propriety and accuracy in the details an incident that has occurred in a foreign land, is no easy task, unless the narrator has actually witnessed it and confines himself strictly to describing what he saw. In such a case the one chance of safety for a writer that has not seen the facts, lies in faithfully reproducing the narrative of an eyewitness. As soon as he ventures to write from an independent standpoint, and to modify the account of his authority, he is certain to import into his version some of those errors that betray the foreigner.

I propose to examine, from this point of view, some details in the account given in Acts of the riot fomented in Ephesus against St. Paul by Demetrius the silversmith. The writer does not profess to be an eyewitness of the scene, but he had abundant opportunity of learning from eyewitnesses all the incidents which he relates in Acts xix. with a multitude of minute details and local touches. If the story was invented, only a person intimately familiar with Ephesus could avoid errors that would provoke a smile from any

native.   The most careful and accurate modern students of
the antiquities of that country, even after close observation
of the ruins, would be the first to profess their inability to
attain local verisimilitude, if they had to invent such a tale.
The nearest approach they could make to verisimilitude
would be to collect in their narrative the details that they
could actually trace from ancient remains and records, and
studiously to avoid or slur over all others.   But, while it
would be impossible for any of us to attain verisimilitude
in relating such a story, it is much easier for us to criticise
such a story when told by another, and, by comparison with
other sources of information, to detect discrepancies between
the details that occur in it and facts that can be otherwise
ascertained.   Such criticism finds plenty of scope in the tale
of Paul and Demetrius.   While, on the one hand, it must
be confessed that our information has hitherto been too
scanty to justify us in asserting the perfect verisimilitude
of the story, yet it is equally certain that no error has
yet been proved to exist, and that a number of accurate
touches have been detected.

The most serious difficulty hithero started has been the
reference to the Asiarchs ; but this touches an exceedingly
obscure and difficult subject, and no recent writer has
ventured to maintain that the reference betrays ignorance.
It certainly is difficult to harmonise the reference with
other known facts ; but it is equally difficult to harmonise
these facts with each other.   For my own part, I accept
the reference as entirely accurate and as a valuable piece
of evidence.

The chief purpose of my remarks is to show the difficulty in which even the highest authority on the antiquities of Ephesus was involved, when he suggested that

the natural and straightforward interpretation of the narrative was incorrect, and ought to be rejected in favour of a rather artificial and far-fetched explanation. The theory which he elaborated only brings out more clearly the coherence and the direct simplicity of the narrative. There is only one way of interpreting it, and that is as embodying almost, if not absolutely, *verbatim* the words of an eyewitness.

The recent edition of the inscriptions of Ephesus gives a vast amount of new information about the city, and adds greatly to our power of criticising the nineteenth chapter of Acts ; and it is noteworthy that the firstfruits of that great work should be the editor's own attempt to prove that there occurs in Acts xix. precisely such an error in detail as a writer ignorant of the country is sure to commit in inventing a tale about it. This view is fatal to the whole theory which I have advanced as to the character and composition of the "Travel-Document." If the proof is conclusive, I should feel constrained to follow ; but the view at least requires rigorous examination, and I hope to show that it is not correct. H., indeed, infers only that the writer misunderstood the words of an eyewitness ; but this inference does not exhaust the consequences that follow from his theory. In opposition to it I shall try to prove, in the first place, that the view held on this detail by the author of Acts xix. is involved in the essence of the story, and must have been got by him from the account of the supposed eyewitness that he used as his authority ; and secondly, that it is no error, but a true and accurate idea, which adds to the general verisimilitude of the narrative.

While I am unable to agree with the theory stated by H., I should like to acknowledge the high interest and value of his paper in the *Expositor.* The importance of closely scrutinising the details of such a document is great, and the results, whether we actually agree with them or not, are sure to be highly suggestive. There are cases where a book or paper, whose actual results cannot be accepted, is far more valuable and suggestive than many statements of certain and indisputable facts are. H.'s paper is one of these cases ; its value in method is quite distinct from its value in results.

3. DEMETRIUS THE NEOPOIOS AND DEMETRIUS THE SILVERSMITH.

I should be very ready to acknowledge that, with regard to the identification which he proposes between the Demetrius of the inscription and the silversmith of Acts xix., H. has made out at least the probability of his case. It would be, of course, almost as difficult to prove an identity between two persons named John Smith in our own country as between two persons named Demetrius on the west coast of Asia Minor. But if he is right in dating his inscription about 50–60 A.D., then the case may be thus stated. Two independent documents mention a Demetrius in Ephesus about 50–60 A.D. In each case the Demetrius is a man of a certain standing in the city, influential and presumably wealthy. In the one case Demetrius is specified as a "silversmith," and as evidently a leader in the trade ; in the other case the Demetrius in question is designated in the ordinary way by his father's and grandfather's name, and by his "thousand." Such was the regular designation of a citizen—the addition of the father's name being almost universal, while the grandfather was less frequently mentioned, chiefly when the citizen bore one of the commoner names. In addition to this, the official position of the second Demetrius, as member and chairman of a board of city magistrates,* is recorded. The variety of style in the references is quite natural, and the fact that nothing in the one case agrees with anything recorded in the other is due to the different character of the documents, and affords no presumption that the two persons are different. The identity of the two is therefore quite possible; and a natural inclination leads us to hope that it may even be called probable.

The whole of the following remarks are written on the assumption that H. is right in dating the inscription about Demetrius in the reign of Nero.† But I cannot agree with a statement which he made in his reply, that "the identification of the Demetrius of the inscription with the silversmith of Acts xix. stands or falls with the date to be assigned to the inscription." The identification certainly falls if H.'s date is wrong; but it does not necessarily stand if his date is right. It merely begins in that case to be a possibility. There were certainly many Ephesians under Nero who were called Demetrius; and it would be an arbitrary assumption that the two references to Demetrius indicate the same person, without assigning some other reasons for the identification. But I have gone so far as to admit H.'s identification as probable. It is

---

* The *neopoioi* were civil magistrates, not religious officials. H. correctly apprehends this. They were, as he says, elected by the people annually.

† But on the date of the inscription see the note at the end of this chapter. I have here cut out a paragraph, and have elsewhere done the same where any passage does not contribute much to the effect. No change in my opinions is indicated thereby.

interesting, and I hope it is true. I say not a word against
it. The one reason why the paper is written lies in the
theory which H. has founded on it, and which may be false,
even though the identification be true.

4. ACTION OF THE PRIESTS OF ARTEMIS.

H.'s next point is, that the inscription belongs to the
very year in which occurred the famous scene in the theatre,
and that " the honour therein voted to him and his colleagues was in recognition of the services rendered by him
and them on behalf of the national goddess "—*i.e.*, as H. proceeds to show, in recognition of the demonstration against the
Apostle which Demetrius (and his colleagues, as H. would
add, expanding the narrative in Acts) organised in the
Great Theatre.

If this be so, we must gain much new light on the events
related in Acts xix. According to H.'s interpretation,
an entirely new aspect is put on the whole scene, and an
aspect which is absolutely at variance with the character
ascribed to it in Acts xix. It is represented to us in Acts
as a spontaneous demonstration by a trade against the
new influence that threatened to undermine its prosperity.
H. makes it out as due to the action of the priests,*
whose " jealousy only waited for an opportunity of attack-
ing the Apostle." " The plan they adopted " was to get
the board of Neopoioi " to organise a demonstration
against the Apostle." Demetrius called together the
silversmiths and " those engaged in kindred trades. He
appeals first to their trade interests, and soon proceeds to
work upon their fanaticism."

---

* In order to represent H. quite accurately, I preserve his own
words as far as possible.

The narrative in Acts xix. in its opening words states the connection between the silversmiths and Artemis : Demetrius "made silver shrines of Diana," and his trade would therefore disappear if her worship decayed. H., however, argues that this phrase is inexplicable and unintelligible, and that it is a bad inference from the words of an earlier narrator and eyewitness, who had described Demetrius as a silversmith by trade, holding the office of Neopoios of Artemis. The title was misunderstood by the author, who, in recasting his authority, altered νεοποιὸς Ἀρτέμιδος into ποιῶν ναοὺς ἀργυροῦς Ἀρτέμιδος. Let us, for the moment, grant this assumption, and substitute the new version for the old. The first thing that then strikes us is, that in this version the narrative does not explain how the trade interests were threatened. Demetrius says to the silversmiths, "By this business we have our wealth" : he then tells them that the worship of Diana is threatened, and the inference is that their trade is in danger. This speech has no meaning unless Demetrius is addressing tradesmen who work for the temple ; and no person who conceived the circumstances vividly, from personal knowledge, could relate the story without putting in the forefront an explanation of the close relation between the trade and the worship of Artemis. Silversmiths were common in all Greek cities ; the silver work of Athens was famous and lucrative, yet it had no relation to the worship of Artemis. There must have been some reason why the silversmiths of Ephesus were peculiarly connected with the temple, and this reason must have been stated at the outset of the tale, for it is assumed throughout as the explanation of the whole proceedings.

We must then suppose that the original authority began

his tale with a statement showing the connection between the trade, whose champion Demetrius makes himself, and the religion with which Demetrius assumes that the interests of that trade are identified. This connection must either be the same as that which is assigned in Acts, or a different one. H. evidently considers that it was a different one, both because he states that the author "misapprehended the document before him," and because he considers that Demetrius drove "a brisk trade in metal statuettes" of the goddess Artemis. This, then, was the connection stated in the original authority. We have to suppose that the author of Acts not merely misapprehended the meaning of *Neopoios*, but also omitted the explanation of the connection of the trade with Artemis-worship, and substituted a different explanation.

The term *Neopoios* was a very common one, and the office existed not merely in Ephesus, but in many others of the Greek cities of Asia. It would be quite as strong a proof of ignorance to interpret *Neopoios* as equivalent to *maker of temples*, as it would now be to confuse between Major-General and Lord Mayor. That the writer of Acts should not understand the meaning of *Neopoios* is hardly probable ; but that he should so arbitrarily and violently alter the account of the eyewitness whom he follows is in the highest degree improbable.

Another objection occurs to me, which in view of H.'s high authority on the antiquities of Ephesus, I hardly venture to state. I have never seen the phrase νεοποιὸς Ἀρτέμιδος, which he assumes to have been used in the original authority. The officials in question are, in all the inscriptions which I remember to have seen, called νεοποιοί simply. I may assume that H. would not have used the other title unless he could justify it from the inscriptions ; but I wish he had quoted an example. *Neopoioi* of Aphrodite at Aphrodisias* do not, in view of the diversity of usage in different cities, seem to me a sufficient justification for a *Neopoios* of Artemis at Ephesus. But considering H.'s accuracy and knowledge of Ephesus, I simply appeal to him for information on this point. I maintain, however, that, if he cannot justify the phrase by the authority of inscriptions, in which these officials occur very frequently, the use of a wrong title would constitute precisely one of those errors in detail, which might be used as a proof that his supposed eyewitness was no eyewitness, but an inventor.†

5. SHRINES OF ARTEMIS.

Is the phrase, " which made silver shrines of Diana," so inexplicable as H. supposes ? He says that none of the commentators have explained it ; and certainly all the references which he quotes from them justify his statement. The explanation has always seemed so obvious that I never thought of looking into a commentator. I have been familiar for years with terra-cotta shrines of Artemis, and had always understood that the richer classes bought silver shrines of a similar character. I claim no originality for the suggestion, which I have always understood to be accepted among archæologists. I think I have read it as stated by Professor Ernst Curtius ; and if I remember

---

* *Corpus Inscr. Græc.*, No. 2811. Cf. Dittenberger, *Sylloge*, 6.

† In his reply H. concedes this point. There is not any authority extant which would justify us in supposing that a well-informed person, about A.D. 57, would have used the phrase νεοποιὸς Ἀρτέμιδος in speaking about these city officials.

rightly he actually quoted the allusion in Acts xix. when publishing a monument of the class in question. I speak, however, from distant recollection, and as I write in Scotland, where no scholar's library exists, I cannot verify the statement.*

Such small shrines in marble abound, and they were especially used as dedicatory offerings in the cultus of that Asiatic goddess who was worshipped under the name of Artemis at Ephesus, and under other names, but with essential identity of character, in many other cities of Greek or semi-Greek character. Scores of examples are enumerated in the *Archäologische Zeitung* for 1880,† and the number might easily be raised to hundreds. Terracotta shrines are not so numerous, partly on account of their more perishable character, and partly from the fact that in many cases part of the shrine was suppressed and left to the imagination, as was sometimes the case even in marble ; so that the shrines thus become little more than statuettes of Artemis.

But the proper dedicatory offering to this goddess was not a simple statuette, but a shrine. I have elsewhere traced the history of this style of representation from the remotest period through its later developments ‡ in the

---

* Mr. Cecil Smith, when I mentioned the point to him, soon found the reference—viz., *Athenische Mittheilungen*, ii., p. 49. The illustration there will convince every one; it shows exactly the kind of *naos* which Demetrius made, except that the material is terracotta

† See Conze's article on *Hermes-Cadmilos*.

‡ In *Journal of Hellenic Studies*, 1882, p. 45 : "The figure at Magnesia, beside Mount Sipylos, commonly called 'Niobe,' is the earliest known example of a hieratic representation of Cybele common among the Greeks. The goddess sits in a niche or naiskos, some-

cult of the goddess who was worshipped in Lydia and Phrygia under various names, such as Artemis, Cybele, Leto, Anaitis,* but who was really the same under all these names. The temples built by Greek architects in Ephesus, Sardis, etc., were beautiful, but did not rival in actual sanctity the simple and primitive shrines which alone were known in the early ages of the cultus; and similarly the beautiful statues in which Greek art idealised their conception of Artemis did not serve the purposes of actual ritual so well as the primitive *xoana* of the nursing-mother (Artemis at Ephesus), or the mother of all nature (Cybele at Sardis), or the other slightly varying types of this goddess.

The innumerable worshippers of the goddess required innumerable dedicatory offerings of the style which was most likely to please her. A great city erected a great shrine with a colossal statue of the goddess; private individuals

---

times alone, sometimes accompanied by one or more figures, among whom is Hermes-Cadmilos, the Grecised form of her favourite and companion Atys. In ruder examples she sits in stiff fashion, holding in one hand the tympanon, in the other the phiale. Beside her are generally one or two lions. In more artistic examples she has laid aside the symbols, which give such unnatural stiffness to the ruder figures, and often caresses with one hand the lion, which climbs up to her knee or lies in her lap. In some cases the lion serves her as a footstool; in other cases two sit in stiff symmetry, one on each side of her throne. Curtius has published an example of the most developed type, which he attributes, probably with justice, to the worship of the Ephesian Artemis."

* She was called Anaitis by the Persian colonists who were settled by Cyrus in the Hermus valley, and who identified the native goddess with the Anaitis of their own land (*Hist. Geogr.*, p. 124). On the identity of Artemis and Leto in the Lydo-Phrygian cults, see my papers "Artemis-Leto and Apollo-Lairbenos" in *Journal of Hellenic Studies*, 1890, pp. 216 ff.

propitiated her with miniature shrines, containing embodiments of her living presence. The vast temple near Ephesus and the tiny terra-cotta shrine were equally acceptable to Artemis; she accepted from her votaries offerings according to their means. She dwelt neither in the vast temple nor in the tiny terra-cotta: she was implicit in the life of nature; she was the reproductive power that kept the great world ever the same amid the constant flux of things. Mother of all and nurse of all, she was most really present wherever the unrestrained life of nature was most freely manifested, in the woods, on the mountains, among the wild beasts. Her worshippers expressed their devotion and their belief in her omnipresence by offering shrines to her, and doubtless by keeping shrines of the same kind in their own homes, certainly also by placing such shrines in graves beside the corpse, as a sign that the dead had once more gone back to the mother who bore them.*

The phrase in Acts xix. informs us that the term *naoi*, literally "dwellings," † was appropriated to the tiny shrines equally with the great temple; the phrase is almost unique, for we are reduced to gather all our information about this religion from scattered hints and passing allusions. Ancient literature, as a rule, says least about those phases of ancient life which were so fundamental and so familiar to all as to be naturally assumed as present in the minds of all readers.

---

* The commentators on Acts, and even Lightfoot in his note on Ignatius, *Ephes.* 9, omit these uses of the shrines, which are really the most important, especially the employment in graves.

† Strictly *ναός* denotes that part of the temple in which the image of the god was placed, and the whole temple as the dwelling of the god.

Precisely in regard to these phases archæology comes to our aid, and interprets the wealth of meaning that underlies the literary references.* But I hope that I have shown how entirely consistent the phrase in Acts is with all that we know about the worship and nature of Artemis : it is one of those vivid touches which reveal the eye-witness, one of the incidental expressions which only a person who speaks with familiar knowledge can use, and which are full of instruction about popular ideas and popular language.

A passage in a document of a slightly later period, the letter of Ignatius to the church of Ephesus, § 9, seems to prove that this use of the term *naos* was widespread.† The light thrown by these words of Ignatius on the phrase used in Acts xix. has not escaped Lightfoot's notice ; but in his commentary there seems to be one slight misconception. He treats the remarkable picture drawn by Ignatius of a religious procession as if it were an intentional picture of the great procession of the goddess at Ephesus. But Ignatius probably had never been at Ephesus, and his picture is no doubt painted after processions which he had seen at Antioch in Syria. It may, however, be safely used in illustration of all such processions, for its traits are generic and not confined to Antioch or to Ephesus. A picture found at Pompeii‡ in a rather mutilated state

---

* According to Professor Mommsen's interpretation of a passage of Horace (*Epist.* I., 6, 51), it contains the only occurrence of the word *pondera* as the name for the stepping-stones across streets, which are one of the first details that strike the modern visitor to Pompeii.

† σύνοδοι πάντες, θεοφόροι καὶ ναοφόροι.

‡ See Helbig, *Wandgemälde Campaniens*, 1476; Schreiber, *Kultur-historischer Bilderatlas*, XVII. 10.

represents a procession in honour of Hercules and Hebe; and in it we see what Ignatius calls *naophoroi*, persons carrying a miniature temple on a salver or board.

When we consider the immense and widespread influence of the Ephesian Artemis, we must acknowledge that vast numbers of pilgrims coming even from considerable distances continually visited her shrine, and that vast numbers of "*naoi*" (I accept the word on the authority of Acts xix. as the technical term used in the trade and by the pilgrims) were needed to supply the unceasing demand. Workers in marble and workers in terra-cotta drove a thriving trade through their connection with the temple, and this connection was directed and organised by Demetrius, evidently as guild-master * (παρείχετο τοῖς τεχνίταις ἐργασίαν οὐκ ὀλίγην).† The author sums up these tradesmen in the phrase, "the workmen of like occupation" (τοὺς περὶ τὰ τοιαῦτα ἐργάτας). We can, however, well imagine that rich pilgrims dedicated shrines of precious metals; and, even without any other evidence, the mere statement in Acts xix. is so natural and so consistent with the facts just stated, as to constitute sufficient proof that this was so. The silver-

---

* H. has some excellent remarks on these guilds in the cities of Asia Minor. The institution still flourishes; and each guild is directed by a master. I have briefly described the guild of street-porters in Smyrna under the Roman empire in the *Amer. Journ. Arch.*, vol. i. A study of these ancient guilds is much needed. Maue in his treatise *Præfectus Fabrum*, and Liebenam in his *Römisches Vereinswesen*, have done a great deal on this subject.

† The reading of *Codex Bezæ* in this verse is in some respects superior in vividness to the accepted text: οὗτος συναθροίσας τοὺς περὶ τὰ τοιαῦτα τεχνίτας, ἔφη πρὸς αὐτούς, Ἄνδρες συντεχνῖται, κ.τ.λ. The form of address is more individualised; but the distinction between τεχνῖται and ἐργάται is lost.

smiths were of course a craft of higher standing, greater skill in delicate work, larger profits, and therefore greater wealth and influence, than the potters and marble-workers. How natural then it is that it should be a silversmith who gathered together a meeting of the associated trades and organised a disturbance! The less educated workmen follow the lead of the great artisan.

On this view every detail confirms the general effect. We are taken direct into the heart of artisan life in Ephesus; and all is so characteristic, so true to common life, and so unlike what would occur to any person writing at a distance, that the conclusion is inevitable : we have here a picture drawn from nature, and copied literally by the author of Acts from the narrative of an eyewitness.

6. Attitude of the Ephesian Officials towards Paul.

On the other hand, look at the picture drawn by H. The riot is got up by the priests through the agency of a leading official and his board of colleagues. That is precisely the idea that would occur to any person inventing such an incident. Paul goes to Ephesus; he preaches at first with effect ; the priests are alarmed, and raise a dangerous riot against him. Such is the picture that every inventor of the biography of a saint * is sure to draw : the priests at once occur to his mind as the natural enemies of his hero. There is nothing characteristic and individual about such an

---

* Though the early saints of Asia Minor are, as a rule, real persons, yet their biographies are, in general, deficient in historical value, being invented, or at least profoundly modified, in later centuries. Only the discovery of early evidence can enable us to learn anything definite about their real history.

account; all is commonplace, and coloured by the religious ideas of a later time.

The first way in which Christianity excited the popular enmity, outside the Jewish community, was by disturbing the existing state of society and trade, and not by making innovations in religion. The rise of a new god and a new worship was a matter of perfect indifference to almost everybody in the cities of the Roman provinces. In the Græco-Roman world every one was quite accustomed to the introduction of new deities from other countries. The process had been going on with extraordinary frequency, and had produced a sort of eclectic religion in all Græco-Roman cities. The priests of Artemis looked on it with indifference. They had not found it injurious to their interests; rather, the growth of each new superstition added to the influence of Artemis and her priests. Isis was no enemy to Artemis.

The narrative of the New Testament has led to a general misapprehension on this point. We are so accustomed to the strong religious feeling of the Jews and the intolerant fanaticism with which they persecuted all dissentient opinion, that we are apt to forget that this feeling was peculiar to them, and beyond any other of their characteristics excited the wonder of the tolerant, easy-going indifferentism of the ordinary pagans, who did not care two straws whether their neighbour worshipped twenty gods or twenty-one. A new deity preached in Ephesus, a new inmate of their eclectic pantheon: it was all a matter of indifference.

Gradually people began to realise that Christianity meant a social revolution, that it did not mean to take its place alongside of the other religions, but to destroy them. The

discovery was made in a homely way, familiar to us all—
viz., through the pocket. Certain trades began, with all
the sensitiveness of the money-market, to find themselves
affected. The gradual progress of opposition to Christianity
is well marked in the Acts, and is precisely in accordance
with the above exposition. When Paul began to preach
in Asia Minor, he at first experienced no opposition except
from the Jews. In Antioch of Pisidia, in Iconium, in
Lystra, in Thessalonica, his experience was always the
same. The Gentiles were indifferent or even friendly, the
Jews bitterly hostile. But in Philippi occurred the incident
of the "maid having a spirit of divination"; and "when
her masters saw that the hope of their gain was gone,"
they accused Paul as a Jew of inciting to illegal conduct
and violation of the Roman law, and turned to their own
account the general dislike felt by both Romans and Greeks
towards the Jews.

Similarly in Ephesus the first opposition against Paul
was roused when the trades connected with Artemis-
worship felt their pockets touched, and then the riot arose.
It was not a religious persecution, but a social and mer-
cenary one. So far am I from thinking with H., that "the
hierarchy would be sensible of the Apostle's influence before
any others suspected it," that I should not be surprised if
priests or leading supporters of the worship of Artemis were
among the Asiarchs, who were "the only influential friends
of Paul at Ephesus." Probably the priests of Artemis
would act like the priests at Lystra ; they would encourage
the "revival," and try to turn it to their own account, as
in so many cases previously such "revivals" of religious
feeling had ultimately only enriched Artemis and her
priesthood.

Another contradiction between the account given in Acts xix. and H.'s theory must be noticed. According to the latter, the officials who organised the riot were rewarded for this action with a special vote of distinction by the senate and the popular assembly. But according to the account in Acts, it was a thoroughly disorderly riot, discouraged by the Asiarchs, and rebuked by the city clerk as a groundless disturbance, which involved the magistrates and the city in danger at the instance of the Roman law (see ver. 40). This contradiction alone would be fatal to the theory against which I am arguing; or rather, if the theory be true, it convicts the author of Acts xix. as guilty of a most inaccurate and prejudiced account, and as an altogether useless authority for history.

I prefer then to follow the version of the incident given in Acts. Far from finding that " the action of Demetrius appears in a new and far more significant light if he really was the Demetrius of the inscription, and if the honour therein voted to him and his colleagues by the senate and people of Ephesus was in recognition of the services rendered by him and them on behalf of the national goddess," I think that this theory both involves us in contradiction to the general situation recorded in Acts, and reduces the incident from a marvellously vivid and true picture of society in Ephesus to a commonplace and uninstructive tale.

If I were to trust my own inference from Acts, I should picture the riot as entirely that of an ignorant mob, fomented by an artisan more far-seeing than his neighbours. It was a riot disapproved of alike by priests and by magistrates: the former saw nothing in Paul to characterize him as dangerous to the goddess (see ver. 37); the latter felt that the riot was contrary to the Roman regulations. The distinction which H. makes between the attitude of the Asiarchs and that of the priests of Artemis towards Paul is entirely groundless, and forms an unfortunate conclusion to a paragraph, great part of which is excellently expressed and thoroughly true. The cultus of the emperors did indeed prepare the way for the Christian Church; but this preparation was quite involuntary. It co-ordinated the various religions of the province into something approximating to a single hierarchy. But to maintain that the officials of the imperial cultus, *i.e.*, the Asiarchs, naturally represented a different point of view from the priests of Artemis is to go against all evidence. These officials were simply provincials, selected chiefly on account of their wealth and sometimes against their will; they did not represent the point of view of the Roman governors, but the average view of the upper classes of the province Many of them no doubt had held priesthoods of the native deities before they became officials of the imperial cultus; in fact, it is probable that the native priesthoods were a sort of stepping-stone to the Asiarchate. The attitude of the Asiarchs towards Paul may then be taken as a fair indication of the tone of the educated classes, among whom I include the higher priests. The attitude of Demetrius and the mob was that of tradesmen whose trade was threatened, and who got up a demonstration on its behalf.

We find, then, that the attitude of the officials and of the educated part of the Ephesian people was that of curiosity and intelligent interest in the new doctrines. This curiosity was in the air at the time throughout the Eastern world; and it is one of the signs of a very early date in the narrative, that it shows no trace of the feeling of dislike to the new religion which soon began to spread abroad. Here and always we find that the spread of Christianity at first was favoured by a measure of intelligence and freedom of mind in those among whom it was preached.

7. FATE OF THE SILVER SHRINES

One objection made by H. must be met. " If these silver shrines were common articles of merchandise, such as pilgrims to the famous temple purchased to take back to their homes, then we might fairly expect to find some specimens still extant among the treasures of our museums." Probably the chief use made of silver shrines was, not to take home, but to dedicate in the temple. They were sold by the priest to the worshippers, and dedicated by the latter to the goddess : similar examples of trade carried on by priests are too familiar to need quotation. Why then have these silver shrines all disappeared ? Simply on account of their value. They have all gone into the melting-pot, many of them being placed there by the priests themselves. Dedicatory offerings were so numerous, that they had to be cleared out from time to time to make room for new *anathemata*. The terra-cotta shrines, being worthless, would be thrown away quietly, the silver would be melted down. Those which remained to a later period met the same fate at other hands, less pious, but equally greedy. H. indeed speaks apparently of silver statuettes of Artemis as common.* The expression, however, is only a careless

---

* His words are (p. 417): " Statuettes " (sharply distinguished by H. from shrines) " of the Ephesian Diana were to be found everywhere in the Greco-Roman world. In fact, these statuettes of the goddess, reproducing all her hideous Oriental features, may be found in bronze, in silver, or in terra-cotta, in every European

and probably unintentional one ; for existing examples of them are so rare as to be unknown to me.

8. GREAT ARTEMIS.

After Demetrius' speech the excited mob began to shout " Great is Artemis ! " and at a later stage they spent about two hours in clamour to the same effect. The phrase is noteworthy. In such circumstances there can be no doubt that some familiar formula would rise to their lips ; it would not be mere chance words that suggested themselves to a whole crowd, but words which were well known to all. We are therefore justified in inferring from this passage that the phrase, " Great is Artemis ! " was a stock expression

---

museum. The type was exceedingly common, and witnessed to the wide extent of the worship. If the writer of the Acts had spoken of Demetrius as driving a brisk trade in these metal statuettes, the narrative would have corresponded with the facts. As it is, the statement that Demetrius was the maker of ' silver shrines ' is either to be set down as a loose mode of expression, or else it awaits explanation.''

In these sentences H. does not explicitly say that statuettes in silver may be found in every museum. But he proceeds to reason as if this were stated, and assumes throughout the rest of his remarks that he has proved silver statuettes to be quite common. In his reply to the article which is here reprinted, he says, "I should like to see and handle some specimens of metal shrines of Artemis discovered at Ephesus. In default of such metal shrines or of any mention of them elsewhere than in this passage, I made bold to suggest metal statuettes. Such metal statuettes are well known in modern museums.'' In this last sentence H. must either mean that silver statuettes are common in museums, or he has abandoned his case. He insists on seeing silver shrines, and till they are shown he declines to believe in their existence. In my criticism I plainly put the case to him that silver statuettes of the Ephesian Artemis were unknown to me, and quoted in a footnote Mr. Cecil Smith's statement (made in answer

in the religion, just as we might argue from a single loyal demonstration that " Long live the Queen ! " was a stock phrase in our own country, or Χριστιανῶν Βασιλέων πολλὰ τὰ ἔτη a current phrase in Constantinople under the Byzantine emperors. Conversely, if we can prove that " Great is Artemis ! " was a stock phrase of Artemis-worship, we shall add one more to the list of vivid, natural, and individualised traits in this scene.

We have very scanty information about the ritual of the goddess of Ephesus and of Western Asia Minor in general ; but recent discoveries have added greatly to our knowledge. The expressions " the great Artemis, " the queen of Ephesus," * were formerly proved to have been actually

---

to a question which I addressed to him on the point), that in the British Museum there is no silver statuette of the Ephesian Artemis, and only one supposed doubtfully to represent the Greek Artemis. Metal statuettes of the Ephesian Artemis do not prove H.'s case, for he himself explicitly demands proof of silverwork. But even metal statuettes of the Ephesian Artemis are unknown to me ; and I ask for proof of H.'s reiterated statement, that they are common in museums. A single example, or even two, will not prove his words to be accurate. Even marble and terra-cotta statuettes of the type which is commonly called the Ephesian Artemis (and which is clearly intended by H.) are, so far as my own experience goes, rare. I know of only four examples in terra-cotta, and Wood (*Ephes.*, p. 270) gives an illustration of a marble statuette which he had seen in private possession at Mylasa. Baumeister's *Denkmäler* and Roscher's *Lexicon der Mythologie*, s. v. *Artemis*, do not mention any statuettes, but only statues, of the Ephesian Artemis. I believe that H. has unintentionally exaggerated the importance of this type. Representations of the other type in niches are common in marble and terra-cotta ; and the value of the metal is a sufficient explanation why none in silver are known. The silver figures quoted in H.'s reply were not of the Ephesian Artemis.

* τῆς μεγάλης θεᾶς Ἀρτέμιδος, *Corp. Inscr. Græc.*, 2963 c. : Ἐφέσου Ἄνασσα, *Ib.*, 6797.

used of the goddess; but proof was wanting that the epithet "great" was so peculiarly and regularly associated with her as to rise naturally to the lips of her worshippers as a sort of formula in her service.

In 1887 Mr. Hogarth, Mr. Brown, and myself found the site of a temple dedicated to a goddess and her son, Artemis-Leto and Apollo-Lairbenos, at the Phrygian city of Dionysopolis. Beside it we found numerous inscriptions of a remarkable type. They were all erected within the sacred precinct by persons bound to the service of the two deities. They agree in representing the authors as having come before the god when polluted with some physical or moral impurity (sometimes of a very gross kind), and when therefore unfit to appear before the god. The offenders are chastised by the god (in some cases at least, perhaps in all cases, with disease); they confess and acknowledge their fault, and thereby appease the god. They are cured of their ailment, or released from their punishment, and finally they relate the facts in an inscription as a pattern and a warning to others not to treat the god lightly.

In publishing these inscriptions,[*] I have drawn out a number of analogies between the formulæ used in them and those hieratic formulæ which we can trace at Ephesus; and have argued that the religion of Ephesus and of Dionysopolis was fundamentally the same. Among the

---

[*] *Journal of Hellenic Studies*, 1889, p. 216 ff., in completion of a paper by Mr. Hogarth, *ib.*, 1887, p. 376 ff. In my paper I have to make one correction in a detail of the fourth inscription. The phrase Ἀτθὶς Ἀγαθημέρου must be translated " Atthis, wife " (not daughter, as I have rendered it) " of Agathemeros." The impurity alluded to is of the same type as in No. 5. Mr. Hogarth's paper was right on this point, though the inscription was imperfect in some other points.

formulæ common to the two cults is the cry, "Great
Apollo!" "Great Artemis!" The former occurs as the
heading of one of these confessions at Dionysopolis, and
was evidently a regular formula of invocation addressed to
the god by a worshipper. In these inscriptions, and in another group found in the Katakekaumene, the great power
of the goddess is even oftener insisted on than that of
her son : *e.g.*, "I thank mother Leto, because she makes
impossibilities possible" is the exclamation of a pious epi-
graphist * at Dionysopolis, and in the Katakekaumene we
find the heading "Great Anaitis" † over a confession of the
type just described. The Oriental colonists of the latter
(as has already been remarked) often applied the Oriental
name Anaitis to the Lydo-Phrygian goddess.

In other seats of Artemis-worship we find that her great
power is insisted on in the same way. The Artemis of
the lakes is called Great Artemis in an inscription.‡ The
Artemis of Therma in Lesbos is invoked by the single
phrase "Great Artemis of Therma" on a stone still standing
by the road between Mitylene and Therma.§

Pamphylia affords a good parallel to Ephesus. The
cult of the Pergæan Artemis closely resembled that of the
Ephesian goddess. The former was styled the Queen
of Perga, and the tribe at Sillyon (a neighbouring town),
which bore the name of the goddess, was called "the tribe
of the great one." ‖

---

* *Journal of Hellenic Studies*, 1883, p. 385.

† *Smyrna Mouseion*, No. υλζ′.

‡ *Hist. Geogr.*, p. 410.

§ Plehn, *Lesbiaca*, p. 117; *Bulletin de Corresp. Hellén.*, 1880,
p. 430.

‖ As this last fact has never been observed, so far as I know, I
shall point out the evidence on which both statements rest. In 1880

These numerous analogies show that the power of the Ephesian goddess was insisted on in the cultus, and that her greatness was vividly present to the mind of her worshippers, and prompted the cry "Great Artemis." The invocations "Great Apollo" at Dionysopolis, "Great Anaitis" in the Katakekaumene, "Great Artemis" in Lesbos, afford complete corroboration of the title "Great Artemis" mentioned in Acts.

9. TEXT OF ACTS XIX. 23-41.

Here we find a discrepancy between the inscriptions and the received text of Acts. The customary phrase was an invocation "Great Artemis," but the text of Acts reads "Great is Artemis," as a formal assertion. There can be no doubt that it would be a far more striking trait if the narrative represented the population as using the precise phrase which has just been proved to have been common in their ritual. Also, we cannot fail to observe that popular shouts are not usually expressed in the indicative. The suspicion suggests itself, that the populace used their ordinary

I published in the *Journal of Hellenic Studies* a paper on the then undeciphered Pamphylian alphabet, in which (p. 246) the title "Queen of Perga" was given as the explanation of the enigmatic legend on some coins of the city. This explanation has been accepted by almost every subsequent writer, and may be regarded as certain. In the same paper (p. 253) the group of letters MHEIAΛE, which occurs several times in an inscription of Sillyon, was explained as the Pamphylian dialetic form of μεγάλη. The latter interpretation has not been so widely accepted, though it has met with the approval of several very good scholars. A recently discovered inscription of Sillyon shows that one of the tribes was called Μεαλεῖτις. It is evidently named after the Μειάλη goddess. The inscription is published in *Bulletin de Corresp. Hellén.*, 1889, p. 486.

phrase, and that their words have been misrepresented by a very slight alteration, viz., the duplication of the letter η, so that μεγάλη Ἄρτεμις became μεγάλη ἡ Ἄρτεμις. We turn, then, to the manuscripts to see whether we can find any confirmation of this suspicion.

The best manuscripts are agreed on this point : they read "Great is Artemis"; but *Codex Bezæ* * preserves the form which, as we see from the inscriptions, was actually used in the cultus. The latter form, moreover, lends more character to the scene. The mob for two hours invoked with loud voice the goddess and queen of Ephesus, but it is much less natural to represent them as shouting in the streets and in the theatre the statement that Artemis is great. The people were praying, not arguing against Paul's doctrines ; and there is a keen sarcasm in the way their praying is described, ἔκραζον λέγοντες 28 and κράζοντες 34. Consistently with the principle we have hitherto followed, we must give in this case the preference to the invocation, and suppose that *Codex Bezæ* alone preserves it, while the other manuscripts have suffered ; and the change has been due to a misunderstanding of the scene,† as if the cry were a controversial assertion in opposition to the doctrine preached by St. Paul. The preservation of the correct form in *Codex Bezæ* would be facilitated, if that MS. represents a

---

* Alone in xix. 34, supported by three cursives in xix. 28.

† Probably the change arose through an accidental duplication of η, and then spread by deliberate preference due to the misunderstanding. If, on the other hand, we suppose that in this case *Codex Bezæ* does not give the original text, but an alteration of the original text, due to the influence of the popular formula, this supposition will strongly confirm the theory maintained in Chap. viii., that the text of *Codex Bezæ* is founded on a revision of the text made in Asia Minor.

text current in the province Asia, where this cry or prayer must long have been familiar to the Christians.

I need hardly spend more time on the point. The Ephesians habitually invoked their goddess as "Great Artemis," and their common formula of prayer rose to their lips on this occasion in the theatre. The reading of *Codex Bezæ*, which alone retains the form actually used by the people, must here be preferred. From whatever point of view we contemplate the narrative, the superior vividness and suitability of this interpretation of the scene becomes apparent ; and, at the risk of wearying the reader, I may add one more consideration. The majority of the people in the theatre were ignorant of what was the matter (xix. 32). They had heard the shouting in the street,* and had with the usual human instinct joined the crowd and filled the theatre. But they did not know that the riot was directed against Paul, and could not therefore share in the feeling which might have prompted the argumentative statement, "Great is Artemis" ; whereas, when they had learned from the shouts that something connected with the goddess was on hand, the customary invocation would naturally suggest itself to them.

The use of the nominative form in place of the vocative Ἄρτεμι, need not cause any surprise or difficulty. The confusion of forms, and the substitution of the nominative form for the vocative, began early in Asia Minor ; and Ἄρτεμις for Ἄρτεμι was adopted even in Greece at no very late date. A similar confusion of nominative and vocative forms occurs in a Cappadocian inscription, which may

---

* On this point, which also is preserved only in *Codex Bezæ*, see below, p. 153.

serve to complete the proof that the formula under consideration was a widely spread invocation. The inscription in question is a dedication to the great Cappadocian god, Zeus of Venasa: "Great Zeus in heaven, be propitious to me Demetrius" (μέγας Ζεὺς ἐν οὐραν[ῷ ἴσθι], εἴλεώς μοι Δημητρίῳ). It lies on a hilltop, which was probably sacred to the god.* Here we have the same formula, introducing a fully expressed prayer, yet the nominative form is used as in the Ephesian and Lesbian invocations.

One other example of the epithet "great" may be added, as illustrating the prevalence of the idea in Asia Minor. At Laodiceia on the Lycus, some coins which bear the effigy of the local deity, Zeus, have the legend Ζεγc Αceιc. M. Waddington is in all probability right in proposing to understand this word as the Semitic Azīza, "mighty." Syrian colonists in the city which was founded by a Greek king of Syria left this trace of their language in the religion of the city.

One striking parallel to the scene in the theatre must not be omitted. In the scene on Mount Carmel, the four hundred and fifty prophets of Baal "called on the name of Baal from morning even until noon, saying, O Baal, hear us . . . and they cried aloud, and cut themselves after their manner with knives" (1 Kings xviii. 26). Except for the wounds inflicted on themselves in the vehemence and agony of Oriental prayer, the loud invocation of the prophets is similar to the prayers of the Ephesians in the theatre; and it is highly probable that even the epithet "great" was used by the former as well as by the latter.

---

* I published it in *Bulletin de Corresp. Hellén.*, 1883, p. 322, doubting the connexion with the worship of Zeus of Venasa. I have since shown that Venasa was the plain round this hill. (*Hist. Geogr.*, p. 292). The above restoration, not ἔστω or ἐστι, seems certain.

10. HISTORICAL CHARACTER OF THE NARRATIVE,
ACTS XIX. 23-41.

The more closely we are able to test the story in Acts,
the more vivid and true to the situation and surroundings
does it prove to be, and the more justified are we in pressing
closely every inference from the little details that occur in
it. I entertain the strong hope that the demonstration
which has now been given of its accuracy in disputed
points, will do away with all future doubt as to the faithful-
ness of the picture that it gives of Ephesian society in A.D.
57. Even though we cannot agree with H.'s conclusions,
our best thanks are due to him for directing our close and
minute attention to this most interesting historical scene,
and to the inscription he has so ingeniously pieced together.
In his paper there are many observations and many passages
of permanent interest and value ; and parts of it which lie
beyond the scope of this chapter give much information
about the state of Ephesus between 50 and 150 A.D. The
finest part of it is his proof that a revival of paganism in
Ephesus began probably as early as A.D. 104. In corroboration of this view he might also have referred to the series of
imperial coins struck under Hadrian, and bearing the name
and image of DIANA EPHESIA. Roman imperial coins
cannot bear the name of a non-Roman deity ; and we
may therefore see in them the proof that the defence of
the Ephesian goddess was formally constituted a part of the
Imperial policy at or before this time.

One of the most interesting facts in the history of religion
under the Empire is the influence that was exerted by the
new religion on the old ; and the progress of discovery is
gathering a store of information on this point, which will,

at some future time, make a remarkable picture. In the
first century we observe a general tone of indifference and
careless ease in the higher classes, the municipal magistrates,
and even the priesthood. Afterwards this security is disturbed. New zeal and earnestness are imparted to paganism;
its ceremonial is more carefully studied ; and even certain
doctrines are adopted from Christianity, and declared to
have been always present in the old worship.

H. in his reply considers that I have " overrated the
tolerance of the local hierarchies."*   I have, however, on
my side at least the record of Acts. The priests of Zeus
Propoleos at Lystra were the foremost in paying respect to
Paul and Barnabas, and in stimulating and directing the
zeal of the populace. They had known of the Apostles'
preaching for some considerable time, for the accepted text
implies that the Apostles had been evangelising for some
time previously, and the text of *Codex Bezæ* asserts that
they had already produced much effect on the people.†
The priests, however, showed no jealousy. They were
willing and ready to patronise the Apostles, to give them
place and honour, and to use the revival of religious feeling
for their own purposes. I have simply interpreted the
attitude of the Ephesian priests according to the statement
in Acts xix. 37,‡ and the contemporary analogy of the
priests at Lystra. H. quotes against my view the opposition offered to the Christians in Bithynia by the priests in
A.D. 112. Such opposition is not indeed recorded, but may

---

* *Expositor*, August 1890, p. 146.

† καὶ ἐκινήθη ὅλον τὸ πλῆθος ἐπὶ τῇ διδαχῇ : addition to xiv. 7.

‡ Paul had neither been guilty of sacrilege (thus becoming amenable to the ordinary procedure of the proconsul), nor of disrespect
to the goddess (thus rousing the anger of the priests).

safely be assumed. But H. leaves out of sight the difference caused by the development of the situation since the period 47–57 A.D. The period of indifference and toleration had been succeeded by that of apprehension and of confirmed hostility. H.'s example tells only against his own argument.*

---

* While I have written throughout on the assumption that the date proposed by H. for the inscription of Demetrius is correct, I feel bound to think that it is rather too early. The form of the symbol $\bar{2}$ is not known to me before the second century, and the two instances which occur of O substituted for Ω point also to the period of confusion between these two letters. The confusion implies that they had ceased to be distinguished in pronunciation, and it is hardly probable that this had taken place so early as A.D. 57. H. would explain the substitution of O for Ω as a mere fault of the engraver, and not as the result of confusion in the pronunciation, quoting the occurrence of A for O and of X for Y. This is quite possible ; but two cases of O for Ω point more naturally to actual confusion in pronunciation. I mentioned these difficulties in a footnote written when I saw the original marble, and added to my article after it was in type. H. has not in his brief reply taken any notice of these difficulties. He rightly insists on the absence of Latin names as a proof of early date; but in regard to this we must remember that, in a thoroughly Hellenised city like Ephesus, Greek names were used at all periods by those who had not actually gained the coveted prize of Roman citizenship. There are no Roman citizens in this official inscription, which may be due to the fact that the Neopoioi were not officials of very high rank.

CHAPTER VIII.

THE ORIGINAL AUTHORITY FOR ST. PAUL'S JOURNEYS: VALUE AND TEXT.

1. RAPID SPREAD OF CHRISTIANITY IN ASIA MINOR.

IN view of the extraordinarily powerful effect which is described in Acts as produced in the country by the preaching of Paul, the question may fairly be put whether any evidence is known which tends either to corroborate or to throw doubt on the account there given. It is very difficult to find any evidence outside of the Christian documents, but anything that is known points to the conclusion that the new religion must have made very rapid progress in Asia Minor during the first century. The testimony of Pliny is, that before 112 Christianity had spread so widely in his province that the pagan ritual was actually interrupted and the temples almost deserted (see p. 198). Various other considerations * point to a similar result as having taken place in Phrygia at a very early time. It is probable, therefore, that the new religion spread with marvellous rapidity from the beginning of St. Paul's preaching in Western Asia Minor. Unless that were so, it is hard to see how the social condition of Asia Minor during the second century could have been produced. On the other hand, no evidence of the early spread of Christianity in the great plains of the Axylon and in North

---

* *E.g.*, the Montanist quarrel could hardly arise in a small sect.

Galatia is known to me; and in regard to part of this region, I have concluded from epigraphic evidence that paganism continued dominant till the third or fourth century.*

With regard to the west coast of Asia, among the great Greek cities like Ephesus and Smyrna, the condition of things was midway between these two extremes. It appears probable that the Christians were both numerous and influential there during the second century; but they do not seem to have had the same dominating influence that we must attribute to them in Phrygia. Can any reason be found for these apparent variations? Where the Greek spirit and education were completely dominant, the new religion spread with considerable rapidity, but a large part of the population was proof against its influence. Where the Greek education was unknown, the new religion seems to have made no progress at all. The regions where it spread most rapidly were those where the people were becoming aware of the beauty of Greek letters and the grandeur of Roman government, where they were awaking from the stagnation and inertness of an Oriental people, and their minds were stirred and receptive of all new ideas, whether Greek philosophy or Jewish or Christian religion. We have seen that St. Paul came into South Galatia just at the time when the Roman spirit was beginning to permeate the country, and that the four places where he is recorded to have founded churches were the four centres of Roman influence.

We cannot fail to be struck with the strong hold that

---

* See a paper on " Phrygian Inscriptions of the Roman period " in *Zeitschrift für vergleichende Sprachforschung*, 1887, pp. 383, 398.

Roman ideas had on the mind of St. Paul. In theory he
recognises the universality of the Church (Col. iii. 11); but
in practice he goes where the Roman Empire goes. We
therefore feel compelled to suppose that St. Paul had
conceived the great idea of Christianity as the religion
of the Roman world ; and that he thought of the various
districts and countries in which he had preached as parts
of the grand unity. He had the mind of an organiser ;
and to him the Christians of his earliest travels were not
men of Iconium and of Antioch—they were a part of the
Roman world, and were addressed by him as such.

2. Distinction of Authorship.

Throughout these chapters a distinction has been drawn
between the author of Acts and the writer of the original
document describing the journeys of St. Paul, which we
assume to have been worked into the book as it has come
down to us. This distinction seems to be proved, both
by other reasons which do not come within our present
purpose, and by the variation in Acts in the use of names
denoting the districts of Asia Minor. The original document employs these names in the Roman sense, while in
the earlier part of Acts the names are used in the popular
Greek sense which was common in the century before and
after Christ. There was at that time great uncertainty in
the usage of the names denoting the great territorial districts
of Asia Minor. Not merely were the boundaries of several
of these districts very uncertain (so that, for example, the
difficulty of drawing a dividing line between Mysia and
Phrygia was proverbial) ; but also several of them had,
according to the Roman provincial system, an extent dif-

ferent from that which they had according to older history, ethnical facts, and popular usage. The only source of diversity which concerns us here is the latter. There is no distinction of practical consequence in the extent of Lycia, Pamphylia, Bithynia; Pontus and Cilicia also do not afford any criterion. Galatia and Asia are the two provinces in regard to which very serious difference of usage existed.*

The use of these names in the Travel-Document has appeared very clearly in the preceding discussion. It appears to agree with the practice of St. Paul's Epistles. It is not possible to demonstrate that in the Epistles every name is used in the Roman sense, where the Roman and the popular sense differ; but in some cases there is no room for doubt, and the invariable presumption that the Roman sense is intended, is fully admitted even by Wendt, though he is an advocate of the North-Galatian theory.†

In Acts ii. 9 the enumeration, " Pontus and Asia, Phrygia and Pamphylia," is distinctly popular and Greek in style. According to the Roman fashion Phrygia was included in Asia, except a small part which belonged to Galatia. In making such an enumeration a Roman would not have omitted Galatia, nor would he have mentioned Phrygia, for

---

* In Greece a similar difference existed in regard to the names Achaia and Macedonia; which to the Romans meant two large provinces, and to the Greeks two much smaller districts.

† So in the latest edition of " Meyer's Commentary," 1888. In the previous edition, Wendt held that the Epistle to the Galatians was written to the churches of Antioch, etc. But even in the latest edition he still admits that Paul used the provincial names according to the Roman sense. He admits this even in the case of Galatia as it is used in 1 Cor. xvi. 1 (see Comm. on Acts xiii. 9); and why he should deny that in the Epistle to the Galatians, Galatia is used in the same sense as in 1 Corinthians, it is difficult to see.

to a Roman Phrygia had no political existence. Mysia and Phrygia and Lydia were in the Roman sense merely geographical terms denoting parts of the province of Asia, which he might sometimes feel himself obliged to use (as, *e.g.*, in Acts xvi. 9), in order to specify more distinctly some exact position within the province, but which he would not employ in an enumeration of countries and provinces like Acts ii. 9 ff.

Asia is a term about which it is very difficult to decide. The Roman province Asia had been formed in 133 B.C., and the name seems to have soon come into popular use, because there was no other term to denote the Ægean coast lands. But during the first century before Christ, the province was greatly increased in size, and it is very difficult to determine after this time whether the name Asia is used in the popular sense of the Ægean coast lands, or denotes the entire Roman province ; in short, whether it includes Phrygia or not. In Acts ii. 9 Asia is pointedly used in the popular sense, excluding Phrygia.

In Acts vi. 9 the use of the term Asia is quite consistent with either the Roman or the popular sense. The Jews in question are probably those educated in the rhetorical schools of Smyrna and Pergamos ; the Phrygian Jews would be less likely to have received a philosophical education and to engage in subtle discussions, but they were numerous, and may be included.

There are only these two verses from which any inference can be drawn as to the usage in Acts i.–xi. ; but even one clear example is a sufficient proof that some parts of these chapters use a geographical nomenclature different from that which is employed in the Travel-Document and in the Epistles.

On one point of great interest this theory perhaps throws some light—viz., on the abrupt ending of Acts in the middle of St. Paul's imprisonment. Probably the original Travel-Document was composed in the sphere of his influence during that imprisonment? If that be so, the author of Acts stopped where his chief authority stopped : perhaps he intended to complete the tale in another work, using different authorities.

3. TEXT OF *CODEX BEZÆ* : ASIA MINOR.

In addition to the points which have already been noticed, it will be convenient to examine some other passages bearing on the antiquities of Asia Minor, in which *Codex Bezæ* differs from the received text of Acts, and thereafter to examine some of the variations in the narrative of St. Paul's adventures in Greece.

The radical change of text in xvi. 9, 10, is very remarkable. The scene is described with a vividness and completeness of detail that almost incline us to think that *Codex Bezæ* gives here the original text. But perhaps the reading of this *Codex* may be best explained as an alteration founded on a tradition still surviving in the churches of Asia, " And [in] a vision by night there appeared to Paul [as it were] a man of Macedonia,* standing [before his face], beseeching him and saying, ' Come over into Macedonia and help us.' [Awaking, therefore, he related the vision to us, and we perceived that] the Lord had called us for to preach the gospel unto them in Macedonia : and [on the morrow] setting sail," etc.

In xviii. 24 *Codex Bezæ* has Ἀπολλώνιος for the common

---

* The changes in *Codex Bezæ* are marked by square brackets.

'Aπολλώς. The latter is the familiar diminutive or pet-name of the former. The same person may be spoken of by both names, as in an English book the same person might be spoken of sometimes as Henry, sometimes as Harry. A similar example occurs in the case of Prisca, as she is called by Paul in Rom. xvi. 3, but who is generally known by the diminutive Priscilla.* Apparently the reviser was offended by the use of the familiar Apollos in a passage of serious and lofty tone, just as in a highly wrought passage of Burke one would be offended by a reference to Will Shakespeare. Accordingly he substituted the full name Apollonius.

In xix. 9 the addition ἀπὸ ὥρας εˊ ἕως δεκάτης can hardly be explained except as a deliberate impertinence (which is improbable), or as founded on an actual tradition, which was believed by the reviser to have survived in Ephesus from the time of St. Paul's residence there. It is quite probable that this tradition is true. The school would be open for Paul's use after the scholars were dismissed. Now schools opened at daybreak, both in Greece and in Rome. Martial was wakened before sunrise by the noise of a school (ix. 68, xii. 57), and Juvenal describes, in his exaggerated style, the teacher at work from midnight onwards, and the scholars, with their lamps, standing round him (vii. 222–6, see Mayor's notes). It is, therefore, not strange that school should be over one hour before midday.

In xix. 14 *Codex Bezæ* reads υἱοὶ Σκευᾶ τινὸς ἱερέως, in

---

* Many examples of two forms applied to one person are collected by O. Crusius in *Jahrbücher für Philologie*, 1891, p. 385 ff. Such *Kosenamen* imply familiarity, sometimes even vulgarity : my friend Mr. Neil thinks that those in ᾶς are contemptuous.

place of the accepted text Σκευᾶ Ἰουδαίου ἀρχιερέως ἑπτὰ υἱοί. The reviser thought it impossible that Sceva should have been high-priest,* and xix. 16 seems to imply that there were only two sons. *Codex Bezæ* here gives a text which is intelligent, consistent, and possible: the accepted text is badly expressed, and even self-contradictory. The context makes it clear that Sceva was a Jew, even though his nationality is not explicitly stated in *Codex Bezæ*.

In xix. 28 *Codex Bezæ* adds a detail, which may probably be taken as true to fact. Demetrius had gathered the craftsmen together and inflamed them by a skilful speech. According to the received text, "They shouted out saying, Great is Diana of the Ephesians; and the city was filled with the confusion, and they rushed with one accord into the theatre." The reviser considered that the first meeting was held in some house or building, whether private or public, and that therefore before they rushed into the theatre they must have gone forth into the street. Accordingly he says, "When they heard [this] they were filled with wrath, [and ran into the street,] and kept crying out, saying, Great Diana of the Ephesians; and the whole city was thrown into confusion †; and they rushed, etc." The addition increases the individuality and the local colour; and possibly an actual tradition, surviving in Ephesus, fixed the house or public *stoa* where the preliminary meeting was held, and the street along which the artisans ran invoking the goddess.

The use of ναοκόρον (*Codex Bezæ*) for νεωκόρον in xix. 35 is remarkable: nothing otherwise is known to suggest that

---

* The word may mean 'belonging to a high-priestly family.'

† συνεχύθη ὅλη ἡ πόλις αἰσχύνης.

this form was used in Ephesus. Coins and inscriptions have νεωκόρος invariably. May we therefore conclude that the reviser did not belong to Ephesus, but to a district where the strange form ναοκόρος was actually in use?

In xx. 4 *Codex Bezæ* reads Ἐφέσιοι for Ἀσιανοί. In the case of Trophimus, we know from xxi. 29 that the change is accurate, and we need have no hesitation in admitting that a local tradition made Tychicus also a native of Ephesus; for the references in 2 Tim. iv. 12, Titus iii. 12, Col. iv. 7, Eph. vi. 21, are favourable to this view. The desire to give due honour to Ephesus in this case would favour the idea that the reviser belonged to, or was closely connected with, that city. But proofs abound of his intimate acquaintance with the topography and circumstances of the South-Galatian churches; and we are bound to conclude that close relations and constant intercommunication were maintained between the church of Ephesus and the churches that lay along the road towards South Galatia and Syria. Hence it does not appear safe to infer more than that the reviser was intimately acquainted with that whole group of churches, and jealous of their honour.*

Codex Bezæ differs widely from other MSS. in the difficult passage, xx. 4, 5, 6. There can be no doubt (1) that its text is clear, consecutive, self-consistent; (2) that it gives the proper and necessary sequence of events which the text of the other MSS. is intended to describe; (3) that none of the other MSS. give a clear and well-expressed version of the facts. The conclusion then is either that

---

* Contrast with his desire to give due honour to Ephesus his desire to state clearly the fault of Berœa. (See p. 160)

Codex Bezæ gives the original text, or that it represents a revision made with great skill and success.

In xx. 15, and xxi. 1, two interesting little additions are made in the text of *Codex Bezæ.* In the former passage Paul is said to have stopped in Trogylia on his voyage between Samos and Miletus. In the latter he is said to have touched at Myra after leaving Patara on his last voyage to Jerusalem. The first of these details is in itself highly probable, for the promontory of Trogyllion or Trogylia projects far out between Samos and Miletus, and the little coasting vessel would naturally touch there, perhaps becalmed, or for some other reason.* The second detail is also natural and probable in a coasting voyage, and geographically accurate. Moreover, the addition of Myra seems to have been made before the extant edition of the *Acta* of Paul and Thekla was composed, and a general consent exists that that edition was in its main outlines composed about A.D. 170 to 190, though personally †

---

* It might appear probable that this reading was in the text used by St. Willibald, who sailed along the same coast on his pilgrimage to Jerusalem about A.D. 754. He visited Ephesus, and walked thence to Pygela; from Pygela he sailed to Strobolis, and thereafter to Patara. The name Strobolis has puzzled the editors (see the edition of the *Hodæporicon*, § 11, in the " Palestine Pilgrims' Series "), who suggest Hierapolis of Phrygia. Strobolis is for (εἰ)ς Τρώγυλιν —a form in accordance with a common analogy; and some cursive MSS. of Acts read Στρογυλίῳ ος Στρογγυλίῳ. Willibald, however, would use a Latin Bible, and this word seems not to have penetrated into the Latin versions. Even if we do not suppose that Willibald's selection of Strobolis and Patara was due to recollection of the narrative in Acts, his voyage is at least an apt illustration of St. Paul's voyage, as showing that these points are natural halting-points for a small coasting vessel.

† I hope to discuss this interesting work fully elsewhere.

the present writer is inclined to date soon after 130 the enlargement and revision of a much older text of the *Acta*.

4. TEXT OF *CODEX BEZÆ*: EUROPE.

To appreciate the force of these results, let us compare a few of the discrepancies between *Codex Bezæ* and the received text in the narrative of St. Paul's travels in Europe. In xvi. 12, according to the received text, Philippi is the "first (*i.e.* leading) city of its division of Macedonia, a colonia"; but in *Codex Bezæ* it is "the head of Macedonia, a city, a colonia."[*] The latter description is not expressed in the proper terms, does not cohere well together, and is actually incorrect. The term "first" was commonly assumed by towns which were, or claimed to be, chief of a district or a province; and Philippi either boasted, or was believed by the reviser to boast, of this distinction; but he is wrong in assigning to it the pre-eminence over the whole of Macedonia. Philippi was merely first in one of the districts into which Roman Macedonia was divided, but not in the whole province. While the received text is right, *Codex Bezæ* shows an alteration made without knowledge of the country and its circumstances, and without proper comprehension of the text. The reviser, unfamiliar with the constitution of the province, understood $Μακεδονίας$ as genitive in apposition with $μερίδος$, whereas it is really partitive genitive depending on it; and he was therefore dissatisfied with the term $μερίδος$ as applied to a province. He might have substituted province ($ἐπαρχίας$) for district ($μερίδος$), but he attained the same end by simply omitting the latter word, for "Macedonia" and "the province Mace-

---

[*] $ἥτις ἐστὶν κεφαλὴ τῆς Μακεδονίας πόλις κολωνία.$

donia" are synonymous. For "first" he substituted the
term "head," which is less technically accurate.* Now the
term "first" was familiar to him in the usage of Asia
Minor.† Why then should he change it for the less accurate
"head"? The reason lay in the ambiguity of the phrase,
which is still a noted difficulty and a cause of disagreement
among scholars. In order to prevent readers from taking
the phrase in the sense of " the city nearest in its district and
which they first reached," the reviser altered the expression,
and substituted an unmistakable term for a doubtful one.
In all probability, the person who made this change was
aware that the interpretation of which he disapproved
was advocated by some, and desired to eliminate the
possibility of mistake. Whether he was right in his view
is even at the present day a matter of controversy ; but
his attitude towards the passage is clear, and his change is
instructive as regards the principles on which he treated the
text of Acts.

The erroneousness of the reading in *Codex Bezæ* would be
st   clearer if we accept Lightfoot's view, and understand
the received text as "the first [*i.e.*, first at which they

---

* In this and various other cases *Codex Bezæ* agrees with some
Syrian texts. I refrain from noticing these agreements, as leading
too far into textual criticism. The constant intercourse maintained
along the line Antioch-Iconium-Ephesus would naturally result in a
close relation between Asia Minor and Syrian texts.

† It is not known to have been used in Macedonia or Achaia,
whereas it is frequent in Asia and Cilicia. Smyrna, and Ephesus,
and Pergamos vied in claiming the title "first city of Asia,'
Nicomedeia and Nicæa that of first of Bithynia, Tarsus and
Anazarbos that of first of Cilicia, or first of the three provinces
Cilicia, Isauria, Lycaonia. Tralles claimed the title " first of the
Greeks" on a coin published by M. Babelon in *Revue Numism.*,
1892, p. 124.

arrived] in the district, a city of Macedonia, a colony." If this was the meaning intended by the writer, then the reviser completely misinterpreted the topographical term, taking it in the sense that was common in Asia Minor and therefore familiar to him.*

Another case in which the reviser has misunderstood the text before him occurs in the Corinthian narrative, xviii. 7. Paul had "reasoned in the synagogue every Sabbath," but when the Jews opposed him, "he departed thence, and went into the house of a certain man named Titus Justus," etc. The meaning is that Paul left the synagogue, and held his meetings for the future at Justus' house. But the reviser thought that a change of Paul's residence was described, and that he ceased to live with Aquila (xviii. 3), and

---

* I do not like Lightfoot's interpretation: I share the reviser's objection to μερίς in the sense of province. It is most natural that there should be subdivisions of the large province Macedonia, and this passage may be taken as a proof that there were. Even if the original division into four was obsolete (which I cannot agree with Lightfoot in thinking that Leake has proved, *Northern Greece*, III., p. 487), another division was very likely to come into use. Still less acceptable is Dr. Hort's remedy. He maintains that μερίς was not used in the sense of "division of a province," and proposes to alter the text to πρώτη τῆς Πιερίδος. But μερίς is, in Egypt at least, a technical term in the sense of "subdivision of a large district, or nome, or province." For example, the title of one of the two Strategoi of the Arsinoitic Nome was στρατηγὸς τῆς Ἡρακλείδου μερίδος (see Wilcken as quoted in *Berlin Sitzungsberichte*, 1892, p. 815). I would accept the phrase of the Travel-Document as an addition to our knowledge of Macedonia, and infer that (1) in the first century the province was sub-divided into μερίδες : (2) Philippi was the capital of a μερίς : (3) the phrase in Acts shows local knowledge : (4) the thought is Pauline, for Paul here and always presses on to the chief centre of civilisation, and the writer emphasises this principle.

migrated to the house of Justus. Accordingly, to make the meaning quite clear, he remodelled the words, and wrote, " departing from Aquila's, he went into the house of a certain man named Justus."*

In the European narrative, also, we find several places in which the received text contains short passages wanting in *Codex Bezæ* : in xvii. 34 a " woman named Damaris " is not in the *Codex* ;† in xviii. 3 it omits " for by their trade they were tent-makers " (may we presume that this fact had perished from the Asian tradition ? Paul is never said to have worked with his hands in Asia or Galatia) ; and in xvii. 18 it omits " because he preached Jesus and the resurrection." The last omission is contrary to the usual practice in this *Codex*, which generally lengthens and emphasises the allusions to teaching.‡ There is certainly nothing in the teaching described which would be thought unsuitable in the Asian churches ; in fact, an Asian document, which is commonly attributed to the second century—the *Acta* of Paul and Thekla (see pp. 155–6)—insists on this character in St. Paul's teaching.

Where anything is added in the European part of the narrative to the text of *Codex Bezæ*, it is either easily gathered from the context (as in xviii. 2, xvi. 35, 39, 40), or it further emphasises the character of Paul's preaching (xviii. 4), or the intervention of supernatural guidance in his course (xvii. 15).

In a few cases the insertion is of more complicated type : *e.g.*, in xvii. 15 *Codex Bezæ* adds, " And he passed by Thes-

---

* μεταβὰς ἀπὸ τοῦ ᾿Ακύλα, εἰσῆλθεν, κ.τ.λ.
† On this point see below, viii., § 5.
‡ *E.g.*, xviii. 4.

salia, for he was prevented from preaching the word unto them." The reviser is struck with the fact that Paul omits Thessaly; he recollects that on his second journey Paul passed by Phrygia and Mysia without preaching there, and he applies the same explanation to this case. He did not observe that in this case Paul probably sailed direct from the coast of Macedonia to Athens. In none of these additions to the language is anything really added to the general sense of the passage, with the single exception of xvi. 30, where the added sense is of very dubious value. The jailer at Philippi, "trembling for fear, fell down at the feet of Paul and Silas, and brought them out [after having secured the other prisoners], and said, 'Sirs, what must I do to be saved?'" The clause in brackets, which is added in *Codex Bezæ*, has an almost comic effect. The jailer carefully looked to his immediate interests before he attended to his future salvation.

It is perhaps a trait not without significance that *Codex Bezæ* is decidedly less favourable to the Berœans than the received text: it says (xvii. 12), "Some of them therefore believed, and some disbelieved." Considering the mutual jealousy between Greeks of different districts which has characterised their history alike in ancient times and at the present day, we may here perhaps see that a native of Asia seizes the opportunity of emphasising the fact that some disbelieved, whereas the received text merely says that "many of them believed." In the latter part of the same verse *Codex Bezæ* loses a distinctly individual trait, characteristic of Macedonia,* viz., the prominent part played by the women. It reads, " And of the Greeks and of those of

---

* See Lightfoot's note in his *Philip.*, p. 55, ed. I.

honourable estate, men and women in considerable numbers believed," instead of "Also of the Greek women of honourable estate, and of men, not a few."

5. *CODEX BEZÆ* FOUNDED ON A CATHOLIC RECENSION.

The omission of Damaris in *Codex Bezæ* (xvii. 34) is specially remarkable. There seems no doubt that this omission is deliberate and intentional. The word εὐσχήμων, which occurs here in *Codex Bezæ* (Διονύσιός [τις] Ἀρεοπαγίτης [εὐσχήμων], καὶ ἕτεροι), seems to be appropriated to women in Acts (compare xvii. 12, xiii. 50); and its use is the last remaining trace of the vanished Damaris. The process of change seems to have been that the word εὐσχήμων was added as a gloss to her name under the influence of xiii. 50, xvii. 12; and then her name was cut out, and the gloss remained in a wrong place in the text.*

In the first place the question occurs, why Damaris was cut out. The omission may be compared with the change in the second part of xvii. 12. The reason for both changes is the same: they are due to dislike to the prominence assigned to women in the accepted text.

Now the prominence of women is, as we have seen, a characteristic of the social system of Asia Minor. This feature in *Codex Bezæ* might therefore seem to be out of keeping with our theory that it is founded on a revision made in that country. But the prominence assigned to women was, firstly, pagan rather than Christian, and secondly, heretical rather than Catholic. It was characteristic of the

---

This explanation is founded on suggestions of Mr. Armitage Robinson.

less advanced and less civilised parts of the country: it
lingered longest in villages and small towns in remote and
mountainous districts; it was extirpated or reduced to a
mere honorary position at an early period in the more
advanced cities, under the influence of the Græco-Roman
civilisation.   Now it was precisely in the educated parts of
the country that Christianity first spread.   Thus in the
second century the situation was produced that the more
advanced districts were Christian, while the uncivilised
districts retained their paganism and their old *mutterrecht*,
even reckoning descent through the mother.*

Further, it is pointed out in chaps. xx. and xxi. that
various developments of religious feeling, which arose in
Asia Minor, were penetrated by the native tone and spirit
of the country, and, in particular, were characterised by
prominent position and influence of women.   In opposition
to these provincial types, the Universal and Catholic type
of Christianity became confirmed in its dislike of the prominence and the public ministration of women.   The dislike
became abhorrence, and there is every probability that the
dislike is as old as the first century, and was intensified
to abhorrence before the middle of the second century.

Under the influence of this feeling the changes in Acts
xvii. 12 and 34 arose in Catholic circles in Asia Minor.

6. Relation of *Codex Bezæ* to Asia Minor.

The explanation just given of the change in xvii. 34
implies that some at least of the alterations in *Codex Bezæ*

---

* Epigraphic proof in the case of Dalisandos, a small town of
Isauria, will be found in a forthcoming paper by my friend Mr.
Headlam, in the special issue of the *Journal of Hellenic Studies*,
1892.

arose through a gradual process, and not through the action of an individual reviser. Possibly all the changes which have been discussed in the preceding pages may have arisen in this way. But some of them are perhaps more naturally explained as the work of a single individual, whom I shall speak of as the reviser.

The freedom with which the reviser treated the text proves that he was a person of some position and authority. The care that he took to suit the text to the facts of the day proves that he desired to make it intelligible to the public. The knowledge that he shows of the topography and the facts of Asia and of South Galatia proves that he was intimately acquainted with the churches from Ephesus on the west, to Iconium and Lystra on the east ; and the felicity with which he treats the text, in all that relates to Asia, seems to be due to his perfect familiarity with the country, for it deserts him when he tries to apply the same treatment to the European narrative. He shows a certain desire to give Ephesus all due glory, and to deny to Berœa any glory that she is not fully entitled to, which proves his Asian bias. He seems to have known certain traditions still surviving in the churches of Asia and South Galatia, whereas none of his changes imply knowledge of any tradition relating to Achaia or Macedonia.

He belonged to the second century, for he alters first century forms and facts to suit those of later time (xiii. 14, xiv. 19). But his knowledge was gained before Lycaonia was disjoined from Galatia between 138 and 161 A.D. As he altered the text freely in order to make it clear to contemporary readers, he would certainly have altered the phrase "the Galatic country," if he had lived so long after the change introduced into the constitution of Galatia and

Lycaonia as to have realised the effect upon the nomenclature. It is conceivable that, if he was living in Asia, he might not for some years realise that what he had once been familiar with as the Galatian district could no longer be called so, and that the old phrase was rapidly becoming unintelligible. But even if we allow for this possibility, the revision can hardly be dated later than A.D. 150-160.

The reviser treated his text with great freedom. He therefore cannot have had any superstitious reverence for the mere letter. His aim was to make it clear and complete ; and for the latter purpose he added some touches where surviving tradition seemed to contain trustworthy additional particulars. Apart from a few cases in which he perhaps had before him a better text than any other MS. has preserved, the value of the reviser's work lies in his presentation of the interpretation put upon Acts in the schools and churches of Asia Minor during the first half of the second century. The book existed then as a whole, and was studied as a work of antiquity, which needed interpretation and modernisation in order to make it readily intelligible. The process of modernising was performed with skill ; it was applied to many passages in which the received text presented real difficulty, and to a few where the received text still defies interpretation. In several cases, chiefly relating to Asia Minor, it produced a text which is really smoother and clearer in expression without actual change of sense ; but in some cases, relating to a foreign country, it was guided by ignorance, and misrepresented and constructed a radically false text.

We can imagine what would have been the result if this process of modernisation had been applied systematically for centuries. The introduction of surviving tradition about matters of fact (as, for example, the hours when St. Paul taught in Ephesus) is not so dangerous, and is sometimes interesting. But the reviser considered himself equally justified in making additions warranted by the doctrinal tradition current in the Asian churches, and shows a distinct tendency to exaggerate the Divine guidance given to Paul, and to specify more precisely than was done in the text the character of his teaching. We cannot doubt that, in all his changes, the reviser was guided by the general consensus of opinion in the churches of Asia, and not by his mere individual opinion. But the results, even of this first revision, are, as a whole, very serious, and, if the process had been performed a second time a century later, would certainly have been ruinous to the character of the text. In another place I shall try to show what was the effect of such a continued process of revision in the case of a work which was (as I believe) composed in the first century, and revised after the middle of the second century, which was extraordinarily popular in Asia Minor, but which was never protected by the reverence that attached in ever-growing degree to the books recognised in course of time as canonical and venerated from the beginning.

If the text of Acts was treated so freely in Asia, the question arises how far a similar freedom of treatment was applied to it in other countries. There is no reason to think that the Asian churches would stand alone in thus treating the text; but there is reason to think that they would be bolder than other churches. During the century following A.D. 70 they had a marked pre-eminence in authority (see p. 171); and they were no doubt conscious of their dignity and weight, and apparently handled the sacred texts more rashly.

POSTSCRIPT: SPITTA'S *APOSTELGESCHICHTE*.

After the preceding chapters were printed, I became acquainted with Spitta's work, *die Apostelgeschichte : ihre Quellen und deren geschichtlicher Wert* (Halle, 1891). It is too late to make in these chapters any use of the book, which I have only time to glance hurriedly into before sending away the last pages of the Preliminary Part. The following points have struck me.

The distinction in the usage of geographical names, which I have pointed out, Chap. VIII., § 2, corresponds to Spitta's distinction of documents A and B. A uses names in the Roman sense, B in the popular or Greek sense. The second part of xix. 10 must be assigned to the editor, who fused A and B (he is called R by Spitta) : the name Asia is used there in the Roman sense. In xix. 26, 27, Asia is used in the popular or Greek sense ; but, as it is there spoken by the artisan Demetrius, we cannot quote this as a proof of the character of B.* It is remarkable how rarely the names of districts in Asia Minor occur in B.

The usage of the participle, which is alluded to above, p. 52, seems to belong to R : Spitta's division makes this necessary in some cases, and easy in all.

Spitta's solution of the problem connected with the account, given in *Galatians*, of St. Paul's visits to Jerusalem is so simple that it carries one away and compels assent, at least for the moment. If it be true, then it follows that the Epistle, which mentions only two visits to Jerusalem, must have been written before that third visit which Paul

---

* Hence I did not mention it in Chap. VIII., § 2.

made at the conclusion of his second journey. This agrees with the date which we have, on independent grounds, assigned to the Epistle (see p. 100) : Paul must have sent the letter to the Galatian churches either from Corinth or from Ephesus, where, during his brief visit, he may have heard news from Antioch and Iconium. Wendt's argument (see p. 106) shrivels away if Spitta's solution is correct.

Almost every case in which, according to our arguments, *Codex Bezæ* presents a reading superior in individuality and accuracy to the accepted text, belongs to B. This is remarkable, and confirms Spitta's view that B is inferior in value to A : it would favour the view that a text, in which the accuracy of some details relating to Asia Minor had been lost, was deliberately improved in all these cases. But, as I have already pointed out, every instance in which we have to attribute to a reviser of the second century such marked improvements in point of individuality and local colour as those in xiv. 13, xix. 28, constitutes a strong proof of my theory that the reviser whose work has been used in the text of *Codex Bezæ* was intimately acquainted with Asia Minor.

Many improvements* in the preceding chapters will become possible if Spitta's theory be accepted ; but on the whole it is agreement in the main issues, rather than difference, that strikes me on a first hasty glance into a few of the chapters. In regard to date, Spitta places B after A.D. 70 and R before A.D. 100 ; while he has apparently no objection to putting A almost as early as I have placed the "original authority for St. Paul's journeys" (see p. 151).

---

* Some details would have to be cut out entirely, *e.g.* the argument advanced as the lesser evil on pp. 107-8, and the note p. 74.

The passage in A, which I have found deficient in clearness, occurs at a junction with B; and the obscurity is probably due to some mutilation of the text (cp. p. 53, and Spitta, p. 171).

Granting Spitta's general theory, I would take A as written down under Paul's immediate influence during his imprisonment, A.D. 62-64; whereas B is a narrative that has passed through more than one intermediary. But much of B must ultimately depend on an eyewitness, though the details have sometimes suffered a loss of vividness. The argument of Chap. VII. acquires new meaning, if Spitta be right, and I am glad that it was completed before I saw his work.

I now feel even more confident than before, that Acts xiii.—xxi. is an authority of the highest character for the historian of Asia Minor. Formerly I looked on it with much suspicion, and refrained entirely, in my *Historical Geography*, from founding an argument on it. Now I have learned that those points which roused suspicion were perfectly true to the first century, but were misjudged by me, because I contemplated them under the influence of prepossessions derived from the facts of the second century

THE CHURCH IN THE ROMAN EMPIRE.

PART II.—A.D. 64–170: BEING

LECTURES AT MANSFIELD COLLEGE, OXFORD
MAY AND JUNE, 1892.

CHAPTER IX.

SUBJECT AND METHOD.

AN apology is due for my boldness in venturing to address such an audience on so difficult and so vexed a subject. But I may almost claim that the topic had been chosen for me by those who had for a time the right to direct my studies. In the task of exploration in Asia Minor the subject was forced on me: unless a large part of my materials and a large part of the history of the country were handed over to others, this subject must engage a great deal of my attention. If there had been at first some one in the circle of my own friends ready to take over my materials and to work them up, as there are still many who could do so with fuller knowledge than I possess, I should not be placed in the difficult position that I now occupy. Every word that I have to say springs ultimately from the desire to do as well as I could the work assigned to me in Asia Minor.

How closely the subject on which I venture to speak is involved in the investigation of the history of Asia Minor may be shown in a single sentence. Asia Minor, and especially the province of Asia, was during the century following A.D. 70, to use the words of Bishop Lightfoot,* "the spiritual centre of Christianity." There the new religion spread most rapidly and affected the largest

---

* *Ignatius and Polycarp*, I., p. 424.

proportion of the whole population ; the conduct of the
Asian communities during that period, their relations with
the imperial government, with their pagan neighbours, and
with other Christian communities, gave to a considerable
extent the tone to the development and organisation of
their Church.   To discuss the relation of the Asian communities to the Empire is practically to discuss the relation
of the Church to the Empire.   This page of history must
be written as a whole.

I. Aspect of History here Treated.

The subject before us has many sides, of which one
alone will here concern us.   These lectures are historical,
not theological.   It is to a page in the history of society
that I ask your attention, and not to a theory of the
development of religious organisation, or doctrine, or ritual.

I want to take Church history for the moment out of the
theological domain, and to look at it from another point
of view.   When it is treated by writers whose interests are
either theological or anti-theological, there is generally a
tendency to treat controversies between sects, and struggles
between opposing churches, too much as a matter of religious dogma.   The diversities of opinion on points of doctrine, often sufficiently minute points, are related in great
detail, by the theologians with the interest of love, by the
anti-theologians with the interest of ridicule.   But, to take
an example from my own country, the historian of Scotland
who described the differences of doctrine, often barely
discernible by the naked eye, between our innumerable
sects, and left the reader to infer that these were the sole,
or even the chief, causes of division between the sects,

would give a very inadequate picture of the facts. He must also describe and explain many social and political differences ; *e.g.*, he must not leave his readers ignorant of the fact that one church as a body took one political side, another as a body took the opposite side.

So in earlier Church history, it has often been the case that differences of race or manners were the cause of division between churches and sects, and slight differences of doctrine or ritual were merely badges on the banners of armies already arrayed against each other. I do not maintain that this is the whole matter, nor even that it is the chief matter ; but I do say that it is a side that deserves and will reward study, and that it does not always receive its fair share of attention. The schism between the Latin and Greek Churches in the ninth century, the schisms between the Greek and the Armenian and other Eastern Churches, are examples of religious movements which were even more important in their political than their theological aspect.

2. CONNEXION BETWEEN CHURCH HISTORY AND THE LIFE OF THE PERIOD.

I do not think that in this work I am venturing away from my proper subject—viz., the study of the character and life of the Roman Empire, especially in the eastern provinces. It is possible to set too narrow bounds to the study of Roman life ; and any bounds are too narrow which exclude from that study what is probably its most important problem—viz., its relations to the system of belief, morality, and society which, beginning in the eastern provinces, gradually spread over the whole Empire.

It must be confessed that this opinion as to the close

connexion between Church history and the general history of the time is not generally held. They are generally considered to be unconnected with each other, and to belong to different fields of study. There has existed, and perhaps still exists, a widespread opinion that Christian writings (like Byzantine history) lie beyond the pale of what is called humane letters, and that the classical scholar has nothing to do with them. We are all only too prone to bound the realm of humane letters by the limits of our individual interests. Is it still necessary to plead that a classical scholar may justifiably spend some part of his time in reading such authors as Cyprian or Tertullian, as interpreters of the society in which they lived, or such authors as Basil of Cæsareia or Gregory of Nazianzos, as aids in understanding the history of Roman Cappadocia? In becoming Christians, these writers did not cease to be men: they only gained that element of thoroughness, sincerity, and enthusiasm, the want of which is so unpleasant in later classical literature; and if they directed these qualities into different channels from those which are most natural now, every such direction of our common human nature must be studied and explained by the circumstances of its time. History only deepens in intensity and interest as we pass from the classical and come down towards the present time. The only reason why it sometimes appears less interesting is that the strands of life become more numerous as time goes on, and the effort to comprehend them separately, and bring them together in the mind to form the complicated thread of human history, grows more serious.

There are many interests of the most fascinating kind in the history of the Roman empire, when we turn away from

the battles and sieges, the murders and suicides, the crimes
of one emperor and the lofty character of another—in
short, from all the great things of history. The machinery
by which for the first time in human history there was
constructed a great and stable empire, more permanent
than the strong arm of the despot who held it together ;
the remarkable system by which such a splendid series
of provincial administrators was produced and trained,
administrators of whom one of the greatest scholars Cambridge ever sent forth—a scholar whom we all grudge to
the politics that absorb him—says that we can find among
them examples occasionally of cruelty, occasionally of
rapacity, but never of incompetence *: that magnificent
system is a fascinating study, but it is inferior in human
interest to the study of social phenomena. The widest
democracy of ancient times was a narrow oligarchy in comparison with our modern states. But the ideas which have
realised themselves among us as the rights of the poorest
and lowest classes were at work under the Roman empire ;
and the central point in the study of Roman imperial
society is the conflict of the new religion with the old. By
a study of Roman imperial society, I do not, of course, mean
superficial talk about Juvenal and the society he describes.
What Juvenal considered to be society was merely the
slowly dying governing caste of earlier Rome, the nobles
who had conquered the world, who had long maintained
their pre-eminence by absorbing into their number every
person of vigour and power enough to raise him above the
level of the lower class, but who at last paid the penalty
that every privileged class seems always to pay, in cor-

---

* Waddington, " Fastes des Provinces Asiatiques," p. 18.

ruption and gradual death. Tacitus and Juvenal paint
the deathbed of pagan Rome; they have no eyes to see
the growth of new Rome, with its universal citizenship,
its universal Church (first of the Emperors, afterwards of
Christ), its "alimentations," its care for the orphan and
the foundling, its recognition of the duty of the State to
see that every one of its members is fed. The Empire outraged the old republican tradition, that the provincial was
naturally inferior to the Roman;* but this, which was its
greatest crime in the eyes of Tacitus, is precisely what
constitutes its importance in the history of the world.
What we are in search of is the historian who will show us
the state of things beyond the exclusive circle of aristocratic
society, among the working classes and the thinking classes;
who will discuss the relation between the Christian and
his next-door neighbour who sacrificed to Rome and the
emperor, and amused himself with the pageantry of Jupiter
and Artemis. I want to be shown what the middle classes
of the community were doing, and still more what they
were thinking. I care little for the university scholar who
immured himself in the university, and dabbled in elegant
literature and gave showy lectures; but I want to see the
man of high university training who went out to move
the world. I get little for my purpose among the pagan
writers; and I must go to the Christian writers, whom I
find full of social enthusiasm, though expressed in strange

* On Horace's protest against this tendency of the Empire, of
which he was vaguely conscious, see Mommsen's speech to the Berlin
Academy on the anniversary of the two emperors, Frederick and
William II., in *Berlin Sitzungsber.*, January 24th, 1889. Horace,
though an adherent of Octavian, never really abandoned his old
republican view; he admired Augustus as the restorer of old Rome,
not as the maker of new Rome.

and to me sometimes repellent forms. They weary me sometimes with doctrine, when I want humanity; but beneath their doctrine the man appears, and when they condescend to the affairs of the world, they are instinct with human feeling. The greatest of them often reach the level of thought where doctrine and life are fused as two aspects of the same thing.

Placed amid the uncongenial society of the Roman Empire, the Christian Church found itself necessarily in opposition to some parts of the Roman law and custom ; negatively it refused to comply with them, positively it even enacted laws for itself which were in flat contradiction to the national laws (as when Callistus, Bishop of Rome, ordered about 220 A.D. that certain marriages should be legal, though the state considered them illegal). The Church was a party of reform and of opposition to the government policy, carried sometimes to the verge of revolutionary movement. Notable differences are found in this respect between the teaching of different periods and different individuals. The question as to the point where disobedience to the imperial law became justifiable, or as to how far the Imperial Government was right in trying to compel obedience and to maintain order, is a very difficult one. The usual answer, that he who thinks as I think is right in disobeying, he who thinks otherwise is wrong, is completely satisfactory to few. We attempt to approach the question from the imperial point of view, and to follow where the evidence leads us.

3. THE AUTHORITIES : DATE.

What then is the evidence? The answer to this question is of primary importance in a subject where the date, the authorship, and the trustworthiness of many of the ancient authorities are all matters of dispute. A few words on these points are necessary as a preliminary. The criticism applied to one class of our authorities—viz., the writings that give (or profess to give) the views of the Christians—has been strict and severe ; it is very important that they should have been subjected to this minute examination, conducted with the learning, acuteness, and ingenuity which belong to German scholarship. But it is unfortunate that some scholars should so habituate themselves to this point of view as to become incapable of taking a wider historical survey of the situation as a whole.

There are some documents whose falseness to the period to which they profess to belong has been clearly demonstrated. All such documents have certain well-marked characteristics. Some purpose or intention of the writer is obvious in them ; and above all, nothing, or next to nothing, for the historian's purpose can be inferred from them. They have no reality or life beneath the surface ; or, to put it in another way, they have no background on which, by closer inspection and minuter study, other facts and figures can be seen to live and move. They attest some single fact in view of which they were composed ; but they give no further evidence to aid the historian. The personages are mere lay figures : they have lived no life ; they have no past and no historical surroundings. But there is another class of documents, whose spuriousness would cause a serious loss to the historian. Such documents suggest a real story underlying the superficial facts : the characters are living men, whose real experiences in the world have caused the facts which appear on the surface ; and from these facts we can work back to their past experiences, their surroundings, the world in which they moved. I know no case in which it has been demonstrated that such a document is spurious.

It is quite true that there are many grave and serious difficulties in documents of this type ; but such difficulties occur in all historical documents. The historian has to accept them, though often he fails entirely to solve them. Not a year passes, hardly a month passes, in which the solution of some puzzle in classical antiquities is not attained through the discovery of new evidence ; and each difficulty solved marks an advance in our knowledge and an increase in our powers. But many of them remain for the future to solve ; with our present resources they must be accepted. These difficulties often take the form of apparent contradictions between authorities. It is a cheap solution to bring down the date of one authority by a century ; but historians have found that this method of explanation raises far more difficulties than it solves, and it has been practically abandoned in almost all branches of history. In them the rule is for the critic to test the genuineness of documents so far as possible apart from his own theories on disputed points, and frame the theory on the basis of the documents.

For example, Juvenal and Martial were contemporaries and acquaintances ; but it is very hard to reconcile and to work into a consistent picture their allusions to the habits and manners of upper-class Roman society in reference to the formal visits of courtesy and the presents given by the host to his visitors (*salutatio* and *sportula*). Even if we take into account the slight difference of time, Martial's writings being published at intervals from 86 to 101 A.D., whereas Juvenal's first book (the one chiefly in question) was published about 103 to 105, no theory of development that can be considered satisfactory has yet been offered. Moreover, Juvenal expressly claims to be describing the manners of the reign of Domitian, 81 to 96, and to avoid as dangerous all references to the age of Trajan, in which he was writing. The attempt to solve this contradiction by bringing down the date of either authority a half-century or a whole century or more would only arouse ridicule; it certainly would not be thought worth serious refutation.

In one branch of history alone do we find still in full vigour, unaffected by sounder methods of inquiry, the superficial and uncritical way of getting rid of such difficulties by tampering with the date of documents and moving them about like pieces on a chessboard. Oddly enough, it is among those to whom the name of critics has been specially applied that this uncritical method is still practised, after it has passed out of credit in all other departments of inquiry. Many consequences of an unexpected kind have resulted indirectly from the practice of this method. For example, it is now generally acknowledged that the tendency of the Tübingen school of criticism was to date the documents and the facts of early Christian history decidedly too late, and most recent critics have carried back the documents to an earlier date. But the question latent in their minds seems always to take the form, " How far back does clear and irrefragable evidence compel us to carry the documents?" They seem to start with the presumption of a late date in their minds, and thus always to have a certain bias, which hinders them from attaining the purely historical point of view. Evidence which formerly was weighed under the bias of a dominant theory seems to retain, even among those who have gradually come to abandon that theory, part of the weight derived from it. It is, as I believe, due to this bias that some German scholars are now gradually settling down to an agreement in dating a number of important documents about midway between the traditional date and the date assigned by the earlier Tübingen school.

To quote another example, similar in character, Neumann* has realised clearly and argued convincingly that the interpretation of Pliny's letter about the Christians which was almost universal in Germany is wrong, and that the letter marks not the beginning, but a stage in the further course of persecution. Yet certain theories† of the growth of church organisation retain their hold on him, although they were elaborated by a long series of investigators, who were biassed in their judgment by the misinterpretation of that cardinal document, which Neumann has more correctly estimated. He assumes the conclusions, after having overthrown one of the premises.

---

* It is impossible to avoid frequent references to Neumann's admirable work on "The Roman State and the Universal Church" (Part I, Leipzig, 1890). It is an excellent collection of materials: much of what he says I agree with, and shall as far as possible avoid repeating ; but his general view of the subject differs greatly from mine. As the book is widely known, I shall mention also some details in which his interpretation of the ancient authorities differs from that which is assumed in this book.

† These theories have affected his view throughout. The heroic dogmatism of his reference on p. 57 to the letter of Ignatius to the Smyrnæans is a fair example : if the word "universal" (καθολικῇ), applied to the Church, occurs in it, the author cannot be Ignatius of Antioch. Where proof is defective, Neumann has not risen superior to the method of supplying the defect by increased boldness in assertion.

With the question of date, that of authorship is to a certain extent bound up ; so far as it is a separate question, it hardly concerns our purpose. For example, the question whether the Epistles attributed to St. John were written by the Apostle will not practically affect the historian's estimate of their value, if once he is convinced that they are first-century productions.

4. THE AUTHORITIES : TRUSTWORTHINESS.

With regard to the trustworthiness of the documents, some words also are needed. We have now for ever passed beyond that stage of historical investigation which consisted in comparing the statements of Christian documents with the Roman writers, and condemning the former in every point where they differed from the authoritative standard of the latter. We have now recognised, once and for all, that the value of the Christian documents for the historian lies in their difference from the Roman writers at least as much as in their agreement ; that a contrast between the version of the same facts given by these two classes of documents was inseparable from their differing points of view, and, so far from disproving, is really the necessary condition for our admitting, the authenticity of the Christian documents. If they agreed, they would lose their value as historical authorities, and they could not possibly be genuine works of the period to which they claim to belong.

In truth we are fortunate, amid the dearth of documentary evidence as to the actual facts of history in the period 50-170, to have so many presentations of the general tone of feeling and thought from very different points of view.

In the Roman writers of the period of history in which our subject lies, we have in general the view of the opposition to the imperial rule; even some writers who nominally take the side of the government are so hopelessly hedged in by the prejudices of the past, so dominated by the glories of republican Rome, so incapable of appreciating the higher elements of the imperial rule, so opposed in heart to those higher elements if they had understood them, that they present themselves as mere apologists of a rule with which they at heart are not in sympathy, and are really the most telling witnesses against the system which they believe themselves to be defending and extolling.

Few authors are more full of interest than the Roman writers of this period. Historical literature has never found a subject more full of picturesque and striking incidents, of strong lights and deep shadows, of vivid contrast of individual characters, of enormous vices and of great virtues in the *dramatis personæ*. Few writers also have shown greater power of telling their story in the way best suited to heighten its effect. No writer has surpassed, hardly any has equalled, Tacitus in power of adding effect to a narrative by the manner in which the incidents are grouped and the action described. Whatever faults a purist may find with the style of the period, its practical effect as a literary instrument can with difficulty be paralleled in the whole range of literature. But their historical view is far from wide. It would not be easy to find a period in which literature was so entirely blind to the great movements that were going on around it. The Romans were destitute of the historical faculty, and of scientific insight or interest: they could make history, but they could not write it.   The early emperors are remarkable figures in themselves, and still more remarkable as they are presented to us by Tacitus and Suetonius; and their individual influence and importance were of course great.   But the permanent Imperial policy was distinct from them and greater than they were, and offers a more serious problem for the modern historian of the Roman empire.   We must determine what was the policy in reference to the prosperity and education of the population, the development of jurisprudence, the organised machinery of government, the training of the officials, the alimentary foundations for poor children, the attempts to cope with great social problems (such as the formally admitted duty of the State to feed its pauper population), the spreading of equal rights and equal citizenship over the whole civilised world, the making of a state religion to guarantee that citizenship.

On such things as these depends our estimate of the Roman Imperial system; and on such points the Roman writers are practically silent.   Among them we find philosophers who aired their rhetoric, rhetoricians who dabbled in moral philosophy, at best pessimists who disbelieved in the present and in the future of the Empire, who made heroes of Cato with his pedantry, of Brutus with his affectation, and Cicero with his superficiality, but who despaired entirely of the possibility of restoring their golden age.   The historians are so occupied with the *great events* of history, the satirists so busy with the vices of upper-class society, the moralists with abstract theorising, the poets with Greek mythology and with the maintenance of their footing in the *atria* of the rich and the favour of the Emperor and his freedmen, that they have neither time to write about the aims of imperial policy nor eyes to see them ; and we gather only indirectly from them some information which we can interpret by other authorities. Here we must trust to our second class of authorities, the inscriptions and the laws.

Lastly, we have the view taken by the adherents of that new religion which grew up within the Empire, formed itself in a great and powerful organisation, and finally took into itself the Imperial Government, its policy, and its laws. As to them, we might with little exaggeration say in one sweeping sentence that, when we find any person who sets himself to do something with energy for the improvement of society, he is either an Emperor or a Christian.

5. RESULTS OF SEPARATING CHURCH HISTORY FROM IMPERIAL HISTORY.

It is safe to say that this last class of authorities has not yet been used so fully as it might be by the modern historians of the Empire, partly, indeed, from doubts with regard to the authenticity and value of the documents, but partly also from preoccupation with the other two classes of authorities. But if classical scholars have more to learn from the Christian writers than has been generally recognised, theologians also have something to learn from the evidence of classical history. The wide and accurate knowledge, and the grasp of the facts of Roman life, shown by the late Bishop Lightfoot and some other scholars whom I need not name, must not blind us to the comparative rarity of such depth of treatment as theirs.

In particular, I feel bound to say that in several of the modern German critics there has been a want of historical sense, and even a failure to grasp the facts of Roman life, which have seriously impaired the value of their work in early Church history, in spite of all their learning and ability. Perhaps the best way to explain my meaning, and to offer myself to criticism and correction if I am wrong, will be to quote a few typical examples.

Baur's "Paul the Apostle of Jesus Christ," with its keen criticism of the historical incidents in St. Paul's life, has been an epoch-making work in the subject. Let us take one specimen of the historical arguments which he uses. There is no more difficult problem for the historian than the relations in which Romans and non-Romans stood to one another in provincial towns : a recent paper of Mommsen's * will give some idea of the utter obscurity in which this subject is involved. But for Baur there is no obscurity. Utterly unconscious of the difficulty of the subject, he moves with perfect ease and unhesitating confidence through the scene with the magistrates at Philippi ; he knows exactly what the colonial magistrates would do and how they would behave ; and he triumphantly disproves the authenticity of a document which might give one who possessed the historic sense a vivid picture of the provincial Roman magistrate suddenly realising that he has treated a Roman like a mere native. Ignorance might be freely pardoned, but not such bold assumption of knowledge.

But this example is perhaps antediluvian ; let us see

* *Ephemeris Epigraphica*, vol. vii., 1892, p. 436ff.

whether all is now changed for the better. I shall come down to a recent date, 1887, and to no mean theologian, Dr. Pfleiderer of the University of Berlin ; and shall select two examples bearing closely on my present subject and helping to make it clear.

1. In one single sentence he states the historical argument about the first epistle attributed to St. Peter. It presupposes that the persons to whom it was addressed were in a situation introduced by an act of Trajan, and therefore the epistle must be later than Trajan. These persons belonged to the provinces or countries of Pontus, Galatia, Cappadocia, Asia, and Bithynia; * and Dr. Pfleiderer boldly sums up these countries as the Roman province of Asia Minor, declares that Pliny was governor of Asia Minor, and that Trajan, in reply to a question addressed to him by Pliny, issued an edict, ordering a persecution of the Christians in the province of Asia Minor. It would not be easy to unite more errors in a single short sentence. (1) There was no such Roman province as Asia Minor. (2) There was for the ancients no such geographical or political entity as Asia Minor. (3) Pliny was governor, not of all the districts mentioned in I. Peter, but of the one province of Bithynia-Pontus. He had no authority in Cappadocia or Galatia or Asia. Therefore, if Trajan's orders extended only to Pliny's province, Dr.

---

* "Urchristenthum," p. 656 : " Der Brief setzt voraus, dass die Kleinasiatischen Leser um ihres Christennamens willen gerichtliche Verfolgungen zu bestehen hatten ; solche Glaubensprozesse aber, bei welchen keine anderweitige Beschuldigung als eben das Christenbekenntniss den Anklagepunkt bildete, sind erstmals von Trajan angeordnet worden, und zwar gerade für die Provinz Kleinasien, wo Plinius Statthalter war, der durch seine Anfrage in dieser Sache das kaiserliche Edikt veranlasste."

Pfleiderer's explanation fails to account for the facts with which he is dealing. (4) Trajan did not issue any edict about the Christians.

In the sequel we shall see how far any unprejudiced reader of the original letters could hold that Trajan first instituted a persecution of the Christians.

2. Arguing that the Epistles of Ignatius are a forgery, Dr. Pfleiderer says that the tale of Ignatius' journey as a prisoner to be exposed to beasts in Rome is an unhistorical fiction; for there is no analogy in the second century to this transportation of the criminal from the place of trial to the Roman amphitheatre.* But it is a commonplace of history that the practice was usual. It was regulated by special enactments, a few of which are preserved to us. If among the small number of cases known to us of Christians exposed to wild beasts no parallel to Ignatius occurs, that is no argument against the general practice. Mommsen expressly argues that the words of the Apocalypse, that Rome was "drunk with the blood of the martyrs," must be understood as referring to those who were condemned in the Eastern provinces and sent to Rome for execution.†

I do not quote these faults from any desire to pick holes in the work of scholars greater than myself, but solely because they are examples of false method. The question as to the date of I. Peter is a historical question, and the

---

* Pfleiderer, "Das Urchristenthum," p. 826 : " Diese ganze Reise des Verurtheilten nach Rom ist eine ungeschichtliche Fiktion ; denn so oft auch Christen zum Thierkampf verurtheilt wurden, so findet sich doch im zweiten Jahrhundert keine Analogie zu diesem Transport aus dem Gerichtsort ins römische Amphitheater."

† See *Provinces of the Roman Empire*, vol. ii., p. 199, of the English Translation.

necessary condition of understanding it properly is to accurately conceive the circumstances and position of those to whom it is addressed. What confidence can be placed in the judgment about the authenticity of a historical document pronounced by a critic who is so hopelessly at sea in regard to elementary facts about the condition of the provinces to which the document relates? But Dr. Pfleiderer cares for none of these things. Ingenious and highly abstract philosophic thought reveals to him the whole evolution of Christian history, and with that knowledge clear in his mind he decides with secure confidence on the authenticity and date of historical documents. In truth historical arguments are to him of little importance and of no interest. His historical argument about I. Peter is a mere *parergon*, a mere make-weight thrown in for the sake of appearance and effect: unreasonable people demand historical arguments about historical documents, and it looks well to give them. The whole value of Dr. Pfleiderer's learned, ingenious, and able work lies in another direction; but for us, who require the theory to be founded on the document, not the document cut to fit the theory, its value is nil.

The false method which has just been alluded to is far too common. In a subject of such difficulty as the history of the early Church, a subject about which the only point that is universally agreed on is its obscurity, not a few writers feel so confident in their own particular theory that they condemn as spurious every piece of evidence that disagrees with it. This condemnation is sometimes justified by a professed examination of the evidence—a mere pretence, because conducted with mind already made up and strained in the outlook for reasons to support their conclusion ; at other times the pretence of examination is discarded, and a document, in spite of the general presumption in its favour on other grounds, is rejected or relegated to a later date, simply and solely because its admission is fatal to the critic's pet theory.

6. The Point of View.

No one can be free from bias in this subject, and perhaps, therefore, it would be best to put you on your guard by stating briefly the general point of view from which these lectures are written.

The Roman Empire and the Church represent to the historian two different attempts to cope with the existing problems of society. The former started from the idea first articulated by Tiberius Gracchus, that every Roman citizen deserved to occupy a situation of decent comfort, and to benefit in some degree by the wealth and prosperity of the whole state. It soon appeared that this idea implied political reform, or rather revolution. Experience further showed that this revolution, and the changed relations to the subject countries which were introduced by it, demanded a new religion.

A religion was needed, for to the ancients a union without a religious bond to hold it together was inconceivable. Every society made its union binding on its members by religious obligations and common ritual. The family tie meant, not common blood, but communion in the same family cultus. Patriotism was another form of adherence to the national religion.

Further, this religion must be a new one ; for no existing

religion was wider than national ;* and no ancient religion wished to proselytise or to take in new members. The object of each was to confine its benefits to a small circle of devotees, and to enlist the aid of the god whom it worshipped against all strangers, all foreigners, all enemies—*i.e.*, against all who were not within the privileged circle. But the new Empire transcended national distinctions and national religions. Roman citizenship included an ever growing proportion of the population in every land round the Mediterranean, till at last it embraced the whole Roman world.

This new unity therefore required a new religion to consecrate it, and to create a common idea and a tie. Half with conscious aim, half driven on unconsciously by the tide of circumstances, the new empire set about creating a new religion. It showed extraordinary skill in constructing the new system out of the old with the least possible change, taking up the existing religions and giving them a place in its scheme. The Emperor represented the majesty, the wisdom, and the beneficent power of Rome : he was in many cases actually represented in different parts of the empire as an incarnation of the god worshipped in that district, the Zeus Larasios of Tralles, the Mên of Juliopolis, the Zeus Olympios of the Greeks in general. Even where this final step was not taken, the imperial cultus was, in the Asian provinces generally, organised as the highest and most authoritative religion, and the emperor was named along with and before the special deity of the district.

---

* Apparent exceptions, such as the worship of Isis, need not be here discussed. The general principle will not be disputed by any

Christianity also created a religion for the Empire, transcending all distinctions of nationality ; but, far from striving to preserve a continuity between the past and the future, it comprehended the past in a universal condemnation, "dust and ashes, dead and done with." It cannot be denied that the Christians were in a historical view unfair to the old religions, and blind to certain fine conceptions lurking in them ; but it is equally certain that the Imperial state religion had no vitality and nothing of the religious character.

The path of development for the empire lay in accepting the religion offered it to complete its organisation. Down to the time of Hadrian there was a certain progress on the part of the Empire towards a recognition of this necessity ; after Hadrian the progress ended, but also after Hadrian the development of the imperial idea ended, until he found a successor in Constantine.

This view * has been the guide in my reading, and has perhaps caused some bias in choosing facts. But I am glad to be able to refer to the eloquent and weighty pages in which Mommsen last year showed † that Christianity was in reality not the enemy but the friend of the Empire, that the Empire grew far stronger when the Emperors

---

* I may quote what I said in the *Expositor*, December 1889, p. 402 : "One of the most remarkable sides of the history of Rome is the growth of ideas which found their realisation and completion in the Christian Empire. Universal citizenship, universal equality, universal religion, a universal Church, all were ideas which the Empire was slowly working out, but which it could not realise till it merged itself in Christianity."

† On pp. 416 ff. of a remarkable review of Neumann, which appeared in the *Historische Zeitschrift*, vol. xxviii., pp. 389-429, under the title of "Der Religionsfrevel nach römischem Recht."

became Christian, that the religious attitude of the earlier centuries was a source of weakness rather than of strength, and the endeavour of the fourth century to make the state religion an abstract monotheism tolerant of all creeds and sects was soon found impracticable.

But when Mommsen implies that the emperors would gladly have tolerated Christianity, but were occasionally forced by popular feeling and popular clamour to depart from their proper policy and persecute Christianity, I cannot follow him. Instances of mere weak yielding to popular feeling undoubtedly occur ; but in a strong government a permanent policy could not be based on such a motive.

The difficulty then is, how is the persecution of Christians by the emperors to be explained ? Lightfoot has urged that Christianity was a *religio illicita*, and as such forbidden by immemorial law. This is true, but it does not constitute a sufficient explanation of the persecution. The same prohibition applied to many other religions which practically were never interfered with. Growing toleration of non-Roman religions was inseparable from the growth of the imperial idea and the gradual merging of Roman citizenship in Imperial citizenship. The exclusiveness of Roman religion, which sprang from the pride of Roman citizenship, necessarily grew weaker along with it. The sense of this growing change was not perhaps consciously and distinctly present to the mind of any Emperor except Hadrian, who is said to have entertained the thought of building temples everywhere to the unseen god.* But it must have been dimly felt by all the emperors, and it

---

* See *Scriptores Historiæ Augustæ*, xviii. (Alex. Severus), 43, 6.

13

certainly lies at the bottom of the growing indifference to
the spread of foreign rites among the Romans.

To explain the proscription of one religion alone, amid
otherwise universal tolerance, is our first object.

Few historical questions have suffered more from loose
expression and loose thought than this.   It is universally
agreed (1) that originally Christians were regarded as a
mere Jewish sect, that the Empire did not concern itself with
questions of Jewish law, and that Christianity benefited by
the freedom and even favour granted to the Jewish religion
by the Roman Government; (2) that at a later period there
was an absolute proscription of Christianity by the empire,
and war to the knife between these two powers.

The question at what time the one treatment was
changed for the other, or whether any intermediate treatment
different from both was in force for a time, is a delicate
one, in which precision in word and in thought is absolutely essential.   Until Mommsen had introduced more
exact ideas as to the terms and forms of Imperial procedure,
such precision was very difficult to practise ; and even now
to attain it is " hard and rare."

The beginning of the declared and inexpiable war
between the Empire and the Christians has been assigned
to very different dates by modern writers.   Some make it
the result of a supposed edict of Septimius Severus, but
Neumann has shown conclusively that no proof exists that
Severus issued any edict on the subject.   It illustrates the
looseness with which the legal and administrative aspects
of this question are treated, that Dr. Harnack,* in review-
ing Neumann, continues to speak of this edict, whose

---

* *Theologische Zeitschrift*, 1890, No. 4, col. 87.

existence Neumann has disproved. There is no proof, and we may add no probability, that Severus did more than answer by rescript questions addressed to him by provincial governors. This is no mere question of words and names; it is a question of prime consequence in understanding the relation of the Empire and of Severus to the Church.

Others date the beginning of this war from the reign of Trajan ;* Neumann recently derives it from Domitian, and dates the supposed change in the attitude of the State to the Church precisely 95 A.D.

Where shall we find a safe point from which to start our investigation? This cannot be a matter of doubt. If we were allowed our choice of a piece of evidence about the view held by the Imperial administration with regard to the Christians, probably those most conversant with Roman history would ask for a private report addressed to the Emperor for purely business reasons, with no thought of publication, by some experienced official, possessing a good acquaintance with the ordinary imperial procedure, and for the Emperor's reply to it. That we possess in Pliny's Report addressed to Trajan from Bithynia, probably in the latter months of the year 112, and Trajan's Rescript to Pliny.

---

* This was the prevailing idea in Germany, and in all scholarship that was dominated by German influence, till Neumann. A slight variety of it is stated by Overbeck, *Studien zur Geschichte der alten Kirche*, p. 94, " Before Nerva it is only by accident through the personal mood of one or another Emperor that the Christian sect found itself at enmity with the state."

CHAPTER X.

PLINY'S REPORT AND TRAJAN'S RESCRIPT.[*]

1. PRELIMINARY CONSIDERATIONS.

A WORD of preliminary is needed on the question of the genuineness of the documents. The question fortunately has been already raised, discussed, and, we may almost say, buried. The correspondence of Pliny with Trajan depends on a single manuscript, of unknown age, found in Paris about 1500, apparently taken to Italy in the next few years, used by several persons before 1508, and never since seen or known. In spite of this suspicious history, the correspondence is indubitably genuine. It contains such a picture of provincial administration that, until Mommsen had written and the publication of the Corpus Inscriptionum Latinarum had been well advanced, no one was able adequately to understand its importance ;[†] and each advance in our knowledge of the imperial organisation only enables us more clearly to appreciate the importance of this unique revelation of Roman provincial government.

The two letters (nos. 96 and 97) which especially concern us now are also genuine. The one is indubitably written in

---

[*] Pliny, "Epist. ad Trajan," 96, 97.

[†] The whole correspondence can be studied best in Mr. Hardy's useful edition, the notes in which bring out the characteristics of provincial administration very well. A few occasional errors are not such as to interfere with the enjoyment and profit of the reader.

Pliny's style. The other shows the direct, incisive manner of the great practical administrator, Trajan, who speaks his meaning without a single unnecessary clause; but we have not the same criteria about the style as we have in the case of Pliny, and we must take into account that such rescripts were perhaps composed in the imperial chancellery from the Emperor's notes or verbal directions. Personally, I must confess that the whole series of Trajan's rescripts to Pliny make on me the impression of having been composed (and doubtless dictated) by one single person; but it is not easy to estimate, and it is certainly not safe to minimise, the degree to which uniformity of style could be impressed on an official bureau under the permanent direction of one powerful genius. The spirit of these documents, so different from that of any later age, is alone a sufficient defence. A forger is confined within the limits of his own knowledge and of the tone and spirit of his time; but these documents become more pregnant with meaning the longer they are studied; and the difficulties which they undoubtedly present are caused partly by the imperfection of our own knowledge, and partly by determined prepossession in favour of some imperfect historical view.

In order to appreciate properly two such documents we must put ourselves in the position of the two parties, and we must clearly conceive their character and their training —the one with the precise, formal, but scrupulously just character of a lawyer of high standing and long practice in the Roman courts, the other the greatest and most clear-sighted administrator that ever wielded the power bequeathed by Augustus. We may be sure that a question on a point of legal procedure addressed by Pliny to Trajan puts before him clearly the legal aspect of the situation ; but he explains nothing which he can assume to be present in the Emperor's mind. We have, then, not merely to translate the documents, which is comparatively easy, but to understand them, which is very difficult. We have to read much between the lines, to conceive very precisely the meaning of certain phrases, and above all to remember that these are business papers, and the writers men of affairs—not philosophers discussing subtleties, nor historians drawing a picture of events for the benefit of future readers. This is by no means a short or easy task ; and I trust therefore to your patience if I enter with even painful minuteness into the discussion of the whole situation, and to your indulgence if, after all, I should fail to grasp thoroughly, or explain clearly, the situation.

2. The Religious Question in Bithynia-Pontus.

In A.D. 112,[*] as we learn incidentally from Pliny's letter, the new religion had spread so widely in Bithynia, not merely in the cities, but also in the villages and the country districts generally, that the temples were almost deserted, and the sacrificial ritual was interrupted. Information against the Christians was lodged with Pliny ; but we are left to guess from what quarter it came, and what precise form it took. He does not expressly tell us whether the accusations were simply couched in the form that the accused were Christians, or whether it was also alleged that they had caused injury and undeserved loss to respectable persons, or had been guilty of grave crimes.

---

[*] Mommsen leaves a choice between the two years 112, 113.

Whatever was the precise character of the charges Pliny entertained them.

It is probable that Pliny, with his strict, precise ideas of the law, and with the careful, zealous attention to duty which belonged to his character, proceeded, immediately on his arrival in the province, to carry out the principles of Roman provincial administration with an energy and thoroughness that formed a strong contrast to the conduct of the preceding governors. The latter had permitted a laxity of administration, which had led to serious disorders and disorganisation throughout the province. Pliny had been sent on a special mission to restore order ; and he showed his activity, we may be sure, from the day he entered on office. The character of his mission—to restore order in a province disorganised by lax administration— lends additional emphasis and meaning to the fact that he rigidly enforced the procedure against the Christians. It also throws a clear light on his explanation to the Emperor that the Christians deserved death for their obstinate and insubordinate spirit, quite apart from any question as to the penalty of their Christianity. They offered a gross instance of the disorder and insubordination which had been allowed to pervade the province, and which Pliny was commissioned to stamp out. Such was his first duty, and it is easy to understand how the Christians must have appeared to him to need energetic and severe treatment as soon as his attention was called to them.

Now Pliny pointedly mentions that an improvement in one branch of trade,—viz. in the sale of fodder for the victims that were kept in stock at the temples to be ready for sacrifice by worshippers—took place in consequence of his energetic measures against the Christians. This curious reference to a rather humble trade suggests that originally complaints had been made to Pliny by the tradesmen whose business was endangered, and that in this way his attention was first drawn to the Christians. He saw that persons engaged in a lawful occupation were interfered with in their trade, and deprived of their proper gains, through the disturbance caused in society and ordinary ways of life by the action of the Christians and the new-fangled ideas and ways which they introduced. Such interference with the settled course of society was certain to rouse the action of the Roman Government wherever it was vigorously administered, and it was, as a rule, in some such way that the Christian religion in its earlier stages attracted the notice and the repressive action of the State.[*]

An example of the attitude which a Roman governor would be likely to assume towards any such interference with the normal course of trade may be quoted from the neighbouring province of Asia. When disturbances were caused at Magnesia on the Mæander by the bakers, who had struck for higher prices, a Roman official (of course the proconsul) prohibited them from forming a union, and ordered them to continue their industry. Such revolutionary conduct was destructive of peace and order, and was always vigorously repressed by the Roman Government. No question was asked whether the bakers had any justification for their demand for higher prices. Their action in depriving the city of the necessary supply of bread must necessarily cause disorder, and was therefore

---

[*] *E.g.*, Paul's troubles at Philippi and at Ephesus were caused in this way. See p. 131.

dangerous. The proconsul, accordingly, ordered them to submit in all respects to the officials charged with the superintendence of the general interests of the city.*

3. First and Second Stage of the Trials.

In the investigations which followed in Bithynia or Pontus,† the earlier cases appear to have been of a uniform type. The first that were accused—they were no doubt the boldest and most prominent adherents of the faith‡— appear to have all, without exception, persisted in avowing their religion. Pliny's procedure was to put three times to them the question whether they were Christians, at the same time threatening them with punishment. When they persisted in declaring themselves Christians, Pliny condemned to death those who were provincials, while those who were Roman citizens he ordered to be transported to Rome to await the Emperor's decision.

More complexity in the cases appeared, when in consequence of the proceedings § new charges were brought;

---

* ἀπαγορεύω μήτε συνέρχεσθαι τοὺς ἀρτοκ[ό]κους κατ' ἑταιρίαν, μήτε προεστηκότας θρασύνεσθαι, πειθαρχεῖν δὲ π[άν]τως τοῖς ὑπὲρ τοῦ κοινῇ συμφέροντος ἐπιταττομένοις, καὶ τὴν ἀναγκαίαν τοῦ ἄρτου ἐργασίαν ἀνενδεῆ παρέχειν τῇ πόλει.—Bull. Correspondance Hellénique, 1883, p. 506. It is unfortunate that this extremely interesting and important document is imperfect, so that the date and the precise circumstances are uncertain.

† On the precise part of the province Bithynia-Pontus, where the trials were held, see p. 224.

‡ They correspond to those *qui fatebantur* in Tacitus, *Annals*, xv. 44 ; see p. 238.

§ *Ipso tractatu* : *i.e.*, new cases resulted from information obtained in the first trials ; but Mr. Hardy's explanation—that the informers were encouraged to fresh accusations—is perhaps correct ; or both results may be summed up in one brief phrase. As I am disposed

and the variety in the cases was still further increased when an anonymous document reached Pliny denouncing a large number of persons.   In the course of the further trials that were thus brought about, some of the defendants at once denied that they were Christians, others at first acknowledged, but yielded (as we may understand from the context) to the threats of the governor, and recanted, saying that they had formerly been Christians, but had ceased to be so, some even twenty-five years ago.   All these offered incense before the statue of the Emperor, and cursed Christ. Pliny now found himself in a difficulty.   He had no doubt as to the procedure when the culprits persisted in claiming the name of Christian, but when they repented he began to hesitate.   Apparently he detained the penitents until he consulted the Emperor, while those who denied that they were or ever had been Christians were dismissed.

This exposition differs to a slight degree from the view held by Neumann,* who says that a change in the form of procedure occurred after the anonymous document of

---

to understand it, *ipso tractatu* corresponds to *indicio eorum* in Tacitus, *Annals*, xv. 44: information obtained in the course of the first trials is meant; but Tacitus lays more stress on the fact that this information was gained through the examination of the accused persons, Pliny on the fact that it was elicited in connection with their cases.   As other cases of later date show, Pliny would begin in each case by identifying the accused, asking his name, station, city, occupation, etc.   See, *e.g.*, *Acta Carpi*, and M. Le Blant, *Supplém. aux Actes des Martyrs*, § 59, in *Mémoires de l'Institut*, tome xxx., part II., 1883.

* "Es lief ein anon. Klagschrift ein: . . . Jetzt begnügt sich Plinius aber nicht mehr mit der Frage, ob die Angeklagten Christen sind, sondern jetzt fragt er sie auch, ob sie es überhaupt einmal waren.   Auch genügt ihm jetzt nicht mehr die einfache Verleugnung, sondern er fordert dass sich dieselbe in der Anrufung, u.s.w. bewähre" (Neumann, p. 20).

accusation (*libellus accusatorius*) was received, and that Pliny, who had previously accepted the denial at once, now in the second series of trials went further, first, asking whether they ever had been Christians, and secondly, requiring them to confirm their denial by distinct acts of conformity to the established religion. But this further procedure need not and cannot be taken as an innovation introduced in the second series of trials. In the first series, where the best known cases appeared, there were only respondents of one class, viz., the confessors (*confitentes* or *fatentes*); in the second series several classes appeared (*plures species inciderunt*). Pliny did not modify his procedure : he acted throughout on a certain view as to the proper law and procedure, and when he began to feel some misgivings whether his knowledge was equal to the complexity and importance of the cases, he stayed the investigations till he could lay his difficulties before the Emperor.

Pliny does not expressly state that there were in the later series of trials any cases of persistent and resolute confession ; but there can be no doubt that there were. It was unnecessary for him to mention them expressly, for his object was merely to indicate the various types : the confessors are mentioned once for all in the original series of cases, and Pliny's way of treating them is described.*

When the simple process of listening to reiterated confession and pronouncing sentence was no longer sufficient, Pliny began to inquire into the course of action, the principles, and the character of the Christians. The

---

* Neumann's view is different. He considers that Pliny reserved all cases of confession in the further series of trials : " Das Urteil über die Christen die fest geblieben hat er offenbar noch nicht gefällt," p. 20.

question here arises, why did he make this inquiry? Was
it from enlightened curiosity and scientific desire to investigate the facts, or was it as an essential necessary part of
the legal proceedings? Pliny's position and legal training
leave no doubt that he conceived the inquiry to be
necessary in order to enable him to decide on their case.
If they persistently confess the Name, Pliny does not think
it essential to inquire further into their behaviour before
condemning them; but if they recant and abjure the Name,
and prove their penitence by acts of conformity with the
religion recognised by the State, then he finds it necessary
to investigate into their previous action and life before he
comes to any determination as to what verdict he should
pronounce. What is his view in acting thus? It is
obviously as follows. Mere penitence for past crime is not
in law a sufficient atonement, and does not deserve full
pardon. A robber who confesses and promises to live a
better life is treated less harshly than a persistent criminal,
but he is not pardoned forthwith; his past life and conduct
are examined into, to see what penalty is appropriate for
him. Similarly Pliny proceeded to investigate into the
past life and conduct of the Christians with a view to
determine what degree of punishment was appropriate.
Having abjured Christianity, they could no longer be
condemned for the Name, as persistent confessors were.
But if they had in their past life been guilty of child-
murder, and cannibalism, and other abominable crimes, they
were still amenable to the law, and must stand further trial.

The analogy with the proceedings at Lugdunum in
A.D. 177 is remarkable. There also the penitents were
not pardoned fully, but an investigation was made into
their past conduct as Christians, and the evidence of slaves

was taken. These slaves were Pagans, belonging to Christian masters. Their evidence was to the effect that the Christians had been guilty of abominable crimes.* Thereupon, those who had abjured their religion were imprisoned as murderers and guilty criminals, and suffered even more than the confessors, who were punished simply as Christians.†

4. PLINY'S ATTITUDE TOWARDS THE CHRISTIANS.

Pliny apparently fully believed at first that the charges currently brought against the Christians were well founded, and that the general proscription, in accordance with which he condemned them instantly after confession, was founded on their detestable rites. He proceeded to inquire into the cases individually ; and he learned first of all from those who recanted, and afterwards from two deaconesses (who, being slaves, were examined under torture), that the rites of the Christian religion were simple and harmless, that their discipline forbade all crimes, that the worshippers bound themselves by a *sacramentum* to do no wrong, and that the charges commonly brought against them of practising child-murder, cannibalism, and other hideous offences at their private meetings were groundless.‡

---

* Θυέστεια δεῖπνα and Οἰδιπόδειοι μίξεις, Eusebius, *Hist. Eccles.*, V. 1.

† Afterwards the governor wrote to ask the Emperor's instructions about those culprits that were Romans, and in explaining the situation mentioned (apparently incidentally, and not with a view to ask for guidance) what he had done with the penitents ; and the Emperor in his rescript ordered that all penitents should be pardoned.

‡ Neumann acutely remarks that from their answers we can gather that the questions put to them were about the very charges which are explicitly mentioned in the proceedings at Lugdunum. See above, note *. The same charges are referred to by Tacitus, *Annals*, xv. 44, as *flagitia*.

Pliny clearly was much impressed with the harmlessness
and simplicity which he discovered in the principles of
the new religion.   But this general impression did not
affect his attitude towards it.   He still considers that it is
a crime, and that those whom he had condemned were
deserving of death for obstinacy, if not for Christianity.
He felicitates himself on the good results that had been
already produced by his action, and he expects that by
a continuation of judicious and rigid enforcement of the
law, the sect may be easily suppressed and order restored.
He found it to be nothing more than a *superstitio prava
immodica.*   It was a *superstitio* (in other words, a non-
Roman worship of non-Roman gods), in the first place
a degrading system (*prava*), and secondly, destructive
of that reasonable and obedient course of life which
becomes both the philosophic mind and the loyal citizen
(*immodica*).   They had indeed been in the habit of holding
social meetings, and feasting in common ; but this illegal
practice they had abandoned as soon as the governor
had issued an edict in accordance with the Emperor's
instructions, forbidding the formation or existence of
sodalitates.   None of the fundamental laws applied to
their case ; they avoided breaking these laws.   The only
question that remains about the system is whether in
itself, apart from its effect on the life and conduct of its
votaries (which is found by Pliny to be morally good), it
requires to be prohibited on political or religious considerations ; and these two were to the Roman essentially
connected, for the State interfered in religious matters
only in so far as they had a political aspect and a bearing
on patriotism and loyalty ; while in other respects the gods
were left to defend themselves (*deorum iniuriæ dis curæ*).

5. THE CASE WAS ADMINISTRATIVE, NOT LEGAL.

Meanwhile Pliny resolved to postpone further proceedings until he learned what was the Emperor's view as to the proper action to take ; and he mentioned in his report that his strongest motive for postponing proceedings lay in the consideration of the large number of persons affected. This leads to the question under what special law, or in virtue of what power, Pliny understood the proceedings to be conducted. He was too strict a lawyer to take the view that the law should be leniently administered because it was disobeyed by a large number of persons ; on the contrary, the Roman practice was guided by the maxim that, when offenders increase in numbers, an example must be made by enforcing the law more strictly and energetically. Accordingly, Pliny cannot have conceived the matter as one coming under some definite law ; he understood it to be a matter of practical administration, and he knew, as every Roman governor knew, by nature and by training, that government must often be a compromise. He might, by too rigidly carrying out the general principle that mere profession of Christianity was dangerous to law and order and deserving of death, increase rather than quiet the disorder, through the number of prosecutions. It was a case in which much was left to his own judgment, in which tact and governing capacity had full opportunity; in short, one where he acted with the full authority vested in a governor and administrator, not as the mere instrument and judge enforcing the penalty of a fixed and definite law.

Pliny must have been under the impression that his

action was in accordance with the general powers and instructions of all governors of provinces, to maintain peace and order, and to seek out and punish all persons whose action disturbed, or was likely to disturb, public order.* Such also is the interpretation of Neumann, who has understood the facts better than any of his predecessors.

This view is confirmed by the character of the correspondence of Pliny with Trajan. He refers to the Emperor, not questions of law, but questions of administration and policy; he asks for relaxation of law or custom in individual cases, and, in general, seeks for guidance in cases which are left to his own judgment and tact. Especially where he thinks an exception might be made to a general principle, he consults the Emperor in matters which appear almost ludicrously slight ; but critics have been too severe on Pliny, for in these cases he is really only criticising the rules laid down for him, and suggesting that they may judiciously bè relaxed. Such examples show how strictly Pliny conceived himself to be bound by the general principles of Imperial policy, and how afraid he was to swerve from them in small matters ; and he may no doubt be taken as a good example of the Roman official. The imperial policy ruled absolutely in the provinces, and

---

* *Digest*, 48, 13, 4, 2 : "Mandatis (*i.e.*, the general instructions given to each governor of a province) autem cavetur de sacrilegiis ut præsides sacrilegos latrones plagiarios conquirant, et ut, prout quisque deliquerit, in eum animadvertant." *Digest*, 1, 18, 13, *pref.*: " Ulpianus libro VII. de officio proconsulis. Congruit bono et gravi præsidi curare, ut pacata atque quieta provincia sit quam regit. Quod non difficile obtinebit, si sollicite agat ut malis hominibus provincia careat, eosque conquirat: nam et sacrilegos latrones plagiarios fures conquirere debet, et prout quisque deliquerit in eum animadvertere.'

the emperors, though not present, were consulted before even slight modifications of the general rules were made. The representatives who governed provinces were not viceroys but merely deputies. This fact is very important in our present subject : the policy throughout the empire towards the Christians was moulded by the wishes and views of the reigning Emperor.

Mommsen has pointed out the power in the Roman constitution which allowed the most prompt and effectual action against the Christians, and which seems to have been always employed in the proceedings taken against them.* The higher magistrates were entrusted with a very large power of immediate action on their own responsibility for checking any disorder or abuse, and for correcting and chastising any person who was acting in a way prejudicial, or likely to be prejudicial, to the State. They could, where they thought it advisable, in such cases inflict personal indignity, such as tearing the clothes and beating; they could order a culprit to be for the moment imprisoned, and they could fine him, or even put him to death, but they were not empowered to inflict lasting punishments (such as exile or imprisonment for a definite term), except in so far as the momentary act of punishment caused permanent results. Especially in the case of religion this magisterial action was widely and almost exclusively employed. The Roman religion was the expression of Roman patriotism, the bond of Roman unity, and the pledge of Roman prosperity. Magisterial action, prompt and vigorous, was a better and shorter way of

---

* See his paper in *Historische Zeitschrift*, xxviii., p. 398, on which the ensuing paragraph is founded.

14

preventing the Roman citizen from neglecting this part of his duties to the State, and of punishing the tempter who made him neglect them, than any appeal to formal law and a formal trial. Hence, although such legal procedure was possible, it was hardly used, was never developed, and has no practical bearing on our present subject. It was by magisterial action alone that Isis-worship was expelled beyond the walls of Rome, that worship of the Celtic deities was forbidden to Roman citizens by Augustus, that Romans who professed the Jewish religion were expelled from the city.

Pliny therefore was acting in virtue of his imperium, which gave him power of life and death over all persons within his province, except Roman citizens; nor is there any reason to think that he was the first governor called upon to act in such cases. The supposition is therefore excluded that any formal law had been enacted to forbid Christianity. We may safely infer also that no express edict of any Emperor had been issued to suppress Christianity.

The inference is confirmed by the way in which Pliny put the case to the Emperor. He was in the habit of quoting or referring to any edict or rescript of any emperor which bore upon any question referred to Trajan; and if the usage of previous proconsuls in Bithynia had given prescriptive force to a point of administration,* he mentioned the fact. But here he refers to no previous edict or law.

An instructive parallel is to be found in Epist. 110. There a point is raised for Trajan's consideration, a point of practical administration, where compromise is advisable or at least allowable. Pliny puts the case as turning on

---

* See Epist. 108.

a point in his instructions (*mandata*) forbidding all dona-
tions from cities to individual citizens. The question is
whether this principle is retrospective, whether prescriptive
right of long standing has any validity, and whether the
public prosecutor of Amisos is justified in demanding that
a donation given twenty years ago should be refunded.

In the case of the Christians, not merely does Pliny not
state any law or edict against which they had offended,
but he points out that they had taken care to avoid offending against the edict which he had, according to the regular
practice, issued on assuming command of the province. In
the edict he had, in accordance with the Emperor's instructions (*mandata*), insisted on strict observance of a law which
had been suffered by preceding governors to fall into abey-
ance—viz., the law forbidding *sodalitates*. Thereupon the
Christians had altered their practice so as to conform to
the law.

6. PLINY'S QUESTIONS AND TRAJAN'S REPLY.

Pliny puts three special questions to the Emperor, which
I have postponed in order to bring them into immediate
connection with the rescript sent in reply by Trajan.

1. Should any discrimination be made between different
culprits on account of youth? In other words, are extenuating circumstances to be taken into account?*

2. Should those who repent be pardoned?

3. What is the precise nature of the offence which is to

* It is assumed throughout both letters that the penalty is death;
the question *quatenus puniri debeat* in the preceding clause means,
not what degree of punishment should be inflicted? but what
distinctions should be made in the infliction of penalty—*i.e.*, should
extenuating circumstances be taken into account, or repentance
ensure pardon?

be investigated and punished? Is the mere Name, without any proof that serious moral offences have been committed, to be punished, or is it definite crimes conjoined with the Name that deserve punishment? In the latter case it is of course implied that the commission of these grave moral offences must be proved by distinct evidence, if denied by the criminals (as it may safely be assumed that they will deny). In the former case the acknowledgment of the Name by the accused is in itself sufficient ground for condemnation.

Trajan does not formally reply to the questions in this form and order; but in his brief review of the situation and the principles of action an answer to each is implicitly contained. After the long discussion which has just been given we can readily understand his view.

1. Pliny's procedure has been correct—*i.e.*, his original assumption that the Name of Christian, if persisted in, deserved the penalty of death, was right.*

2. No universal rule applicable to all cases can be laid down—*i.e.*, extenuating circumstances are to be considered according to the discretion of the governor.

3. Penitence deserves pardon, if shown in act by compliance with rites of the Roman religion.

4. The governor is not to search for the Christians; but if they are formally accused by an avowed (not by an anonymous) accuser, the penalty must be inflicted.

This rescript does not initiate procedure against the Christians. It is absurd to suppose that Trajan for the first time laid down the principle, " The Christians are criminals

---

* Neumann has rightly emphasized in the strongest terms the original action of Pliny, p. 22, n. 3, " *Es kann nicht scharf genug betont werden.*"

deserving death ; but you may shut your eyes to them until
an accuser insists on your opening them." Trajan's language
is that of one who feels unable to contravene or to abrogate
an existing principle of the imperial government, but who
desires this principle to be applied with mildness and not
insisted on. Neumann has rightly perceived that this is
the true meaning of Trajan's rescript, and in this respect
has made a great advance on previous critics. It is one of
the most astounding facts in modern historical investigation
that so many modern, and especially German, critics of high
standing and authority,* have reiterated that Trajan was
the first to make the Name a crime, and that any Christian
document which refers to the Name as a ground for death
must be later than his rescript.†

7. THE CHRISTIANS WERE NOT PUNISHED AS A *SODALITAS*.

Trajan, like Pliny in his early trials, condemns the
Christians simply on their confession without further question, trial, or proof. They are outlaws ; they are treated

---

* Even those who have not fully adopted this erroneous view have
often been affected to some degree by it. On the history of the
view see Lightfoot's note, *Ignat.* and *Polyc.*, i., p. 7. M. Doulcet,
in his *Essai sur les Rapports de l'Église Chrétienne avec l'État
Romain*, 1883, p. 52, reckoned Wieseler the only scholar who declined
to accept this view ; but Lightfoot mentions others. It would be unfair to refrain from alluding to the many English scholars. Lightfoot,
Salmon, Hort, etc., who, in writings or in lectures, have interpreted
Pliny and Trajan more correctly. But in general their treatment of
the question has suffered to some slight degree from their treating
it as a matter of formal and positive law, instead of as a question of
practical administration.

† The inference has been drawn especially about First Peter; see
above, p. 187.

like brigands caught in the act. It is necessary to insist on this point, because many high authorities differ from the view here stated. Practically the question comes to this : were the Christians condemned for violating the general law (recently confirmed by Pliny's edict in accordance with the imperial *mandata*), which regulated and confined within very narrow limits the right of forming associations (*collegia*, *sodalitates*), or were they condemned simply for the Name ? A want of clearness and a wavering between these two essentially different forms of trial are apparent in much that has been written on the subject. The same writers who in one page recognise that the Name is punished, on the next page speak of the edict against *sodalitates* as the ground on which the Christians were punished.*

In answer to this question, the following considerations suggest themselves :—

1. If the Christians had been punished by Pliny as an illegal association (*sodalitas*), he must have put some questions on the point to them. Even the most arbitrary of governors could not condemn a criminal to death for violating a law without some show of trial, some statement of the law, and some show of testimony, good or bad, that the criminal had broken the law ; much less can we suppose that a strict lawyer like Pliny would act in so illegal a way. Even a confession of guilt was regarded by the Roman law in some cases † as insufficient to entail condemnation.

---

* In the original form of these lectures I criticised Mr. Hardy's excursus on the subject ; but he has informed me that he has, since the book appeared, modified his opinion there expressed.

† Viz., *in judicio*; but in cognitions (pp. 216, 398), acknowledgment of the charge sufficed to ensure condemnation.

2. Pliny could not have asked Trajan what was their crime, and how he should treat them, if he had conceived them to be a *sodalitas*. It had already been made abundantly clear to him by repeated rescripts that Trajan would not permit the smallest infraction or exception to the law.*

3. Pliny expressly mentions that the Christians had of their own accord given up a weekly meeting and a common meal, which would have constituted them a *sodalitas*.

4. Trajan would not in his rescript have ordered Pliny to abstain from seeking out the Christians, if he had understood them to be a *sodalitas*. He regarded the prohibition of *sodalitates* as a fundamental point in strong government

8. PROCEDURE.

The question may suggest itself, if Pliny was acting on a principle of administration carried out by previous governors, whether of Bithynia or elsewhere, are we not obliged in accordance with what has just been stated, to conclude that he would have quoted the action of previous governors as justifying him? The answer is clear. He does refer to it, and explains why he is uncertain as to its character : he had never taken part in investigations (*cognitiones*) of the case of Christians. Many points are involved in this short statement.†

---

* Trajan would not permit the formation of a body of one hundred and fifty firemen in a great city like Nicomedeia (Epist. 33, 34); he also forbade poor people to join together for a common meal at common expense (Epist. 102, 103). All such unions were dangerous, as liable to cause common action and to assume a political character.

† The import of the phrase is, as a rule, disguised by the rendering "I have never been present at" such cases. The meaning in this report is : " I never occupied such an official position as to be called on to decide or advise in the case of Christians, and therefore I am ignorant of the precise nature of the proceedings."

In the first place, Pliny and Trajan were obviously well aware that such investigations were of ordinary occurrence.[*]

Secondly, these cases were *cognitiones*, not formal trials according to law, *judicia*. Pliny's experience as a lawyer had lain in the *judicia* before the centumviral courts, with a few political cases before the Senate. *Cognitiones* might indeed fall within the jurisdiction of the Senate and consuls ; but it seems pretty certain that trials of Christians were left to the Emperor or his delegates.[†]

The Emperor often delegated such *cognitiones*, even in Rome, to the prefect of the city, and necessarily in the provinces to the governors. Pliny could not be fully cognisant of the law in such cases. He had not hitherto governed a province, nor had he been prefect of the city. The *cognitiones* held by the Emperor were conducted in private,[‡] and only the result was known publicly. Pliny

---

[*] As to the number of such cases, the words do not justify any inference. I cannot agree with Mr. Hardy, who says that Pliny's statement proves conclusively that the trials of Christians had been neither frequent nor important, otherwise Pliny would not have been ignorant of their procedure. The following paragraphs will prove that the inference is unjustifiable.

[†] Hence almost all cases of Christians that we know of came before governors of provinces, prefects of the city, or the Emperors in person (see Mommsen, *Historische Zeitschrift*, xxviii., p. 414).

[‡] This was generally, and probably always, the case. See Mommsen, *Röm. Staatsrecht*, ii., p. 926, ed. ii. Mr. Furneaux is certainly wrong (Tacitus, *Annals*, vol. ii. p. 577) when he speaks of such standing *quæstiones de Christianis* as we have in Pliny's letter. The process against the Christians was invariably, so far as evidence goes, Imperial cognition, exercised personally by the Emperor or delegated to the *præfectus urbi* or to the provincial governors. *Judicium* before a *quæstio* was never employed.

could not have been acquainted with the procedure in such *cognitiones*, except as a member of the *consilium*, which the emperors often employed for consultation. But though he had never actually taken part in such cases, he naturally, as a Roman lawyer and official, had a general idea of their character and procedure.

In conducting these investigations Pliny followed a definite procedure. He put the question three times to each person, giving full opportunity of repentance. What was his reason for following this course?

A possible interpretation of his action is that he was, from motives of pure humanity, anxious to avoid inflicting the penalty of death. There is no doubt that this kind of action would be quite in accordance with his private character. But we must remember that Pliny in this case is the Roman magistrate and judge, and that he is a man in whom long experience as a lawyer and judge had rendered dominant and habitual the strict law-abiding spirit of the Roman. On the judicial bench Pliny was no longer the kind and generous, though rather weak and affected, man whom we see in his carefully studied letters ; he is the Roman officer, trained in the law-courts in the straitest Roman formalism and pragmatical spirit of minute legality. He had not the loftier character which could discern the spirit behind the letter of the law. To him it was second nature to act according to the prescribed forms, and in this case we must assume that he did so. He indeed says that he had never before taken part in such trials ; but, as we have already seen, this does not imply entire ignorance of the forms of procedure. It merely means that he did not feel himself complete master in this branch of law. He could trust his law to the extent of executing

100 or 200 persons,* but when it came to a case of thousands he was not so confident.

Moreover, Pliny is here reporting his procedure to the Emperor, and there can be no doubt that he conceives himself to be playing the strict official. Nothing could be more foreign to the Roman ideal than to allow that conduct on the tribunal should be influenced by individual emotions of compassion or humanity. Severity, degenerating even into cruelty, is characteristic of the best and most upright class of Roman governors : lenity, as a general rule, was the result only of weakness, of partiality, or of carelessness. Pliny certainly was most careful and conscientious ; and equally certainly he did not consider that his procedure would seem to the Emperor to imply weakness. We observe also that the same procedure obtained in numerous other trials of later date, which we cannot think were modelled after Pliny's example. The only possible hypothesis seems to be that Pliny was acting according to a standing procedure which had grown up through use and wont. A succession of governors and emperors, applying the general view that Christianity was subversive of law and order, and acting with the same general intention of maintaining law and order, had, with the usual legal constructiveness characteristic of the Romans, brought about a general procedure which had all the force of legal precedent.

One objection which might perhaps suggest itself hardly deserves notice. If the procedure had already become habitual, how should Pliny require to consult the Emperor about it? If any answer is needed after the above discussion

* On the numbers see p. 220.

of his position, we might quote the fact that in A.D. 177 the governor of Gallia Lugdunensis consulted Marcus Aurelius, and received a rescript correcting his action in a fundamental point. Even Septimius Severus was probably consulted by his delegates; for his action towards the Christians took the form of one or more rescripts. The governors wished to act as the Emperor would act if he were present; and hence in this matter, where details were left greatly to their individual judgment, they frequently asked advice.

9. ADDITIONAL DETAILS.

Some details must be noticed before we leave the subject. The regular morning meetings which Pliny speaks about, and which, as we know, must have been weekly meetings, were not abandoned, and Pliny obviously accepts them as strictly legal. Amid the strict regulations about societies, the Roman Government expressly allowed to all people the right of meeting for purely religious purposes.* The morning meeting of the Christians was religious; but the evening meeting was social, including a common meal, and therefore constituted the Christian community a *sodalitas.* The Christians abandoned the illegal meeting, but continued the legal one.† This fact is one of the utmost consequence. It shows that the Christian communities

---

* Unless, of course, the religion was a forbidden one; but the Empire had quite given up in practice, though not in theory, the old objection to non-Roman religions as illicit.

† Neumann indeed considers that the Christians suspended even the morning meeting for religious purposes. This seems not to be required by the Latin words, while it is inconsistent with the principles of the Christians to suppose that they discontinued their Sunday worship.

were quite alive to the necessity of acting according to the law, and of using the forms of the law to screen themselves as far as was consistent with their principles.

Pliny's language permits no inference as to the number of executions, and we are left entirely to individual estimate of probability. How many examples would be sufficient to produce the effect described by Pliny in restoring the disused worship of the ancestral gods, and reintroducing the disused temple ritual?

Probably the history of the Church may show that I have not exaggerated in speaking of 100 or 200. If some sort of remote analogy may be found in the number of witches burned in Scotland at no very remote period, I may seem to have understated the probabilities. A certain lapse of time is also required to produce the effect described.

It is also quite impossible to attain certainty as to Pliny's treatment of the confessors, whether he employed torture, or condemned them to be exposed in the amphitheatre, or took the more merciful course of ordering them to instant execution.* Probably he would follow the usual course, which was to utilise condemned criminals for the public games.

Trajan's letter to Pliny applied only to the single province. A copy, of course, was permanently preserved in the governor's office; but in the ordinary course of events the document would not have any wider publicity or influence. Accident, however, gave this rescript an unusual

---

* The latter is the ordinary, but not the necessary, sense of *duci iussi*. The phrase is perhaps used more generally, "I ordered them to be taken whither the law directed." The torture applied to the deaconesses was not punishment, but the preliminary required by the Roman law before the evidence of slaves could be accepted.

importance both in ancient and in modern times. It was published (of course by the Emperor's permission) after a few years in the collected correspondence of Pliny and Trajan. It thus reached a wider public; and officials, who were always eager to act according to the imperial wishes, would take it as representing Trajan's settled policy. Tertullian was able to quote this letter; whereas he merely refers by inference to the supposed reports of Pilate to Tiberius, and of Aurelius to the Senate, assuming that, if sought in the imperial archives, they may be found. The importance of Trajan's rescript is twofold, being due, partly to its internal character, partly to the chance which preserved it to our time. An entirely fictitious importance has been attached to it, as if it were the first imperial rescript about the Christians and defined for the first time the Imperial attitude towards them.* Its real importance is very different. It marks the end of the old system of uncompromising hostility.

A question suggests itself which is of interest in estimating Pliny's character, but which does not directly bear on our purpose. Was his intention in consulting the Emperor merely to learn his views, or had he any wish and hope that the policy towards the Christians should be reconsidered? Personally, I can feel no doubt that the latter alternative is correct. It would of course be unbecoming and unprofessional to hint that the imperial policy should be reconsidered; but Pliny goes as far as he could go without directly suggesting it, and he has conceded to the

---

* We need not doubt that anxious reports from many governors had reached Rome long ere this, coming especially from Asia Minor; and that the matter had engaged the serious attention of the Emperors.

prevailing anti-Christian prejudice enough to avoid the appearance of hinting. The only respectful course for him was to profess ignorance, and ask for instructions ; and thus we have the astonishing change in his attitude, that, beginning with unhesitating condemnation, he ends by addressing to the Emperor the charmingly simple question, " Am I to punish them for the Name, or for crimes co-existing with the Name ? " He apologises more for consulting the Emperor on this case, involving the lives of many thousands, than he does for any of the other quesitons, many rather insignificant, which he addresses to him. The apology seems unsuitably elaborate ; and we cannot really appreciate the letter, till we understand that the writer is desirous to have the policy changed, and yet shrinks from seeming in any way to suggest a change.

Considering the confidence which Trajan reposed in Pliny and the friendship he entertained for him, we shall not err in believing that this letter exercised some influence on him. Trajan's reply inaugurated a policy milder in practice towards the Christians ; and it is a pleasant thought that a writer, whose life gives us a finer conception than any other of the character of the Roman gentleman under the Empire, should be, in the last months of his life, so closely identified with the change of policy and with the first step in the *rapprochement* between the Empire and the Church.

10. RECAPITULATION.

In view of the importance and the complication of the subject, it will be convenient to sum up our results here :—

1. There was no express law or formal edict against the Christians in particular.

2. They were not prosecuted or punished for contravening any formal law of a wider character interpreted as applying to the Christians.

3. They were judged and condemned by Pliny, with Trajan's full approval, by virtue of the *imperium* delegated to him, and in accordance with the instructions issued to governors of provinces, to search out and punish sacrilegious persons, thieves, brigands, and kidnappers.

4. They had before this been classed generically as outlaws (*hostes publici*), and enemies to the fundamental principles of society and government, of law and order ; and the admission of the Name Christian in itself entailed condemnation.

5. This treatment was accepted as a settled principle of the imperial policy, not established by the capricious action of a single Emperor.

6. While Trajan felt bound to carry out the established principle, his personal view was opposed to it, at least to such an extent that he ordered Pliny to shut his eyes to the Christian offence, until his attention was expressly directed to an individual case by a formal accuser, who appeared openly to demand the interference of the imperial government against a malefactor.

7. A definite form of procedure had established itself through use and wont.

8. Pliny, when for the first time required to take part in such a case, used the regular procedure, either through his own general knowledge of a branch of official duty not specially familiar to him, or as following the advice of his *consilium* and the precedents which they might quote.

11. TOPOGRAPHY.

The province which Pliny governed, officially entitled *Bithynia et Pontus*, was of very wide extent, reaching from the river Rhyndacos on the west to beyond Amisos on the east. The question suggests itself whether his experiences, with regard to the Christians, extended over the whole province, or was confined to part of it. Mommsen has shown that Pliny visited the eastern part of his province in the summer and autumn of 112, and that letters 96 and 97 were written during this visit, perhaps from Amisos.* It is therefore clear that the events which led to Pliny's letter took place there, and that the description of the great power acquired by the new religion in the province applies to Eastern Pontus at least. But it would not be right to restrict his description to this part of the province. The general impression made by the letter is, that it describes a condition of things which was true of the province as a whole, and was not confined to a small district. Pliny speaks of the cities (*civitates*) in general as being much affected by Christianity.

In the letter Pliny alludes to two distinct stages in his proceedings against the Christians. In the first stage he acted without hesitation, and had no thought of appealing to the Emperor for advice. But facts that came to his knowledge in the second stage led him to hesitate, and to stop further proceedings until he heard from the Emperor. We may, then, feel fairly confident that the second stage of the proceedings belonged to Eastern Pontus, and that

* See Mommsen's paper on Pliny's life in *Hermes*, iii., p. 59. The letters which immediately precede and follow 96 and 97 were written from Amisos.

the two deaconesses whose evidence produced such an effect on Pliny belonged to the church of Amisos, or of the immediate neighbourhood. This fact suggests some reflections on the geographical distribution of Christianity in the north of Asia Minor.

We have seen, on page 10, that Amisos was the point on the north coast to which the new religion might naturally be expected to spread earliest. We now find that Amisos is the place where, in A.D. 112 or 113, renegades were found in considerable number ; and that some of these claimed to have abandoned that religion even twenty-five years previously. Christianity, therefore, was already of some standing in Amisos in A.D. 87 or 88.

We have seen that in the earlier stage of the proceedings all the accused persons were confessors : renegades appeared only in the later stage in Eastern Pontus. This implies, probably, that in the western parts Christianity was more recent, and that greater boldness was required to be a Christian ; whereas about Amisos the religion had spread more widely, and was more powerful, so that there might even be advantages in belonging to such a strong and closely united sect. We are therefore again brought, by a new line of argument, to the conclusion that Amisos was the first city on the Black Sea to which Christianity spread.

As to the date when this took place, it was, on the one hand, some time before 87-88 ; and, on the other hand, it would naturally be later than the spread of Christianity along the main Eastern highway to Ephesus and other Asian cities, about 55-57. We may fairly place the entrance of the new religion into Amisos about 65-75 A.D.

15

CHAPTER XI.

THE ACTION OF NERO TOWARDS THE CHRISTIANS.

WE have learned from Pliny that actions against the Christians had become habitual before the accession of Trajan, and that a form of procedure had grown up. Neumann, though differing in some respects from our estimate of Pliny's evidence, is quite agreed on this point. The next question that comes up is, when did this habitual action originate. Neumann dates its origin in A.D. 95, and supposes it to be founded on an edict of the Emperor Domitian. But we have already seen that Pliny's action was not founded on any law or edict, but was that of a practical ruler and governor interpreting a fixed but unwritten principle of policy. Moreover, the opposition of the Empire is too settled and confirmed to be explained in this way. An edict of Domitian might be overturned by a word from Trajan ;* but Trajan clearly regarded the proscription of the Christians as a fundamental principle of the Imperial policy, which he did not choose, or shrank from trying, to alter.

We cannot then accept Neumann's view, and must look for some more deep-seated reason for the hostility of the Empire to the new religion. Our authorities for the time of Domitian are so scanty that we are reduced to hypothesis about it ; and we have to go back to the reign of Nero to find another well-attested moment in the Imperial action.

---

* See Mommsen, *Staatsrecht*, ii., p. 1069, ed. ii.

I. TACITUS, *ANNALS*, XV. 44.

In the famous chapter of Tacitus about the persecution of the Christians under Nero in 64 A.D., we have a document very different in character from Pliny's report to Trajan; and the difficulties which face us in the attempt to estimate rightly its meaning and value are of a different order.

1. It is written for publication, and composed with a view to literary effect; and the question arises in several points, how much is to be attributed to rhetoric and how much to faithful description of the facts?

2. It is written more than fifty years after the events by an historian, who was a child when they took place, and who was entirely dependent on the evidence of others. In regard to many points, a doubt arises whether Tacitus may not have been attributing to the earlier period the knowledge and the feelings of the time when he was writing; and it is at least certain that Tacitus could not, even if he tried, altogether free himself from the additional experiences of fifty years. He must write from a more developed point of view.

Any question as to Tacitus' veracity in matters of fact need not trouble us. He certainly took the greatest care to seek out good authorities and to compare them with each other, and to state facts as they occurred.*

Nor need we touch on the genuineness of the chapter.

---

* The bias which undoubtedly exists in his work is founded on his inability even to see, much more to sympathise with, the finer sides of Imperial policy In matters of detail and fact he was a very careful investigator, and tried to be an accurate recorder, though his straining after literary effect often veils his description of facts.

There have been, and perhaps always will be, occasional doubts ; but they belong to the curiosities of literature.

As to the extent to which Tacitus' account is coloured by the circumstances of his own time, the most diverse opinions have been held. It has been maintained* that Tacitus took his materials for describing the Christians of Nero's time from the letter of Pliny, which we have just been discussing, that he adopted from him the term *fatebantur,* deepened Pliny's *superstitio prava immodica* into *superstitio exitiabilis,* and used the *flagitia* which Pliny speaks of as an explanation of the popular hatred of the Christians. Bauer has even used this theory as a proof that the letter of Pliny is genuine.

In direct contradiction to this theory it has been stated † that "the ignorance of Tacitus on this subject is more remarkable because his friend Pliny had already learned the ways of Christians while governor in Asia Minor." This implies the view that Tacitus had strictly adhered to the ignorant accounts of contemporaries, and had intro- duced nothing of the knowledge which was possessed by some, at least, of his contemporaries.‡

We shall neither accuse Tacitus of ignorance about what

---

* By B. Bauer, *Christus und die Cæsaren,* 1877, p. 273. Not having access to the book, I follow the account given by Arnold, " *Die neronische Christenverfolgung,*" p. 105.

† By Holbrooke, Tac. *Ann.,* note on xv. 44.

‡ There can be no doubt that Tacitus possessed as much know- ledge of the Christians as any Roman did at this period, because (1) he had been proconsul of Asia, the chief stronghold of Christianity, about 112–116, before he is believed to have composed the *Annals* (see the inscription of Mylasa quoted in *Bull. de Corr. Hell.,* 1890, p. 621) ; (2) he is known to have taken great pains to collect evidence for his history, and to have consulted Pliny about another point in preparation for his earlier great work.

was known to Pliny, nor shall we credit him with thrusting Pliny's ideas into a period to which they were foreign. We shall try whether it be not possible to believe Tacitus, when he claims to be describing the state of public eeling and belief in A.D. 64 ; even though we also consider that he was probably quite aware of Pliny's investigation and its results. We hold that Tacitus wished and tried to describe the events of this year 64 and of other years as they occurred ; though .we quite acknowledge that he could not divest himself of his knowledge, and could not possibly write exactly as he would have written if the *Annals* had been composed in the reign of Nero.

It is not possible to determine the meaning of Tacitus' words with the same certainty as in the case of Pliny's letters. Here, as usual, the attempt to disentangle from the rhetoric of Tacitus the precise and exact facts which he is describing cannot be successful, for it is hardly possible to rise above individual subjective judgment, and attain an interpretation which shall be quite certain. In such a case it is of the first consequence to determine from independent witnesses, even to a small extent, the exact state of the facts. Several other writers have, on authority quite independent of Tacitus, alluded to or described the action of Nero towards the Christians. The earliest of these is Clement of Rome, a contemporary and probably an eyewitness ; but his reference is too slight and general, and is not confined to this persecution alone. It will be considered in a later chapter.

2. THE EVIDENCE OF SUETONIUS.

The chief independent witness is Suetonius, who was certainly acquainted with the work of Tacitus, with whom he undoubtedly had personal acquaintance. He has apparently used and followed the authority of Tacitus in some few passages, * and it is a quite fair assumption that he was acquainted with Tacitus' view. Among a list of police regulations to ensure good order in Rome,† he mentions the punishment of the Christians, a class of persons characterised by a novel and mischievous superstition. His list enumerates what he evidently considers as examples of good administration. They are all of the nature of permanent police regulations for maintaining order and good conduct. He mentions the sumptuary regulations, the institution of the *sportula* in place of the *publica cena*, the prohibition of the sale of any cooked food except vegetables in the cook shops, the infliction of punishments on Christians, the prohibition of the disorderly revels of the charioteers, etc. Every other regulation which is mentioned in the list is the permanent institution of a custom, or the lasting suppression of an abuse. It would be quite inconsistent with the others to introduce in the midst of them a statement which meant only that a number of Christians were executed on the charge of causing a fire. The fair and natural interpretation of Suetonius' words is, that he considered Nero to have maintained a steady prosecution of a mischievous class of persons, in virtue of his duty to maintain peace and order in the

---

* See especially *Vespas*, § 4, where he speaks of the general expectation of the period that out of Judæa were to spring they that should rule the world. Cp. Tac., *Hist.*, v. 13 ; Teuffel-Schwabe, *röm. Litteratur*, § 347, 8 ; Arnold, *" Die neronische Christenverfolgung,"* p. 38. I shall have occasion often to quote, and sometimes to criticise, the latter useful monograph.

† *Ner*, § 16.

city, and to have intended that this prosecution should be permanent. Such a steady prosecution implies a permanent settled policy; and if the chapter of Suetonius had been the only extant passage of a pagan writer referring to the subject, the view which is here stated would in all probability have been universally accepted. As we see, this interpretation is in perfect harmony with all we have gathered from Pliny.

Contrast with this Suetonius' account of the action taken by Claudius in the case of the disturbances which took place among the Jews in Rome about A.D. 52.* This measure, which is obviously a single act suited to a special occasion, and does not involve the institution of any general rule, is mentioned along with the taking away of freedom from Lycia, the giving of freedom to Rhodes, the remission of tribute of the Ilians, the permitting of the German ambassadors to sit beside the Armenian and Parthian envoys in the orchestra. The whole list is of the same kind,—individual and single exertions of authority in special cases. None of them involves a general principle or the institution of a permanent rule applicable to all cases of a class.

Comparison of these two passages of Suetonius shows that he considered the action of Nero as different in character from that of Claudius. The latter expelled all Jews from Rome; but, as we know from other authorities, this was a mere single isolated act, and involved no lasting

---

* *Claud.*, § 25. Here we have, according to the generally accepted view, a proof that the Christians were still considered under Claudius to be a mere Jewish sect; and dissensions between Christians and Jews were described in the authorities employed by Suetonius as " continued disturbances among the Jews."

judgment. The former, on the contrary laid down a permanent principle regulating the attitude of the government towards the parties affected, viz., the Christians ; and this inference would certainly have been drawn by all historians had it not been for the authority of Tacitus, who has been interpreted as contradicting the view naturally suggested by Suetonius. Now, even if Tacitus' words were as strongly opposed to this view as is usually thought, It might be plausibly argued that Suetonius was almost certainly acquainted with Tacitus' opinion, and intentionally dissents from it ; and, as he used excellent authorities, his express contradiction must be accepted. But I believe that Tacitus' description has in parts been misunderstood, and that there is no serious contradiction, but a slightly different and more detailed version of the same facts. Suetonius gives merely a brief statement of the permanent administrative principle into which Nero's action ultimately resolved itself. Tacitus prefixes to his account of the same result a description of the origin and gradual development of Nero's action ; and the picture which he draws is so impressive and so powerful as to concentrate attention, and withdraw the mind of the reader from the final stage and the implied result of the Emperor's action.

3. First Stage in Nero's Action.

Let us then turn to Tacitus' account, and try to disentangle the facts as they were conceived by him. To do so successfully, we must try as much as possible to look from Tacitus' point of view, and to assume the tone and the emotion with which he looked down from the lofty, serene height of philosophy on the toil, and zeal, and earnestness, and enthusiastic errors of miserable Christians.

According to Tacitus, Nero wished to divert from himself the indignation which was universally entertained against him as the author of the conflagration which destroyed great part of Rome in A.D. 64. He turned to his purpose the popular dislike of the new sect of fanatics, who were generally detested on account of the abominable crimes of which they were supposed to be guilty,* and who were nicknamed by the populace " Christians." He laid the blame of the fire on them, as being enemies of society, eager to injure the city.

The Christians, therefore, were sought out. Those first of all who openly confessed the charge of Christianity were hurried to trial. Then on the information elicited at their trial,† many others were involved in their fate,‡ far

---

* Tacitus probably exaggerates the popular hatred (p. 346).

† The word *indicium* is obviously not used in its strict sense of evidence given by a criminal who denounces his accomplices on promise of impunity, nor can we suppose that the first arrested Christians voluntarily called attention to others; hence we must understand information elicited from them during their trial.

‡ I see no reason either to adopt the almost universally accepted emendation *convicti* for *coniuncti*, or to have recourse to Boissier's awkward *coniuncti reperti sunt.* Tacitus' rhetoric is responsible for the doubts. We must accept the MS. reading (corrected in all but the original and important MS.). Tacitus does not expressly state in precise terms that the accused were condemned: "they were hurried to trial; they were executed with novel refinements of punishment." Had he said merely this he could not have been misunderstood; all would have recognised the rhetorical device which leaves the essential point of condemnation to the reader, and hurries on to the final scene. But, in order to picture the hurry still more effectively, a sentence referring to a second class of criminals is interposed between the two clauses which describe the trial and the punishment respectively; and so we have the form: "First, some were tried; then others were involved in the same fate: they were executed," etc. Cuq alone prefers the MS. reading,

less on the charge of incendiarism, than of hostility to society and hatred of the world.* Their punishment was turned into an amusement to divert the populace ; for example, they were made to play the part of Actæon torn by his dogs, or were fixed on crosses † to be set on fire, and to serve as torches at nightly festivities held in the Vatican Gardens.

4. SECOND STAGE : CHARGE OF HOSTILITY TO SOCIETY.

But the trials and punishments of the Christians continued even after all pretence of connection with the fire had been abandoned. The safety of the people, it was argued, required that these enemies of society should be

---

interpreting *coniuncti* as a legal term in the sense of " called on to answer the same charge." Arnold, with some justice, protests against the technical term in this highly rhetorical passage. I should rather understand a bold Tacitean, not technical, but poetical usage, such as *Ann.*, xiii. 17 : *Nox eadem necem Britannici et rogum coniunxit* (cp. *Ann.*, vi. 26, iv. 57, 33, etc., for various bold uses of this verb). " They were put side by side with " (or immediately after) " the first class of culprits."

* *Haud perinde* is to be interpreted on the analogy of xiii. 21, where Agrippina, defending herself against Silana's accusation that she had plotted against her own son Nero, says *neque proinde a parentibus liberi quam ab impudica adulteri mutantur.* " Parents are not so ready to change their children as a shameless woman like Silana is to change her lovers "—*i.e.*, while Agrippina would not actually deny that parents occasionally turn away from their own children, the other case is infinitely more common. So here Tacitus is not prepared to assert that no one was actually involved in, and convicted on, the charge of incendiarism ; but the other charge was far more common.

† Arnold's alteration, *sunt, flammandi utque*, is, I think, a change in the right direction ; but the general sense is not doubtful.

severely dealt with ; and more general charges of employing
unlawful means to affect the minds of their victims among
the people and turn them from the ways of their fathers,
were brought against them, and easily proved. There can
be no question that this action was at first popular with
the mob. It furnished them with an object on which to
direct for the moment the rage and frenzy aroused by the
great fire ; and popular feeling was already against the
Christians. But, as Tacitus emphatically says, and as Pliny
afterwards attests, the judgment of the mob on the origin
of the fire was not permanently blinded : Nero was the
real culprit, and not these miserable victims. At last
popular feeling veered round, and the Roman public began
to feel compassion for the Christians. Guilty indeed they
were, and well deserved was their punishment; but the
people thought that they were being exterminated rather
to gratify the cruelty of an individual than from consideration of the common weal.

On this interpretation we observe a remarkable analogy
to the action of the English law-courts and people during
the "Popish Plot" in 1679—action which in respect of
brutality, injustice, and unreasoning credulity, furnishes a
fit parallel to the Neronian trials. We have first a frenzy
of terror and rage against the Christians, who are tried on
the charge of incendiarism. In the fear and excitement of
the people, witnesses were easily found, and immediately
believed. Soon, however, some variety in the accusations
was needed, and this was supplied by the hatred of society
(*odium humani generis*), of which the Christians were universally believed to be guilty. The new charge was
obviously as easily proved and as readily credited as the
first. But gradually popular feeling changed both in Rome

in 64 and in England in 1679. The number of executions sated the people, and a reaction occurred.

To understand the development of Nero's action, it is necessary to conceive clearly and precisely what is meant by the hatred of the world with which the Christians were charged (*odium humani generis*). It was not the mere abstract emotion of which they were accused, but the actions in which that emotion manifested itself. To the Romans *genus humanum* meant, not mankind in general, but the Roman world—men who lived according to Roman manners and laws; the rest of the human race were enemies and barbarians. The Christians then were enemies to civilised man and to the customs and laws which regulated civilised society. They were bent on relaxing the bonds that held society together; they introduced divisions into families, and set children against their parents; and this end they attained by nefarious means, working on the minds of their devotees by magical arts.* All this they did with a view to practise their abominable crimes (*flagitia*) more freely. So elastic an accusation was easily proved in the excited state of popular feeling. The Christians were in truth hostile to certain customs practised freely in Roman society, but considered by them as vicious or irreligious; and the principle was readily admitted that he that is an enemy to a part is an enemy to the whole. The Christians

---

* *Odium humani generis* was, as Arnold aptly points out, the crime of poisoners and magicians, p. 23, n. 1. The punishments inflicted on the Christians under Nero are those ordered for magicians. Paullus, *Sentent.* V. 23, 17, " *Magicæ artis conscios summo supplicio affici placuit, id est, bestiis obici aut cruci suffigi. Ipsi autem magi vivi exuruntur.*" Constantine ordered that *feralis pestis absumat* those who used magic arts (*Cod. Theodos.*, ix. 16, 5); and also that *haruspices* should be burned (*ib.* ix. 16, 1).

were bent on destroying civilisation, and civilisation must in self-defence destroy them.*

The crime of employing magical arts to compass their nefarious purposes was closely connected with this, and was even more easily proved. The extraordinary influence which the new religion acquired over its votaries, the marvellous reformation which it wrought in its converts, the enthusiastic devotion and unbending resolution of the whole body, were all proofs that supernatural means and forbidden arts were employed.

Tacitus has been criticised on the ground that there is no authority to prove that such *flagitia* were attributed to the Christians earlier than the second century.

Putting out of sight that in 1 Peter ii. 12, "they speak against you as evildoers," † these popular accusations are distinctly referred to, we may reply that numerous historical examples show that such crimes were likely to be attributed to the private meetings of the Christians from the beginning. It is a real difficulty to understand how Fronto, the monitor of Marcus Aurelius, could credit these *flagitia* ; ‡ but there is needed no proof that Tacitus is right in attributing the belief to the vulgar of the year 64. We find in his words a strong proof that he is giving the views held in 64, and not those which he himself entertained. We need not suppose that so careful an investigator credited them, especially as he so carefully and specially restricts the belief to the vulgar and the past.

---

* In this connection the phrase *utilitate publica* is important. Obviously Nero assigned the common interest as the reason for his continued persecution of the Christians.

† καταλαλοῦντες ὑμῶν ὡς κακοποιῶν.

‡ According to the representation of his words by Minucius Felix, *Oct.* 9 and 31.

5. CRIME WHICH THE CHRISTIANS CONFESSED.

Some other points in Tacitus' description need a word. As to the words *qui fatebantur,* what crime did they confess? Arnold understands that they acknowledged the charge of incendiarism, and gave information against other Christians as guilty of the same crime. *Credat Judæus Apella* : to me this seems absolutely incredible ; and the suggestion which Arnold makes that the Christians were partially implicated in, or at least privy to, the criminal act appears impossible. Moreover, this view is contrary to the recorded facts. If so many of the Christians acknowledged the crime on their trial and denounced others, their complicity in the crime would necessarily have been accepted by the popular opinion. But Arnold himself shows clearly that the popular opinion remained ultimately unshaken about the author of the fire, and that the revulsion of popular feeling which finally occurred was due to the growing conviction that the Christians were innocent and ill-treated. Such a conviction could never have grown up if the Christians had in numbers confessed the crime.

The difficulty, which requires from Arnold seven pages of examination, seems to arise entirely from the compression of Tacitus' style, and to disappear as soon as we make explicit the thought which is in his mind, and which he expects his readers to have in their minds—viz., "The Christians were sought out." Assuming this step as implied in the context,* Tacitus then proceeds, "Those who ac-

---

* This thought is implied in the brief introductory sentence: *abolendo rumori Nero subdidit reos et pœnis affecit Christianos ; primum correpti qui fatebantur.* This is the sequence of the

knowledged the charge (of being Christians) were hurried to trial." The form of expression, assuming, but not making explicit in words, a thought implied in the circumstances, is quite in the style of Tacitus.

There is here implied, precisely as in Pliny's letter, a distinction between two classes of Christians—those who made no secret of their religion, but openly professed, and, we may perhaps add, taught and preached it, and those who were not known to their neighbours as Christians. We may safely conclude that the latter were the great majority. It is clear that in outward appearance they must have avoided all show of difference from their pagan neighbours. Situated as they were in the midst of a society where numberless little acts of life daily expressed respect for the common religion, these persons must in outward show have conformed with the common fashion and the ordinary usages of politeness, though strictly taken such usages implied belief in an idolatrous worship.* It is of course well known that much controversy existed in the Church during the early centuries as to how far such conformity with the usages and conventions of society was right or permissible; and it is obviously a very delicate point, on which considerable difference of honest opinion is sure to exist, as to where such conformity ceases to be mere compliance with polite conventions, and becomes an acknowledgment of false religion.

---

narrative, for all that is interposed between *Christianos* and *primum* is a parenthetical description of the Christians. When the parenthesis is omitted, the sense of *fatebantur* is clear. Hardly any one before Arnold felt a difficulty.

* For example, the pagan formula D(is) M(anibus) was sometimes used on Christian graves. See below, p. 435f.

6. CHARACTER, DURATION, AND EXTENT OF THE NERONIAN PERSECUTION.

The analogy between the narrative of Tacitus and that of Pliny is great ;* but the inference drawn from it that Tacitus coloured his narrative through his knowledge of the situation in the second century is incorrect.   There is an even more striking analogy in certain respects between the conduct of Pliny and that of the governor of Gallia Lugdunensis in A.D. 177.†   In each case the resemblance is due to the essential similarity in the circumstances, and not to the colour imparted by the narrator.

In the words of Tacitus, taken by themselves, there is nothing to suggest that the prosecution of the Christians continued for several years ; but at the same time there is nothing inconsistent with this conclusion, which was suggested by the words of Suetonius.   As we have seen, Tacitus asserts that the larger number (as the passage has been interpreted above, the far larger number) of the accused must have been condemned on the ground of hatred of the world and hostility to society.   This went on till the Roman populace was sick of it, and began to pity the sufferers.   Here we have the one expression in the whole paragraph that can safely be used as an indication of

---

* Besides the points mentioned already in this chapter (*fate-bantur, indicio, flagitia*) Tacitus uses the phrase *superstitio exitiabilis*, Pliny *superstitio prava immodica*.

† See above, p. 204.   The similarity would certainly be much more striking if we had the report addressed by the governor to Marcus Aurelius ; but we only know the situation as it appeared to the Christians in Lugdunum.

the extent of the persecution. The phrase *ingens multitudo* alone might quite well be interpreted, in a writer like Tacitus, as indicating that the number arrested and tried was great in view of the charge—viz., incendiarism, in which, as a rule, only a small number of persons are likely to unite. But it can have been no inconsiderable number and no short period which brought satiety to a populace accustomed to find their greatest amusement in public butcheries, frequently recurring on a colossal scale. Accordingly those writers who would minimise the whole occurrence and treat it as the execution of a few Jews, find this statement a difficulty. Schiller treats it as absolutely false and incredible ; and he considers that any novelty or intensification of cruelty in the form of execution would be only an additional amusement to the jaded nerves of the mob.* It certainly is a statement well deserving of careful thought; but probably few will agree with Schiller in thinking it absolutely incredible that the Roman populace could ever grow tired of butchery, or could ever feel that a persecuted class had been unfairly treated. It must, however, be confessed that there is no third alternative. Either Schiller is right and the statement incredible, or else there must have been a great and long-continued massacre.

On these grounds we conclude that if Tacitus has correctly represented his authorities, the persecution of Nero, begun for the sake of diverting popular attention, was continued as a permanent police measure under the form of a general prosecution of Christians as a sect dangerous to the public safety.

* Schiller, *Gesch. d. Kaiserreichs unter der Regierung des Nero*, p. 437. I quote it from Arnold, not having access to the book.

16

7. PRINCIPLE OF NERO'S ACTION.

As we have seen, Pliny implies that the attitude of the Government towards the Christians was governed by a principle which was already in existence before Trajan's time. The next question that awaits us is whether the principle is the same as that introduced by Nero.

The answer must be in the negative. Pliny and Trajan both assume that Christianity is in itself a crime deserving of death. No question is asked, no investigation is made, about crimes committed by the Christians; the acknowledgment of the Name entails immediate condemnation. But under Nero it is otherwise. The trial is held, and the condemnation is pronounced, in respect not of the Name, but of serious offences naturally connected with the Name (*flagitia cohærentia nomini*). These offences are, in the first place, incendiarism, and secondly, hostility to civilised society, which, as we saw, implied the practice of magic and tampering with the established customs of society.

Now we can admit that a certain rhetorical manner veils the bare facts in Tacitus's narrative; but we cannot admit that he has seriously misrepresented them. We have founded our interpretation on the view that he is accurate and trustworthy, and we cannot now abandon it.

The action which he attributes to Nero is essentially different from the practice of Trajan's time. Tacitus was familiar with the later practice; and, since he describes Nero's action as different from it, we must conclude that he is following older authorities. Unless they had been conclusive on this point, he would naturally have described the action of Nero as similar to that of his own time.

The chapter of Tacitus describes the action of A.D. 64; and Nero reigned four years longer. Now the development is easy from the stage described by Tacitus (in which proof is required that an accused Christian has committed some act of hostility to society) to the further stage implied by Pliny (in which it is assumed that Christians are all guilty of such hostility, and may be condemned offhand on confession of the Name). Was this further step taken in the later years of Nero, and mentioned, as we must then suppose, by Tacitus in a later chapter?

Within the reign of Nero there is hardly enough time for such a development. The persecution began in 64, and it was obviously at an end when Nero left Rome towards the end of 66.* It had been continued by the Emperor after the people had become sick of it; and when his personal influence was withdrawn, it can hardly have continued. Flavius Sabinus, who was prefect of the city at the time, was not a person likely to urge it on actively, and the populace was opposed to it.

It is true that Sulpicius Severus, whose account of the Neronian persecution is founded on Tacitus, and stated almost in his words, proceeds, "This was the beginning of severe measures against the Christians. Afterwards the religion was forbidden by formal laws, and the profession of Christianity was made illegal by published edicts."† But the value of this late evidence depends entirely on its

---

* This does not mean that executions of Christians ceased entirely, but that they were sporadic. The fact remains always that Christianity, as a disturbing influence, was opposed and punished by the State, whenever anything of a marked character drew the attention of the Government to it.

† *Chron.*, ii. 29.

source; and there can be no doubt that this author's account of the Neronian persecution has no authority, except in so far as he quotes from Tacitus. Now this statement was certainly not founded on anything that was said in the *Annals*; for the chapter, xv. 44, has the appearance of summing up the whole subject of Nero's attitude towards the Christians, and there seems to be no opportunity for Tacitus to resume it in the conclusion of the work.*

There are then only two alternatives in regard to the statement of Sulpicius Severus. Either it is a pure amplification of his own, inconsistent with Tacitus and possessing no authority, or it must be interpreted as referring to the action of subsequent emperors. I incline to the latter alternative. Sulpicius having described the beginning of persecution under Nero, adds a sentence briefly describing the repressive measures, more marked in theory, but not more terrible in action, which were decreed by later emperors.

But, as we have inferred from Suetonius, Nero introduced the principle of punishing the Christians. Is the account given by Tacitus consistent with this? The answer must be affirmative. In any single trial the general principle must have been laid down that certain acts, which all Christians were regularly guilty of, were worthy of death. Even after Nero left Rome, the prefect of the city would

---

* The extant part of the *Annals* brings down the history till the summer or autumn of 66. Before the end of 66 Nero went away to Greece, and only returned in 68, just in time to hear of the revolt of Vindex. During the few weeks of his reign that remained, his attention must have been absorbed with more pressing needs than the trials of Christians.

be bound to follow the example set by the Emperor ; for it would be treason to dispute or disregard it.*

When Nero had once established the principle in Rome, his action served as a precedent in every province. There is no need to suppose a general edict or a formal law. The precedent would be quoted in every case where a Christian was accused. Charges such as had been brought against Paul in so many places were certainly brought frequently against others ; and the action of the Emperor in Rome would give the tone to the action of the provincial governors.

We conclude, therefore, that between 68 and 96 the attitude of the State towards the Christians was more clearly defined, and that the process was changed, so that proof of definite crimes committed by the Christians (*flagitia cohærentia nomini*) was no longer required, but acknowledgment of the Name alone sufficed for condemnation. Nero treats a great many Christians as criminals, and punishes them for their crimes. Pliny and Trajan treat them as outlaws and brigands, and punish them without a reference to crimes.

8. EVIDENCE OF CHRISTIAN DOCUMENTS.

Finally, we have to ask what is the evidence of contemporary Christian documents. In the Apocalypse and in First Peter the development has taken place, and Christians suffer for the Name. Both these documents have been referred to this period, the former by many recent critics,

---

* If the widely entertained opinion, that St. Paul was executed in A.D. 67 or 68, be right, we have an example of the trials which took place during Nero's absence before one of his delegates, probably the prefect of the city.

the latter by tradition, which supposes St. Peter to have perished in the Neronian persecution. But in the following chapter we shall try to show that both belong to the latter part of the first century. As to the other documents of this period (admitting, as we do, the authenticity of the Pastoral Epistles), we find in them no hint about persecution for the Name. Persecution is indeed alluded to as imminent on all; but it is not an organised persecution directed by the Government, nor do we find explicit references to punishment for the Name simply. The advice given by St. Paul as to the relations of the Christians to the society in which they are placed, is always in accordance with the situation which we have described as occupied by them under Nero. They should avoid, as far as is consistent with religion, the appearance of interfering with the present social order. The proper rule of life is to accept the world's facts, not as in themselves right, but as indifferent, and to waste no time and thought on them. Slaves must be obedient. In society Christians are to observe the courtesies of life, though these had often a religious appearance.

The most developed and pointed expressions in Paul are perhaps 1 Tim. vi. 1, where slaves are counselled to " count their own masters worthy of all honour, that the name of God and the doctrine be not blasphemed," and Titus ii. 4, 5, where the young women are advised to maintain strictly the proper relations of family life, " that the word of God be not blasphemed." In both cases the position of Christians in pagan households is not merely not excluded, but is even the prominent idea.* The es-

---

* In the former passage heathen masters are expressly meant, for Christian masters are distinguished in the next verse. In the latter the analogy of 1 Peter iii. 1 shows what the true significance is.

tablished social order must, where possible, be respected, for any vain interference with it will give rise to calumnies and accusations against the Christians who bear the name of God, and against the doctrine which they teach.

James ii. 6 stands on the same plane as the passage which has just been quoted from 1 Timothy : "Do not the rich persecute you, and themselves drag you before the judgment-seats ? Do not they blaspheme the honourable name by the which ye are called?" Here and in 1 Tim. vi. 1, the name is not spoken of in the tone used twenty years later, when it becomes almost a technical formula.* The danger about 65–70 is that calumnies and false charges be circulated, and the Christians tried for these imputed crimes. In such trials recantation is not sought for, and would be no palliation of the crimes charged against the Christians.

All these familiar passages suit the close of the Neronian period, as we have described it. It would, however, require a special chapter to go over the Epistles of Paul from this point of view, and to show their agreement with the facts which we have elicited from Tacitus and Suetonius. As in all early Christian literature, the persecutions to which the Christians are liable occupy much less space than might perhaps be expected ; only in a passing word or an obscure implication is any attention paid to them. But through the period that engages our attention paucity of references to persecutions can never be taken as a proof that none were going on. Probably "the doctrine" would never have surmounted them, if the attention of its teachers had been much given to them.

---

* That stage is marked in these pages by using the capital. James, strictly, does not bear on our present subject, see p. 349.

Incidentally we may here note that the tone of the Pastoral Epistles in this respect is consistent only with an early date. It is difficult for the historian of the Empire to admit that they were composed after that development of the Imperial policy towards the Christians which occurred (as we shall see in the following chapter) under the Flavian Emperors.

But as this remark touches on a keenly controverted point, a little more space may fitly be devoted to the subject. I take Holtzmann's *Pastoralbriefe*, p. 267, as the most complete statement of the opposite view, that the references to persecution denote a late date towards the middle of the second century.*

The seeking out of the Christians ($\delta\iota\omega\xi\iota\varsigma$, $\delta\iota\omega\gamma\mu\delta\varsigma$) is alluded to in 2 Tim. iii. 12 ($\delta\iota\omega\chi\theta\dot{\eta}\sigma\sigma\nu\tau\alpha\iota$); but it was practised from the first day of the Neronian persecution. The suffering of affliction and persecution ($\kappa\alpha\kappa\sigma\pi\alpha\theta\epsilon\hat{\iota}\nu$) is the lot of all Christians (2 Tim. iii. 12, etc.); but the kind of suffering is expressly defined as the same to which Paul himself was exposed, and Holtzmann cannot surely be serious when he quotes these passages as a proof of a second century date (2 Tim. iii. 11, iv. 17, 18). There were some who showed cowardice, and shrank from enduring the persecution; but we need not ask for proof that recantation occurred in Nero's time, as well as in the second or the third century. The suffering is endured by

---

* Among Holtzmann's indications of later date, none appear strong. An analogy to Apuleius does not tell much in favour of the date he assigns, 112-150. Every analogy to anything mentioned in later literature is taken, most uncritically and unhistorically, as a proof that an early date is impossible. Such analogies often merely prove general similarity in the situation; see p. 204-5.

the Christian as if he were a malefactor, and this treatment is complained of as unjust (2 Tim. ii. 9); but that is exactly the tone of the Neronian period, and the Greek word κακοῦργος refers expressly to the *flagitia*, for which the Christians were condemned under Nero, and for which they were no longer condemned in A.D. 112. Finally Holtzmann quotes rightly the analogy between 1 Peter ii. 12 and 1 Tim. vi. 1, Titus ii. 5,* and between 1 Peter iv. 15 and 2 Tim. ii. 9. But it is precisely these verses in 1 Peter which mark that epistle as retaining traces of earlier feeling, and as standing in the transition from the Neronian period to the formulated persecution of the Flavian period, when the Name is explicitly prohibited. Moreover, the *flagitia* were a standing reproach in all periods.

Holtzmann appeals to the use of βασιλεῖς in the plural in 1 Tim. ii. 2, as a proof that conjoint emperors were reigning at the time. It is undoubtedly true that the use of the plural often furnishes an excellent and conclusive criterion of date. On this ground we may probably date the *Acta* of Carpus and Papylus, the *True Word* of Celsus, and several other documents, in the joint reign of M. Aurelius and L. Verus. Even though the singular βασιλεύς be used in the same document, the argument is still valid; for the singular was the ordinary usage, into which a writer was apt to slip.† This rule can be proved

---

* Βλασφημεῖν is used in Clement, *Epist.*, § 47; but that is no proof that the Epistles to Timothy were composed at the same time as Clement's letter to the Corinthians. I do not know what date Holtzmann assigns to Clement's *Epistle*, or whether he quotes this analogy as a proof of the date of Timothy.

† I cannot therefore agree with the inference that Lightfoot draws from the use of the singular by Celsus. See his *Ignat. and Polyc.*, i. p. 530, 593 n, edition II.

by the usage of Athenagoras, and many other writers.*
But the case is quite different in 1 Tim. ii. 2; the writer
directs that a general rule be observed to pray "for all
men; for kings and all that are in high place." The term
βασιλέων without the article cannot be understood as denoting "the emperors who are reigning at the present
time;" it means "emperors (or sovereigns) in general."

Where any definite information has reached us, we find
that the accusations made against the Christians throughout the reigns of Claudius and Nero are, as a rule, of the
type just described—*e.g.*, at Philippi, "these men set forth
customs which it is not lawful for us to receive or observe,
being Romans" (Acts xvi. 21); at Thessalonica "they that
have turned the world upside down." On the other hand,
where the accusation was a purely religious one—as at
Corinth, "this man persuadeth men to worship God contrary to the law" (Acts xviii. 13)—the Roman governor
refused to listen to a charge that was not on "a matter of
wrong or of wicked villany." So St. Paul's judges in Palestine agreed that there was no real charge against him, and
that, if he had not appealed to the Emperor, he might
have been set free.

One charge especially, which soon afterwards became a
standing one and the regular test and touchstone of persecution, is never alluded to under Nero: this was the refusal
to comply with the established and official worship of the
emperors. That religion, though widely and willingly
practised in the provinces, was not yet explicitly adopted
by the State as a political institution. Disrespect to the

---

* Many of the cases are rightly quoted by Holtzmann, p. 269; see
also Neumann, p. 58 n.

Emperor had indeed already been treated in Rome as treason (*majestas*, ἀσέβεια) ; but there is no evidence that as yet this charge had been brought against the Christians,* or that compliance with the rites of the Imperial religion was formally proposed to them as the test of their faith. That treatment belongs to the later period, and marks the stage when they are condemned for the Name, and when their death constitutes them "Witnesses" (μάρτυρες) to the Name. Under Nero they are not martyrs in the strict sense ; they are only sufferers.

The action of Nero inaugurates a new era in the relation of the Empire towards Christianity ; or, to speak more precisely, the Empire then for the first time adopted a definite attitude towards the new religion. So says Suetonius, and Tacitus does not disagree. Hitherto the Roman officials had, on the whole, treated the Christians with indifference, or even with favour mingled with contempt (see p. 133). Where they acted harshly, either they were influenced by the enmity of influential Jews, or they punished the Christians as being connected with disturbances, which were due in whole or in part to their presence and action. But after 64 A.D. the example set by the Emperor necessarily guided the action of all Roman officials towards the Christians. As yet, however, the religion was not in itself a crime.

---

* Treason is, indeed, involved in the charge at Thessalonica : "These all act contrary to the decrees of Cæsar, saying that there is another King, one Jesus." But this and similar instances are quite different in type from the charge of treason founded on refusal to worship the Emperor. They belong to an early period, before the charge had been formulated in its developed shape.

CHAPTER XII.

THE FLAVIAN POLICY TOWARDS THE CHURCH.

DURING the two years that immediately followed the death of Nero, the anarchy and confusion of the struggle for power would naturally prevent any development in the Imperial policy. The attention of the rival emperors and of the governors of provinces must have been almost entirely concentrated on the great struggle ; and none but the most pressing business of government can have been attended to. We thus reach the year 70, when the Flavian dynasty was firmly settled in power. Here unfortunately we lose the guidance of Tacitus, whose *Histories* of the Flavian period would have doubtless cleared away the obscurity which envelops this critical time in the relations of the Church to the Empire. We possess only the brief biographies of Suetonius, which are personal studies, not formal history, Xiphilin's epitome of the history of Dion Cassius, and various other even poorer documents. In the dearth of contemporary and trustworthy authorities we are compelled, unless we leave this period a blank, to have recourse to hypothesis. The development in the State action, which has been alluded to on p. 242, must fall between 70 and 96. What can we learn or conjecture about the way in which it took place ?

1. Tacitus' Conception of the Flavian Policy.

It will serve our purpose best to begin by considering the attitude of Tacitus as a historian towards the Christians. In *Annals*, xv. 44, he introduces them into his pages.* After mentioning the names popularly applied to them and the hatred popularly entertained towards them, he describes their origin and early history. From this elaborate and careful introduction we may infer, first, that Tacitus, with the fuller knowledge of their importance as a factor in Roman history which he possessed in A.D. 120,† considered this to be the moment when they entered on the stage of his history; and, second, that the carefulness and parade with which the new factor is introduced mark the entrance of a figure which is to play some important part in the tragedy.‡ In the conclusion of the *Annals*, as we have seen, this figure can have played no part; but in the *Histories* there can be no doubt that the Christians were mentioned several times. Although this work is lost, except for the years 68–70, we have in the pages of Sulpicius Severus, as has been proved by Bernays,§ an epitome of one important passage. This fourth century writer used Tacitus carefully : he made extracts almost *verbatim* from the account of the Neronian persecution in the *Annals*,

---

* In the *Histories*, which were written before the *Annals*, the Christians were certainly mentioned as a developed sect. Tacitus wrote the *Annals* to lead up to the completed *Histories*.

† Taking this as a rough date for the composition of *Annals*, xv.

‡ We must remember that in the ancient plays every important figure is formally introduced to the audience at its first appearance.

§ See his paper, a masterpiece of analysis, *über die Chronik des Sulpicius Severus*, republished in his *Gesammelte Abhandlungen*.

xv. 44 ; and Bernays has discussed his relation to Tacitus, and has shown that there are strong signs of a Tacitean origin in Sulpicius' narrative of the council of war, which was held after the capture of Jerusalem. In this council different opinions were expressed. Some thought that the temple should be left uninjured. Others, and among them Titus himself, expressed the view that the Temple especially ought to be destroyed, in order that the religions * of the Jews and of the Christians might be more completely extirpated ; for these religions, though opposed to each other, had yet the same origin. The Christians had arisen from amongst the Jews ; and, when the root was torn up, the stem would easily be destroyed.

This speech cannot be supposed to embody the actual words of Titus. Very probably it was composed by Tacitus himself ; but its importance is even greater in that case, for it would then embody the historian's mature conception of the nature of the Flavian policy towards the Christians, as shown in the whole course of their rule. Whether then it gives an abstract of Titus' actual speech, reported by some member of the council, or was composed by Tacitus, it is a historical document of the utmost importance, and we must examine it carefully. In Titus' speech the difference between Judaism and Christianity is fully recognised ; but the fact is not grasped that the latter was quite independent of the Temple and of Jerusalem as a centre. Titus had only a superficial knowledge of the Christians and their principles, gained entirely from his experience in Palestine ; and the circumstances of

---

* Tacitus, of course, called them *superstitiones*, but Sulpicius altered the term to *religiones*.

Palestinian Christianity quite explain his idea of its connexion with the Temple.

Further, Titus regarded both the Jewish and the Christian religions as evils to be extirpated ; but he believed that they had a local home and centre, with which their organisation was connected and on which they were dependent.

The hypothesis is inevitably forced on us that, when Christianity was found to be independent of a centre at Jerusalem, and to flourish unchecked after the Temple was destroyed, the enmity that underlies the speech of Titus would be carried into vigorous action. If that were not so, the speech of Titus loses all its force and appropriateness ; but, if our hypothesis as to the subsequent policy is correct, his speech appears as a fitting and dramatic introduction, worthily put into the mouth of the conqueror of Jerusalem. In the following books Tacitus would show how the emperors, when settled in Rome, and masters of the information about the Christians contained in the Imperial archives and steadily accumulating during their reign, resumed the Neronian vigour of repression.*

---

* The passage in which Severus describes the subsequent development of Nero's policy towards the Christians has been quoted above (p. 243) ; and Bernays has taught us how much use that chronicler made of Tacitus. Is he in this passage, with its reference to laws and edicts, giving his own general impression derived from the *Histories* of Tacitus? It is possible that he is ; but if so, we must take exception to the words *edicts* and *laws*. We must hold that Sulpicius uses these terms loosely and inaccurately ; and perhaps a chronicler of the fourth century was quite as likely to use the words loosely, as we have found some modern writers to be, even while they aim at scrupulous and rigid accuracy. (See above, p. 194.)

Mommsen also is strongly inclined to the opinion that the account of the council of war which Sulpicius Severus gives (flatly contradicted as it is by the contemporary Jewish historian Josephus), is derived from Tacitus ; and he unreservedly adopts the view, that " the Jewish insurrection had too clearly brought to light the dangers involved in this formation of a national religious union—on the one hand rigidly concentrated, on the other spreading over the whole East, and having ramifications even in the West."*

2. Confirmation of Nero's Policy by Vespasian.

Our hypothesis is that this development took place under Vespasian, after some years of his reign had elapsed. But the brief remainder of his reign, and the short reign of Titus, did not impress themselves on the memory of the Christians.† Hence Domitian alone was remembered as the persecutor, ranking along with Nero ; and the execration and condemnation, which were deserved by his personal character and conduct in other respects, have been apportioned to him in the popular memory of Christian times on account of a policy to which he was only the heir. His action was not due to his personal idiosyncrasies ; it was

---

* *Provinces*, ii., p. 216.   I have slightly altered the printed translation.

† But of course there probably were, even in the interval 68-75 A.D., isolated cases of accusation and trial, and, no doubt, condemnation, of Christians.   The reference of Hilary to a persecution under Vespasian is only a slip in expression.   A writer of the fourth century, who enumerates as three types of the persecutor Nero, Vespasian, and Decius, must not be quoted as a witness to a persecution under Vespasian (as is hesitatingly done by Lightfoot, *Ignat. and Pol.*, i., p. 15).   He meant Domitian, who was the second type.

the natural development of the Imperial policy, and the
facts and reasons on which it was founded were stored in
the Imperial archives, and were, of course, consulted by
Trajan before he replied to Pliny. It is possible that a
reference to Vespasian's actions occurs in a mutilated
passage of Suetonius, where it is said that "never in the
death of any one did Vespasian [take pleasure, and in
the case of] merited punishments he even wept and
groaned."* The words in brackets are restored to fill
up an obvious gap in the text of the MSS.; but this
restoration is not sufficient. We have here indubitably
a reference to some class or individuals, whose punishment Vespasian felt himself compelled to accept while
he regretted it; for it is inconceivable that Vespasian,
a Roman, a soldier of long experience in the bloody
wars of Britain and Judea, wept and groaned at every
"merited" execution, as the restored text would imply.
We think of the punishments which by the principle
of Nero attached to the Christians; we saw from the
way in which Suetonius mentioned Nero's measure that
he considered it a good one; he uses the same term
supplicia in both places. Does not the second passage
(*Vesp.* 15) look back to the first (*Nero* 16), and is not
Suetonius here continuing in his own way the same
subject?† A more detailed reference did not enter into his

---

* Suetonius, *Vesp.*, 15. *Neque cæde cuiusquam umquam
[lætatus est et] iustis suppliciis inlacrimavit etiam et ingemuit.*
Some fill the gap with the single word *lætatus*, but *neque* at the
beginning looks forward necessarily to *et* following.

† This suggestion is so obvious that I have no doubt it has been
already made.

17

plan.   The principle was instituted by Nero.   It continued permanently ; and Suetonius would, according to his usual practice, not again allude to it, were it not for the detail, interesting to a biographer, that Vespasian wept while he confirmed its operation.

What form did the confirmation take? As yet Nero's principle was merely unwritten law, according to which the governors, when any case came before them, judged it according to the precedent set them by the Emperor.   The punishment of Christians was administrative, not judicial. The same character continues to attach to it under the Flavian Emperors and under Trajan (see p. 207).   Hence we need not suppose that any edict or law was passed ; only rescripts were issued to inquiring governors.   But such repressive measures could not remain in the form which Nero gave them : they must develop to their logical conclusion ; and the followers of a sect, whose tendency was to unsettle the foundations and principles of Roman society, were held as outlaws, and the very name treated as a crime. Such seems the natural course foreshadowed in the speech which the great historian puts into the mouth of Titus ; and such is the state of administrative procedure, when Pliny was first called on to conduct *cognitiones* in the case of Christians.

If the theory just stated be not accepted, the only possible alternative seems to be that under Nero the attitude of the Roman State towards the Christians was determined finally.   We have rejected this alternative (see p. 243), for Tacitus's evidence on the point is conclusive against it, though the weight of Suetonius' evidence is rather in its favour.

3. The Persecution of Domitian.

It may safely be asserted that it is only the date of the proscription which is hypothetical; its occurrence at some time before the downfall of the Flavian dynasty is certain. The persecution of Domitian burned itself ineradicably into the memory of history; it may be doubted by the critic, but not by the historian. He that has only an eye for details, that "sees hairs and pores, examines bit by bit," will always find the evidence defective for almost every detail and fact of the persecution. But the historian who can discern

> "How parts relate to parts, or they to whole,
> The body's harmony, the beaming soul,"

can never feel any doubt as to the general character of Domitian's action towards the Christians, and will always see in it the same type of absolute proscription of the Name, which was taken by Pliny and Trajan as predetermined. So strong and early a tradition as that which constitutes Domitian the second great persecutor cannot be discredited without wrecking the foundations of ancient history. Those who discredit it must, to be consistent, resolve to dismiss nine-tenths of what appears in books as ancient history, including most that is interesting and valuable.

It is urged that it was the interest of the Christians to represent the two worst emperors, Nero and Domitian, as the two great persecutors; and therefore their evidence is dismissed as unworthy of credit. Pliny tortured the two Christian deaconesses, before he would accept their evidence; but he applied the same process to heathen slaves. To be consistent let us apply the same standard to all our authorities; and we then must begin with Thucydides, who had the strongest motives for misrepresenting the Athenian policy. If it were contended that ancient history as a whole is uncertain and unknowable, no reply need be made; but the same measure must be applied to it throughout; and on the ordinary standards of history, Domitian's persecution is as certain as that of Nero.*

The only passage in which any pagan writer mentions punishments inflicted by Domitian for religious reasons, occurs in the Epitome of the history of Dion Cassius, made in the eleventh century by the monk Xiphilin. Dion mentioned that Flavius Clemens, consul A.D. 95 and cousin of the Emperor, and his wife Flavia Domitilla, niece of the Emperor, were tried on a charge of sacrilege (ἀθεότης).† Clemens was executed, and Domitilla was banished. A great many others were put to death or deprived of their property on the same charge, among

---

* Schiller is consistent in disbelieving the evidence for both. He considers that ἀθεότης and ἀσέβεια are used indifferently in this period as translations of the Latin *impietas,* which quite explains his consistent scepticism. If we take from the words of the ancient historians only such vague and loose ideas as a schoolboy gets from his lexicon, we cannot find much evidence in them. See his *Gesch. der röm. Kaiserzeit,* i., p. 537. Neumann (pp. 14 and 17) points out the stricter sense in which these Greek terms were used.

† Neumann (p. 17) has observed that this is the technical sense of the word ἀθεότης. We might at first expect that ἀσέβεια would be the rendering of the Latin *sacrilegium*; but it was pre-occupied as the translation of *majestas.* The word ἱεροσυλία, which was in earlier times (*e.g.,* Acts xix. 37) used to represent *sacrilegium,* was too loose a rendering; and the use of this old term in *Acta Pauli et Theklae* (see p. 401) stamps the episode in which it occurs as early.

them being Acilius Glabrio, consul in A.D. 91, who had after his consulship been sent into exile. Dion mentions that the persons against whom this charge was brought had gone astray after the manners of the Jews. We see, therefore, that a number of Roman citizens had changed their religion, and that the charge on which they were tried was sacrilege.

The first question which has to be determined is what was the religion which these Romans had adopted. Was it Judaism or Christianity, or did some adopt one religion, some another?

It is certain that Clemens and Domitilla suffered as Christians. The evidence is complete and conclusive, and there is practical agreement on almost all hands among modern writers on this point.*

The question as to Acilius Glabrio's religion is more difficult, and opinion is much more divided. But in the account given by Dion it is difficult to separate his offence

---

* Domitilla's memory as a martyr was preserved, and the catacomb on the Ardeatine Way, where she was buried, was called afterwards by her name. It is known from inscriptions that the ground in which this catacomb was situated belonged to her. De Rossi's discoveries on this point will be found most conveniently summarised in Lightfoot's *Clement*, i., p. 35 ff. Eusebius mentions that Domitilla was a Christian (*H. E.*, iii. 18, and *Chron.*, pp. 162-3, anno 2112). Christian tradition speaks of both Clemens and Domitilla as Christian, and Syncellus, p. 650 (Bonn edition), records this (the divergent accounts of Domitilla's relationship are explained, probably rightly, by Lightfoot); while the Christianity of Clemens is not so well attested as that of Domitilla, there is at least no doubt that suspicions of this contributed to cause his trial and prompted the charges on which he was condemned. The *Acta Nerei et Achillei* also attests the fact of their religion. On Suetonius' view, see below, p. 271.

from that of Clemens and the others.* Dion reported by Xiphilin is not a very high authority ; but, so far as his evidence goes, it is that Acilius belonged to the same class of criminals as Clemens and others,† and that they were Christians. Moreover, when we read of De Rossi's recent excavations, we can hardly refuse to follow Dion. De Rossi found that the original centre of a group of catacombs beside the Via Salaria consisted of a gamma-shaped crypt attached to a small chapel. In the chapel was buried the person who gave sanctity to the whole group of catacombs, and near whom other Christians wished to repose.‡ The crypt was the burial-place of the family on whose property the chapel and the series of catacombs were situated, and to which apparently the person buried in the chapel belonged. The fragmentary inscriptions found here hardly leave room for doubt that the family was that of the Acilii Glabriones. Who then was buried in the

---

* Lightfoot's attempt to separate them seems to me to be unsuccessful. (*Clem.*, i., p. 81, n. 6.)

† An additional charge was brought against Acilius, of having fought in the arena during his consulship, and thus (we may infer) injured the " majesty " of Rome. He was, therefore, accused both of sacrilege and treason.

‡ The eager desire of the Christians to be buried near the grave of some saint or martyr (*sanctis martyribus sociari*) is a well-known and widely prevalent fact. (See Le Blant, *Suppl. aux Actes des Martyrs*, p. 272.) In this case, of course, there is no certain proof that the saint or martyr, who was buried in the chapel, belonged to the family which owned the land. Many cases occurred where a martyr's body was bought or taken by Christians not of his kindred. Several are mentioned in extant *Acta*. (See Le Blant, p. 282.) But the probability is, of course, strong that the Acilii obtained the body of their own relative, and made it the central point of a new family sepulchre. The comparison of Dion with the discoveries of De Rossi makes the case very strong, but not conclusive.

chapel? Surely we may, with Dion, connect the charge against Acilius with that against Clemens and Domitilla, and consider that the body of the consul of 91 was brought back from his place of exile, and buried in Rome. It was the regular practice to leave the corpses of criminals free to their friends to tend and bury.

Those persons who are actually named by Dion as having perished on the charge of going astray after Jewish customs prove therefore to be Christians. Taking his words in connection with the persistent tradition about Domitian's persecution, we cannot doubt that in A.D. 95 many Roman citizens were put to death on suspicion of being Christians, or at least of being connected with Christians.

4. BIAS OF DION CASSIUS.

In the next place we have to face the question, why then does Dion speak only of Jewish manners? This fact ceases to present any serious difficulty when we observe that he seems to have studiously refrained throughout his history from referring explicitly to the Christians.*

This silence is obviously intentional. When Dion wrote in the third century, the Christians were of course perfectly well known; and there were many occasions on which an unbiassed historian must have alluded to them. Whether Dion approved or disapproved of them, it was undeniable

---

* The name occurs three times in Xiphilin's epitome, but in each case he is plainly supplementing Dion from other authorities. It may be taken as certain that Xiphilin would not omit any reference to the Christians that occurred in Dion. He found none, but introduces references from other sources where he felt bound to complete Dion. The evidence deduced from Zonaras, who also used Dion, confirms this conclusion.

that they had been a factor of some consequence in the State
from the time of Nero onwards.   His silence may be compared with the peculiar language of Ælius Aristides, who also
makes a point of not naming the Christians, though he
mentions "them in Palestine," in a passage where I cannot
doubt that the Christians are at least included in the general
description.*   It was apparently a fashion and an affectation
among a certain class of Greek men of letters about 160–240
to ignore the existence of the Christians, and to pretend to
confuse them with the Jews.   These high-souled philosophic
Greeks would not even know the name, for it was a solecism
to use such a vulgar and barbarian word as Χριστιανός.

We conclude then that Dion was biassed, and that his
attitude as an historian has a certain leaning which we
must always make allowance for in estimating his testimony.   In regard to the events of A.D. 95, we see that
it would be quite in his style to describe the crime of
Christians by the vague phrase "manners of the Jews";
and we therefore can find in his words no serious discrepancy
with the inference which has been drawn from the individual
cases mentioned by him.

5. Difference of Policy towards Jews and Christians.

On the other hand, if we take Dion's phrase to imply
that he considered Clemens, Acilius, and many others to
have been put to death for becoming Jewish proselytes, we
are involved in insuperable difficulties, and must reject his
evidence as wholly incredible.   It is in itself improbable that

---

* *Or.*, xlvi. πρὸς Πλάτωνα ὑπὲρ τῶν τεττάρων, vol. ii., p. 394 ff. (ed.
Dindorf). This much-controverted passage is discussed more fully
below, p. 351 ff.

many Romans had become Jewish proselytes; and it is difficult to account for the entire failure of corroborative evidence.
A disposition among some classes of Romans to coquet with
Jewish habits is indeed attested; but it was not carried to
a degree which would render Dion's account probable.

It is true that under Domitian the Jews suffered much
extortionate and harsh treatment. The Jewish poll-tax,
which since the Jewish war, 67–70 A.D., had been levied for
the benefit of Capitoline Jupiter, was exacted with great
severity. Proselytes, who strictly were not liable, and
persons of Jewish origin, who had given up their faith,*
are said to have been compelled to pay. The exaction
was accompanied with much hardship, with insult, and even
with violence to the person of suspects.† But the object
was to enrich the treasury; for after the enormous extravagance of Nero, finance became one of the most important concerns of the Imperial policy. Hence it was
that the poll-tax was levied from as many as possible; but
for this very reason there appears to have been no slaying
of Jews. Finance and not religion dictated the action
towards them; and potential taxpayers would not be
slain by a needy government, except in rare cases as a
warning to others to pay more readily.‡

---

* The whole history of the Jewish race precludes us from the
supposition that these Jews had apostatised to paganism. They
can have been only Jewish Christians.

† The extreme violence which was applied to reluctant taxpayers
is described by M. Le Blant in his *Actes des Martyrs*, p. 162 ff.

‡ See the passage quoted in preceding note. Schiller, i., p. 537,
on the contrary, considers that the intention was to weaken the
numbers and power of the Jews: *Dass die Regierung durch
Erhöhung und strenge Beitreibung der Judensteuer in Rom selbst
die Juden zu decimieren und zu controllieren suchte.*

Finally, another alternative remains for consideration—viz., that Christians and Jews were in A.D. 95 still confused with each other by the Romans, and that Dion (who of course was well aware of the difference between them) merely retained the phrase employed by his authorities. In that case the whole view which we have taken as to the attitude of the State towards the Christians during the first century is shown to be erroneous. Many high authorities have maintained that the Imperial Government continued till the time of Pliny and Trajan to consider Christians as a mere sect of the Jews, to speak about both as Jews, and to treat both in the same way. Neumann has correctly observed that this view is inconsistent with the spirit of Pliny's and Trajan's letters; but he only moves back a few years the discovery of the Christians by the Government. He thinks it certain that the Christians were reckoned by the Roman Government to be a mere sect of the Jews down to the reign of Domitian; or even if their existence was known, the same regulations applied to them as to the Jews.* The question as to the attitude of the Government towards the Christians had not yet been raised. Hitherto, indeed, the Christians had been affected along with the Jews by occasional measures directed against the latter; but on the whole they lived in freedom, protected by the screen of the legalised Jewish religion. Even under Domitian, Neumann considers that for a time the Christians were still classed among the Jews, and compelled to pay the Jewish poll-tax, and that the strict exaction of the tax revealed to the Government the extent to which Christianity had spread. In the last year but one of Domitian's reign it

---

* Neumann, p. 5 ff., p. 14 ff.

was decided that the propagation of the Jewish-Christian religion should be restrained by the law. The Jews, on the other hand, were still tolerated, but Jewish proselytising was forbidden.

We cannot admit that the Roman Government did not begin until A.D. 95 to understand that Christians were not a mere sect of the Jews, and to consider what should be its policy towards the former. The following reasons seem conclusive against Neumann's view.

(1) The nature of the Imperial Government, the ability with which it was conducted, the success which it attained in Romanising the provinces, are inconsistent with the supposition that it continued until A.D. 95 so ignorant about the Christians. The remarkable success of their provincial administration could not have been achieved without intimate knowledge of the provincial peoples and manners. The correspondence of Pliny shows how carefully the ways of the people were reported to the Emperor ; and all such information was certainly collected and preserved in the Imperial archives. It seems almost as absurd to say that the Imperial policy treated Christians until 95 under the mistaken idea that they were Jews, as it would be for some historian of future ages to argue that the British Government continued until the twentieth century to mix up the Brahmo Somaj with Brahminism. This *à priori* argument, however, must yield if evidence is against it. What then is the evidence ?

(2) The evidence of the historians, where accessible, is that Christians were distinguished by the Government and the populace as early as A.D. 64. Tacitus and Suetonius are agreed on this point. Again we saw that in A.D. 70 (according to Tacitus probably) Titus was familiar with

the distinction. Before 79 an idle person could write on a
Pompeian wall the name of the Christians. The facts
indeed are few, but all (with the one exception of Dion's
phrase) are on one side. On the other side there is mere
theory, supported by Dion's words.

(3) The treatment of the Jews was quite different from
that which, as we have seen, was employed towards the
Christians. The Jewish religion had always been recognised
as legal by the Imperial policy ; and the Jews were released
from all duties which were contrary to their religion. Even
the great rebellion, A.D. 67–70, entailed no essential change.
The religion continued to be legal, and no Jew was required
to do anything contrary to it (p. 355). It is true that the
old temple-tax was now levied as tribute to the temple
of Capitoline Jupiter ; and this exaction gave rise to heart-
burning among the Jews and harsh usage at the hands of
the collectors. But, when once the tax was paid, the Jew
was free to worship as he pleased. Harsh taxation was not
inconsistent with religious toleration. (See p. 265.)

6. The Executions of A.D. 95 an Incident of the General Policy.

While we have to differ from Neumann on this point, we
find him in other respects quite agreed with the view which
we have taken as to the executions of A.D. 95. They were
the result of action by the State against the Christians on
the ground of their religion. We cannot, however, consider
that these executions are by themselves sufficient to
explain the persistent tradition which makes Domitian the
second great persecutor, or to account for the facts which
will be further described in the following chapter.

The execution and banishment of Christians in A.D. 95, so far as the record in Dion goes, would appear to have been confined to Roman citizens. The obvious explanation of this is that mere execution of ordinary Christians was not mentioned by Dion any more than he would mention the execution of so many thieves. The attitude of the State towards the Christians during the Flavian period cannot be better described than in the words of Mommsen : " The persecution of the Christians was a standing matter, as was that of robbers." * It was inherent in the nature of the Imperial constitution that it should stamp out Christianity, just as it was inherent in its nature that it should stamp out brigandage. The desultory and fitful nature of the persecutions arose naturally from the situation. The repression of brigandage was as uncertain as the repression of Christianity. Both were permanent evils ; and some governors made more or less energetic attempts to carry out completely the fundamental principle which proscribed both, while others made little or no attempt to cope with either. Many governors boasted, or were anxious to boast, that they had brought back from their province their lictors' axes unstained with blood. † Under their rule little can have been done to punish either Christians or brigands. The Imperial system was inconsistent with the Christian principles of life and society ; collision between them was inevitable. The actual moment when the collision first took place was due to accident—viz., to the position of Nero in regard to the popular feeling in A.D. 64 ; but sooner or later it had to take place. Other circumstances determined

---

* *Provinces of the Roman Empire*, ii., p. 199, of the translation.
† See Le Blant, *Actes des Martyrs*, p. 127.

the precise year of the collision, but the nature of the two powers determined its necessity.

Dion then would have defended his silence about the Christians in general on the ground that they were as far beneath the notice of history as were thieves and other malefactors. Only when Roman citizens were involved did it enter into his plan to allude to the proceedings. But much may be gathered from what he does record; and we may fairly ask what would be done to non-Romans, if noble citizens, consuls and relatives of the Emperor, were put to death on the charge of being Christians? A formal trial must be granted to all Romans, in which the exact accusation was plainly stated, and the character and degree of the crime considered in the sentence; but that gives no reason for thinking that a similar careful trial would be accorded to non-Romans. In their case the magistrate simply made the investigation necessary for attaining certainty about the facts, and forthwith exercised on the parties the powers that belonged to him as the guardian of law and order. The charge against these Romans in A.D. 95 was sacrilege. Now Mommsen has shown conclusively that there was no regular process in Roman law for trying such a crime; and the trial therefore could not be before an ordinary *quæstio*. A special procedure was required, and there can be no doubt that it was of the following character: the Emperor judged at least the case of his own relatives, and as the ultimate source and arbiter of right he pronounced the fitting decision, or as the supreme magistrate he took what steps he thought right to vindicate propriety and order. But no allusion seems to have been made to crimes connected with, or springing out of, Christianity; the trials were directly concerned with the religion of the accused; and the fact that Romans had become Christians was reckoned as sacrilege and punished with death. This decision of the supreme fountain of law and right must, when applied by magistrates to the case of non-Romans, have taken the form according to which Pliny in his first *cognitiones* acted, and which he understood to be already settled.

We need not consider that the trials of A.D. 95 were the first that Domitian (or his delegates) held. The only reason why we hear of them is that persons of such high rank were implicated.

7. Evidence of Suetonius about the Executions of A.D. 95.

Suetonius also mentions the execution of Flavius Clemens and Acilius Glabrio. His references, though disappointingly brief, are sufficient to show that the account given in Xiphilin's Epitome of Dion is neither complete nor entirely trustworthy. Suetonius evidently considered that the reason for the execution of both lay in Domitian's dread of conspiracy and treason. We have seen, even in Xiphilin's bald version, that Acilius must have been accused of treason as well as sacrilege; and Suetonius declares that he was put to death on a charge of fomenting disturbance or revolution.* About Clemens he only says that Domitian suddenly, on a very light suspicion, put him to death; but the context shows beyond a doubt that the suspicion was that Clemens was plotting. What is the

---

* *Quasi molitores rerum novarum.* The word *quasi*, in a writer of Suetonius' period, does not imply a false appearance, but a real ground of accusation.

relation between this charge of treason and conspiracy, as related by Suetonius, and the charge of sacrilege, which Dion (as represented by Xiphilin) considered to be the chief part of the accusation? Are the two accounts flatly contradictory, or do they present two different aspects of the same fact? We have seen that the two accounts of Nero's persecution, by Tacitus and by Suetonius, complete each other; and we shall find that the same is the case with the different accounts of Dion and Suetonius.

Throughout the first century, one of the chief motives in the policy of the emperors within the city was dread of conspiracy among the Roman nobles in favour of a rival. Under the Flavian dynasty it was especially among the philosophers, and those nobles whose tastes lay in that direction, that conspiracy was feared. The philosophic temperament was connected with preservation of the memory of the old Roman republic, and with thoughts of freedom and unwillingness to submit to despotism. Even interest in past history was considered a dangerous symptom, and Tacitus is said to have felt it unsafe to write while Domitian lived. This policy was carried to an extreme by Domitian, who expelled the teachers of philosophy from Rome about A.D. 93, and put to death many of the Romans who had shown philosophic interests; but it did not originate in mere capricious tyranny. It was the permanent Flavian policy, and an example of its effect appeared in the execution of Helvidius Priscus by Vespasian.

Now there is great probability that, in the middle and end of the first century, many of the philosophic class among the Roman nobles took an interest in the speculations and doctrines of Jews and Christians and of the East in general. That Seneca had some slight acquaintance

with Christian teaching appears to be plain from his
writings, though it would be as absurd to say that he ever
had any inclination towards Christianity as it would be to
say that the extant correspondence of Paul and Seneca is
genuine. So long as philosophy retained its spirit of
opposition to the Government, and asserted the right of the
individual against absolute despotism, it had a certain
affinity with the position of Christianity in the Empire.
Hence it came about that an inclination towards the
doctrines of Christianity was a mark of the class which
Domitian most dreaded, and an interest in foreign religions
became a point in the accusations brought against many
Roman nobles whose attitude had roused his suspicion.
To Suetonius the important point in these trials was the
general fact of suspected conspiracy, whereas in Xiphilin's
version one isolated detail, referring to religion (in which
the monk was interested), is mentioned alone. But even
in Xiphilin we see that treason (the crime of injuring
the *majestas* of the State) must have been included in
the charge against Acilius; and at an earlier point in
his Epitome he made it clear that the exile into which
Acilius had been sent several years before was due to
that cause exclusively. Domitian's suspicions were roused
by certain omens which had happened to Acilius during
his consulship, A.D. 91.*

These considerations explain Suetonius' phrase about
the death of Flavius Clemens. The groundless suspicion
on which he was executed was of conspiracy; and the

---

* It is true that the same prodigies happened to his colleague in
the consulship, Trajan, who was not banished; but we have too little
information to enable us to understand why " one should be taken
and the other left."

"utterly contemptible indolence," which according to Suetonius characterised him, would appear to the historian a sufficient disproof of the suspicion.

But it must be admitted that Suetonius' words are not consistent with the idea that he was aware of Clemens being a Christian. We must then conclude that Clemens had been able to preserve the secret of his religion, and that Suetonius did not think it had been proved;* and Lightfoot is in all probability correct in saying that the "indolence" of Clemens was "the result of his equivocal position." By avoiding public duties to the utmost, he escaped showing his reluctance to comply with the pagan ceremonies constantly required of public officials, and thus incurred the charge of indolence.

8. THE FLAVIAN ACTION WAS POLITICAL IN CHARACTER.

The comparison of the scanty records, then, points to the view that the real motive of the Flavian policy towards the Christian was political, and not religious. The Christians were a politically dangerous body; and, if that be so, the danger must have lain especially in the fact that they were an organised and united body. It is therefore inaccurate to speak of the Flavian action as directed against the Christians. That phrase might be used about Nero, but the Flavian action was, if we can trust our inferences from the

---

* Probably Dion also did not believe that the charges brought by Domitian against Clemens, Acilius, and others had been proved. They profited in the eyes of the later Romans by the general belief that Domitian's action had been that of a jealous and groundlessly suspicious tyrant.

authorities, directed against the Church as an organised unity.*

One of the marked features of the reign of Domitian is the attention which he devoted to the restoration of the national cultus.† In this respect his policy was the same as that of Augustus; and, like him, he looked on the Imperial cultus as part of the national religion. He himself delighted to be identified with Jupiter, and to be idolised as the Divine Providence in human form; and it is recorded that Caligula, Domitian, and Diocletian were the three emperors who delighted to be styled *dominus et deus.* Though a certain element of individual caprice is discernible in the extent to which Domitian pushed the personal reference, yet the policy is not peculiar to him, but was a fixed and highly important part of the general Imperial policy, which treated religion as a part of the machinery of government. In this point of view, refusal to comply with the prescribed forms of respect to the Emperor was a refusal to be a member of the Roman unity, and constituted disloyalty and treason. As we have already seen, Pliny found the procedure already established that a charge of Christianity should be tested by calling on the accused to perform the ceremonies of loyal service and worship to the Emperor. Christianity was disloyalty; and, conversely, the mere rendering of the duties of loyalty disproved Christianity.

The scanty evidence which we have found, therefore, seems to point to the view that Christianity was, under Domitian, treated as treasonable. This implies that the

---

* This point is of the utmost importance in our subject, and will engage further attention in Chapter XV.

† See Schiller, *Geschichte,* i., p. 536.

trials now assumed a new form. Individual Christians were no longer proved guilty of acts which showed hostility to the existing system of society ; but the whole principles and constitution of the sect were condemned as hostile to the established order, and mere membership of the sect, if persisted in, was reckoned as treasonable. The Christians, as a body were outlaws, and were treated as such as soon as their adherence to the sect was recognised ; and the trial was conducted only with the view of establishing the fact that the accused persons were Christians. Such was the *cognitio* which Pliny applied as a regular process to the first cases that were brought before him.

We have not found the slightest reference to this aspect of the case against the Christians in the case of Nero's action ;* and we can hardly suppose that, if the action had assumed that character, Tacitus would have given the account which we read in *Annals*, xv. 44. Alike as historian and as proconsul of Asia, he must have been aware of the later character of procedure against the Christians ; and, if he so pointedly describes Nero's action as being of a different character, we must infer that he had found good reason to consider that the procedure with which he was familiar had been developed and systematised at a later time. Suetonius, on the other hand, in his brief allusion, lays stress only on the fact that the permanent

---

* It is true also that we have as yet no complete proof that under Domitian procedure against the Christians had assumed this aspect ; but we have no detailed account in the latter case, as we have in regard to Nero, and the evidence does show that some reference to religion was made by Domitian. The Christian authorities quoted in the following chapter prove that his action had assumed fully the character which we find in Pliny.

principle of condemning Christians originated under Nero, and does not count it part of his duty as a biographer to recount the development which the principle underwent.

It is obvious how widely the view here taken of a practically continuous proscription of the Christians from 64 onwards differs from that which is ordinarily accepted— viz., that there were two isolated persecutions, one by Nero in 64, and the other by Domitian in 95. How then is it that the Christians are silent about this continuous persecution? No names of martyrs are preserved,* no facts are recorded which have not been attributed to one or other of these two individual outbursts of fury. There is a Christian literature ; there are Christian historians. Are their silence and their record not conclusive? Partly, I think, their silence is not conclusive, partly, I think, their evidence has been misinterpreted. Their silence is not conclusive, because the thoughts of the first century Christians were so absorbed in life, in teaching, in the imminent end of the world, that memory and history had small place with them. The moment, as it passed, sank out of sight and out of mind, in contemplation of the pressing future. Hence there survived in recollection only a few isolated facts about a very few of the greatest figures in their history ; and these survived only in vague and dubious tradition. When history began for the Christians late in the second century, hardly any historical authorities later than the Acts of the Apostles

---

* The single exception is St. Paul, whose death is, by Lightfoot and others, dated about 67. If this date is right, the event proves the continuance of the principle after Nero's personal direction was withdrawn. Nero was in Corinth on November 28th, 67, as we know from an inscription published by M. Holleaux, *Discours prononcé par Néron*, Lyon, 1889, p. 13 ; see above, p. 243f.

remained, and the events of Christian history during a long period after A.D. 62 had perished from memory. So far from exaggerating, the Christian historians give a very defective account of the sufferings of that period. From the silence, therefore, of the authorities, no argument against the view here advanced can be drawn.

But we have a few contemporary Christian documents, which are indeed not of the type of formal history, but which, being written by persons absorbed in the practical problems of life, as we have supposed the Christians to be, throw some light on that life. Persons whom we have assumed to be living a life so real could not compose abstract, philosophical, or moral, or even religious treatises. There must beat in their work the pulse of actual life. Here we have an infallible test of genuineness. The period was unique in its character, and unsurpassed in the violence of contending emotions ; the writers were men of affairs, living in deadly earnest ; the resulting literature must bear the stamp of the period, and must prove or disprove the view here advanced of the war between the Church and the Empire.

NOTE.—The phrases used in the text—"resumption of the Neronian policy by Vespasian," and "continuity of persecution after Nero"—are not mutually contradictory. Nero's precedent guided provincial governors in cases that were brought before them, until, in some way unknown to us, the question was again raised and decided by Vespasian in a more developed way. Similarly, it was again raised by Pliny for Trajan's consideration, and by Licinius Silvanus Granianus for Hadrian's.

CHAPTER XIII.

CHRISTIAN AUTHORITIES FOR THE FLAVIAN PERIOD.

THE scanty indications which can be gathered from Pagan authorities, and from the few facts established by evidence independent of the contemporary Christian writers, are not sufficient to prove, though they certainly point the way to, the view which we have taken of the policy of the Flavian Emperors towards the Church. The real proof of that view lies in the indications of the feeling which was roused in the minds of the Christians by the Flavian action—a feeling so intense as to be almost without parallel in history.

I. THE FIRST EPISTLE OF PETER.

If the view, which will be stated about 1 Peter, be found even approximately correct, it will afford a very strong, almost a conclusive, proof of the general accuracy of our theory on the relations of the State to the Church. On the other hand, the extreme views—that 1 Peter belongs to a very early date, about A.D. 40-64, or to a very late date under Trajan—are absolutely inconsistent with our theory; while the view that 1 Peter was written between 64 and 67, would involve a modification of our theory, and an admission of the view which we have deliberately rejected (see p. 242), that the development from the condemnation of Christians for definite crimes, to the absolute proscription of the Name, took place before the conclusion of Nero's reign.

It is not easy to state, in precise and brief terms, the view which is here taken of 1 Peter. There is great danger of over-emphasising one aspect, and omitting others entirely. I must therefore beg for indulgence, while I state once for all, that in this chapter our concern is with only one side of a group of documents which are, to an unusual degree, many-sided ; and that, forced as I am to leave out of view much of the character of the documents, I am far from ignoring or disparaging that which I do not explicitly mention. My point is that, if the points which I lay stress on are not absolutely false, the inferences here stated must follow.

I shall first state shortly my view of the character of this Epistle, and shall thereafter criticise two different views : the criticism will serve to render more precise my own view and the reasons for it.

The First Epistle of St. Peter is addressed to all the Christian communities of Asia Minor north of the Taurus.* They are regarded as exposed to persecution (i. 6), not merely in the form of dislike and malevolence on the part of neighbours, though that is, of course, an additional and trying element of the situation, but persecution to the death (iv. 15, 16), after trial and question (iii. 15). † The persecution is general, and extends over the whole Church (v. 9). The Christians are not merely tried when a private accuser comes forward against them, but are sought out for

---

* See above, pp. 110, 187.

† The Greek, ἀπολογίαν and αἰτοῦντι λόγον, is more precise than the English version.　For other views, see below, p. 291 ff.

trial by the Roman officials (v. 8, iii. 15).* They suffer for the Name (iv. 14–16) pure and simple ; the trial takes the form of an inquiry into their religion,† giving them the opportunity of "glorifying God in this Name."

The picture is here complete. We have the fully developed kind of trial which we suppose to have been instituted about 75–80, and which was carried out by Pliny as part of the fixed policy of the Empire towards the Christians. These circumstances are essentially different from those of the Neronian period. The resulting action was indeed much the same ; many Christians were in each case executed in barbarous ways ; but the legal and political aspects of the situation were very different.

But 1 Peter does not look back over a period of persecution. It rather looks forward to it as the condition in which the Christians have to live. The State is absolutely hostile, raging against them, seeking them out for destruction (v. 8, 9) ; but it is not yet regarded, as it is in later documents, as inexorably and inevitably, from its very nature, opposed to the Christians. By steadily avoiding all just cause of offence, by convincing the world of their good works, by strict obedience to the laws of the State, to the Emperor, and to the provincial governors, they may put

---

* A trial which involved the penalty of death could take place only before Roman officials of high rank. They that are sought out for such a trial must be sought out by order of Roman officials.

† iv. 14–16 refers obviously to trials issuing in death. Christians are to face gladly the accusation of bearing the Name and the death that it entails, and to fear only such crimes as would justify their execution. The passage loses much of its significance, unless the question put to the accused is of the type, "Are you a Christian?" The words, περὶ τῆς ἐν ὑμῖν ἐλπίδος, iii. 15, define the subject of the enquiry.

their slanderers to silence, and emerge from their fiery
trials (ii. 11–15). It is clear from this analysis of the
situation that the writer stands at the beginning of the
new period. He still clings to the idea that the Christians
are persecuted because they are believed to be guilty of
great crimes; the old charges of the Neronian time are
still in his memory, and he hopes that, if the absurdity of
these charges be fully brought home to the minds of men,
the persecution must be stopped. Hence he reiterates
St. Paul's advice.* The social order is not to be interfered
with : slaves are to respect their masters in spite of bad
treatment ; divisions within the family on account of religion
are to be avoided. This attitude belongs to one whose
experience has been gained in the first period of Christianity, in the time of Claudius and Nero, and who is now
at the beginning of a new period. He recognises the fact
that Christians now suffer as witnesses to the Name, and
for the Name pure and simple ; but he hardly realises all
that was thereby implied.

The First Epistle of Peter then must have been written
soon after Vespasian's resumption of the Neronian policy
in a more precise and definite form. It implies relations
between Church and State which are later than the
Neronian period, but which have only recently begun.

If the date about A.D. 80, to which we ascribe 1 Peter,
is correct, either the author cannot be the Apostle Peter,
or the usual view, according to which Peter perished at
Rome in the Neronian persecution, is not correct. Now
while the tradition that St. Peter perished in Rome is strong
and early, the tradition about the date of his death is not

---

* See above, p. 246.

so clear.* The earliest authority for the date is Origen, who places his martyrdom under Nero before that of Paul. Tertullian also seems in one passage to assign it to the time of Nero; but in another passage he mentions the tradition of the Roman Church that Clement was ordained by St. Peter.† The latter passage is the strongest evidence which we possess on the point, and it clearly proves that the Roman tradition during the latter part of the second century placed the martyrdom much later than the time of Nero.‡ The tradition that he lived for a long time in Rome is also strong, and, as Dr. Harnack justly says, "it is difficult to suppose that so large a body of tradition has no foundation in fact."§ But conclusive reasons show that he cannot have been in Rome long before the Neronian persecution ; and therefore a long residence there is impossible unless he lived to a much later date.

The only early tradition with regard to St. Peter's later life, then, is that which was accepted by the Roman Church during the second century, and it is to the effect that St. Peter lived in Rome till long after the time of Nero. The tradition that he died under Nero is not a real tradition, but an historical theory, framed at the time when all recol-

---

* In the original lectures this date was treated as inconsistent with Petrine authorship. A conversation with Dr. Hort suggested the view now taken. In the rest of this paragraph I am indebted to Lightfoot, *Clement*, ii., p. 494 ff.

† Origen in Eusebius, *H. E.*, iii. 1 ; Tertullian, *Scorp.*, 15 (about 215 A.D.) ; in *de præscript*, 32 (about 199, Noeldechen, *Abfassungs-zeit d. Schr. Tert.*), he mentions the Roman tradition.

‡ In the extreme uncertainty of the history of the early Roman episcopate it is not possible to fix an exact date for the ordination of Clement.

§ Harnack on " Peter " in the *Encycl. Brit.*, ninth edition.

lection of the true relations between the State and the Christians had perished, and when it was believed that there had been two separate and single persecutions, one by Nero, and one by Domitian in his later years. As to the date of the Epistle there is no tradition, and it is merely a modern theory, keenly contested by many, that places the composition about A.D. 64.

It has been said that Clement, *ad. Cor.*, 4, mentions Peter's death before Paul's, and that his order is naturally taken as chronological. I see no reason to think that in mentioning " the good apostles " Clement must be supposed to follow chronological order. It may have been the natural order for a Roman, even then, to mention Peter first. The passage is quite as effective in expression if Peter's death was more recent than Paul's.*

The history of the spread of Christianity imperatively demands for 1 Peter a later date than A.D. 64. When it was written the new religion had been diffused over all the provinces of Asia Minor, north of Taurus. The impression that we get from Acts is, that the evangelisation of Asia Minor originated from St. Paul ; and that from his initiative the new religion gradually spread over the country through the action of many other missionaries (Acts xix. 10). Moreover, missionaries not trained by him were at work

---

* It is remarkable that Lightfoot, *Clement*, i., p. 344, should say, " Whether Tertullian, when he states that the Roman Church recorded Clement to have been ordained by St. Peter, was influenced, etc., or whether it was his own independent inference, etc., we have no means of determining." Surely we have means of determining— viz., by believing Tertullian's plain statement, that he is doing neither of the things suggested by Lightfoot, but is quoting the tradition current in Rome. His own "independent inference" seems rather to have been that Peter died under Nero, *Scorp.*, 15.

in South Galatia and in Ephesus as early as 54–56 A.D. (Gal. v. 7–10.; Acts xviii. 25). If we can assume that this account is not absolutely unhistorical, and that Christianity was extending along the main line of intercourse across the Empire between 50 and 60, it is inconceivable that, before A.D. 64, (1) it had spread away from that line across the country through the northern provinces; (2) so much organisation and intercommunication had grown up as is implied in 1 Peter, where a person writing from Rome is familiar with the condition and wants of the congregations, and advises them with some authority.

We have already seen that Christianity is not likely to have reached Amisos before A.D. 65 ; and if we assume that this great further development had taken place in time for 1 Peter to be written about 75–80, we are straining historical probability as far as the evidence will reasonably permit. So far as an opinion is possible, they that make Peter write to the congregations of Pontus during Nero's reign remove the story of early Christianity from the sphere of history into that of the marvellous and supernatural; and it lies outside of the plan of this work to follow them.

It is no argument against the date when we consider Christianity to have reached Amisos, that it must have reached Rome as early as A.D. 55-6. In the state of the Empire Rome was easier to reach than Amisos ;* and all movements of thought spread first to Rome. Nor does it constitute any real objection to our dating, that, in the Pastoral Epistles, the new religion is spoken of as spreading to Dalmatia and other places off the main line of communication. Assuming the genuineness of these Epistles,

---

* See *Hist. Geogr.*, p. 26.

we must attribute this rapid spread of Christianity in the
years following Paul's release to his extraordinary activity
and energy ; and concurrently therewith we place the
evangelisation of Amisos and the north coast of Asia
Minor.

Moreover, the strong analogies which 1 *Peter* shows to
James, *Romans*, and *Ephesians*, implying that the writer
was familiar with all these letters, are more easily
explicable if 1 *Peter* was composed about A.D. 80.
Holtzmann indeed uses them as an argument against the
Petrine authorship of the Epistle, and Lightfoot* has not
cleared away the difficulty which they cause if the composition of 1 *Peter* is assigned to A.D. 63 or 64.

It seems difficult to explain this character in 1 Peter, and
the influence which these three Epistles have exercised on
it, except in the way which Holtzmann has done.   These
Epistles were known to the writer, and were esteemed by
him as works of high authority and value.   A certain lapse
of time for the formation of this authoritative character
seems required ; but it is entirely in keeping with the view
we take of the organisation of the Church during the
Flavian period that these letters should have acquired that
character before A.D. 80 (see p. 367).

That this Epistle was written from Rome, I cannot doubt.
It is impregnated with Roman thought to a degree beyond
any other book in the Bible ; the relation to the State and
its officers forms an unusually large part of the whole.   It
seems, if I may venture to hold an opinion on such a point,
to presuppose a more organised and inter-connected state
of the entire Church than most documents included in the

* *Clement*, ii., p. 499.

New Testament, more so than even the Pastoral Epistles. It is far advanced on the path that leads to the letter of Clement to the Corinthians. The reference to Rome as "Babylon"* implies a developed state of symbolic expression approximating to that of the Apocalypse. The letter is addressed to "the elect who are sojourners of the Dispersion" in Asia Minor. The congregations of Asia Minor were composed of persons that had been Pagans (iv. 2, 3). It is contrary to all reasonable probability that they contained any appreciably large Jewish element; and if Acts is a historical authority of any value whatever, the Jewish population was, as a body, strenuously opposed to the Christians of Asia Minor. How then can a Jew, like Peter, speak of these congregations by the Jewish title Diaspora? It is because, writing after the destruction of Jerusalem, and recognising the utter change that had thereby been produced both for Judaism and for the possible development of Christianity, he now appreciated the unique position and the importance of the Asia Minor churches (see p. 171), and regarded them as the chief guarantee for the unity which had once—in his view—centred in Jerusalem, and was now scattered abroad (see p. 110).

There are several points in this Epistle which have a more vivid and forcible character, if we date it as late as A.D. 75–80; whereas if it belongs to a period earlier than A.D. 64, their natural force has to be, to some degree,

---

* That Babylon should be understood as the Chaldæan city appears to conflict so entirely with all record and early tradition, as to hardly need discussion. But that a Jew, whose life had been spent in Palestine and Chaldæa, should write so *romanised* a letter is even more improbable.

modified.   In the reference to the Devil (v. 8) we have a step towards the strongly developed idea of the World, which is described below (see § 5).   In this case the expression is more purely metaphorical and ethical ; but the action of agents seeking and arresting Christians is included, and gives point and pertinence to the metaphor.   The State, however, is not yet conceived as the irreconcilable enemy (see p. 296).

Again, the reference to hospitality (iv. 8, 9) has more force, if the Epistle was written after the Church had begun to appreciate, with full consciousness, the importance of intercommunication.   Paul appreciated this very early, and insists on it frequently (Rom. xii. 13 ; 1 Tim. iii. 2 ; Titus i. 8 ; *cp.* Hebr. xiii. 2) ; but it is not so easy to imagine Peter appreciating it, until the destruction of Jerusalem made it clear that the local unity of a central sanctuary was exchanged for the ideal unity of constant intercourse and mutual welcome.*   Otherwise we must take iv. 8, 9, as merely urging in a general way the duty of hospitality, which hardly needs such prominence, considering the state of contemporary society.

The date of 1 Peter seems clearly fixed.   If it was written by St. Peter, reasons founded on his character and history confirm the late date.   If it be proved that he died before A.D. 70, we should have to assign the composition (like 2 Peter) to another author.

2. LATER DATE ASSIGNED TO 1 PETER.

Many critics have fully realised that the Epistle does not suit the time of Nero, but, misled by the false interpretation

---

* Hence Clement urges on the Corinthians the duty of φιλοξενία, §1, 10–12, 35.   See above, p. 10.

of Pliny's report to Trajan, have dated its composition too late. Holtzmann's article in Schenkel's *Bibel-Lexikon*, iv., p. 296, may be taken as the best statement of the historical arguments on which this Epistle has been assigned to the period of Trajan or Hadrian.

1. "In the Epistle, iv. 15, the Christians of Bithynia and other provinces are warned against murder, theft, and other crimes ; and, according to Pliny, the Christians of Bithynia were in the habit of taking an oath to avoid such crimes."

Such is one of Holtzmann's arguments, which would be irresistible, if he could add the proof that the Christians first began to avoid these crimes about 112. This essential part of his argument he has omitted.

2. "In the Epistle trials of Christians are alluded to,. iii. 15, and such trials were held by Pliny in Bithynia."

Again Holtzmann omits the essential part of his argument—viz., the proof that such trials were first held by Pliny. When we find a series of trials of Christians before Roman officials, beginning with that of Jesus and reaching through the time of Paul and the whole of the first century, we can see no cogency in Holtzmann's reasoning.

3. "In the Epistle it is implied that the issue in these trials turns on the simple question whether the accused is a Christian, and that question first came to the front under Trajan."

The first part of this argument we fully accept. It states, in brief, the essential and critical point, which distinguishes the language of this Epistle from all earlier references to persecution. But we have seen that, while the trials of Trajan's time were certainly conducted on this principle, the procedure was then settled by long usage.

Such are the reasons which lead Holtzmann and many

19

others to date 1 Peter about 115–135.* We can see no validity in them. On the contrary, we observe that the tendency of Trajan's rescript was to put an end to the state of things implied in the Epistle. He forbade the seeking out of Christians, which is expressly referred to in iii. 15, v. 8. We cannot, indeed, prove that this prohibition, addressed to a single governor, immediately became universal; but no one who has studied the character of Trajan will doubt, that the principle which he formulated to Pliny resulted from a consideration of the whole evidence as collected and arranged in the Imperial archives, and was the fixed rule of his policy. Moreover, Hadrian confirmed still more emphatically the prohibition. If 1 Peter is not earlier than A.D. 112, we cannot place it earlier than 161 (see below, p. 337), a date which requires no notice, and has never been seriously proposed.

3. Official Action implied in 1 Peter.

Many writers have sought to minimise and to explain away the references to persecution in this Epistle. Having accepted too readily the dominant view as to the relations between the Empire and the Church, they could not resist the argument that, if 1 Peter implies a developed persecution by the State, it must be as late as Trajan. Yet

---

* The rest of his reasons go to prove only the disagreement between the Epistle and the facts of the Neronian period. So far we cannot disagree from his conclusion, though his statement that during that period action against the Christians was confined to Rome is incorrect: we have seen (1) that it was inherent in the Imperial system that the Emperor's action should form a model for all provincial governors; (2) that Suetonius considered Nero to have laid down a permanent principle of action against the Christians.

they rightly appreciated the marks of an early date in the Epistle, and, thereby feeling bound to place it in the first century, they naturally and inevitably estimated too lightly the references to persecution. As the best expression of this view, a few sentences may be quoted from Dr. Marcus Dods' *Introduction to the New Testament*, p. 200. My personal respect for the writer, and my high admiration for most of his work, make me reluctant in this case to differ from him so completely; but the same clearness, preciseness, and completeness of statement, which raise his work to high rank, make him in this case a perfect exponent of the view that sacrifices the natural force in order to preserve the orthodox dating. He admits that "the letter was written to Christians, who were suffering for their religion"; but maintains that "the persecution to which they were being subjected does not appear to have been instituted by the magistrate or governor of the district in which they lived, but to have been of a social kind. They had refused to join their old associates in 'excess of riot' (iv. 4), and were therefore calumniated. They were spoken of as evildoers (iii. 16, ii. 12); and they were urged by Peter to prove by their conduct that these accusations were false. These accusations, therefore, were social calumnies, and not legal indictments. Indeed, Peter hints (iii. 13), that to be free from persecution they have only to continue in well-doing, each in his own position, whether as servant (ii. 18–25), as wife (iii. 1–6), or as husband (iii. 7). There is no allusion to trial before the authorities, nor to imprisonment, nor to death. Even the strongest passage adduced in favour of these views (iv. 16) will not bear such an interpretation. It is 'reproach' that they suffered as Christians, and the fear is that they would be 'ashamed' of this reproach, and their deliverance from it was still to be by unmurmuring patience and continuance in well-doing (iv. 19)."

In answer to this view, attention may be directed to the following points :

1. The Christians are addressed as persons exposed to suffer death. The words, "Let none of you suffer as a murderer, or as a thief; but, if (a man suffer) as a Christian, let him glorify God in this Name" (iv. 15, 16), have no satisfactory meaning, unless those to whom they are addressed are liable to execution : the verb in the second clause is understood from the preceding clause, and must have the same sense. Moreover, if we suppose that "suffer" in the second clause could have the milder sense attributed to it by Dr. Dods, the whole sentence then implies : " Do not commit murder and be executed for it ; and if your neighbours make fun of you as a Christian, do not be ashamed of this name." What a feeble production does this noble letter then become ! A leader of the religion writes to his co-religionists in a distant land, advising them to abstain from murder and theft, and to disregard their neighbours' jeers. This is the meaning of what Dr. Dods calls "the strongest passage" in that letter, about which Lightfoot says that " no other book of the New Testament, except the Apocalypse, is so burdened with the subject [of persecution] : the leading purpose of the letter is to console and encourage his distant correspondents under the fiery trial which awaited them." * Had all manhood and steadfastness disappeared from Peter, or from the Asian Christians, that he should write to them

---

* *Clement*, ii., p. 498.

like this, about a situation which was prevented from being comfortable by their neighbours' discourtesy and rudeness ? All reality of tone, all nobleness, all power, disappear from this letter, unless it be addressed to those who are liable to suffer unto death as Christians.

2. In the Roman Empire the right of capital punishment belonged only to a small number of high officials. No Asian Christian was liable to suffer death except through the action of the governor of his province. If the Christians are liable to suffer unto death, persecution by the State must be in process.

3. The charges enumerated in iv. 15 are those which the writer thought likely to be brought against the Christians. He had known the Neronian system, when the Christians were tried and convicted of definite criminal acts ; and he knew also the charges currently made against them by popular scandal. In this way he is led to the phrase of iii. 15 and iv. 15 : " Murder, theft, gross crimes,* tampering with the slaves and the families of others †—these and similar charges will be brought against

---

* These charges are all implied in the accusation of Θυέστεια δεῖπνα. See pp. 205, 237.

† The remarkable word ἀλλοτριοεπίσκοπος has never been explained. It appears to be a rendering in Greek of a charge brought against the Christians, which had no single term to denote it, and for which this bold compound was framed by the writer. I cannot doubt that it refers to the charge of tampering with family relationships, causing disunion and discord, rousing discontent and disobedience among slaves, and so on. We have already seen (pp. 236 and 282) how much importance this charge had, and how strenuously Paul and Peter urge the Christians not to provoke or justify it. Professor Mommsen writes that *speculator alieni* of Tertullian, *Scorp.*, 12, is a wide term, which might denote even a thief and a kidnapper (*plagiarius, qui servos alienos intercipit*) ; though I do not know

you.   Give no colour to them by your life; avoid the risk
of perishing by such a disgraceful death;* but be proud
when you are called on to make your defence concerning
the hope that is in you (iii. 15), and to be executed as
Christians." †

It would be a useful, but far too long, task to go over the
whole Epistle, pointing out how vividly various passages
in it express the character of Roman action against the
Christians : the official action, and the terror caused by its
awful surroundings, the pressure of public opinion and
popular dislike, the open expression of opinion by the
circle of spectators round the tribunal, and the social persecution which became powerful and serious as a concomitant
to legal proceedings, but which would be of little consequence unless abetted and completed by official judgment.
The alliance between popular and judicial action was
necessary for any real persecution in the Roman Empire.
This does not naturally occur to us ; but it will be shown in
Ch. XV. that the thoroughness of persecution was, to a very

---

whether he would approve of the connotation which I give to the
Greek and the Latin term in this case.   The other Latin renderings,
alienorum appetitor, curas alienas agens, are vague and useless
guesses.   (On this subject see Ch. XV., § 1.)

* M. Le Blant, in his *Supplém. aux Actes des Martyrs*, p. 173,
alludes to the dislike expressed by St. Felicitas and other martyrs
to be executed along with criminals ; they gloried in suffering as
Christians, but shrank from even the appearance of being executed
for crimes (*Acta Perpetuæ*, 15).   The same feeling actuates the
expression of 1 Peter iv. 15.

† The two passages, iii. 15 and iv. 15, must be taken in connection.
'Απολογίαν is a strong term, strictly a legal term, a defence against a
formal accusation.   Unless formal trials were in the writer's mind,
I do not think he would express himself thus ; though any less
formal challenge is included.

great extent, dependent on the co-operation of the populace. Such is the state of things that is presupposed
throughout 1 Peter : the mixture of official and popular
action is very clearly expressed. But the official action, as
a necessary part of the situation,* is clearly implied in the
language of iii. 15, 16, iv. 15, etc. ; and to ignore it is to
sacrifice much of the character of a letter, which is instructive beyond all others with regard to the position of the
Christians in the Empire, after the development of official
action had taken place.

As to the argument which is founded by Dr. Dods on
the advice to avoid persecution by continuance in well-
doing, I trust that a satisfactory explanation of the advice
has been give on p. 281-2.

4. The Evidence of the Apocalypse.

We turn next to a work of notorious difficulty, the
Apocalypse. Here the moving spirit of the vision is the
sufferings of the Church. The scene lies wholly in the Eastern
Provinces, and especially in Asia among the seven churches ;
for Rome is on the extreme horizon, and is conceived only
as the distant metropolis where the martyrs are sent to
suffer the death decreed against them. Only in this way, as
Mommsen † has pointed out, can the reference to Rome as
the woman drunk with the blood of the saints and witnesses
of Jesus be explained (xvii. 6). In this phrase there is

---

* On this subject, as a whole, see below, p. 373. The developed
language of James must not be quoted in this connexion. James
wrote to Jews, whose situation was utterly different. (See p. 349)
Peter wrote to Gentile Christians.

† *Provinces of the Roman Empire,* ii. 199, of the English
translation.

implied a wide-spread persecution with many victims; and the sufferers are witnesses to the Name, not persons condemned, even though unjustly, for specific crimes. Many other passages imply that the Church was exposed to a long-continued persecution to the death (vi. 9; vii. 14; xii. 11; xiii. 15; xvi. 6; xvii. 6; xviii. 24; xx. 4, etc.); and the persecution is likely to last (vi. 11).

The victims of this persecution are witnesses to the Name, or the word of God (ii. 13; vi. 9; xii. 11; xvii. 6), which implies that their death springs directly from their acknowledgment of their religion, and not from conviction, even on false evidence, for specific crimes (*flagitia*). But it is also implied that the persecutor is worshipped as a God by all people * except the Christians (xiii. 8), and that the martyrs are slain because they do not worship the Beast—*i.e.*, the Roman Emperor (xiii. 15). Hence their refusal to worship the Beast and their witness to their own God are united in one act; and this implies that worship of the Beast formed a test, the refusal of which was equivalent to a confession and witness. Here we touch on the feature which for our purposes is of the first importance—viz., the absolute and irreconcilable opposition between the Church and the Empire. The latter is the very incarnation and manifestation of evil. The one characteristic, by which it concerns the Church, is the hatred and the firm resolution

---

* Incidentally we note that this expression is a typical instance of the fact which we have already observed (p. 236). The mind of the writer is practically restricted to the Roman world. The expression "all that dwell on the earth" has not the nature of an exaggeration, for it is in accord with the unconscious restrictions of the writer's view. He thinks, like a Roman, that *genus humanum* is the Roman world. The nations which did not worship the Emperor were never present to his mind.

with which it seeks to destroy Christianity. There is no wish for reconciliation with the persecuting power, only for vengeance on it (vi. 9–11 ; ix. 4) ; there is no thought of the possibility of bringing the State to a milder policy by convincing it of the harmlessness of Christianity.

The visions in the Apocalypse may be taken as an historical authority, for they arise directly out of the situation of the Church. Moreover, every detail of persecution that occurs in the visions may be paralleled from the messages to the churches which are prefixed to them. The messages indeed do not refer in such clear terms to persecution. But the single example of a martyr quoted by name, Antipas of Pergamos (ii. 13), shows what is meant by the "patience" of Ephesus and the "tribulation" of Smyrna. Antipas remained for some reason (perhaps as being the first of his class) * personally and individually in the memory of the Asian Church. Moreover, the persecution has been long-standing (ii. 13), and is to continue for a time (ii. 10). Again, the importance attached during this persecution to the worship of the Emperor, and the hatred for this special form of idolatry as the special enemy, have dictated the phrase addressed to the church of Pergamos, "Thou dwellest where the throne of Satan," *i.e.*, the temple of Rome and Augustus, "is" (ii. 13).†

But on the whole surprisingly little space or attention is

---

* Neumann (p. 15) infers unjustifiably that Antipas was the only martyr that had as yet suffered at Pergamos.

† We may note in passing that this phrase belongs rather to the first century than the second. In the first century the supremacy of Pergamos in the Imperial cultus is certain or highly probable ; but in the second century it would rather appear that Ephesus succeeded to its place, and became the most important seat of the worship.

given in these messages to the subject of persecution, and this same character attaches to all letters addressed to the early churches.* Incidental allusions occur to the sufferings, but other subjects are more important to the writers. If the early Christians had given much thought to their persecutions, they would not have conquered the world.

The date of the Apocalypse, and the question whether it is a product of Jewish or of purely Christian feeling, have been much debated. The hypothesis has even been advanced by Vischer and others that the Apocalypse was originally composed about A.D. 70, as a pure Jewish and non-Christian work, which was enlarged and retouched about A.D. 95, so as to become a Christian work. But this extreme hypothesis can certainly not be adopted. The Christian character is so imbedded in the structure of the Apocalypse that it cannot be taken out of it even in the most superficial way, except by such gross violence as is unworthy of sound criticism. The experiment has been made by Vischer; and his work has the great value of showing conclusively that the thing is impossible. The Apocalypse is a Christian document from its inception to its completion.

This does not, however, imply that John, in composing the Revelation, made no use of already existing *Apocalypses.* Vischer's investigation has shown conclusively that John was greatly influenced by older Jewish works of this character; though he errs in regard to the manner in which John used them. The Revelation, as we have it,

---

* Except, of course, on the supposition that 1 Peter was written before official action became regular. In that case surprisingly much space and attention are devoted to the subject in that Epistle.

is not a revised edition of a Jewish document. It is the work of a Christian writer, who was familiar with Jewish *Apocalypses,* and adapted to his own purposes much that was contained in some one or more of them ; but this writer treated the material with a mastery and freedom that made his work in its entirety a Christian document, however strong are the traces of the older form in parts of it.

Spitta, in his *Offenbarung des Johannes,* has justly appreciated the erroneous side of Vischer's hypothesis. He considers that John's Apocalypse was at first composed as an independent Christian document about A.D. 60, and that this Christian Apocalypse was enlarged by a redactor, who incorporated along with it two Jewish Apocalypses, one composed about B.C. 65, the other about A.D. 40. The redactor made considerable additions of his own to effect a harmonious junction between the fragments of these three works. This theory, while avoiding the difficulties into which Vischer fell, is involved in others even more serious. Its artificiality is so extreme as to make it incapable of proof and on the face of it improbable, since Spitta has not succeeded in finding any sufficiently clear marks to distinguish one document from another. The separation between the work of the two supposed Christian writers is especially hazardous and hypercritical.

According to Spitta, the last two chapters are a patchwork of fragments from all four sources. Yet this patchwork has always been considered to be one of the most poetic and highly wrought passages in the Bible. A patchwork which rises to that rank is no mere piecing together of fragments ; it is an original work, in which ideas learned from various sources are fused into a truly original production.

Spitta's theory, however, is at least a strong confirmation of the arguments which we have advanced against Vischer's theory in its actual form; and we are in agreement with much that is contained in each of them, while considering that both require considerable modification.

But the decisive argument against the actual form of Spitta's theory is that the supposed first Christian document is quite unsuitable to the year 60. It is most improbable that the Christians of Asia were at that date so highly organised in numerous congregations as they were when the letters to the seven churches were composed; and it is contrary to all evidence that they were at that time exposed to serious persecution and actual execution. Spitta supposes (p. 477) that the churches of Asia were persecuted even to death by the Jews, and compelled to take the yoke of the law upon them; and he shows that, in the message sent to the churches, Jesus does not threaten the Jews with judgment, but encourages His faithful people to resist to death. The idea that in great cities of the Roman Empire, some of them the residence of high Roman officials, Ephesus, Pergamos, Smyrna, etc., the Jews could persecute and kill the Christians in the public and open way that is implied in the Apocalypse, does not require serious refutation. We need only recommend Dr. Spitta to devote a little more time to the study of Roman Imperial history and administration, in order to learn that, defective as was the Roman Empire in some respects, it was not so utterly unfit for the fundamental duties of government, as to allow the extreme license and organised riot that are implied by his theory.

But, even if the hypothesis be true, that the Apocalypse is the re-edition issued about 90–96 A.D. of an older work or works, whether composed by Jews or by Jewish Christians, it still continues authoritative for the later period.

If the Apocalypse was originally a Christian document, there can remain no doubt that the preceding exposition forces us to date it not earlier than about A.D. 90.* The external circumstances in which it is environed are those which characterise the fully developed policy of the Flavian Emperors, and are different from those of the Neronian period. It looks back, unlike 1 Peter, over a period of persecution. As a Christian document, the Apocalypse is an historical impossibility about A.D. 70. The Church did not at that time stand opposed to the Empire and "the World" in declared inexpiable war; the idea that Christianity might spread peaceably through the Empire was still dominant, as we see both in the Epistles of Paul † and in 1 Peter. Accordingly, if the Apocalypse is placed under Nero or Vespasian, the feeling that rules in it could be attributed only to the Jewish hatred against the Empire, which led to the rebellion of 67–70; and then it must lose the Christian character which we find to be inherent in it. Moreover, the circumstances and details are not in accordance with Jewish feeling. We must agree with Völter that these imply "a persecution which leads to imprisonment and death"; ‡ and no such relation existed between the Jews and the Empire.

---

* The earliest authority extant—viz., Irenæus—dates it in the later years of Domitian, *i.e.*, 90–96.

† His earlier Epistles to the Thessalonians do not show this character; but in the later Epistles there is a distinct progress towards it, until it becomes strongly marked in the Pastoral Epistles.

‡ *Streitschrift gegen Harnack und Vischer*, p. 34. "Es ist vielmehr eine Verfolgung (cf. xii. 12) gemeint, die zu Gefängniss und Tod führt (xiii. 9, 10, 15)."

On the other hand, the Apocalypse is equally an
historical impossibility much after the year 112, when
Trajan revised and toned down the harshness of the
previous policy,* modifying it in execution without abro-
gating it in principle. As we shall see, there then began
a gradual *rapprochement* between the Church and the
Empire, and the idea that rules in the Epistles of Paul
and Peter again became dominant in a much more
advanced and defined form.

One marked development in the procedure against the
Christians seems to have taken place between the composition of 1 Peter and that of the Apocalypse. The
worship of the Emperor is not alluded to in the former,
whereas it is prominent in the latter. Precisely in the
interval between them lies the accession of Domitian,
and, as we have seen, it was his desire to be regarded as
a god in human form, and to be styled *dominus et deus.*
We shall probably not err in attributing to his influence
the final development of procedure in regard to the
Christians.

5. THE FIRST EPISTLE OF JOHN.

From the Apocalypse we naturally turn to the Epistles
attributed to St. John. There can be no doubt that the same
hand can be traced in the First Epistle and the Fourth
Gospel. No two works in the whole range of literature show
clearer signs of the genius of one writer, and no other pair

Völter's words, " nur bei Christen erklärt sich das und auch
bei ihnen nur in der Zeit seit Trajan," are half right and half wrong.
The error is founded on the strange misinterpretation of the two
letters of Pliny and Trajan, which prevails so widely, and which
Neumann has happily abandoned.

of works are so completely in a class by themselves, apart
from the work of their own and of every other time. One
work alone stands near them, the Apocalypse ; and while
identity of authorship is very far from being so clear, as in
the case of the Gospel and Epistle, yet there is a closer
relation between the three works than exists between any
of them and any fourth work. We must expect to find
a close connection in time and circumstances of origin
between the First Epistle and the Apocalypse.

The First Epistle of John was in all probability "addressed
primarily to the circle of Asiatic Churches, of which Ephesus
was the centre." * It may be expected to contain some
reference to the persecution of the Christians by Domitian.
No explicit reference, however, occurs ; and it has even
been concluded that the situation was entirely different.
" Outward dangers were overcome. The world was indeed
perilous ; but it was rather by its seductions than by its
hostility. There is no trace of any recent or impending
persecution." † Therefore, it may be argued, either they
belong to a later date, or they prove that the author knew
of no such persecution in Asia as we have found ourselves
obliged to suppose.

We answer that even the attribution to a later date does
not explain the attitude of the writer in respect of the
relations with the Empire, unless we bring him down to a
decidedly later date than the most extreme critics advocate.
Throughout the second century, as will be shown in the
following chapters, Christianity continued to be forbidden,
and the confession of the Name on trial constituted at once,

---

* Westcott, *Epistles of St. John*, p. 32.
† Westcott, p. 33.

without any further proceedings, a sufficient ground for condemnation to death. A writer who was advising and admonishing any congregation during the second century must, if he referred at all to their relations with the State, refer to the proscription of the Church ; and if he could admonish the congregation at that time without referring to their relations with the State, he might equally well do so during the first century. Herein then lies the real explanation. The author has no thought to spend on the relation of his congregations to the Empire and the law, his mind is entirely occupied with another subject—viz., the inner life ; and he has no thought of advising them as to their behaviour towards the State.

But, though he does not allude to persecution, he does not leave us in the dark as to the feeling with which he regarded the State. The State is summed up in " The World." As Bishop Westcott says, " In the Emperor the World * found a personal embodiment and claimed Divine honour." Accordingly, when St. John says, " Marvel not, brethren, that † the World hateth you," and goes on to state that the passage from the World to Christianity is a passage from death to life, and from hatred of the Church to love of the Church, we shall see in the paragraph iii. 13 ff., first, what was the attitude of the Empire towards the Church 90–100 A.D. ; and secondly, how little thought St. John bestowed on it. The transcendentalism of his thought, and the remoteness of his position from that of

---

* *Epistles of St. John*, p. 255. I have slightly modified his phrase (which is " the world ") for the sake of uniformity.

† I have modified the translation to bring out clearly that the hatred is assumed as a fact ; a literal rendering of εἰ in English is apt to conceal this.

the practical preacher who tells his congregation how they are to behave in the presence of the persecutor, cannot be better expressed than in the words of Westcott himself, p. 34 : "According to his view, . . . the World [including the "Empire"] exists indeed, but more as a semblance than as a reality. It is overcome finally and for ever. It is on the point of vanishing. . . . And over against 'the World' there is the Church. . . . By this, therefore, all that need be done to proclaim the Gospel to those without, is done naturally and effectively in virtue of its very existence. It must overcome the darkness by shining. . . . St. Paul wrote while the conflict was undecided. St. John has seen its close." * Fully to appreciate the writer whose attitude is described in these words, and to realise his perfect indifference to, and want of concern with, the superficial aspect of the facts of the day, we must remember that he was writing under Domitian, who banished him to an islet in the Ægean Sea, and who was addressed by his subjects as "our Lord and God." When we do so, this paragraph, written to explain why missionary work is not urged by John as it was by Paul, also explains why the enmity of the Empire is treated so lightly, and occupies a hardly appreciable place in his mind.

We now see that the attitude of the Epistles to the Empire is the same as that of the Apocalypse; and we also realise that it would be a mistake to argue, from the absence of any explicit reference in them to persecution, that they were composed in a season of peace, when persecution was at an end. Any apparent discrepancy

---

* I would only add to this last sentence, "with the eye of a seer," *Epistles of St. John*, p. 34. I have, as before, made the change of a capital in "the World."

between the Epistles and the Apocalypse, in reference to the relations of Church and State, lies in the difference of their point of view. In the words we have just quoted, the first Epistle sees the World "only as a semblance, finally overcome, and on the point of vanishing." The Apocalypse explains how this is so, by the vision of the Divine scheme of things, in which the World, the persecutor, is conquered and evanescent, while permanence and reality belong only to the Church which the World has vainly tried to destroy. In this vision the Empire and its action towards the Church must be expressly described. But neither in the Apocalypse nor in the Epistle is it described with the intention of advising Christians as to their behaviour in the face of persecution. The writer is always remote from that point of view, and on a higher plane of thought.

6. Hebrews and Barnabas.

The Epistle to the Hebrews throws little light on the relation between the State and the Church, nor does this subject throw much light on that enigmatic work. The persons addressed have been exposed to taunts and afflictions (x. 33), and have endured a great conflict. Yet the general tone, perhaps, implies that worse and more serious trials have been experienced by Christians elsewhere, and that the persons addressed may expect a more terrible trial in the immediate future. The whole spirit of the advice given them seems to be directed to prepare them for serious persecution, and therefore the writer must already be familiar with persecution of that type.

By the language of xii. 4 this impression is confirmed. The persons addressed were up to the present not sufferers

of persecution that had been carried as far as death.*
But the example of the heroes and heroines of old, who by
faith were enabled to resist death and extreme torments, is
urged upon them at such length, and with such earnestness,
as to show that the writer considers them to be threatened
by a similar fate.

This summary practically assumes the point, and dis-
regards the difficulty. It gives far too much definiteness to
what is expressed in fainter outlines and in a less precise
way. But, if it at all correctly represents the tone of
the Epistle, the date of composition appears to be about
64–66. But, first, there is in the Epistle an absence of
expressions which are specially and obviously appropriate
to the character of the Neronian trials; and, secondly, a
certain poverty of meaning is on this supposition attributed
to x. 33 (ὀνειδισμοῖς τε καὶ θλίψεσιν θεατριζόμενοι), which may
however be in keeping with the rather rhetorical style of
this writer. Yet no other date suits better, for there is an
equal absence of expressions that would be suitable if the
letter were composed at some critical period of later history
—*e.g.*, under Domitian. Moreover, it is probably easier to
understand the want of definiteness in the writer's attitude
towards the State, if he belonged to an earlier period.
Perhaps the reason for this difficulty of fitting the letter
to any special date lies in its style, which is further away
from the realities of life, and more rhetorical and abstract
than the letters of St. Paul.

The Epistle of Barnabas is assigned by Weizsäcker and
Lightfoot to the reign of Vespasian. The date is reckoned

---

* The sense which Wordsworth, for example, gets from this verse
by pressing the force of the aorist seems to me quite unacceptable,
for it is not consistent with οὔπω.

by them from the passage in which Daniel is quoted : " Ten
kingdoms shall reign upon the earth, and after them shall
rise up a little horn, who shall lay low three of the kings in
one." The writer quoted this to prove that the last day
was approaching, for this sign was in actual fulfilment when
he was writing. Weizsäcker and Lightfoot differ in the
details of their explanation, and the latter certainly is more
satisfactory. In one respect they seem both to miss the
truth. Both say that Vespasian is the tenth king—*i.e.,* the
tenth Roman Emperor ; but they differ about the three
kings that are laid low by the little horn. Weizsäcker finds
them in Galba, Otho, and Vitellius, overthrown by Vespasian. The objections to this are obvious. Vespasian is
made to do double duty, as one of the ten kings, and also
as the little horn ; moreover, Vespasian did not in any
sense lay low Galba, but vindicated his memory. Lightfoot explains the little horn as the returning Nero, who was
expected to destroy the three Flavii, Vespasian, Titus, and
Domitian, conceived to reign together as Augustus and two
Cæsars. In this explanation a difficulty suggests itself. It
is clearly implied that the three who are to be destroyed at
a blow are all included in the ten, whereas on this explanation an eleventh and twelfth, viz., Titus and Domitian,
have to be added to make up the three. But little change
is needed. We have only to bear in mind that, in the time
of Vespasian, Otho and Vitellius were not regarded as
Emperors, for Vespasian claimed to succeed Galba directly,
and to avenge his death on the two usurpers.* Vespasian
therefore was the eighth, Titus the ninth, and Domitian the

* It was a later idea to reckon Vitellius and Otho among the
twelve Cæsars. To do so in the time of the Flavian Emperors would
have been treason.

tenth king; and three kings reigning together between 70 and 79 were according to widespread belief destined all to perish together at the hands of the expected Nero. This remarkable situation fulfilled the sign of the prophet Daniel, and portended the approaching end of the world; and this part of the Epistle of Barnabas was therefore written under Vespasian.

The subject of the Epistle gives little or no occasion for alluding to the relation of the Christians to the State. Only in the concluding part, "the Two Ways," is there any opening for such allusion; and here we find little or nothing bearing on the subject, except the advice to "be subject to masters as the image of God" (§ 19). The impression here given is that the writer, like Paul and Peter, insists on the strict observance of the actually existing laws. The Christians are not to give any countenance to changes of the established order; they are to accept the present situation, and to remember that their own world is a different one.

7. THE EPISTLE OF CLEMENT.

The evidence of Clement, in the letter to the Corinthian Church, written, perhaps, about A.D. 97,[*] is very important. After quoting from ancient Jewish history various examples of the evils wrought by jealousy, he proceeds:—

"But let us come to those champions who lived very near to our time. Let us set before us the noble examples which belong to our generation." He quotes at some

---

[*] Lightfoot argues convincingly that Clement wrote under Nerva, i., p. 352; but elsewhere he regularly speaks of the *Epistle* as composed in the latter years of Domitian.

length the sufferings of St. Peter and St. Paul; and he then proceeds : " Unto these men of holy lives was gathered a vast multitude of the elect." The idea of two distinct and isolated persecutions is forced upon these words in accordance with the tradition of the second century, which mentions only two great persecutors, Nero and Domitian.* But Clement is most naturally understood as referring to a continuous persecution throughout his own generation, keener perhaps at one time than at others.

It appears probable that after the death of Domitian, as after the persecution of Nero, there was a temporary cessation of a policy which had been carried to an extreme. There was in each case a certain revulsion of feeling, which is expressly attested in the earlier case by Tacitus, and which may be inferred in the second case both from Clement's expression "the sudden and repeated calamities and reverses which befel us," † and from the statement of Dion that Nerva dismissed those who were awaiting their trial on the charge of sacrilege. Hence Clement was apparently writing during a lull in the storm of persecution ; while it was at its height, he had no time to attend to the reports which reached him about the Corinthian church. But Clement knows well that the present is only a momentary lull ; he says in § 6 that " we are in the same lists [with those who have been slain], and the same contest awaiteth us."

---

* Lightfoot, though on the whole he takes this view, remarks about the " vast multitude of the elect," that " the reference must be chiefly, though not solely, to the sufferers in the Neronian persecution."

† Lightfoot translates as if the text were γινομένας, but in the text he reads γενομένας, which alone has MS. authority, and which he expressly prefers, i., p. 352, ii., p. 8, although the Syriac translation has a present

Clement has been interpreted * as implying that there had never been a persecution at Corinth: "a profound and rich peace had been given to all." But the context shows that here the thought in the writer's mind is not of persecutions. He is speaking of that peace and freedom from dissensions which formerly characterised the Church of Corinth, but which characterised it no longer.

8. The Letters of Ignatius.

One other work remains, which throws much light on the spirit of this time, but it is a work whose date and authenticity are more keenly contested than those of any other in Christian literature. The letters of Ignatius have certainly formed a subject for forgery to work upon on an extraordinary scale. But, after Lightfoot's arguments, it is clear that the supposition of a forgery in the case of the seven central documents entails the belief that a tale coherent, probable in itself, and yet unusual in some points, was constructed as a basis, that the letters are written on this foundation, and, without ever formally referring to the incidents of this tale, pre-suppose them as having actually occurred ; that this tale disappeared from memory ; that it was flatly contradicted by a later forger, who remodelled the original forgery, and also by all tradition ; and that it remained for scholars in recent years, and especially for Lightfoot, to disentangle this tale from the obscure language of the genuine letters, and thus enable us to comprehend the skill of the most skilful forger known in history. He that is not prepared to admit all this is

---

* By Gebhardt and Harnack, in *Prolegomena* to their edition of *Clement*, p. lvii.

bound to admit the genuineness of what Lightfoot calls the Middle Recension.

Strange to say, it is not possible to prove from the actual words of Ignatius that a general persecution was going on at the time. The situation in which he was placed made any such allusion unnecessary. No exhortation to face persecution could strengthen the effect of his mere example. In his letter to the Romans, § 5, Ignatius refers to previous cases in which the beasts had "refused through fear to touch" martyrs exposed to them. The passage does not, indeed, explicitly mention that the victims were Christians; but it is natural and probable that he should refer to martyrs. This shrinking of the beasts from human beings is often referred to in the best and most authentic Acts of Martyrs; and M. Le Blant has discussed the subject with his usual learning and critical sense.* But if we except this letter, no direct reference to persecution occurs; though there is a general implication that Ignatius is suffering the common lot of Christians. His attention is almost exclusively devoted in the other six letters to the affairs and the future of the churches to whom he writes. But even where he makes no express reference to it, Ignatius leaves the feeling in the reader's mind that persecution and suffering are general.

A subtle difference exists, in respect of our subject, between the two groups of letters, the four written from Smyrna, and the three from Troas.† In the latter nothing occurs for our purpose; the former abound in delicate

---

* *Actes des Martyrs*, p. 86 and 95; see below, p. 404.

† Incidentally we may notice this difference in thought as a proof of genuineness: it implies a difference of situation, such as is inexplicable on the theory of forgery.

phrases, the most explicit of which may be quoted. The life of the Christian is a life of suffering, the climax of his life and the crowning honour of which he gradually makes himself worthy is martyrdom, and Ignatius is far from confident that he is worthy of it (*Trall.*, 4). Suffering and persecution are the education of the Christian,* and through them he becomes a true disciple (*Ephes.*, 3; *Magn.*, 8, 9). The teacher, then, is the person or church which has gone through most suffering, and shown true discipleship; and Ignatius distinguishes Ephesus and Rome as his teachers (*Ephes.*, 3; *Rom.*, 3). Ignatius is still in danger, not having as yet completely proved his steadfastness, whereas Ephesus is proved and firmly fixed, the implication being that it has been specially distinguished by the number of its martyrs (*Ephes.*, 12); and, moreover, Ephesus has been the highway of martyrs, the chief city of the province where many, even from other parts, appeared before the proconsul for trial, and at the same time the port whence they were sent to Rome (see p. 318). A detailed comparison is made in *Magn.*, 8, 9, between the prophets and the Christians of the age. The prophets were persecuted, and the Christians endure patiently in order to become true disciples. When such is the principle of the Christian life, that suffering is the best training, it is the devil's teaching to make any compromise with the world, and to ask pardon for one who has been condemned, as the State would express it, or promoted to the crowning glory, as the Church should consider it (*Trall.*, 4).

The impression which had been produced by persecution

---

* He repeats in a new sense the principle of Æschylus, to suffer is to learn, *Agam.*, 170, and often.

on the feeling of the Christians towards the Empire is very strongly marked in the letters of Ignatius. Outside of the Apocalypse the irreconcilable opposition between the State and Christianity is nowhere more strongly expressed than in them ; and there runs throughout both groups of writings the same identification of the State with the World,* and the same rejection of the slightest compromise with the World. The same magnificent audacity towards the State, the same refusal to accept what seemed to men to be the plain facts of the situation,† the same perfect assurance of victory characterise both. In both the point of view is that the Church is the powerful party, and that the State is the criminal. The Church must act with the strong hand, not with gentle persuasion, in its dealings with the State.‡ Christians must not speak of Christ and desire the World.§ The opposition between the Church and the World is of course a commonplace of Christianity, and in itself would be no indication of the period to which the letters of Ignatius belong ; but it would be difficult to find at any time, except 90–112, a form so extreme as the thought reaches in Ignatius. He considers that even the slight recognition of the State, which is implied in asking for clemency to a condemned Christian,

---

* I do not mean that in these documents the World means the State, and nothing else : the State is the most definite, concrete, and pressing form in which all that is implied in the phrase "the World" faces and opposes the Christians. The point of view in Ignatius and John is that the State is wholly summed up in "the World," that it is absolutely and exclusively bad, and opposed to the Church.

† οὐδὲν φαινόμενον καλόν.—*Rom.*, 3.

‡ οὐ πεισμονῆς τὸ ἔργον ἀλλὰ μεγέθους ἐστὶν ὁ χριστιανισμὸς, ὅταν μισῆται ὑπὸ κόσμου.—*Rom.*, 3.

§ μὴ λαλεῖτε Ἰησοῦν Χριστὸν κοσμὸν δὲ ἐπιθυμεῖτε.—*Rom.*, 7.

is treason to religion, and an unworthy compliance with the temptations of the World.

The character and the thought of the letters of Ignatius, then, are those of a person whose mind had been formed in the period of the Flavian persecution, amid the same circumstances which led to the writing of the Apocalypse ; but at the same time there are some subtle indications that the feeling of Ignatius was, in this respect, not entirely shared by the Church. The Church in Rome, in spite of its glorious past history, is, as Ignatius hints (*Rom.*, 2), disposed to seek favour with men, and to gain influence at the expense of compromise with the world. The obscure paragraph in *Trall.*, 4, seems to be a reply to a hope expressed by the Trallians through their messenger-bishop, that a person so important and distinguished as Ignatius might, after all, be spared to the Church through the exertions of the influential Romans.* Moreover, Ignatius seems always to feel it necessary to explain his attitude in respect to martyrdom, and to justify it. Hence arises the violence of expression which has offended many readers ; for a man is sometimes apt to compensate by strength of expression for weakness of reasoning, and Ignatius felt that the reasoning which we hypothetically attribute to the Trallians might be generally considered truer than his own. The very influence attributed to the Roman Church indicates a time when the policy of the State was not so uncompromisingly hostile as we suppose it to have been before A.D. 112. If we were asked to specify the period which is best suited by these indications, we should have to name

---

* This expression may have suggested the composition of the immediately following letter to the Romans (see Lightfoot, ii., p. 186). I assume that the order of the letters in Eusebius is chronological.

the conclusion of Trajan's reign or the earlier years of Hadrian's. We observe also that the Church in Antioch got peace from persecution soon after Ignatius was taken away;* and he heard this news at Troas. This indicates a sporadic, rather than a settled action; and takes us into the period of concession.

The opinion with regard to the letters of Ignatius which has been advocated by Dr. Harnack is hardly consistent with this view. He quite admits the genuineness of the letters, but considers that there is no trustworthy evidence for dating Ignatius' martyrdom in the reign of Trajan; he therefore places the journey to Rome and the composition of the letters about 130–40.† It seems, however, improbable, if Ignatius had written so late, that his tone should be so different from that of the *Apology* of Aristides, and so like that of the Apocalypse. The tone that was roused by the Flavian persecution might naturally continue for some years after the relaxation of its severity by Trajan about 112; but it is difficult to admit that letters composed about 135 should be unaffected by the new spirit, of which Hadrian was the most thorough exponent. If the evidence of our ancient authorities with regard to the date of Ignatius pointed to the later date, we should have to accept it, and modify the view which is expressed in these and the following chapters. But

* On this subject also there is a distinction between the letters from Smyrna and those from the Troad: *cp. Philad.*, 10; *Smyrna*, 11; *Polyc.*, 7; *Ephes.*, 21; *Magn.*, 14; *Trall.*, 13; *Rom.*, 9.

† The possible confusion between the successive Emperors Nerva Trajan and Trajan Hadrian (according to their official names) has been appealed to as favouring the substitution of Trajan for Hadrian in tradition. See Harnack in *Theolog. Literature*, 1891, col. 304*n*; he quotes the analogous case of the *Apology* of Aristides.

the evidence, though (as Dr. Harnack has shown) it is scanty and inconclusive, points to the same date which our view of the relations between Church and State indicates as most natural ; and therefore we adhere to the tradition, and date the letters not later than Trajan, and preferably between 112 and 117.

Ignatius is the only individual Christian who is described as having been sent for public exhibition in the amphitheatre at Rome. But it is a well-attested fact that criminals were often utilised in this way ; and the condemned Christians were treated by the Government in the same way as other criminals. The wider popularity of sports, both shows of wild beasts (*venationes*) with other exhibitions of the Roman style, and athletic contests in the Greek style, was one of many results of the spread of Græco-Roman civilisation in the Eastern provinces during the second century. It is therefore probable that, in the age of the Antonines, criminals in the Eastern provinces were, with growing frequency, reserved for sports at home. There even grew up a custom among provincial governors of obliging one another in case of need with a gift of criminals for exhibition in the hunting scenes of the amphitheatre; and this custom had to be formally prohibited by a rescript of Severus and Caracalla 198–209 A.D. But in the time of Domitian and Trajan the case was different ; such criminals were not much needed in the Eastern provinces, while they were in great request in Rome.*

The enormous scale of the exhibitions in the Flavian amphitheatre, which is commonly known as the Colisseum,

---

* Provincial governors were strictly forbidden from releasing criminals who had been condemned to the beasts, as a concession to the populace. *Digest*, 48, 19, 31.

was probably the reason why this practice became so common at that time. The building was dedicated in A.D. 80, and Martial's earliest extant work, the *Liber Spectaculorum*, describes some of the more remarkable sights which were shown on the occasion. The reign of Trajan was also distinguished for the great scale of these disgusting exhibitions, which were a recognised part of the means employed by the Imperial policy for amusing and instructing the people under its fatherly care (Lft, i. 354).

But though Ignatius is the only individual case which is known to us, the evidence of the Apocalypse, as explained by Mommsen, is clear that this practice was a common one in the case of Christians ; and we have one passing reference to it in a hitherto unexplained expression used by Ignatius in writing to the Church at Ephesus: "Ye are a high road of them that are on their way to die unto God."* Ephesus was the chief port for the trade from the interior of Asia Minor, the leading city of Asia, and the place where the Roman governor was by regulation obliged to enter the province. Ignatius himself did not pass through it ; but the road by which he travelled was apparently an unusual one, due to some special circumstances. In ordinary circumstances, probably, he would have been sent from Syria by sea direct to Italy ; but he was conducted over land by Philadelphia, Smyrna, Troas, and Philippi to Rome.† Ephesus is the sea-end of the road along which

---

* πάροδός ἐστε τῶν εἰς Θεὸν ἀναιρουμένων.—*Ephes.*, 12.

† It is needless to conjecture, with Zahn (*Ign. v. Ant.*, p. 253, with whom Lightfoot is half disposed to agree, i., p. 362, ii., p. 211), that Ignatius sailed from Seleuceia to a Cilician or Pamphylian harbour. (1) The natural route to Philadelphia is by the Syrian and Cilician Gates ; and, unless there is evidence for an unusual route, we must suppose that the regular road was followed. (2) The

most of the criminals sent to Rome from the province of
Asia would be led, and at Ephesus they would find ships
to take them to Ostia.*

---

words of Eusebius, *H. E.*, iii. 36, more naturally suggest the land
route, whatever be the value of his evidence.   (3) The words in
Rom., 5, " by land and sea," are rightly explained by Lightfoot, ii.,
p. 211, as referring to the entire journey.

* The expression which Ignatius uses about Ephesus is similar
to that which Clement uses of Corinth, § 1 : τίς γαρ παρεπιδημήσας
πρὸς ὑμᾶς τὴν ὑμῶν . . . πίστιν οὐκ ἐδοκίμασεν ; on this passage Lightfoot remarks in his commentary : " Corinth was a natural halting-
place on the journey between Rome and the East " ; and in § 10
and § 35 he alludes to the frequent occasion which the Church at
Corinth had, to show hospitality to travellers.

CHAPTER XIV.

THE POLICY OF HADRIAN, PIUS, AND MARCUS.

I. HADRIAN, AUGUST 11TH, 117, TO JULY 10TH, 138, A.D.

THE most important evidence about Hadrian's attitude towards the Christians is his rescript addressed to Minucius Fundanus, who was proconsul of Asia about A.D. 124, a few years after Tacitus had filled the same office, and about twelve years after Trajan's rescript to Pliny had been issued. A word is needed on the question whether this important document is genuine. The external evidence is, as Lightfoot says, " exceptionally strong : " it was quoted in full by Justin Martyr in his first *Apology*, addressed about A.D. 140 to Antoninus Pius, and was mentioned by Melito in his *Apology* addressed to Marcus Aurelius about thirty years later. Such evidence, of course, cannot be disbelieved, if the genuineness of the documents is admitted. But some modern critics, such as Keim, Aubé, Lipsius, Overbeck, who have adopted a false view of the relations between the Church and the Empire, find that the rescript is very inconvenient for them. It is too clear and explicit to be misinterpreted in the way that they have misinterpreted Pliny's report and Trajan's rescript and it is irreconcilable with their view. Accordingly they declare that it must be a forgery. Justin refers to it only in the last chapter of his *Apology*, and this can easily be cut off. Hence for no reason except to save a hasty theory from being still-born, the last chapter of the *Apology* is pronounced spurious. It would be difficult to surpass the childishness of the argument against the genuineness of the conclusion of Justin's *Apology*, but Keim surpasses it in his discussion of Melito's reference to the rescript. This reference cannot be eliminated from Melito's *Apology*, nor can the *Apology* be pronounced spurious. The only resource, therefore, is to consider that the rescript had been forged before Melito wrote, and was accepted by him as genuine. Now after Keim has cut away from Justin the chapter where the rescript is quoted, he finds, of course, that Justin does not refer to the rescript. Accordingly he argues that, as Justin knows nothing about Imperial letters, whereas Melito quotes the letter to Fundanus, the letter must have been forged in the interval.* It is really adding insult to injury, first to deprive Justin of his chapter appealing to the rescript, and then to quote him as a proof that the rescript had not yet come into existence. Justin does not quote Trajan's letter to Pliny, therefore it also must, by parity of reasoning, be spurious ; and we can date its origin as accurately as the origin of Hadrian's letter. Athenagoras, about 177, did not know of Trajan's letter, whereas Tertullian quotes it in his *Apology* about 197 ; therefore it had been forged in the interval. How easy it is on this principle to prove and date the forgery of every ancient document !

The result of the polemic against the rescript is to bring

---

* "*Als Entstehungszeit wird man die Jahre von der justin'schen Apologie, welcher keine Kaiserbriefe kennt und ein Hauptmotiv zur Entstehung derselben bot, bis zum Beginn des aurel'schen Verfolgungssturmes (Frühjahr, 177) ansehen dürfen, etwa 160-176, am ehesten doch das Jahr, 176.*"—Keim, *Aus dem Urchrist*, p. 183.

out more clearly its inconsistency with the views advocated by Keim, Aubé, etc., as to the relations of the Church to the Empire, and to relieve us from the necessity of discussing them. With regard to the perfect conformity of the rescript with the general history of the time, a very strong opinion has been pronounced by Mommsen, who says * that "the groundless suspicions cast on the genuineness of this document are the best proof how little capable recent writers are of understanding the attitude in which the Roman Government stood to the Christians." Lightfoot's remark of older date † is in full agreement with the opinion of the great historian : "not only is this rescript no stumbling-block when confronted with the history of the times. Some such action on the part of the Emperor is required to explain this history. . . . Short of actually rescinding the policy which made the profession of Christianity a crime, there must have been a vast amount of legal discouragement."

This rescript is on the same lines as that of Trajan, but goes beyond it in several points.

(1) Its intention is defined as being to prevent innocent persons from being harassed and false accusers from being allowed free scope.

(2) The provincials may indeed prosecute their suit against Christians before the tribunal of the governors, but they must bring forward evidence, and not confine themselves to petitions and shouting, "Away with the Christians!"

(3) Proof is required that the Christians have offended against the law.

---

* *Histor. Zft.*, xxviii., p. 420.
† *Ignatius*, i., p. 462 (478, ed. ii.).

(4) If the prosecutor fails to make good his case, he must be punished as a false accuser.

There is in this rescript a studied vagueness in regard to the crimes of which proof is required. It is not expressly admitted, as it was by Trajan, that the Name is a crime ; on the other hand, that established principle is not rescinded. As to the offence against the law which must be proved against the Christians, it is quite open to any governor to consider that the Name is an offence ; but it would also be quite possible for him to infer from the rescript that some more definite crime must be proved. With this uncertainty facing him, the accuser might well dread failure and the consequent penalty. Everything would depend on the personal character of the judge ; and we can quite under-stand how one governor might readily find the case proved when the accused acknowledged the Name, whereas another might point out to the accused how they could answer the questions in such a way as to escape all penalty without violating their religion.*

* This is said to have been done by Cincius Severus. (See Ter-tullian, *ad Scap.*, iv.) He was, perhaps, proconsul of Africa between 180 and 190. (See Tissot, *Fastes de Prov. Afr.*) An example may be given of the methods which Cincius Severus might suggest to the Christians. The oath *per genium Cæsaris* was forbidden to Christians, and was not used by them ; but the oath *per salutem Cæsaris* was lawful for them, and was a proper and widely recognised form among the pagans. A governor who was friendly towards the Christians might accept a solemn oath *per salutem imperatoris* or *imperatorum* as a sufficient guarantee of loyalty, and might enter in his records (Plin., *ad Traj.*, 96, 4 ; *Digest.*, 48, 17, 1, 2) that the accused person had complied with the test of loyalty, and shown due respect to the cultus of the emperors, while an unfriendly governor might demand a more satisfactory proof of loyalty. Ter-tullian approves of the oath *per salutem*, Apol., § 32, *sed et juramus sicut non per genios Cæsarum, ita per salutem eorum.* (The

The Emperor himself, the Olympian god who roamed over the Empire, looking into every religion, initiated into various mysteries, was quite alive to the fact that the State religion was a sham, and, looked at as a religion, a failure ; but he knew also that it was the keystone of the Imperial policy, and he could not or would not face the task of altering it.   He leaves the religious question quite open, and lets the rival sects fight it out for him to watch. In this ordinance about a religion he never alludes to the idea of religion.   No other person could have written such a rescript ; and without any evidence we might have identified it as Hadrian's.   That a Christian should have forged such a document without introducing some reference to religion is most improbable ; and had the idea not been maintained by such distinguished scholars as Keim, Lipsius, Overbeck, etc., we might have been tempted to use stronger language.

Such action as that of Hadrian's was, of course, quite illogical, and could not continue as a permanent policy. The rescript was a sarcasm, and none knew this better than Hadrian himself.   But sarcasm is not government, and the Empire had to be governed.

The rescript left to Hadrian's successors a difficult problem in their relations with the Christians.   It did not settle any principle ; and one of the most important clauses in it was susceptible of very various interpretations.   The most certain points in it were that Trajan's prohibition of seeking out the Christians was confirmed, and that the

---

Apologeticum was written in 197 A.D., when two Cæsars were reigning.)   Dio Cassius, xliv., 50, says, οἱ τήν τε ὑγίειαν τήν τε τύχην ὤμνυσαν.   Numerous inscriptions show how common was the formula ὑπὲρ σωτηρίας τοῦ Αὐτοκράτορος.

prosecutor who failed to make out his case was to be punished for false accusation (*calumnia*). But still the settled principle remained in operation, that any Christian might be ordered to execution at any time by any governor of a province. The most important effect of such acts as those of Trajan and Hadrian was to require some definite person, willing to take on himself the invidious character of accuser (which had hitherto been almost equivalent to murderer) of some definite person.

There are many indications that various circumstances might originate a short and temporary enforcement of the general law and practice. But apart from this, in the period on which we are now engaged, the Christians must have been, to a considerable extent, protected against accusers by their own strength and union. The professional accuser (*delator*), though necessitated and encouraged by the Roman laws,* was always highly unpopular.† Even in our own country a private prosecutor has always to face a certain prepossession against him, which can be overcome only by a complete proof of the justice of his plea. But in the Mediterranean lands there is a much stronger feeling, for law and police are tacitly regarded as enemies to the individual citizen to an extent that we can hardly understand, at least after we have ceased to be boys at school ; and the same feeling existed in ancient times. Occasionally revenge produced a *delator*; but usually an accuser was actuated by hopes of gain. In free Rome of the Republic, political advancement was sometimes the inducement ; but generally the actual rewards in money or position,

---

* There was no public accuser, and many laws were inoperative unless private initiative set them in motion.

† Compare Horace, *Sat. I.*, 4, 66.

promised in several individual laws to successful prose-cutors, elicited *delatores*. In the case of prosecutions on the charge of Christianity, no such rewards were to be obtained ; the *delator* would not win permanent approval even from those who hated the Christians, and who might encourage him at the moment. An isolated accuser would have much to lose, and could, in general, have little chance of gaining anything. Finally, the hatred of a united and energetic body like the Christians would, in itself, be a serious penalty, and, in places where Chris-tianity was very strong, might be a sufficient deterrent to any single prosecutor. The hatred which was popularly entertained for the Christians during the century following 64 A.D. was too intense not to contain a considerable element of fear. In modern history, the *Judenhass* and *Judenhetze* are strongest where the Jews are thought dangerous.

An example of the strong feeling entertained by the Christians against any who had been instrumental in procuring the condemnation of Christians, is found in the action taken in A.D. 320 against those who, in the great persecution by Diocletian and Maximian, had played the part of informers or accusers, or had delivered up to de-struction copies of the sacred books (*traditores*).

How then were accusers found in the face of such deterrent motives ? In the first place, from disturbance of trade. This is a subject on which we have very little information ; but that trade was highly developed and very influential in the Asiatic societies is obvious. We have already referred to the strike of the bakers in Magnesia (p. 200), which produced such serious consequences as to require the intervention of the proconsul. The circum-stances which led to the outbreak of persecutions in the

second century are almost wholly unknown to us, and no
case in point later than the hypothetical one of 112 (which
has been already alluded to) is known ; yet it is highly
probable that combined action of a whole trade was
occasionally instrumental in prompting the action of the
Government against the Christians.

In the second place, motives of a personal nature, such as
revenge, might occasionally induce individuals to face the
odium and appear as *delatores.* An example of this occurs
in the case of Ptolemæus, who was prosecuted before the
prefect of the city, Lollius Urbicus, about 152.*

But the great danger lay in popular excitement produced
by some sudden cause, some general calamity, or signs,
prodigies, and prophecies, which either made the multitude
by a unanimous impulse act as accuser, or raised individuals
beyond the influence of motives which, in saner moments
would weigh with them. As Tertullian puts it : " If the
Tiber rises, if the Nile does not rise, if the heavens give
no rain, if there is an earthquake, famine, or pestilence,
straightway the cry is, ' The Christians to the lions ! ' " †

Hence we see how strong Hadrian's rescript was, for it
expressly forbade the shouts of a crowd to be received as an
accusation, and required some definite individual to appear
and to take the risk of punishment if he failed to prove his
case.

That proceedings against the Christians were not quite
discontinued under Hadrian must be taken as certain. The
general principle of proscription had not been abrogated,

---

* See Borghesi, *Œuvres,* ix., 295; *Justin,* ii. *Apolog.,* 2. Lightfoot,
Ignat. i. p. 509, gives the date 155-160, after Borghesi, viii. 545 ; but
in the later vol. (1884) Borghesi inclines to an earlier date.

† *Apolog.,* 40.

and the evidence as to this and the following reigns is clear. Lightfoot is on this point not so accurate and logical as he generally is,* except in his concluding phrase, that our knowledge is too scanty to permit the inference that no prosecutions of Christians took place under Hadrian. But when he disposes of all the *Acta* which assign martyrdoms to this reign, on the ground that " the reign of Hadrian was a convenient receptacle for these real or supposed martyrdoms which were without a date," it is impossible to follow him. The reign of Domitian, who in all later time was one of the typical persecutors, was equally convenient, and was comparatively empty ; so also was the reign of Trajan. There occur under Hadrian more martyrdoms about which detailed *Acta* are preserved, than under Domitian or Trajan ; but the reason is that Hadrian was later, and nearer the time when Christian historians flourished. More actual names of individuals were remembered under his reign ; but even in their case, hardly anything of perfectly authentic character is preserved. The *Acta* are fabulous, or nearly so ; but that does not warrant the rejection of the tradition as unhistorical, or the assertion that martyrs attested by the older martyrologies are purely fictitious (pp. 405*n*, 434*n*).

Nor can we accept Lightfoot's explanation that here " misinterpretation of Eusebius' words " by Jerome originated the belief in a persecution under Hadrian. Eusebius' statement is that Quadratus composed his *Apology* because " certain wicked men were endeavouring to molest our people " ; and Lightfoot holds that " the implication is that they were thwarted in their endeavours." This seems too

---

* *Ignat. and Pol.*, i., p. 507.

strong an inference. Quadratus, a private citizen in Athens, could become aware of such endeavours only through their resulting in action. Hadrian did not hold a public discussion as to his policy, but the Christians, finding that he was disposed to relax in some degree the severity of the standing policy, and hoping that he would listen to argument, began to defend their cause in formal *Apologies.* That Eusebius knew few facts regarding Hadrian's action is certain ; but his comparative ignorance was due to the dearth of authorities. The *Apology* of Aristides is itself the best proof that a defence and a protest against the accepted policy were thought necessary by the Christians.* But after all deductions are made, the fact remains that the lot of the Christians in this reign must have been comparatively a happy one after their experiences before A.D. 112.

Rescripts such as that addressed by Hadrian to Fundanus were secret and confidential documents. We learn the exact terms of some, in whole or in part, in ways not contemplated by the writers, and quite apart from their nature. Trajan's was published—of course with the Emperor's permission—in the collected correspondence that passed between him and Pliny ; and many fragments of others are quoted in the law books, and thus preserved to us. Hadrian's was quoted by Justin Martyr about twenty years or less after it was written. How had it become known to the Christians? This is a point of some interest, but an answer cannot be given with certainty. Possibly Hadrian himself may have intentionally allowed

* The view of Professor Rendel Harris is that Aristides addressed, not Hadrian, but the succeeding Emperor Hadrianus Antoninus, in the beginning of his reign.

it to be brought to their knowledge. But, so far as I can judge, it is more probable that its terms became known to them through their influence in the province of Asia and in the bureau (*officium*) of the proconsul. That supposition is quite in accordance with the general impression we receive, that the new religion was very widespread and influential in this and the neighbouring provinces before the middle of the second century. We find an example which has some bearing on this point in the case of Florinus, who was listening to Polycarp's lectures in Smyrna along with Irenæus, while he was attending the Imperial court and enjoying high favour there. The exact date and the precise circumstances are as yet a matter of conjecture. In the great uncertainty about Irenæus' birth and early life the facts may belong to any time between 135 and 150. But it is quite probable that an inscription may any day be found giving a clue to the circumstances and time when an imperial visit, otherwise unknown to us, was made to Asia during this period.*

It is of course possible that the Christians bought a copy of the rescript. Many instances are recorded in which they purchased from the clerks (*commentarienses*) copies of the official shorthand report of the proceedings at trials of martyrs, and these official *Acta* form the groundwork of many of the tales of martyrs, and are even reproduced verbatim in some of the best and most authentic accounts.†
The rescript would certainly be preserved in the proconsular archives of the province of Asia.‡

* This is a fair example how much may reasonably be expected from the progress of investigation and discovery.

† Le Blant, *Actes des Martyrs*, pp. 65 and 70.

‡ *Archivum proconsulis* is the phrase used by St. Augustin in reference to Africa (*contra Cresconium*, iii. 80 (70), Le Blant, pp. 63–4.

2. ANTONINUS PIUS, JULY 10TH, 138, TO MARCH 7TH, A.D. 161.

The more liberal procedure of Trajan and Hadrian was, on the whole, maintained in this reign. The general tone of the rescript to Fundanus seems to have characterised the letters addressed by Antoninus Pius to several cities of Greece and Thrace, forbidding disorderly procedure against the Christians.* These letters confirmed the section in Hadrian's rescript, ordering that mere tumultuous shouting should not be taken as a formal accusation of the Christians. They required that the proper procedure before the governors of the provinces should be observed, and forbade any riotous action on the part of the populace. In this very restriction, however, it is implied that the regular formal procedure was still maintained, and was, in the opinion of the Emperor, fully adequate to the requirements of the case. As to the facts which occasioned these letters, we may assume with some confidence that tumultuous action, similar to that which took place at Smyrna in A.D. 155 against Polycarp, had occurred in various other cities about the same time; and the Emperor wrote to the Athenians, Larissæans, Thessalonians, and the Greek cities in general,†

---

* The reasoning of Neumann (p. 28), Overbeck (*Studien zur Geschichte*, etc., p. 146 ff.), and others, about these letters is vitiated by their wrong interpretation of the phrase μηδὲν νεωτερίζειν. This does not indicate "innovations," as they understand it, but riotous and tumultuous action. In the Latin original *novæ res* was, no doubt, the phrase. Lightfoot rightly translates the phrase, *Ignat.*, i., 459. The letters are mentioned by Melito, in a lost *Apology* addressed to Marcus Aurelius, and quoted by Eusebius, *H. E.*, iv., 26.

† Among these Smyrna is included. The phrase is not "cities of the province Achaia," but "all Hellenes," which includes those of the Ægean coast. Compare the coin on which the people of Tralles claim to be the "First of the Greeks," see above, p. 157 n.

reminding them of the actual state of public law, and warning them against stretching municipal action too far, and encroaching on the powers of the Imperial Government (see p. 393*f*).*

The action of the citizens of Smyrna was in direct disobedience to the rescript of Hadrian; but the rescript was in advance of public feeling, and was therefore liable to be disregarded. It seems also clear that the proconsul was a weak official. This is shown by his attitude towards the mob. His inclination and sense of duty urged him to give Polycarp a further hearing and a formal trial, if he could "prevail upon the people;" but their shouts impelled him to order, or rather to permit, immediate execution.† We may suppose that the passions and fears of the mob were strongly excited by some recent great calamity, for many events of that kind are mentioned in the reign of Pius.‡ In Smyrna a serious earthquake had occurred not long before, A.D. 151 or 152 apparently.§

This series of outbreaks of popular feeling in the Greek cities points to some widely spread cause; and the circumstances of the following reign show that the cause was

---

* This point of view is involved in νεωτερίζειν and *novæ res*. The precise time when the letters to the cities were written is not recorded. Melito implies that it was after the assumption of Marcus Aurelius as Cæsar in A.D. 147; and the reasoning in the text shows that it was probably soon after the action of the Smyrnæans in A.D. 155.

† See § 10 of the letter of the Smyrnæans.

‡ *Script. Hist. Aug.*, iii., *Vit. Anton.*, 9.

§ Lightfoot, *Ignat.* i., p. 461, following Waddington, *Fastes*, § 141; but the latter gets his date from the forged letter of Antoninus to the Koinon of Asia, which he assigns to A.D. 152, whereas Mommsen and Lightfoot, p. 483, put it in 158. Probably the date for the earthquake is pretty accurate.

a general revival of paganism in a more philosophic and reasoned form.

A larger body of detailed information is extant about the sufferings of individual martyrs under Antoninus Pius than under Hadrian. Lightfoot has clearly shown this,* but we need not infer that the Christians really suffered more. We are now coming nearer the period when regular contemporary registration of Christian history began ; and moreover, the extraordinary personal importance of Polycarp secured the preservation of the facts of his death.

The language of Justin and of Minucius Felix is conclusive as to the existence of persecution in this reign. In his first *Apology* Justin appeals direct to the Emperor against the principle now enforced that the mere Name is a capital offence. He argues against it on the ground of justice and legality, and quotes the rescript to Fundanus as a proof that Hadrian was opposed to it. He did not find it serve his purpose to quote Trajan's rescript, which expressly affirmed the principle ; and his silence about the rescript is no argument that he did not know it. The later rescript of Hadrian might fairly be considered as overruling the earlier.† But he does not refer to the actual seeking out of Christians as practised by the Government officials, and we shall see that in this respect the authorities for the succeeding reign differ greatly from him.

A procedure conforming to the rescripts of Hadrian

---

* *Ignat. and Pol.*, i., p. 509.

† I need not quote all the passages in *Justin*, which are numerous. (See Lightfoot, *Ignat. and Pol.*, i., p. 534.) The date of Minucius not later than A.D. 160 appears to Lightfoot established by the passages quoted by Schwenke. I have not the right to express any opinion on the date of Minucius ; but, if the words are pressed in that way, they point to a period before A.D. 147.

and Antoninus was employed in the case of Ptolemæus and Lucius. Neither of them was sought out by the prefect, Lollius Urbicus, but private accusers came forward against the former, and the latter offered himself voluntarily.* The exception in the case of Polycarp has been shown to be an infraction of the established rule.

A good example of the action which a Roman official might take at the time is furnished by the case of Pudens, who, as Neumann has shown, was probably proconsul of Cyrene and Crete a few years before 166.† He expressly declared that he was forbidden by the instructions (*mandatum*) of the Emperor to investigate the case of a Christian, unless a formal accuser appeared; and, after tearing up the document of accusation which was sent along with the prisoner, he dismissed him on the ground that no individual prosecutor had come forward.

3. MARCUS AURELIUS, MARCH 7TH, 161, TO MARCH 17TH, 180.

The larger policy of Trajan and Hadrian was not understood by Marcus Aurelius. His ideal was to be the true Roman; and a decided reaction towards the older narrow Roman policy is apparent during his reign. He could not of course "stem the torrent of descending time"; ideas

---

* Lollius was, according to Borghesi, *præfectus urbi* about 152. See note, p. 327.

† Tertullian, *ad Scap.*, iv. The usual view is that Pudens was proconsul of Africa when the incident occurred; but Neumann's reasoning establishes the strong probability of his case. If the usual view were correct, Pudens' proconsulate would have to be dated under Commodus; for his action is contrary to the character of procedure under Marcus, but similar in style to that of Cincius Severus, which has been quoted previously (p. 323).

enlarged, policy widened, and the conception of Rome developed insensibly and inevitably. But philosophic leanings now no longer inclined toward Christianity and against the Imperial rule, as in the Flavian period. The Cynics indeed were still in opposition to the narrower policy, and championed the cosmopolitan spirit, which was steadily marching towards its final triumph. But popular *dilettante* Greek philosophy was no longer on the side of the opposition. It was now seated on the throne; and for the time the Imperial policy coquetted with other favourites, and lost sight of the goal towards which history was moving.

Christian thought was diametrically opposed to the Greek ideals of social life;* and for a time, while the retrogressive tendency in the Imperial policy lasted, a union took place of the Roman power and the Greek philosophic influence, in opposition to the Christian re‑organisation of society. They allied themselves with the current religions, and tried to make explicit in the ceremonial paganism the higher ideas, which certainly were latent beneath the gross and detestable exterior of its mystic rites. Paganism, which the Imperial policy had throughout the first century, from Augustus to Domitian, tried in vain to galvanise into life, began even under Hadrian to feel, under the stimulus of opposition to Christianity, the pulse of returning life. The mysteries set before the initiated a doctrine which might compete with Christian doctrine, and might prove that the higher truths of life and morality had been stolen from

---

* I do not refer here to questions of morality. The introduction of the purest morality into Greek ideals would have left them still essentially opposed to the Christian principles of society.

them by the Christians. Already in 134 A.D., Hadrian was greatly interested in watching the contest between the doctrines of Christianity and the mysticism of the religion of Serapis, which he considered to be of much the same character and rank.*

It seems clear that during this reign the active pursuit of the Christians became a marked feature. Celsus in his *True Word* speaks of them as being sought out for execution.†

The evidence of the Christian writers is to the same effect. Melito, about 170–171, refers to new edicts, according to which the Christians are pursued.‡ Such persecution he declares to be unprecedented.

It would also appear, if Melito can be trusted, that rewards were promised to informers from the property of the accused; for the informers are said to be greedy for property of others, and to spoil the innocent by day and by night.

Athenagoras, about 177–180, also refers to the harassing, plundering, and persecution of the Christians, and the fines imposed on them (which are probably the rewards given to informers). He speaks also in strong terms about the Name being suffcent proof of guilt, and entailing death.§

---

* See the letter to Servianus, quoted in *Script. Hist. Aug.*, xxix., (*Vita Saturnini*) 8 ; Lightfoot, *Ignat. and Pol.*, i., p. 480.

† See Origen, *c. Celsum*, viii., 69. The date of Celsus' work has been the subject of much discussion, but it may be probably placed in this reign, when conjoint Emperors were in power, either in 161–169, or 177–180. The variation between the singular and the plural in referring to the sovereign authority is characteristic of many documents of the period. (See p. 249.)

‡ Quoted by Eusebius, *H. E.*, iv., 26: καινὰ δόγματα, προστάγματα.

§ *Libellus pro Christianis*, I. etc.

Theophilus of Antioch, about 180, also mentions that the Christians were pursued and sought out in his time.*

The *Acts of Martyrs* give similar evidence. The governor of Gallia Lugdunensis sought out the Christians in 177 ; and already at the beginning of the reign, Justin Martyr and four companions were brought before Junius Rusticus, Prefect of the City in 163. In the beginning of the *Acta Justini*, it is said that the arrest was made in accordance with decrees enforcing worship of idols on the part of the Christians. It is clearly implied that the accused were sought out by officers in consequence of these decrees, and were not formally accused by any individual. Having acknowledged their religion, they are ordered to sacrifice, and the order is repeated with threats of severe punishment.

The seeking out of Christians, then, is a marked feature in all documents relating to the time of Marcus Aurelius ; whereas there is not a trace of evidence that it was practised under Antoninus Pius, and it had been forbidden by Trajan and Hadrian. Keim has correctly observed that it begins under Marcus Aurelius ; † but we hold that this was the re-introduction of the Flavian practice, the only logical course when Christianity was a crime.

---

* The word διώκουσι, which he uses, reminds us that the officials charged with this duty and commanded by the *Eirenarch* were styled διωγμῖται. See O. Hirschfeld, *die Sicherheitspolizei im röm. Kaiserreich*, p. 28 (*Berl. Sitzungsber.*, 1891, p. 872).

† "*Unter M. Aurel kam die Verfolgung des ' Atheismus' recht im Schwung und unter ihm erst kam es zur Aufsuchung der Christen.*"—*Aus dem Urchrist.*, p. 99. Justin, in his first *Apology*, written under Pius, is emphatic about the Name being a capital crime ; but he makes no reference to the seeking out of Christians or to rewards for accusers.

These facts prove clearly that new methods were introduced by Marcus Aurelius, at least in the sense that proceedings against the Christians were enforced more actively, though the penalties remained the same. The question arises how this was brought about. Was it by a general edict? Was it by a clause inserted in the general instructions to governors? Or did the governors merely act on the knowledge that the Emperor was inclined to act logically in respect of the Christians, and, as they were criminals deserving death, to seek them out actively?

Some expressions occurring in the documents of the period would, if taken strictly, imply that an edict on the subject was issued. But probably they are simply rather loose phrases, which must not be taken too strictly. Melito, who speaks of " new decrees " in one place, uses in another the term " instructions." * The latter term is probably the right one ; the action towards the Christians was guided by the Imperial instructions to provincial governors (*mandata*). These instructions, as has been shown, were susceptible of varying interpretation, according to the feeling of the governor and the tone of the reigning Emperor. During this reign the general revival of religious feeling would naturally lead to a stricter and logical interpretation of the instructions ; especially as it would rapidly become known that the Emperor was not opposed to this course.

The question remains, whether there was any actual change made in the instructions by Marcus? Neumann considers, p. 33 *n.*, that there had previously been actually a clause in the instructions, forbidding the seeking out of

---

* καινὰ δόγματα, *nova decreta*, in the former case, προστάγματα, *mandata*, in the latter. In *Acta Justini*, i., also the word is προστάγματα.

Christians, and that this prohibition was abrogated by Marcus. He quotes the action of Pudens, as above described; but it is very doubtful whether the proof is sufficient. Such a clause may perhaps have been inserted in the instructions issued by Hadrian and Pius to their lieutenants in the provinces; but the variability of procedure would rather suggest that the inconsistencies which we have described continued to exist throughout this whole century, and that none of the Emperors did anything beyond replying by rescript to questions which their lieutenants addressed to them. The lieutenants had the general instructions to seek out and punish sacrilegious persons, etc., and Christians were sacrilegious. The lieutenants might then either carry out the instructions logically, or observe the rescripts of Trajan and Hadrian forbidding the hunting out of Christians. Under Marcus the logical course was the rule.

We conclude, then, that no actual change was made by Marcus Aurelius in the wording of the clauses that regulated the attitude of the provincial governors towards the Christians. He did not professedly alter the policy of his immediate predecessors, and yet the spirit of that policy was, for a time, changed.

Far more cases of persecution are known in this than in the preceding reign; but no stress can be laid on this fact. Contemporary record of historical facts had now begun among the Christians, and the interest in preserving Christian documents and the *Acta* of martyrs dates from about the sixth decade of this century. The principle of proscription still continued; and persecution had never ceased even under the most tolerant Emperors.

Neumann's view (p. 32) is very different. He traces the

intensification of persecution in this reign to a rescript, dated, according to his view, in A.D. 176, forbidding the introduction of new religious rites which tended to unsettle the minds of the people. This view we cannot accept. (1) It does not explain the facts, for the seeking out of Christians seems to have been practised before 176 (*Acta Justini,* 163, *Melito,* perhaps 170). (2) The rescript was merely a reply to some question addressed to the Emperor, and does not appear to have been the basis of procedure against Christians, for it was approved by Christian Emperors, and retained in the Digest. (3) In 177 the Christians at Lugdunum do not appear to have been punished for proselytising ; nor did they suffer the milder penalties of this rescript.* The procedure is the same as of old, but carried out with more activity.

Coincident with the change of policy there was a revival of the old charge of *flagitia* against the Christians. It is quoted from Fronto, the tutor of Marcus, and it is mentioned in connection with the persecution at Lugdunum in 177. The evidence of slaves was used in support of it ; and the statements made even by Christian writers, not very much later, about actual scandals, suggest that the revival was only an exaggeration of real evils.

4. THE APOLOGISTS.

With Hadrian's rescript begins the age of *Apologies—* *i.e.,* formal defences of the faith. Christianity had now a hearing granted to it. Before 112, when the religion was

---

* Neumann quotes the expression of the populace at Lugdunum, ξένην τινὰ καὶ καινὴν εἰσάγουσι θρησκείαν, Euseb., *H. E.,* v., 1, 63 ; but this phrase was not used in the trial, nor did the thought affect the proceedings. Neumann follows Keim in his dating, see p. 321 *n.*

absolutely condemned, an *Apology* would have been absurd. Now that the Imperial policy was hesitating about its attitude, and a trial was allowed, defence and argument might have some effect ; and a long series of formal pleadings in defence were addressed to the Government, beginning, perhaps, about 129, when Aristides presented his *Apology* to Hadrian during his visit to Athens.*

Defence and argument imply a recognition of the authority to which it is addressed. The spirit of which we discerned some slight indications in Ignatius' letters (see p. 315), had developed greatly before the first *Apology* was presented. In the age which produced 1 John and Apocalypse, and which nourished the spirit of Ignatius, an *Apology* would have been treason to religion. The irreconcilable opposition to the actual system, and the aspiration after an absolutely new era and a new society, had now been given up. The Church responded to the tone of Hadrian's action : mutual allowance and an approximation between the two great enemies began.

The Apologists always express or imply with regard to the character of Trajan's action the same view that we have taken. It is indeed true that the Apologists were special pleaders, and that their testimony in certain respects must be discounted to a certain degree. But they were advocates of at least fair ability and good sense ;

---

* The *Apology* is noticed in Euseb., *H. E.*, iv., 3, and dated in *Chron.*, A.D. 125 ; but Hadrian's second visit is the only one that can be thought of. Professor Rendel Harris brings down the date to 140. Eusebius seems to treat Hadrian's rescript as the effect of the *Apology* ; but this is, no doubt, pure conjecture, and we rathe consider the *Apology* as elicited by the rescript.

misrepresentation of the Imperial action was subject to immediate contradiction, and could only injure their cause. They would naturally darken the colours of the picture which they drew of contemporary paganism; they saw only the bad side of it, and no student of ancient life can accept their account as complete. But, if the view that Trajan was the institutor of formal persecution were correct, it is hard to see how sane men could think to effect any good by misstating plain facts of recent history to the Emperors. The Apologists of the second century stand on a much higher intellectual level, if our interpretation of the evidence is correct.

The objection may be urged against the credit of the Apologists that Tertullian speaks of Marcus Aurelius in terms much more favourable than facts seem to warrant.* But, as we have seen, Marcus did not formally make any change in the policy of his predecessors, though he favoured a more severe interpretation of the clauses on which that policy was based; and he ranks, in a general view, with Trajan, Hadrian, and Pius, as contrasted with the uncompromising spirit of the Flavian Emperors; and this is all that Tertullian asserts.†

Moreover, it is obvious that Tertullian firmly believed in the existence of a letter from Aurelius to the Senate, ascribing to Christian soldiers the merit of a great deliverance from imminent danger during his German wars. It is impossible, and, unless new documents are discovered (of which hope need not be abandoned), it must always

---

* *Apolog.*, 5.
† Tertullian expressly notes that Marcus did not alter the general principle of condemning Christians. This is exactly what we have to remark about all these Emperors.

remain impossible, to discover the truth of that famous
legend. So much is certain : (1) such a deliverance did
occur, and was universally attributed to the special in-
terposition of Heaven ; (2) there were many Christian
soldiers in the army ;* (3) the Christians at the time
attributed the deliverance to the prayers of these soldiers,†
(4) pagan historians narrated the almost miraculous event,
but explained it differently. It is not safe to assert absolutely, what is the most simple explanation, that Tertullian
merely assumes that there existed a letter of Marcus to
the Senate, declaring that the deliverance had followed the
prayers of the Christians, and denouncing penalties against
their accusers. This explanation is apparently simple ;
but it leaves unsolved the greatest difficulty of the case—
viz., how could Tertullian entertain the belief which he
expresses so positively in a document addressed to the
Senate, if it were contrary to all facts and all non-Christian
evidence and belief ? It is clear that Tertullian was not
conscious that any opinion different from his own existed,
or that any member of the Senate would be likely to

---

* In accordance with the method of recruiting the Roman army,
as deduced by Mommsen, *Hermes*, 1884, pp. 8 ff, and stated very
precisely for Africa by Cagnat, *l'Armée Romaine d'Afrique*,
pp. 353 ff., Legio XII. Fulminata, whose permanent station
(*stativa*) was at Melitene, would be originally recruited from the
Eastern provinces ; but after Hadrian (Mommsen, p. 21) the
recruiting for it would be almost wholly restricted to the adjacent
provinces of Asia Minor. Christianity was specially strong in
these provinces ; "and," as Mommsen remarks (*Histor. Zft.*,
xxviii., p. 419, *n.* 2), "the camp and the court were always centres
of Christianising influence."

† Apollinaris is strictly contemporary ; Tertullian wrote within
about twenty-three years of the event.

challenge his statement. There seems to be more in the story than we can as yet fathom.

The Apologists do not ask for a change of law; they ask for a regulation of practice to accord with the law of the State. They demand for Christians a fair trial on some definite charge, attested by witnesses, with permission to make and prove their defence. They ask to be brought under the ordinary law; and they inveigh against the exercise of arbitrary authority against them on no definite charge. This, the most elementary right of citizens, had been absolutely denied them by the Flavian policy, which treated them as brigands. Trajan had left the Flavian principle unaltered, but had exempted them from active pursuit. The Apologists justly argue against the illogical nature of a policy which treats them like brigands when any one formally accuses them, but does not take the trouble to look for them: if they are brigands, it is the duty of the State to hunt them down. Even Hadrian had shrunk from the decisive step of clearly stating that Christianity was not in itself a crime; and this is the step which the Apologists urge upon the Emperors whom they address.

In support of this claim the Apologists advance various arguments : (1) that their religion has a high moral tone, and is absolutely inconsistent with the gross crimes which were currently charged against them; (2) that it is of a higher moral character than Paganism, and is therefore an educative influence in the State; (3) that Christians are loyal citizens, and, though they are compelled by their religion to abstain from some of the conventional signs of loyalty, yet in all essential points they discharge its duties fully; (4) that a name is not in itself a crime, and that even a brigand is not punished for the name he bears, but only after the truth has been proved in regard to his actions.

An essential point in the Christian doctrine was the unity and brotherhood of all men ; and the same idea was being gradually wrought into the Imperial system. Trajan and Hadrian, two Spaniards, free from the narrower Roman tradition, were, not unnaturally, the leaders in the policy of mercy towards the party that carried out most logically the idea which they themselves did much to work out in practice. Tatian expresses this idea more clearly than any other of the Apologists, and contrasts it with the theories of Greek philosophy, which always clung to the old separation of states, and the belief that moderate size was of the essence of a state. In § 28 he professes the cosmopolitan doctrine, and rejects the narrower systems which separate state from state. The true philosophy maintains that there should be one common polity for all, and one universal system of law and custom. The Christian doctrine, § 29, puts an end to the servitude that is in the world, and rescues mankind from a multiplicity of rulers. Its aim, § 32, is universal education, not education confined to the rich, as among the Greeks and Romans ; its principle is free education to the poor, and it makes no distinction of sex, but admits all to its universal system of education. He defends, § 33, the Christian custom of women studying philosophy.*

---

* Tatian did not address any Emperor ; but he employs similar arguments with the other Apologists, sometimes expressing them more sharply. Tertullian's *Apologeticum* would need a chapter to itself.

CHAPTER XV.

CAUSE AND EXTENT OF PERSECUTION.

WE have now determined the main facts in regard to
the action of the State towards the Christians
before A.D. 170. We have next to inquire into the reason
why the Empire proscribed this sect. The question is
presented to us as a paradox : the Empire being remarkably
tolerant, as a general rule, in religious matters, what reason
was there for the persecution of this religion ?

I. POPULAR HATRED OF THE CHRISTIANS.

There can be no doubt that the dislike generally entertained towards the Christians was an element in determining the attitude of the Emperors and their delegates
towards them. The governors, and even the Emperors to
a less degree, acted in some cases simply to conciliate the
populace, and keep it in good humour. The action of Nero
was, as we have seen, turned against the Christians through
his wish to supplant one passion by another in the popular
mind. Having private reasons for seeking to divert the
populace, he tortured for their amusement a class of persons
whom they hated.

We have found reason to think that at first Christianity
was received in Asia Minor, and perhaps in the West
generally, without any detestation, and even with considerable favour. The growth of the opposite feeling was due
to various social causes, among which probably the strongest

were (1) loss incurred by tradesmen whose business was interfered with by the habits which Christianity inculcated ; (2) annoyance caused in pagan families by the conversion of individual members. In the latter case it is clear that the anger felt by the pagan members of any family would, as a rule, be proportionate to the degree of affection that had existed before the family was disunited. The stronger the love that had held together the family, the stronger the hatred that would be felt against those who had introduced discord into it.

Spurred on by such causes, private individuals tried to revenge themselves on those whom they considered to have injured them, whether by riotous and illegal action (Acts xiv. 19, xvii. 5, xix. 23 ff.), by action before the magistrates of provincial cities, who were not empowered to inflict severe penalties (Acts xvi. 19), or by moving the Roman law (Acts xix. 38).

Various methods of prosecution before ordinary tribunals might be, and frequently were, employed by individuals who felt themselves aggrieved. Some of these have been already referred to (p. 250 f.). Riotous conduct, disturbance of the public peace, sedition, and sacrilege, were charges that readily suggested themselves (Acts xix. 37), and might be tried with good hopes of success ; but a purely religious charge was derided by the Roman officials (Acts xviii. 15–17). * We have seen that

---

* St. Paul's experience in Corinth of the favour of the Roman courts as a defence against the Jews seems to have produced a powerful effect on his thought and teaching. This event divides the two letters to the Thessalonians by a deep chasm from the group of Galatians, Corinthians, Romans. There is a remarkable change of feeling as we pass from one group to the other.

charges of breaking up the peace of family life formed the subject of anxious consideration and advice both to St. Paul and to St. Peter (see pp. 246, 281); and we cannot doubt that such charges had often been carried into court. The father or husband or master dealt in private with the individual members of his family;* but he must go before the courts in order to punish the person who had tampered with their beliefs and habits. In such actions probably the accusation of unjustifiable interference with the sphere of duties and rights belonging to another,† though not recognised as a criminal category, would be useful to excite odium and bad feeling, a practice in which extreme licence was conceded to pleaders in Roman courts.

The persecution of Nero made the situation of the Christians distinctly worse, without altering its general character. The Emperor's action in allowing certain charges, moral, rather than criminal, to be urged against Christians, constituted a precedent, and exercised a strong influence on all provincial governors in judging such cases; but still the same method remained in practice, and the governors in Asia Minor still stood as judges between the Christian and his accuser; "for praise to them that do well" (1 Peter ii. 15). Christians suffered by being convicted as criminals, and not as Christians; defence lay in a life above suspicion (1 Peter iv. 25).

---

* Tacitus, *Annals*, xiii., 32. Pomponia was judged by her husband *prisco instituto*, A.D. 58.

† The Latin term, *alienum speculari*, and the noun, *alieni speculator*, suggested the extraordinary Greek rendering ἀλλοτριοεπίσκοπος, 1 Peter iv. 15, which is quite unintelligible, except as a rough attempt to translate a foreign term that had no recognised equivalent in Greek (see p. 293 *n*).

It is not true that mere social annoyances could have had a serious character, until, through Nero's example, they were abetted and completed by action on the part of the Roman administration ; and it is regrettable that several excellent authorities have countenanced this unhistorical view.* It is true that James implies persecution of a more serious character, as taking place before the Neronian policy had come into force ; but James wrote to Jews, who were not governed solely by Roman law, but who, down to A.D. 70, administered justice to a certain extent among themselves, according to their own sacred law, even in Roman cities of the Eastern provinces. Of course the most serious penalties, and especially death, were beyond the independent Jewish jurisdiction ; but still much suffering could be legally inflicted by Jews on other Jews, unless the victims possessed the Roman citizenship. † Hence the situation of Jewish Christians before A.D. 64 was much more serious than that of Gentile Christians ; but after that year official Roman action could be invoked with confident expectation of success against both classes, and after A.D. 70 the self-governing privileges of the Jews were entirely withdrawn.

---

* Weiss' commentary on 1 Peter (*die katholischen Briefe,* Leipzig, 1892), whatever be its merits in a textual or theological view, is a distinct retrogression from Holtzmann and other critics when regarded as a historical investigation. On Spitta, see p. 300.

† The Jews could act against the Roman Paul only by rousing official Roman action on some pretext. Gallio probably did not allow the case to go far enough to find out whether Paul was Roman, but dismissed the case to the Jewish tribunals. In the case of Jesus, the Jews could not make the matter a serious one, except before the Roman tribunal. The Jews, even in Palestine, could not suffer to death (Heb. xii. 4), except before a Roman governor.

Experiences of the kind described, though annoying in themselves, could never have been a serious evil or danger to the Christians ; and the Apologists of the second century argue in favour of the restoration of this procedure (*Justin*, i., 3 ; *Tatian*, 4, etc.), claiming a fair statement of charges against each Christian, an open trial, and liberty of defence against the accusation. While this kind of persecution alone was available against them, the Christians had fair treatment and toleration from the Roman officials, and on the whole looked to them for protection. Paul himself suffered personally a good deal of hard treatment ; but he is an exceptional case. A poor Jewish stranger, almost a beggar, whose language in public had led to much disorder among the Jews, and who was exposed to the enmity of rich and influential Jews, must not be taken as a fair instance of what known citizens would suffer in their own land.

It was not merely the populace who felt this dislike to the Christians ; the governors of provinces, the officials of every class, the Emperors themselves, shared it. Even such a humane spirit as Pliny was so shocked by the demeanour of the Christians on their trial that he mentioned it to Trajan, as in itself a sufficient reason for condemnation. The Greeks were difficult enough to deal with. Cicero speaks of their perverse humour, with which all Romans who had dealings with them must reckon ; * and every proconsul of Asia could tell many a tale of the unreasonable ways of the Greeks in the

---

* Perversitas, *Fam III.*, i., 4. Every Turkish governor would give the same account now. Greeks under his power make his life a burden to him.

coast cities. But the Roman governors found the Christians much more difficult to manage than the Greeks.

Popular feeling, therefore, was strongly on the side of persecution ; and there can be no doubt that the reason for the severity of Marcus Aurelius lay in the dislike which he shared with the educated and uneducated classes alike. Void of insight into social questions, and raised above enthusiasm by philosophy, Marcus honestly carried out against the Christians the principles in which he believed.

It would be a mistake to look for the reason of the antipathy towards the Christians in their disobedience to any single law. The Christians were so diametrically opposed to the general tendencies of the Government and of the ancient social system, they violated in such an unshrinking, unfeeling, uncompromising way the principles which society and philosophy set most store by, that to prosecute them under any one law, or to think of them as ordinary criminals guilty on one single count, was to minimise their offence in an apparently absurd degree. It was true that a Christian was guilty of treason against the Emperor, and as such deserved death ; but to put his crime on that footing was to class him with many noble and high-minded Romans, who had been condemned for the same offence. It was true that he practised a foreign and degrading superstition ; and that he induced many Roman citizens to desert their patriotic loyalty to the religion of their country and their fathers, and to go astray after a fantastic and exaggerated devotion ; but the worshippers of Isis and of Sabazios did something of the same kind, and the fashion was to treat this offence with contemptuous toleration. It was true that Christians cut themselves off from all Greek culture, from everything that was good and noble; that they broke up family ties, and set brother against brother; that their words, thoughts, and acts were alike void of good result for society; that they stood aloof from the pleasures, the religion, and the duties of educated or loyal citizens; held no official position; comforted none who were in sorrow; healed no dissensions; gave no good counsel; made poverty and beggary into virtues; practised robbery under the guise of equality, and shameless vice under the cloak of rigid virtue; made evil into good, and reckoned ugliness as beauty; laid claim to be the true philosophers; and spoke villainous Greek. But, as the very man who paints this picture implies, so did the Cynics;* yet the Cynics were merely satirised and ridiculed.

The combination of so many and various faults, combined with the power given them by their close union, and the fear which mingled with and embittered the general hatred, rendered them pre-eminently the object of popular fury; it seemed absurd to apply to such people any ordinary judicial process. Hence the Flavian proscription, which treated them like brigands, met with general approval. One cry alone was adequate to the case—*Christianos ad leones.* If they gave only annoyance to the world during their life, let them at least afford society some compensation by amusing it at their death.

Some of the traits in the picture drawn by Aristides

---

* Aristides, ὑπὲρ τῶν τεττάρων, vol. ii., p. 400 f. (Dind.) So unsuitable do some of the traits appear to Lightfoot, that he refuses to accept it as a picture of the Christians, and declares that the Cynics were the model for Aristides to paint from (*Ignat.*, i., p. 533). But I cannot separate the picture wholly from the Christians, nor believe that the Cynics alone could have aroused the deep-seated hatred which is here expressed. They were not sufficiently power-

partake (to put it mildly) of exaggeration and prejudice; but if we wish to understand this question we must approach the subject from the point of view of the Empire, and of the educated classes of pagan society, and try to realise their views. We must, for the moment, assume the attitude of those who found the fabric of society assailed by the Christians with a bitter undistinguishing hostility and contempt, which the student of classical antiquity must feel to have been not wholly deserved.

But action that consists only in occasionally yielding to pressure from popular passions does not constitute a policy. We have seen that a permanent proscription of the Name of Christian was implied in Pliny's first action; and it is impossible to suppose that the permanent policy of such a government as the Roman was determined by mere feelings of personal and popular dislike. We cannot suppose that these passions weighed with Trajan, when he reaffirmed the general principle of proscription. Hadrian and Pius expressly forbade that popular clamour should weigh against a Christian; but they both left the general principle in force. The direct and strong antagonism

---

ful to cause fear; and only an enemy which is also feared can rouse such intense hatred. The Cynics and the Christians were united in the mind of Aristides and his compeers as two members of one class, differing in some respects, but, on the whole, of the same type, and this picture gives the features common to the class. The Greek philosophers objected to the cosmopolitan spirit and superiority to the narrow Greek state, which characterised both Cynics and Christians. Neumann, pp. 35-6, has caught excellently the spirit of this passage, following a fragment of Bernays, *Gesammelte Abhandl.*, ii., p. 362, which seems to imply a change from the view expressed in *Lucian und die Kyniker*. In that work Bernays considered the description to be intended for the Cynics alone.

23

against the State which rules in Apocalypse and Ignatius cannot be thus explained. We must look deeper for the real ground of the Imperial action, which, as we have seen, was probably determined about 75–80 A.D.

2. REAL CAUSES OF STATE PERSECUTION.

The success of the Imperial Government in the provinces rested greatly on its power of accommodating itself to the ways and manners and religion of the subjects; it accepted and found a place in its system for all gods and all cults. Religious intolerance was opposed to the fundamental principles of the Imperial rule, and few traces of it can be discerned. It proscribed the Christians, and it proscribed the Druids. In these two cases there must have seemed to the Imperial Government to be some characteristic which required exceptional treatment. In both cases there was present the same dangerous principle : both maintained an extra-Imperial unity, and were proscribed on political,* not on religious, grounds.

On the other hand, the Jews must have appeared to the Government to resemble the Christians very closely. Almost every trait in the picture drawn by Aristides applies to them, and they also were the object of general hatred. But so far from yielding to the popular feeling in this case, the Imperial policy protected the Jews on many occasions from the popular dislike.

---

* Mommsen says (*Provinces*, i., p. 105) "the institution of the Gallic annual festival in the purely Roman capital . . . was evidently a countermove of the Government against the old religion of the country, with its annual council of priests at Chartres, the centre of the Gallic land." See also Duruy in *Revue Archéologique*, April 1880, p. 247 (347).

If the Jews appeared to the Empire to resemble the Christians so much, and yet were treated so differently, the reason for the difference in treatment must have lain in those points in which the Christians differed from the Jews in the estimate of the Imperial Government.* In so far the Jews were merely a body professing a different religion; the Emperors allowed them the completest toleration. But so long as the Jews maintained an articulated organisation, centred in the Temple at Jerusalem, they maintained a unity distinct from that of the Empire; and this fact was brought home to the Emperors by the great rebellion of 65–70. The Flavian policy (see p. 254) made a distinction between the Jewish religion and the Jewish organised unity; the former was protected, but the latter was proscribed. Titus conceived that the destruction of the temple would destroy the unity centred in it; and he substituted the temple of Jupiter for the temple at Jerusalem, collecting for the former the tax hitherto contributed by the Jews for the latter.

With the Jews it was found possible to separate their religion from their organisation. The destruction of the temple, indeed, had to be completed under Hadrian by the destruction of Jerusalem, and the foundation of a new Roman city there. But, to a great extent after 70, and completely after 134, the Jews accepted the situation assigned them by the State—religious toleration on condition of acquiescence in the unity of the Empire.

---

* Tacitus, indeed, says (*Hist.*, v., 5) that the Jewish rites *antiquitate defenduntur*; but he is not here professing to explain formally why the Empire favoured the Jews. The distinction in this point of antiquity between Judaism and Christianity had more weight in philosophy than in government.

Titus at first entertained the belief that the Christians also had their centre in the temple, and that their unity would perish with it (p. 254). But soon the Flavian Government recognised that their united organisation was no whit weakened by the destruction of the temple. The Christians still continued, no less than before, to maintain a unity independent of, and contrary to, the Imperial unity, and to consolidate steadily a wide-reaching organisation. Such an organisation was contrary to the fundamental principle of Roman government. Rome had throughout its career made it a fixed principle to rule by dividing; all subjects must look to Rome alone; none might look towards their neighbours, or enter into any agreement or connection with them. But the Christians looked to a non-Roman unity; they decided on common action independent of Rome; they looked on themselves as Christians first, and Roman subjects afterwards; and, when Rome refused to accept this secondary allegiance, they ceased to feel themselves Roman subjects at all. When this was the case, it seems idle to look about for reasons why Rome should proscribe the Christians. If it was true to itself, it must compel obedience; and to do so meant death to all firm Christians. In the past the success of the Roman Government had been greatly due to the rigour with which it suppressed all organisations; and the Church was a living embodiment of the tendency which hitherto Rome had succeeded in crushing. Either Rome must now compel obedience, or it must acknowledge that the Christian unity was stronger than the Empire.

This disobedience to the principles of Roman administration is only one form of that spirit of insubordination and obstinacy, which is so often attributed to the Christians

by the ancient writers, and which seemed to Pliny to justify
their condemnation. In his note on the passage (Pliny, *ad
Traj.*, 96), Mr. Hardy rightly remarks that "the feature of
Christianity which Pliny here points out as a sufficient
reason * for punishing them, was exactly the point which,
as Christianity grew, made it seem politically dangerous to
the authority of the Empire, and which, more than religious
intolerance, was at the root of later persecutions." We
ask why it should be left for Pliny to make the discovery
that the Christian principles were dangerous. He was not
the first governor of a province in which Christians were
numerous. He was not the character to display special
insight into the probable political outcome of new principles, or to be specially jealous of the authority of the
Empire. He was not a practised administrator. He had
never before held a province. He had been a skilful financier and good lawyer, whose entire official life had been
spent in Rome with the single exception of the necessary
months of military service as a tribune, and even this
term he had spent in managing the accounts of the legion.
He had been selected for this government because the
finances of the cities were in a bad state, and a trustworthy
and hardworking officer and good financier was needed to
administer the province. It is not too much to say that,
if Pliny perceived forthwith the disobedience that was inherent in the new religion, every governor of any Asiatic
province, every Emperor of Rome, and every prefect of
the city, must have made the same discovery for himself
long before 112.

* I have made one slight, but significant, change, substituting
"a sufficient reason" for "his personal reason." Compare note on
p. 214; also *excursus*, p. 374.

The cause here suggested, obvious as it appears, has been ridiculed as impossible by Aubé, who thinks it inconceivable that Nero should already have begun to suspect that the growth of the organised Christian religion might prove dangerous to the Empire. It is difficult to reply to such an argument. For my own part, I can see nothing improbable even in this supposition, and still less in the theory that the Flavian Emperors considered Christianity to involve a dangerous principle. I should only be surprised if the watchful Roman administration had failed to recognise at a very early moment that the principles of the new sect were opposed to its policy. Trajan refused to permit an organisation of 150 firemen in Nicomedeia, or to allow a few poor people to improve their fare by dining in company, on the express ground that such organisations involved political danger. The Christians so managed their organisation as to elude the law prohibiting *sodalitates* ; * but they could not elude the notice of the Emperors.

How can we understand the marvellous power which the Empire showed of Romanising the provinces, except on the supposition that it showed great practical ability in dealing with the various views and principles of different peoples ? and how is such practical ability to be explained, except on the supposition that the Imperial Government was keenly alive to the character and probable effect of any such system ? The Emperors were aiming at a great end ; they pursued it with all the experience and wisdom of Roman law and Roman organisation ; and they punished rigorously those who impeded their action.

---

* The discontinuance of Agapæ (see p. 215) for this reason in Bithynia may safely be taken as a type of the action of other Christians in this respect.

The principle of government just described is connected with, but still must be distinguished from, the restrictions imposed on the formation of *collegia* and *sodalitates*. The same jealousy on the part of the Government and the same distrust of the loyalty of the people underlies both. While Rome was a republic, all citizens had the right of forming associations at will; but as soon as the Empire began, it distrusted such associations, and Julius restricted them within the narrowest limits;* for the Roman Government now considered the Roman people as a danger to be guarded against. The old rule of prohibiting all attempts at union among the subject populations, appears under the Empire mainly under the form of prohibiting *collegia* and *sodalitates*; but it was really of much wider scope, and this prohibition was only one special application of a general principle.

This jealous principle of Roman administration was fatal to all vigorous life and political education among the subject peoples. It was an inheritance from the old narrow Roman system, which regarded the subject peoples merely as conducive to the benefit of Rome. The true interest of the Empire lay in abandoning this narrow and jealous spirit, and training the provincials to higher conceptions of political duty than mere obedience to the laws and the magistrates. Only in this way could it carry out

---

* Benefit clubs among poor people, associations for mutual assistance, alone were permitted; and these were allowed to meet only once a month for any purpose beyond religious ritual, which was of course unimpeded. The commonest kind of these clubs were Burial Societies; but it would be a mistake to suppose that these were the only examples of their class. The use of the term *collegia funeraticia* (a purely modern name) has sometimes led to the false idea that these alone were permitted. They were *collegia tenuiorum*.

its mission of creating a great unified state, characterised by universal citizenship and patriotism (see p. 192 *n.*). Here, as in many other cases, the Church carried out the ideas and forms towards which the Empire was tending, but which it could not realise without the aid of Christianity.

Political and religious facts were in ancient time far more closely connected than they are now. It was under the protection of religion that law, social rules, and politics, gradually developed. Before they had strength to exist apart, they maintained themselves as religious principles, enforced by religious sanctions and terrors. Thus the right of free general intercourse and free union among all subjects of the Empire, had for a long time no existence except as a religious fact.

The strength of the Imperial Government lay in its recognising, more fully than any administration before or since has done, the duty of maintaining a tolerable standard of comfort among the poorer classes of citizens. But while it showed great zeal as regards their physical comfort, it was less attentive to the other duty of educating them. The education imparted on a definite plan by the State did not go beyond a regular series of amusements, some of a rather brutalising tendency. Christianity came in to the help of the Imperial Government, urging the duty of educating, as well as feeding and amusing, the mass of the population. The theory of universal education for the people has never been more boldly and thoroughly stated than by Tatian (see p. 345). The weak side of the Empire —the cause of the ruin of the first Empire—was the moral deterioration of the lower classes: Christianity, if adopted in time, might have prevented this result.

3. ORGANISATION OF THE CHURCH.

The administrative forms in which the Church gradually came to be organised were determined by the state of society and the spirit of the age. In the conflict with the civil Government these forms were, in a sense, forced on it ; but it would be an error to suppose that they were forced on it in mere self-defence against a powerful enemy. They were accepted actively, not passively. The Church gradually became conscious of the real character of the task which it had undertaken. It came gradually to realise that it was a world-wide institution, and must organise a world-wide system of administration. It grew as a vigorous and healthy organism, which worked out its own purposes, and maintained itself against the disintegrating influence of surrounding forces ; but the line of its growth was determined by its environment.*

The analogy between the Church and the State organisations is close and real. But it would be a mistake to attribute it to conscious imitation, or even to seek in Roman institutions the origin of Church institutions that resemble them. The Christians would have indignantly rejected all idea of such imitation.

Hermas states (*Vis.*, ii., 4, 1) the view held by the early

---

* As I cannot hope to hit the passionless scientific truth in a subject so difficult as the present, or to avoid conflicting with widely felt emotions, where such deep and such opposite feelings are entertained, I shall simply indicate, in as unemotional and external way as I can, the view that seems best to explain the attitude of the State to the Christians. The Church is here treated not as a religious body, but as a practical organisation for social duties and needs, and as brought in contact with the State.

Church as to its own origin. The Church appears as an old woman, " because she was created first of all, and for her sake was the world made." The Church was to Hermas a well-articulated organism, and not a collection of individual Christians with no bond of union beyond certain common rites and beliefs ; yet its organisation was not constructed by the early Christians, but was a pre-existing, Divinely created idea, independent of the existence of actual Christians to embody it in the world.

But all the more surely and truly were the Christians under the influence of Roman administrative forms and ideas, that they were entirely unconscious of the fact. The secret of the extraordinary power exerted by the Roman Government in the provinces lay in the subtle way in which the skilful administrative devices, shown by it for the first time to the provinces, filled and dominated the minds of the provincials. After the Roman system was known, its influence took possession of the public mind, and is apparent both in every new foundation for administrative purposes, and even in the gradual modification of the previously existing organisations. Those institutions of the Church which belonged to its Jewish origin steadily became more and more Roman in character. Roman ideas were in the air, and, had the Church not been influenced by them, it would have been neither vigorous nor progressive. After all, Hermas' view and the one here stated differ little from each other. We are trying to express the same fact ; but in these pages the Divine is treated as a development, whereas to Hermas it was immutable and eternal, like a Platonic idea.

Like the Empire, the Church fully recognised the duty of the community to see that all its members were fed ;

and this was one of the earliest forms in which the question of practical organisation began to press on it (Acts vi.). Further organisation was required when many communities existed in different lands, all considering themselves as a brotherhood. Such separation involved, in the course of natural growth, the development of differences of custom and opinion in details; and in life details are often of more apparent value than principles. Questions arise in the relation of community with community. If these are not settled with judgment and skill permanent differences spring up. In the actual development of a Church scattered wide over the world, the officials whose duty it was to guide the communications between the communities necessarily played a decisive part in framing the organisation through which the brotherhood developed into the Church. As it was completed in its main elements by A.D. 170, the organisation of the Church may be described thus :—

1. Each individual community was ruled by a gradation of officials, at whose head was the bishop ; and the bishop represented the community.

2. All communities were parts of a unity, which was co-extensive with the [Roman?] world. A name for this unity, the Universal or Catholic Church, is first found in Ignatius, and the idea was familiar to a pagan writer like Celsus (perhaps 161–9 A.D.).

3. Councils determined and expressed the common views of a number of communities.

4. Any law of the Empire which conflicted with the principles of the Church must give way.

5. All laws of the Empire which were not in conflict with the religion of the Church were to be obeyed.

In this completed organisation the bishops were established as the ruling heads of the several parts, divided in space but not in idea, which constituted the Church in the Roman world. The history of this organisation is, to a great extent, the history of the episcopal power. The bishops soon became the directors of the Church as a party struggling against the Government. I should gladly have avoided this peculiarly difficult part of the subject, but it is not possible to discuss the relations of Church and State without showing the nature of these typical officers in the proscribed organisation. The view which I take is, that the central idea in the development of the episcopal office lay in the duty of each community to maintain communication with other communities. The officials who performed this duty became the guardians of unity. They acquired importance first in the universal Church ; and thereafter, partly in virtue of this extra-congregational position, partly through other causes, they became the heads of the individual communities.

Such a vast organisation of a perfectly new kind, with no analogy in previously existing institutions, was naturally slow in development. We regard the ideas underlying it as originating with Paul. The first step was taken when he crossed Taurus ; the next more conscious step was the result of the trial in Corinth, after which his thought developed from the stage of *Thessalonians* to that of *Galatians, Corinthians,* and *Romans.* The critical stage was passed when the destruction of Jerusalem annihilated all possibility of a localised centre for Christianity, and made it clear that the centralisation of the Church could reside only in an idea—viz., a process of intercommunication, union, and brotherhood (p. 288).

It would be hardly possible to exaggerate the share which frequent intercourse from a very early stage between the separate congregations had in moulding the development of the Church. Most of the documents in the New Testament are products and monuments of this intercourse; all attest in numberless details the vivid interest which the scattered communities took in one another. From the first the Christian idea was to annihilate the separation due to space, and hold the most distant brother as near as the nearest. Clear consciousness of the importance of this idea first appears in the Pastoral Epistles,* and is still stronger in writings of A.D. 80–100, as 1 Peter and Clement. In these works of the first century the idea is expressed in a simpler form than in writings of the second century, where it has a stereotyped and conventionalised character, with a developed and regulated appearance.

The close relations between different congregations is brought into strong relief by the circumstances disclosed in the letters of Ignatius : the welcome extended everywhere to him; the loving messages sent when he was writing to other churches (*Rom.* ix.); the deputations sent from churches off his road to meet him and convoy him (*Rom.* ix., etc.); the rapidity with which news of his pro-

---

* Its prominence in them is one of the many characteristics which distinguish them from the older Epistles, and which would make us gladly date these Epistles ten or twelve years after A.D. 67 (later they cannot be, on account of the undeveloped type of persecution which appears in them). But it does not appear worth while to sacrifice the tradition, and the claim they make to be the work of Paul, for the sake of a few years. We must accept the difficulty involved in their developed character. There is no person who is so likely to have originated these ideas as Paul, in the intense activity of his later years, A.D. 64–67.

gress was sent round, so that deputations from Ephesus, Magnesia, and Tralles were ready to visit him in Smyrna; the news from Antioch which reached him in Troas, but which was unknown to him in Smyrna; the directions which he gave to call a council of the church in Smyrna, and send a messenger * to congratulate the church in Antioch; the knowledge that his fate is known to and is engaging the efforts of the church in Rome. Such details in the letters and in other authorities presuppose regular intercommunication and union of the closest kind along the great routes across the Empire. Lucian was familiar with this intercourse among the Christians; and his language about it implies that it seemed to him the crowning proof of the detestable and perverted energy of the sect.† Lightfoot has correctly emphasised this class of facts, but he does not sufficiently bring out they were the regular and characteristic practice of the Christians; hence he quotes the passages of Lucian as proof that Lucian was acquainted with the story of Ignatius. But Lucian might have gained his knowledge from many other similar incidents as well as from the story of Ignatius; and the only safe inference from his words is, that the picture of life given in the letters of Ignatius is true.

This close connection could not be maintained by mere unregulated voluntary efforts; organised action alone was able to keep it up. The early system of government by the presiding Council of Elders was slowly developed to cope with the pressing need; and the episcopal organisation was thus gradually elaborated.

---

* *Smyrn.*, 11; *Philad.*, 10; *Polyc.*, 7. He is called θεοπρεσβεύτης, θεοδρόμος.

† *De Morte Peregrini*, 12 and 41.

The word *episkopos* means overseer. Originally, when the deliberative council of elders resolved to perform some action, they would naturally direct one of their number to superintend it. This presbyter was an *episkopos* for the occasion. Any presbyter might be also an *episkopos*, and the terms were therefore applied to the same persons, and yet conveyed essentially different meanings. The *episkopos* appointed to perform any duty was necessarily single, for the modern idea of a committee was unknown;* any presbyter might become an *episkopos* for an occasion, yet the latter term conveyed an idea of singleness and of executive authority which was wanting to the former. On the other hand, the idea of an order of *episkopoi* at this stage, like the order of presbyters, is self-contradictory. The *episkopos* was necessarily single, and yet there might be many *episkopoi* for distinct duties. Such appears to be the natural interpretation of the term, as it was used in ancient life.

It was natural that proved aptness and power in an individual presbyter should lead to his having executive duties frequently assigned to him. The Imperial idea was in the air ; and the tried *episkopos* tended to become permanent, and to concentrate executive duties in his hands. The process was gradual, and no violent change took place. The authority of the *episkopos* was long a delegated authority, and his influence dependent mainly on personal qualities. In such a gradual process it is natural

---

* Bodies of 3, 5, 10, or more officers were frequent in Rome ; but they were not committees. Each individual possessed the full powers of the whole body. The act of one was authoritative as the act of all ; each could thwart the power of his colleagues ; no idea of acting by vote of the majority existed.

that the position of *episkopoi* should vary much, that the position of the same individual should be susceptible of being understood and described differently by different observers, and that the *episkopos* became permanent in fact before the principle of permanence was admitted.

The hospitality which is assigned as a duty to the *episkopos* in 1 Tim. iii. 1 ff., Titus i. 5 ff., was closely connected with the maintenance of external relations (see p. 288); and the composition of the letters sent by one community to another was also assigned to him. Hence a copy of the message given to Hermas was ordered to be sent to Clement, who should send it to foreign cities, for to him had been entrusted the duty (viz., of communicating with other communities) ;* while Hermas, with the presbyters who preside over the Church (among whom Clement is, as we believe, included), was to read it to the Romans. This duty was likely to be permanently assigned to the same individual, for uniformity of tone could not otherwise be secured.

The scanty and unsatisfactory evidence of the first century points to the practical permanence of the *episkopos* as already usual, but is inconsistent with the idea that the *episkopos* was considered as separate in principle from his co-presbyters (as he continued for centuries to term them). He was only a presbyter on whom certain duties had been imposed. There was in practice one permanent *episkopos* in a community, when 1 Peter ii. 25 was written, and when the messages were sent to the *angeloi* of the seven Asian Churches; but the *episkopos* was very far re-

---

* *Vis.*, ii., 4, 3, I cannot doubt that, to a Roman Christian of the period, Clement must mean the famous Clement. Either Hermas wrote before Clement's death, or he intended that his book should appear to be of that period.

moved from the monarchical bishop of A.D. 170, and we find not a trace to suggest that he exercised any authority *ex officio* within the community. He represented it in certain cases; he wrote in its name; but the words purported to be spoken by the community. Letters addressed to it were sent to him; but the contents referred solely to the community, and made no allusion to the *episkopos*. His position was ostensibly a humble one within the community; and yet its real influence and its future possibilities must have been obvious to him that had eyes to see beneath the superficial aspect.* The importance of the *episkopos* would be estimated by a writer according to the degree in which his attention was occupied with the unity of the Church.† In Hermas the Church is thought of rather as distinguished from the wicked. He divides the world, one might almost say, into Christian and non-Christian, and heretics are to him mistaken teachers, as they are to Paul in Philip. i. 15–18. The organisation and practical mainte-

---

* Such is the nature of the office as it appears in *Apoc.* i. 16, 20. Spitta considers that the interpretation of the stars as bishops belongs to the revision, 90-112, not to the original Christian document, 60 A.D. His arguments, p. 37 f., are founded on a misapprehension of the delicate contrasts in the position of the *episkopoi*. Again, when Ignatius writes to Polycarp a private letter, he, in the middle of it, begins to address the whole community, being accustomed to regard Polycarp as its representative. Ignatius does not write as bishop, but as an individual, and in his own name: the church in Antioch has now no bishop.

† From Clement alone the permanence of his duties could not be inferred; but it is the natural inference from a comparison of Clement and Hermas' language about him. But it would be as wrong to draw from Clement, as it would be to draw from Polycarp's letter to the Philippians with its similar language (see Lightfoot, *Ignat.*, i., p. 594), any inference against the permanent concentration of episcopal duties in the hands of an individual.

24

nance of unity is not a thought that weighs much with him ; and he merely speaks in a general way of the heads of the community, οἱ προηγούμενοι τῆς ἐκκλησίας.

The language of Ignatius is more developed ; though there is, as a rule, some tendency to read him by the light of later facts. He is not a historian, describing facts ; he is a preacher, giving advice as to what ought to be. He lays most stress on the points which he conceived to be lacking. He speaks with the forethought of a legislator, and the monition of a prophet, and he has caught with marvellous prescience the line of development which the Church must follow. And surely, if ever man was likely to forget self entirely, and to be filled with wider thought, it was Ignatius, when life for him was over, and with full consciousness he was about to sacrifice it for the Church. He was deeply touched by the deputations that visited him ; he realised the power that a united Church might exercise ; and he saw that still closer organisation, through fuller recognition of the bishops' power, was needed. The episcopal authority was to him the centre of order and the guarantee of unity in the Church.* Except through the *episkopoi*, no common policy could be carried out. He insists, then, that the bishop should guide the community ; but he says that this principle is a special revelation,† and

---

* Lightfoot has rightly urged that Ignatius did not think (like Irenæus) that the bishops' duty was to preserve pure and transmit faithfully the doctrine of the Church, *Ignat.*, i., p. 382, ed I., 396, ed. II. " Unity " prompts his words.

† *Philad.*, 7 : " I learnt it not from flesh of man ; it was the preaching of the Spirit, who spake on this wise : Do nothing without the bishop . . . cherish union," etc. It is clear that disunion and disobedience prevailed in Philadelphia.

his reiteration seems a proof that urgency was necessary.[*]
I can find in Ignatius no proof that the bishops were regarded as *ex officio* supreme even in Asia, where he was
evidently much impressed by the good organisation of the
Churches. His words are quite consistent with the view
that the respect actually paid in each community to the
bishop depended on his individual character.[†]

The really striking development implied by Ignatius
is, that a much clearer distinction between bishop and
presbyter had now become generally recognised. This
distinction was ready to become a difference of rank and
order; and he first recognised that this was so. Others
looked at the bishops under prepossessions derived from
the past: he estimated them in view of what they might
become in the future.

For our purpose, the important point is the aspect
which the institution would wear in the estimation of the
Emperors. It was illegal; it was a device for doing more
efficiently what the State forbade to be done at all. How
far its character was known to the Government, we cannot tell; but that the Emperors studied this political
phenomenon—the Christian organisation—I cannot, in
the nature of the Roman administration, doubt. That
they must condemn an organisation such as we have
described, judging it by the fundamental principle of
Roman government, is certain. That the policy of the

---

[*] Cp. Dr. Sanday's true remark, *Expositor*, December, 1888, p. 326.
[†] We notice that the Ephesians are urged to meet together, and
to obey bishop and presbyters (20); but they had not been in the
habit of meeting often enough (13). Advice implies fault. Tralles
is praised for obeying its bishop, and advised also to obey the
presbyters

Flavian Emperors is inexplicable in any other way seems equally certain.   An organisation, strong, even if only rudimentary, is required to explain the Imperial history ; and such an organisation is attested by the Christian documents.   Trajan found himself unable to resist the evidence that this organisation was dangerous and illegal ; yet his instinctive perception of wider issues prevented him from logically carrying out the principle.   All sides of the evidence work in with one another, and all are derived from the simplest and fullest interpretation of the documents as they lie before us.   Christianity was proscribed, not as a religion, but as interfering with that organisation of society which the Empire inculcated and protected.

The question whether the Christian sect was treasonable was not first raised under the Flavian Emperors.   It had been agitated from an early period, and was naturally revived on every occasion when the character of the sect formed a subject of consideration to the Government.

The earliest charge against Christians was that of setting up a king of their own in opposition to the Emperor.   Jesus was condemned on this ground ; and it reappears in Acts xvii. 7.   Eusebius mentions that a similar charge against the grandchildren of Judas, the Lord's brother, was investigated by Domitian, and dismissed.*

Again, according to the old Roman view, it was justifiable, and even required, that the magistrates should proceed actively against Romans who had deserted the national

---

* Euseb., *H. E.*, iii., 20, gives it on the authority of Hegesippus, which carries it back to the second century.   This is a sign that the Christian sect was studied by the Imperial Government.   It was found to involve no serious danger, but to embody a dangerous principle.

religion,* and also against those who had been concerned in converting them. But, in fact, it would appear that this was not a frequent ground on which to found proceedings against the Christians. The feeling of pride in Roman citizenship and the exclusiveness against non-Roman rites, became much weaker as the citizenship was widened. Moreover, religious feeling in the Empire was very weak during the first century. The attempted revival of the national religion under Augustus was not lasting. Tiberius preserved the tradition of Augustus' policy ; but the mad sacrilege of Caligula must have weakened it fatally. Under Domitian, however, the revival of the national worship was a marked feature of the Imperial policy.

While the sect was condemned, it did not appear sufficiently important to require any special measures to put it down. The Government was content to lay down the principle that Christians should be dealt with by all governors under the general instructions (see p. 208). But the Roman administration maintained a very small staff of officials, and the public safety was very insufficiently attended to (see p. 24). Brigandage was rife, and brigands were followed in a very spiritless and variable way. Christians, who were classed along with brigands, profited by the remissness of the Government. In practice the execution of the general principle would greatly depend on popular co-operation ; and though popular feeling was strongly against the Christians, popular action was of a

---

* Mommsen quotes as examples the expulsion of Jews from Rome by Hispallus, *prætor*, B.C. 139, by Tiberius, and by Claudius, the action against the Bacchanalia, the expulsion of the worship of Isis beyond the walls of Rome, etc. See *Histor. Zft.*, xxviii., 402 ff.

very uncertain character (see p. 325). The proscription exercised a strong influence on the Church, causing it to unite still more closely through mutual sympathy and the tendency among the persecuted to help one another; but it was unable to diminish seriously the numbers of the Christians. It merely made the Church stronger, more self-reliant, and more spirited (pp. 296, 314).

NOTE.—Many Christian confessors went to extremes in showing their contempt and hatred for their judges; and the *Acta* fully explain the indignation which their conduct roused in Pliny, conscious as he was of his own lofty motives, and of the wisdom of the Imperial policy. Their answers to plain questions were evasive and indirect; they lectured Roman dignitaries as if the latter were the criminals and they themselves the judges; and they even used violent reproaches and coarse insulting gestures. A Roman court presented a terrible aspect, for torture in court was a regular part of procedure, and the actual surroundings were a grim commentary on Pliny's threats (*supplicia minatus:* Le Blant, *Actes*, p. 118). Christians who were not terrified into recantation must have been usually thrown into extreme excitement. A master of human feeling has described the effect produced on a singularly cool, intrepid, self-restrained Scot—Henry Morton—by his unjust trial before Claverhouse. But the racial character of these Christians was not cool and self-restrained, but enthusiastic and able to see only one side of a case. Exceptions occur: Polycarp's gentle dignity and undisturbed calm are contrasted by the narrator with the nervous and hysterical conduct of others, and seem to him to be on the same lofty plane of feeling as the action of Jesus. Southern races are prone to licence of speech and gesture, by which they relieve the emotions which among us are often relieved by profane or inane expletives (a waggoner will attribute to the female relatives of his waggon, when it bumps over a stone, conduct such as Catullus attributes to the female connections of his enemy Mamurra). M. Le Blant, in some excellent remarks on the subject, *l.c.* 89 f., quotes the rude and violent language of Jerome and Gregory Naz. against Rufinus, Vigilantius, and Julian. Drilling of Christians in the single answer to all questions of a judge is mentioned (Le Blant, p. 290).

CHAPTER XVI.

THE ACTA OF PAUL AND THEKLA.

I.—THE ACTA IN THEIR EXTANT FORM.

THE *Acta Pauli et Theklæ* is the only extant literary work which throws light on the character of popular Christianity in Asia Minor during the period that we have been studying. Thekla became the type of the female Christian teacher, preacher, and baptiser, and her story was quoted as early as the second century as a justification of the right of women to teach and to baptise ; and Tertullian seeks to invalidate its authority * by pointing out that the presbyter who confessed having constructed the work from love of Paul, was deposed from his office. So late as the ninth century, Nicetas of Paphlagonia mentions that Thekla baptised in Isauria, but that this was a special privilege reserved to her alone among women. Respect for and worship of Thekla was then rather opposed to the practice of the Catholic Church in respect of women ; but it was far too deep-seated in the popular mind to be disturbed. But the objectionable features of the tale could be explained away (as they were by Nicetas); and attention was directed more to features of the tale which

---

* Tertullian, *de Bapt.*, 17 (about 195 A.D.). It is generally held that Tertullian refers to the work which has been preserved to us ; but in *Acta Sanctorum*, September 23rd, pp. 550 f., the extant *Acta* is treated as a forged compilation, made in the fourth century from the work known to Tertullian.

were more in accordance with the spirit of later Catholicism. Finally, in process of time, the objectionable features were toned down and eliminated, so that in the extant MSS. not a single trace remains of Thekla's administering the rite of baptism to others. To render this work useful as an authority for the feeling of the second century, we must then try to restore the character which it had when Tertullian read it.

The extant *Acta*, of which numerous MSS. are known to exist,* including versions in Greek, Latin, Syriac, Arabic, and Slavonic, represent on the whole one single document, though differences far beyond mere textual variety exist between the different versions and MSS. The general tendency of recent criticism (see, *e.g.*, Lipsius, *die apokryphen Apostelgesch.*, ii., p. 424, to which, and to his edition of the text, it is needless to say how much I am indebted ; Lightfoot, *Ignat. and Polyc.*, i., p. 623*n.* ; Dr. Gwynn in Smith's *Dict. Christ. Biog.*, iv., pp. 882 ff., etc.), is to place this document in the latter part of the second century. To judge on such a point we may best begin by a brief analysis of the document.

Thekla belonged to one of the noblest families in Iconium. Her mother was called Theokleia, which seems to be only a Grecised form of the same name ; neither father nor brother nor sister has any part in the extant tale. When Paul came to Iconium he lived in the house of Onesiphorus,† and his preaching was audible to Thekla, who sat at a window in her mother's house, and refused to stir from it or to take

---

* Professor Rendel Harris told me that he had seen at Mount Sinai eight or nine MSS. None have been collated.

† On his journey to Iconium and welcome by Onesiphorus, see above, p. 31. Titus intimated Paul's intended visit.

food. No entreaties moved her. Her betrothed lover, Thamyris, after vainly trying to bring her back to her ordinary mode of life, went out to observe Paul. Two false friends of Paul, Demas and Hermogenes, advised him to accuse Paul of being a Christian, and next day he took Paul before the proconsul, Castelius, and accused him of dissuading women from marriage—*i.e.*, of tampering with the customs of society. Castelius remanded Paul for further examination, and in the night he was visited secretly by Thekla. She was found at his feet next morning by Theokleia and Thamyris. Both culprits were taken before Castelius, who ordered Paul to be scourged and expelled from the city, and Thekla, as her mother suggested and urged, to be burned. Men and women vied in preparing the pyre to burn Thekla in the theatre. She, after having a vision of the Lord in the appearance of Paul, was put on the pyre ; but the flames did not burn her, and a storm came on, quenched the fire, and killed many of the spectators.*

Paul and the family of Onesiphorus spent many days fasting in a tomb on the road that leads to Daphne. When they were famishing Paul took off his coat, and sent a slave into the city to buy bread ; the slave met Thekla in the street (her intermediate adventures are not mentioned), and brought her to Paul. She wished to cut her hair and follow Paul, but he refused to permit this. She then asked him to baptise her, which he refused to do.

Paul and Thekla then went to Antioch. The high-priest of Syria, Alexander, saw them as they entered, and, struck

---

* The versions vary. Some read, " so that many died "; others, " so that many were in danger of death."

with passion for Thekla, proposed to purchase her from Paul, who replied, "I do not know the woman of whom thou speakest, nor is she mine." Paul at this point disappears from the action; Thekla was left alone. Alexander put his arm round her and kissed her; and she tore his garment and the crown which he wore on his head. Alexander took her before the proconsul, who condemned her to be thrown to wild beasts. General pity was felt among the people, and the women loudly exclaimed, "Evil judgment! impious judgment!" Thekla asked to be safe from personal violence till her death; and a rich lady, Queen Tryphæna, took her in charge, and became much attached to her, as come to replace her lost daughter. On the day of the preliminary procession Thekla was fastened on the back of a lioness, which licked her feet. On the following day took place the exhibition of beasts (*venatio*). Tryphæna long refused to give up Thekla, but was at last obliged to let the soldiers take her away. In the arena, where she was exposed nude, except for a cincture, the lioness crouched at her feet, and fought for her, killing a bear and a lion, and dying in her defence. A leopard which attacked her burst asunder.* Then other beasts came against her, and she saw a trench full of water, and jumped in, saying, " I baptise myself." † The people were afraid that the seals would eat her, and the proconsul wept. But a cloud of fire encompassed her, and veiled her nakedness from the gaze of the crowd, and lightnings killed the seals. The other animals fell into a stupor. Then she was fastened to fierce bulls, who were goaded to madness by

---

* The leopard occurs only in the Syriac version.
† I retain purposely the inconsequence of the incidents.

red-hot irons; but the fire consumed the fastenings. Here Tryphæna fainted, and Thekla was released, for the officials were afraid of the anger of the Emperor, who was a relative of Tryphæna. Thekla went home with the Queen, refused, in spite of her entreaties, to remain more than eight days with her, converted the whole household, and then, modifying her dress to look like a man's, she went to Myra to meet Paul. Thereafter she returned to Iconium, offered to give her mother the wealth she had received from Tryphæna, and then went to Seleuceia.

The rest of her life is variously related. Some authorities merely say that she converted many and died at Seleuceia; others give a long narrative containing some very feeble miracles; others make her undertake a journey to Rome; the Syriac and Latin versions add nothing.

When I am told that this production belongs to the same age, the same country, the same period of thought as the *Acta* of Carpus and Papylus, and the pathetic letter of the Lugdunensians to the churches of Asia; that it is only a few years later than the simple and noble letter of the Smyrnæans, which so moved Scaliger " that he seemed to be no longer master of himself," * I confess that I can only wonder. That the tale contains much that is fine is true; but it also contains much rubbish, much that is glaringly incongruous with the finest parts. Still more must one marvel that Zahn should be willing to accept it, with a few omissions, as a work of the first century.

In examining this work we shall not look at its doctrinal aspect. Obviously a work which has been exposed to modifications such as have been alluded to is peculiarly

---

* I take the quotation from Lightfoot, *Ignat. and Polyc.*, i., 589 (604).

liable to alteration in doctrinal points; and dogma therefore will be a dangerous guide in attempting to analyse it. The most remarkable disagreement exists between those who have tried to estimate precisely its dogmatic position. Schlau considers that the *Acta* is a polemic by a Catholic writer against Gnostic libertinism: works such as 1 *Timothy*, falsely attributed to Paul, had discredited him in Church circles, and the writer's object was to present a picture of Paul according to the Catholic taste. Lipsius considers that the *Acta* was originally a Gnostic composition, designed to inculcate the doctrine of absolute virginity and abstinence even from marriage, and abstinence from the use of flesh and wine; and that this original work was re-edited in the third century with its doctrines toned down to avoid offending the Catholic taste; he refuses to believe that there were at the time in question any Catholics in whose eyes St. Paul was discredited (a scepticism in which he will find supporters), or that the Catholic taste desired that an apostle should be of the type attributed in the *Acta* to Paul. Dr. Gwynn* maintains that the work is written by an orthodox and well-meaning, but not clear-headed, author, who was unable to understand Paul's doctrine.

It will be allowed that examination of the *Acta* from the side of dogma has not led to such consensus of opinion as to preclude a different theory moving on a different plane of thought, and founded mainly on archæological arguments. It may conduce to clearness to begin by stating the view † which will be supported in the ensuing pages.

---

* In *Dict. Christ. Biogr.*, iv., 891: he quotes Dr. Salmon, *Introduction to New Testament*, ed. ii., p. 420, as in agreement.

† Several points in it have been maintained by others; the novelty lies in some of the arguments on which it is founded.

1. *Acta Pauli et Theklæ* goes back ultimately to a document of the first century.

2. The original document, whose contents can now be only conjectured, mentioned facts of history and antiquities which had probably passed quite out of knowledge before the end of the first century, and which have been rediscovered only during the last twenty years.

3. This document, not being protected by canonical character and popular veneration, was subjected to alterations, due partly to change of views in the Church, partly to the growth of the Thekla legend, which was a myth (ἱερὸς λόγος), explaining and justifying the gradual spread of the worship of Saint Thekla.

4. The scene of the original tale, be it history, or romance, or *Dichtung und Wahrheit,* lay in Iconium and Antioch of Pisidia, and the action begins during Paul's first visit to Iconium.

5. In the versions preserved to us, Antioch of Syria has been substituted for Antioch of Pisidia through a misunderstanding on the part of an enlarger and editor, who is much older than Basil of Seleuceia (fifth century).

In treating this subject the following questions must be clearly held apart from each other : 1. Is the work, as we have it, explicable as the production of a single author ? No difficulty will be felt in answering this in the negative.

2. If it is not a single work by a single author, what are the parts, and to what dates are they to be assigned ?

3. Do the earliest parts form, or appear to have originally belonged to, a complete literary work, or can they be explained as traditional survivals of a popular legend living on in the popular memory, and worked up into literary form at a later time ?

4. If the earliest parts once belonged to a work of literature, what historical value did the work possess? The existence of such a work, and its truth as history, are distinct points.

We shall, as the best method of answering the last three questions, and of corroborating the answer given to the first, examine the work minutely to discover indications of the date to which each must be assigned.

2. QUEEN TRYPHÆNA.

In the action of the romance the *dénoûment* turns on the protection granted to Thekla by Queen Tryphæna, who became a second mother to the Christian virgin, and saved her honour and her life. It is impossible to imagine a form of the romance in which the figure of the queen is wanting; she must have been a character in the tale from the beginning.

Von Gutschmid was the first to point out that Queen Tryphæna was probably a historical character. He appealed to certain rare coins of the kingdom of Pontus, which show on the obverse the bust of a king with the title *ΒΑΣΙΛΕΩΣ ΠΟΛΕΜΩΝΟΣ*, on the reverse the bust of a queen with the title *ΒΑΣΙΛΙΣΣΗΣ ΤΡΥΦΑΙΝΗΣ* ; * and he argued that this queen, whose bust appears on Pontic coins, was the Queen Tryphæna of the *Acta*.

There were obvious difficulties in the identification. The Tryphæna of the coins was queen of the independent kingdom of Pontus; and the Tryphæna of the romance was apparently a Roman subject, resident in the city of

---

* *Rhein. Mus.*, 1864, p. 178: the types imply that the Queen reigned by her own hereditary right, and not simply as Queen-Consort. Lipsius, p. 464, speaks of Cilicia, not Pontus; but Gutschmid is right, and the coins are Pontic.

Antioch. The former was a powerful sovereign, for Polemon is known to have reigned in Pontus until A.D. 63, whereas the latter complains of her friendlessness and helplessness. The former was apparently a Greek ; the latter was a near relation of the reigning Emperor. Polemon's wife could not on any reasonable hypothesis be an elderly woman in A.D. 50, as Tryphæna in the tale is represented.

Von Gutschmid advanced an hypothesis to get rid of some of these difficulties, and to establish a relationship between the Pontic queen and the Emperor Claudius ; and all subsequent scholars, when writing on the *Acta* of Paul and Thekla, have confined themselves to reproducing his hypothesis.* We shall not here repeat it, as subsequent investigations have completely disproved it. Nor shall we recapitulate the gradual progress of discovery, in which the chief parts have been played by Von Sallet, Waddington, and Mommsen ; though it would be a matter of interest to observe how evidence slowly accumulated, and one fact after another was gradually established ; and it would also be important to show the nature of the evidence, for the facts are not all equally firmly established, and some may yet require some modification from further discovery. We may accept and briefly repeat the account given by Mommsen† of this queen, as being in all essential points

---

* Zahn, in *Götting. Gelehrte Anzeigen*, 1877, p. 1307, argues on the supposition that it has been demonstrated as certain.

† *Ephemeris Epigraphica*, i., pp. 270 ff. ; ii., pp. 259 ff. Lipsius refers, p. 465*n.*, to the Tryphæna whom Mommsen describes, as a person bearing the same name as the Tryphæna of the *Acta* and of Gutschmid. He did not discover that she is the true Pontic queen, of whom Gutschmid gave such a boldly hypothetical history, in which the only true points were her name and her identity with the queen of the *Acta*. On a few small points I tacitly differ from Mommsen.

well established ; and we may do so with more confidence
because none of the facts on which his account is founded
are derived from the Christian *Acta*, nor have any of the
successive investigators observed that the facts which they
have discovered bear on this document.

Queen Tryphæna belonged to a family which played an
important part in the history of Asia Minor in the two
centuries immediately before and after Christ ; and it will
be a really important step in our knowledge of the diffusion
of Christianity in Asia Minor, if we succeed in establishing
its relations with this dynasty. Our knowledge of the
dynasty rests almost wholly on the evidence of inscriptions
and coins ; in literature there occurs hardly any reference
to it. It left no mark on the history of the world, and had
no place in the memory of posterity. It is in the last
degree improbable that any person so late as A.D. 150
remembered the existence of this queen,* or that a tale
in which she was a prominent character first received literary
form so late as the latter part of the second century.† It is a
striking instance of the historical value of the early Christian
documents, that the only deep mark this dynasty has left
on literature is in a Christian work ; and I hope to succeed
in showing that several facts with regard to Tryphæna's
fate, which are stated in the *Acta* and are nowhere else
attested, are so suitable to the well-established facts of her
life, that they deserve to be accepted as historical.

* One exception probably was the Sophist of Smyrna, M. Antonius
Polemon, whose magnificent progresses in almost royal state between
Laodiceia (the original seat of the family) and Smyrna are described
in very interesting terms by Philostratus. He, no doubt, thought a
good deal about his royal relatives ; and it is possible that Tryphæna
was his great-grandmother.

† Zahn, *l.c.*, has put this point well.

In the first place, we must observe how well certain traits in the *Acta* agree with the historical position of this dynasty. This family owed its importance to the Imperial policy in Asia Minor. As we have seen (p. 34), the romanisation of the central parts of Asia Minor was in progress actively between A.D. 30 and 70 ; and the attention of the Emperors was closely directed on it. It was part of their policy to interpose what are in modern slang called " buffer-states " between the Roman boundaries and their great enemy in the East, the Parthians. It was important that these States should be governed by sovereigns closely united by feeling, interest, and family ties with the Empire. The influence exercised by this lonely widow among the Roman officers, the deference paid her, and the fear of the Emperor's anger if anything should happen to her, are in perfect agreement with the historical situation.

In the second place, it would be an effective argument to show how the difficulties of reconciling the Tryphæna of the *Acta* with the historical Tryphæna have disappeared one by one in the gradual progress of discovery ; but it would require too minute discussion of the facts. One example, however, is too striking to be omitted. This Polemon, who appears along with Tryphæna on Pontic coins, was a mere boy in the year 37, and must have been a comparatively young man at the time at which the action of the Christian tale is laid. But Tryphæna in the tale is an elderly woman. How could so young a king have an elderly wife? This difficulty was cleared away by M. Waddington's observation that the queen on the coins is a mature woman, while the king is represented as a mere boy ; and that the pair are not wife and husband, but mother and son.

25

Queen Tryphæna was daughter of Polemon, King of part of Lycaonia and Cilicia, and also of Pontus. She married Cotys, King of Thrace, and became the mother of three kings, Thracian, Pontic, and Armenian. She was in her own right queen of Pontus, but only queen-consort in Thrace, hence her name does not appear on Thracian coins. She was probably about forty-six years of age when her son Polemon was made king of Pontus in A.D. 37; * and the latter was then perhaps about nineteen years old. In A.D. 50 she was therefore nearly sixty. This suits the *Acta* perfectly.

A young king who comes of age after his mother has exercised for some years the sovereign power during his minority, does not always find it easy to get on amicably with her. Tryphæna, whose mother Pythodoris had reigned for many years as sole sovereign after her husband's death, was not unlikely to be rather too exacting in her demands on her son's obedience. It is certain that, though we hear a little about Polemon, we never hear in history of the Pontic queen. It therefore appears that Tryphæna did not continue to exercise in Pontus the commanding influence which her mother had possessed, while it is quite natural that she may have desired to exert a similar influence. The queen in the *Acta* complains of her friendlessness. There is then every probability that this is historically true; and that she had quarrelled with her son, who found that she insisted too much on her rights, and retired to a life of seclusion on her own private estates in one of her father's kingdoms.

---

* I have placed in an *excursus* a brief outline of Mommsen's history of the family, to avoid encumbering the text with facts not strictly belonging to my subject, yet having a bearing on it.

Tryphæna was cousin, once removed, of the Emperor Claudius, her mother Pythodoris being his full cousin. The relationship was through the Antonian family, for the mothers of Pythodoris and of Claudius were sisters, both being daughters of Marcus Antonius the Triumvir, and bearing the name Antonia. The connection with the great enemy of Augustus was no great advantage to Tryphæna in her earlier years, when Augustus and Tiberius ruled the empire. The very name of the Triumvir was long proscribed and forbidden to be mentioned on monuments or uttered by loyal citizens.* Memory of Antonius was indeed permitted at least as early as A.D. 20, possibly even before the death of Augustus ; but still he was not mentioned by Augustus in the *monumentum Ancyranum.*† It was not till the accession of Caligula, his great-grandson, in A.D. 37, that it became a really great advantage to belong to the Antonian family, whose members were honoured and promoted by the young Emperor. His successor, Claudius, continued the same policy ; and during this reign it is quite in accordance with the scanty evidence that the picture given in the *Acta* should be strictly true : the widowed queen, though aged and living in retirement, retained the prestige due to her relationship to the reigning Emperor, to her former power as a reigning queen, and probably also to her personal ability and energy.‡

---

* See Mommsen, *Res Gestæ D. Aug.*, ed. II., p. 180.

† Tacitus, *Annals*, iii., 18 ; Mommsen, *l. c.*, p. vi. and p. 181.

‡ Her family undoubtedly showed high ability both before and after her time. Her mother was certainly a remarkable woman ; and the inscriptions which attest Tryphæna's relations with Cyzicos make it probable that she had something of her mother's character. The respect shown to her at Cyzicos illustrates the dignity ascribed to her in the *Acta.*

Further, there is every probability that within a few years the situation changed. In 54 A.D. Claudius died, and Nero succeeded him ; and the new Emperor rather made a point of throwing contempt and ridicule on his predecessor. After a few years he even stripped Polemon of his kingdom of Pontus, leaving him, however, a principality among the mountain districts of western Cilicia. The picture given in the *Acta* of Tryphæna's situation, while true to the time in which the scene is laid, ceased to be so after a very few years had passed ; after 54 she was no longer a relative of the Emperor, and in all probability she lost much of her personal influence with the Roman officials.

It is not possible to account for this accuracy in details * by the supposition that it is a skilful archæological forgery. Such an accurate restoration of a past epoch would be utterly different in type from other ancient forgeries, and beyond the limits of ancient thought and knowledge. The tale must be founded on fact, and committed to writing by some person not far removed from the events, able to compose a history, or at least a poetical idealisation of history. No other hypothesis seems consistent with the fidelity to a transitory and soon-forgotten epoch of history. We must hold that the tale is, at least in part, historical, that Thekla was a real person, and that she was brought into relations with the greatest figures of the Galatic province about A.D. 50—viz., Paul, Queen Tryphæna, and the Roman governor.

---

* Her name is correctly given. As a Roman lady, she was Antonia Tryphæna, but as a queen she dropped the Antonia. So M. Antonius Polemon, as her son was certainly called, became King Polemon.

Two points occur to the critic in regard to which the Tryphæna of the *Acta* differs from the historical Tryphæna.

1. In the *Acta*, § 30, the Queen says, " There is no one to aid me, neither child, for my child has died,* nor relative, for I am a widow." The real queen had at this period three sons living as kings, and powerful relatives. But these words must be taken as the exaggerated expression of grief uttered by a lonely old woman, who feels that her sons have not remained true to her, and are as good as dead to her ; and they are, if pressed, actually inconsistent with the tale itself, for in § 36 she is said to be the Emperor's relative. Moreover, in the long process of alteration through which the work has passed, a little additional colouring was liable to be added to the cry of the widow. The explanatory phrases read like literary additions. The original words then were, probably, " There is no one to help me, neither child nor relative."

2. Tryphæna in the legend seems to reside at Antioch of Pisidia. The family to which she belonged is not known to have had any connection with Antioch ; and we have seen that the natural place of retirement for the historical Queen would be some of the hereditary possessions of her family. We could understand her retiring to estates beside Laodiceia on the Lycus, where immense property was owned by M. Antonius Polemon as late as the second century, or to estates near Iconium ; but that she should be residing at Antioch is not in keeping with what is known of the family. This difficulty will disappear in the course of the investigation into the original form of the tale.

---

* The Greek also permits the rendering, " for my children have died."

3. LOCALITIES OF THE TALE OF THEKLA.

The action of the tale was originally placed at Paul's first visit to Iconium. The general impression is that he is a stranger in the city, and yet various details point to a later visit. This contradiction points to additions or alterations made in an older tale through misunderstanding. With this is connected the doubt whether the Antioch of the tale is the Syrian or the Pisidian. If the scene is laid in the first journey the Pisidian Antioch must be meant, and indubitably the general impression is to that effect. But, if the scene is laid in any other journey, the Antioch of § 1 must be the Syrian; and the other references are naturally interpreted accordingly. The doubt was felt at a very early time, and Basil of Seleuceia says that the Syrian Antioch was really the city alluded to, though Pisidian Antioch claimed to be the scene of Thekla's trial. His opinion was evidently founded on some definite argument; and this argument was probably as follows. We have seen, p. 31 ff., that the meeting of Paul and Onesiphorus was originally described in terms true to the road-system of the first century, but unintelligible afterwards, and that the original text was afterwards changed considerably. The idea taken from the passage in later time was that Onesiphorus went out from Iconium along the road to Lystra, and therefore met Paul on his way from Lystra. This implies that he was coming from the Syrian Antioch, and therefore that the journey was either the second or third. Basil was familiar with the topography of a country so near his own Isaurian home, and naturally argued in this way. The fact that Isauria was subject to the See of Antioch, and not, like Lycaonia, to Constantinople, may also have prejudiced him in favour of the Syrian Antioch.

The reference to Daphne, and the title Syriarch, applied to the president of the games at Antioch, belong to a remodelling of the tale, executed by a person who believed that the Syrian city was meant.

In the first century no Roman governor resided either at Antioch or at Iconium; and, if a governor played any part in the action at either city, a document of historical character would give, either expressly * or incidentally, some explanation of the unusual fact that he was present. The course of the tale explains why a governor was at Antioch; but there is nothing to show why he should be at Iconium. This circumstance alone would be enough to prove that the trial at Iconium before the governor is quite unhistorical; and this conclusion is confirmed by numerous details in the scene.

We infer from these facts that a tale, originally belonging to Paul's first journey, and occurring in Galatic Phrygia (Iconium and Pisidian Antioch), was afterwards remodelled so as to relate to the second or third journey, and to have its scene in part at Syrian Antioch.

4. The Trials at Iconium.

The double trial and attempted execution of Thekla before two Roman governors in two cities stamp the tale as unhistorical, and also suggests a double origin, for a single inventor would be content with one governor and one trial. Now we have seen that the governor of

---

* So, in the opening of *Acta Carpi*, the proconsul's presence at Pergamos is noticed, and the notice is an explanation.

Iconium must be unhistorical ; and, when we eliminate him, the trial and punishment there must also disappear, for only a Roman governor had authority to pass a capital sentence (p. 281*n.*).　Moreover, the salvation of Thekla is not rightly worked into the tale.　No explanation is given as to what happened to her when the fire was quenched ; and in the following paragraph we find her walking in the streets of Iconium, just as if she were an ordinary inhabitant, and not a convicted criminal under sentence of death.　We conclude, then, that the trial at Antioch and the trial at Iconium spring from different origins, and that the latter was unskilfully inserted in a tale where the former previously had a place.

We now turn to the trial and punishment of Paul in Iconium.　The charges against him are double and self-contradictory.　First, Demas and Hermogenes advise Thamyris to accuse Paul of being a Christian, as this will prove fatal to him.　Such a detail could not originate until a much later date than A.D. 50 ; for the charge was an impossible one at that period.　The other charge—of being a magician and of unlawfully interfering with the conduct and feelings of women and the established habits of society—is characteristic of that early period (pp. 236, 282, 410), and points to an origin not later than A.D. 80. The implication that the charge of magic, § 15, is the same as that of interfering with the feeling and action of others, § 16, is true of the period 50–70 A.D.

Expulsion from the city is a ridiculously small penalty for a provincial governor to inflict, if he considered the charge proved.　But in A.D. 50, in Iconium, the charge could only be made before the city magistrates ; and they could not inflict a severer penalty.　They might send

him for trial by the governor, or they might expel him
from the city. We conclude, then, that the Roman
governor has been unskilfully put into an older tale, in
which the judges were the city magistrates,* and which was
more in keeping with Acts xiv. 3–5 (especially as given in
Codex Bezæ) ; also that the accusation suggested by Demas
is a later addition.

The trial of Thekla in Iconium is an anachronism from
beginning to end. The punishment pre-supposes the
presence of a Roman governor ; and there was no governor
in Iconium. The bitter spirit of the mother, who urges
the governor to burn her daughter as an example to other
women in future, is quite unnatural. The natural course
of events is that Thekla should be dealt with in private
by her own family (p. 348*n.*). There was really no charge
against her to come before a court, much less before a
Roman governor. Now, when we turn to one of the
earliest independent accounts of the legend of Thekla,
contained in a Homily attributed to Chrysostom,† we find
that the account there given is very different from that
contained in the *Acta*, and agrees perfectly with what we
must consider the natural course in the time of Claudius.
Far more stress is in the Homily laid on private action in
the family. Her parents, her lover, her relatives, and her
domestics, all urged and entreated her. Finally, she was
taken before the *dikastai*,* who attempted to terrify her

---

* Basil uses sometimes the term *dikastes*, sometimes *proconsul*.
In *Acta Pionii*, *dikastai* tried the case at Smyrna, and sent it for
trial before the proconsul.

† *Opera*, Montfaucon, vol. ii., pp. 896-9, ed. II., pp. 749-51, ed. I.
Opinion seems universal that the Homily is not in his style ; and we
are thus deprived of a date, which would have been welcome. It is
quite probable that the Homily may be as old as A.D. 300.

with threats of punishment, and then dismissed her. She then wandered away, trying to find Paul, and guiding herself by rumours as to his probable destination. Her lover pursued her, and overtook her. When she was on the point of becoming a victim to his violence she prayed to Heaven; and here, unfortunately, the fragment ends. We cannot hesitate to accept this as the original tale. The author must have had access to an older form of the tale of Thekla in which there was no Roman governor, no condemnation and punishment, and no miraculous rescue from the flames. Apparently the family tried all means of persuasion and home influence, and even the terror of a law court. At this trial it would be natural that the mother, provoked by Thekla's long-continued obstinacy, should be desirous that such punishment as was in the power of the *dikastai* should be inflicted on her; but this trait, retained in the extant *Acta*, becomes unnatural when the punishment is death by fire. Finally, it is probable that her wandering forth was permitted in pursuance of a plan of cure, which was founded on the belief that, if Thamyris once succeeded, even by violence, in forcing her to submit to his embraces, the influence gained over her by the enchanter and magician Paul would be destroyed.

In this version all is natural, simple, and suitable to the time and place. We accept the visit to Paul by night, and the bribing of the porter and gaoler; and we observe that the bracelets and the silver mirror are objects that would be ready at hand to a maiden of rich family. We also notice the characteristic trait that the domestics entreat her with tears. The inscriptions of the country, with their common reservation of a place in the family tomb for domestic slaves, prove that close and intimate ties connected the household slaves with the master's family. On the other hand, the details of the attempt to burn Thekla are poor, and either unnatural or borrowed.[*] The vision is a stock incident, not very successfully introduced, and rather like an invention of the second century (founded on the *Acta* of Carpos and Agathonike).

The meeting of Paul with Thekla in the grave at Iconium disappears, when the old form of the tale is restored ; and, with the meeting, their journey to Antioch in company is eliminated, as well as the detestable incident of Paul's denial and desertion of Thekla, when she was exposed to the insults of Alexander. These last details have perhaps arisen from a misunderstanding. Thekla, when seized by Alexander's attendants, called in her distress on Paul ; and the dull wit of a later time thought that this implied his bodily presence.

5. THE TRIAL OF THEKLA AT ANTIOCH.

In the Antiochian part of the tale we are struck at once with the fact that Thekla does not suffer for any act of a religious character, and throughout the scene of the trial no reference is made to her religion (except in some later points : Gwynn, p. 889). An inventor of a legend about a Christian heroine would never have imagined a scene in which religion played no part. We feel here at once the touch of reality and life. The trial at Antioch is on a very different plane of thought and feeling from that at Iconium.

---

[*] One detail seems borrowed from the case of Polycarp. See Lightfoot, i., p. 623*n*.

The central difficulty is the presence of a Roman governor. We cannot get rid of him as we did of the Iconian governor ; for the crime—which was sacrilege—and the sentence alike imperatively demand his presence. But the action fully explains why he was in Antioch. The occasion was a great festival containing an exhibition of wild beasts (*venatio*), which, in a provincial city not the capital of the province, was a remarkable event. The festival, with its Roman *venatio*, had evidently a political character, being part of the government scheme for the romanisation of Southern Galatia. The governor had visited Antioch to make the event more imposing ; and all the chief persons in Galatic Phrygia had come to pay their respects to him and to the Imperial authority which he represented. Among the rest, Queen Tryphæna had come from her estates near Iconium for this great occasion. Thus the solution of one difficulty solves another (p. 389).

Alexander, the *agonothetes* or president at this festival, must have been a person of great importance, and a leading figure in the State religion, which was the bond of loyalty and union in the Empire. In the Greek MSS. he is styled Syriarch, which belongs to the later modification. It is quite possible that, in the original text, he was the Galatarch, or high-priest of the Galatic province. Two of the Latin MSS. mention that he was the giver of the *venatio* ;* and this detail is true to common practice. The president frequently added at his own expense to the magnificence of the festival at which he presided.

Alexander, accompanied of course by a great train of

---

* Probably the text of D. also did so ; but it has been corrupted. *Alexandro præsens sedente* should be corrected to *Alexandro præsens* (*munu*)*s edente.*

attendants, saw Thekla entering Iconium, and was struck
with her beauty. A young woman alone in the street of
an eastern town was obviously a dancing-girl of no respectable character ; and as such Alexander accosted her and
kissed her. The act was originally a piece of gallantry, a
kindness and an honour to a person of her class ; and we
notice that the accounts given of it make it more heinous
and offensive in the later texts than in the earlier. Considering the person and the occasion, we must not attribute
any ugly character to it ; for Alexander was apparently
on his way to the festival. Thekla loudly invoked the
right of a stranger and guest—a touch true to ancient
feeling. She explained her position, as belonging to a
noble Iconian family, and engaged in the service of " the
God." Finally, when Alexander persisted in his attentions,
she tore his dress, and pulled off the crown which marked
his sacred office.*

The reason given by Thekla was the only one that
could, in this Oriental land, explain the appearance
unattended in the streets of a lady of good character and
birth. She was one of the inspired servants ($\theta\epsilon o\phi\acute{o}\rho\eta\tau o\iota$),
who were a recognised and wide-spread accompaniment
of the Asian religion. In accordance with the service
imposed on her by " the God," she was observing a rule
of chastity. In this religion the observance of absolute
and perfect purity was a recognised rite, though, as a
rule, such inspired female servants of the God were bound
to precisely the opposite way of life during their period

---

* M. Le Blant wrongly considers him a *stephanephoros* (*Actes des
Martyrs*, p. 320). That official was a municipal magistrate, whereas
the president of such a festival belonged to the provincial organisation of the Imperial religion.

of service, and were not considered dishonoured thereby.* This trait takes us into the midst of popular life, and makes the original part of the *Acta* a unique document for illustrating the spirit prevalent in Galatic Phrygia in A.D. 50. If one compares it with the tale of the sacrifice at Lystra and the legend of Baucis and Philemon, and then reads the *Attis* of Catullus, one appreciates better the character of Phrygian thought, its difference from Greek, and the fascination which it possesses.

Alexander's attendants arrested Thekla, and carried her before the governor. The case was susceptible of a serious interpretation. She had assaulted a representative of the Imperial authority, wearing his official priestly dress, on the morning of a great ceremony at which he was about to preside. The offence was sacrilege, and, as such, was in the category of dangerous crimes commended to the special care of all governors (p. 208). The governor was satisfied as to the facts by the confession of the accused (pp. 214, 238); a severe example would bring home to all minds the terror of Roman authority; and the penalty of exposing Thekla at the *venatio* given by Alexander seemed peculiarly appropriate to the offence. Such a sentence was probably new to the country, where Roman customs were only coming into use; and it is interesting to observe the effect produced. The whole city was astonished; and the women were specially active in protesting against the sentence as iniquitous.† The

---

* An inscription of Tralles shows the general type. A woman of good birth (proved by her Latin name) erects a dedicatory offering to Zeus, as having, like her ancestors, παλλακεύσασα καὶ κατὰ χρησμόν. See *Bull. de Corresp. Hellénique*, 1882, p. 276.

† The Syriac and Latin versions keep this detail; the Greek has

question suggests itself, how the women could be present at the trial. The trial was evidently held in public at the actual festival before the whole assembled multitude ; the case had been carried straight before the governor, and decided by him sitting in his official place at the festival,* being one of an administrative, and not of a strictly judicial, character (p. 207).

The general sympathy had some effect. The governor granted Thekla the privilege, ordinarily reserved for criminals of higher rank, of being confined in a private house instead of a prison. It was only too evident what reason a condemned female prisoner had to dread the gaoler's brutality ; † and, to enable her to fulfil her service of purity, the noblest lady in the assembly, Queen

---

lost it. From the recurrence of their protest in §§ 28, 32, we gather their view, that Thekla represented them, what she had done they might be ordered by " the God " to do, and her action was covered by the Divine command which all who received it must obey (see p. 403). Harnack has seen the analogy between the sympathy of the women here, and the sympathy of the crowd for Agathonike in *Acta Carpi*, and rightly inclines to think the latter an imitation. He remarks on the motivelessness of the pity for Agathonike, who was voluntarily rushing on death.

* Similarly Polycarp was heard and condemned in the Stadium at Smyrna. M. Le Blant quotes many examples, *l.c.* p. 116.

† Moreover, the ingenuity of Roman practice had in A.D. 31 perverted a humane scruple (*triumvirali supplicio adfici virginem inauditum habebatur*) into a reason for detestable brutality to the young daughter of Sejanus (Tacitus, *Ann.*, v., 9) ; and this act constituted a precedent, which might defend numerous cases of similar brutality to Christian virgins in later time. There is no reason to disbelieve these cases, as Neumann does, p. 142*n.* They are attested by too weighty evidence, though of course the fantastic developments given to them in later hagiography are inane. If such things were done to the innocent daughter of a Roman noble, why not to a Christian criminal ?

Tryphæna, offered to be security for her appearance at the proper moment. This kind of confinement (*custodia libera, privata*) was common. A guarantee (*fide-jussor*) was required ; and ordinarily it would be difficult to find one in the case of a person condemned to death.* Only exceptional circumstances could have saved Thekla from the public prison; but the details here, though unusual, bear the stamp of reality and truth.

The opening ceremony of the games in the Stadium †consisted in a procession, in which were displayed the ornaments of the show and the officials who directed it. This is true to Roman custom. Tertullian speaks of " the ostentatious preliminary display of the games to which the name procession specially belongs," *Spect.* 7 ; and Juvenal describes it x. 35. In one point the *Acta* goes beyond our other authorities. These do not mention that the animals were ever shown in the procession, and it is unnatural that wild beasts should be taken through the streets, whether in cages or otherwise. Here, as in many other details, the Latin version retains a far more accurate account than the Greek. The latter represents Thekla as forming part of the procession, bound to a lioness ; whereas the Latin says

---

* Roman law was very severe in the case of a prisoner's escape, and the guard in charge was, strictly, liable to the fate of the escaped prisoner. Hadrian distinguished (expressly in the case of military guards, and by implication in the case of others) between fault, carelessness, and accident, on the part of the guards, and discriminated penalties accordingly (*Digest.*, 48, 3, 12).

† *Stadium* in the Greek, *amphitheatre* in the Latin. No remains of either were seen by Hamilton or by Laborde ; nor did I, in a very short visit, see any. But such a city must have had some place for public exhibitions. Probably it was a στάδιον ἀμφιθέατρον, a species of building, about which I hope in 1893 to write in *Bulletin de Corresp. Hellénique.*

that Thekla was placed on the top of the cage where the lioness was confined in the amphitheatre, and that, when she was in that position, the procession entered the arena. The lioness protruded its tongue between the bars of the cage, and licked Thekla's feet. The extent to which the ignorant creative fancy of later hagiography has distorted the original document into unnatural form is well exemplified in this case. Lipsius does not quote the complete Syriac version; but we cannot doubt that the Latin approximates far more closely than the Greek to the original text. I see no reason to treat the incident as one that may not have actually occurred. The lioness had been brought from a distance, and it must have been kept in a portable cage during the journey. This cage was put in the arena during the procession.

When Thekla was thus exhibited in the arena, a tablet was placed beside her with the inscription " SACRILEGA." Similarly at Lugdunum in 177, it is mentioned that in front of Attalus was placed the inscription " CHRISTIANUS."* The Greek rendering ἱερόσυλος recalls the language of Acts xix. 37 (see p. 260*n*.).

6. Punishment and Escape of Thekla.

On the day of the procession Tryphæna produced Thekla to take part in it, and received her back to her house to spend the final night. We cannot accept as original the statement that Tryphæna accompanied her

---

* Cp. also Mark xv. 26. M. Le Blant quotes the gloss: *elogium, titulus cujuslibet rei* (*Actes*, p. 172: the word *elogium, eulogium,* is used in D). He also compares the Greek text with Matt. xxvii. 37, forgetting, however, that he is quoting the valueless words of the Metaphrast.

26

during the procession. This is the exaggeration of a later enlarger, who did not comprehend the situation ; it is an improbability of the most glaring kind that this noble lady should go into the arena. Moreover, it is inconsistent with the tale, for Tryphæna's great affection began during the next night,* when her lost daughter appeared and bade her take Thekla as a new-found daughter.

At dawn of the following day Alexander appeared to require Thekla's presence in the arena. The fact that so high an official came in person can be explained only as a special mark of respect to the queen ; it was not thought courteous to send the officers of the law. But Tryphæna now refused to give up her prisoner, and did not yield until the governor sent soldiers.† Tryphæna then led her by the hand to the stadium. She, of course, was accompanied by a numerous retinue of her attendants, who are alluded to at a later stage.

When Thekla was exposed in the arena she was stripped, and a cincture was given her. When she was released her clothes were given back to her. This account, as M. Le Blant remarks, is true to Roman custom ; and he quotes

---

* The Latin version D is very much superior to the Greek text. This could not be gathered from Lipsius' notes. I regret that I am obliged to write without having any of the Latin texts except D before me.

† The Latin versions have *stratorem* (two corruptly). I believe that this is due to the influence of such a document as *Acta Procos. Cypriani*, and marks these versions as being later than the middle of the third century. A *strator* would be an anachronism in the first century. Ulpian says that no proconsul is allowed to have *stratores*, but soldiers must perform their duties in the provinces (*Digest*, i., 16, 4, 1) ; and probably this rule applied also to Imperial provinces like Galatia. The prohibition seems to have been relaxed between 228 and 258 A.D.

the case of an executioner who was burned to death, because
he had not given a cincture to a noble Roman woman
when she was led to execution, but had compelled her to
go absolutely nude.* The simple and pathetic prayer
of Thekla, standing exposed in the arena (it is given in
the Syriac version alone; see p. 413) is not in the later
hagiographical style, and is probably genuine, in whole or
in great part. Thekla in it speaks unconsciously as representing her whole sex; in her exposure the nature and
rights of womanhood are outraged. A similar view is
taken by the women who defended her cause; and this
ethical idea, of a non-religious type, which runs through
the action, is one of the strongest proofs that the tale is no
artificial creation of unhistorical hagiography. It is the
only existing document that gives us any insight into
popular feeling in central Asia Minor during this century;
and it is also the only evidence we possess of the ideas and
action of women at this period in the country where their
position was so high and their influence so great.

The scene in the arena gives excellent opening to later
additions. Marvels of the common type are related of the
strange escape of Thekla from death; and the incident of
the seals slain by lightning is extremely grotesque and
puerile. It is doubtful whether any details can be assigned
to the original composition, except that the lioness spared
her, and that in her subsequent danger Queen Tryphæna
fainted. There can be no doubt that this was the cause of
Thekla's rescue from the first, as it still is in the most
corrupt form of the tale. It is improbable that the lioness
was baptized by Thekla, according to the statement of

---

* Le Blant, *Actes*, p. 247; *Ammianus*, 28, 1, 28: to refuse the
cincture (*subligaculum*) was *nefas admisisse*.

Jerome.* This grotesque detail is quite incongruous with later views; and is also quite as far removed from primitive simplicity as it is from later hagiographical inanity. It can only be treated as a fault of memory on Jerome's part, who remembered that Tertullian referred to it in his treatise *on baptism*, and mixed up the baptizing with the lion.

The precise form in which the incident was originally related cannot be discovered; but the following considerations suggest themselves :—

1. Zahn is probably right in suspecting that Ignatius refers to this incident when he speaks of beasts, " as they have done to some, refusing to touch them through fear." † Such an occurrence may be accepted as quite possible. The capricious conduct of beasts suddenly released from confinement and darkness, and brought into the glare of the arena amid the shouts of the spectators is natural ; and is vouched for by narratives of perfect credibility.‡ We believe, that this incident was embodied in a literary form early enough to be known to Ignatius.

2. A remarkable analogy to the case of Thekla occurs in that of an African martyr, Marciana. A lion was sent against her in the arena. It sprang on her and placed its paws on her breast, and then, after smelling her,§ let her

---

* Lipsius accepts the statement. Jerome, *de vir. illustr.*, c. 7.

† Zahn in *Götting. Gelehrte Anzeigen*, 1877, p. 1308 ; Ignatius, *Rom.*, 5.

‡ See p. 312. The narrative of Tacitus, *Hist.*, ii., 61, is specially appropriate. Mariccus was spared by the beasts to whom he was exposed, and the crowd believed that this was the effect of his divine power. Cp. Le Blant, *Actes*, pp. 86 and 95.

§ *Acta Sanctorum*, 9 Jan., p. 569. M. le Blant's reference, *Actes*, p. 86, directed me to this document. His view with regard to the scene differs from mine. The lion, having licked Thekla's feet, might recognise her in the arena by smell.

alone. Immediately afterwards a bull wounded her, and then a leopard killed her. This action of the lion was interpreted afterwards in a more miraculous sense : an old Spanish hymn speaks of the lion " coming to worship, not to devour the Virgin." *

The tale of Marciana is unhistorical.† It contains various miracles of a rather absurd type. Possibly her fate in the arena was modelled on that of Thekla ; and perhaps the incident of the lion was told in *Acta Theklæ* originally in this simple and natural form, which afterwards was replaced by other details of a more marvellous kind, suited to the taste of later centuries. In this small city of an eastern province it is not probable that the *venatio* would be on a large scale ; probably it was given at the expense of the president, as was commonly the case, and as is here stated in the Latin version. There was therefore probably only one lion ; and this single lion was esteemed a great rarity and a proof of unusual magnificence. The Syriac version speaks only of one lion. Bears were found in the mountains not far from Antioch,‡ and it is quite probable

---

* *Adoraturus, non comesturus, Virginem,* where, as M. le Blant observes, the old *odoratus* has undergone only a slight change. The hymn is quoted in *Acta Sanctorum, l.c.*

† In such a case one need not conclude that the person is a myth, but that details had perished, and were in demand, and were supplied from the analogy of other documents and general probability. M. le Blant has shown that details, historical in one tale, were adopted unhistorically in others, *Actes,* p. 88, etc.

‡ I have actually seen a bear further east in a solitary glen of the Anti-taurus ; and in one case among the Phrygian mountains a Turk professed to point out traces of a bear in a cave, and asserted that bears were occasionally found. I felt far from certain that he was not speaking from a wish to please me, mistaking, as these people often do, curiosity about a point for a desire that the point should be of some suggested character.

that there was a bear in the *venatio,* and that the original intention, before a criminal turned up in the person of Thekla, was to exhibit a fight between the two.* All versions of the tale mention the bear and its fight with the lioness. The Syriac version alone mentions a leopard. This is probably an addition ; and we remember that the Syrian Ignatius makes the earliest known reference to leopards,† which therefore must have been well known in Syria. Panthers were frequently found in Taurus at that time ; ‡ and I have heard men assert that they are still found in the country, but have never known any person who had actually seen a panther there. As no reference occurs to the panther, we may set down the leopard as an addition made by the Syrian translator. The numerous other animals are likewise due to later exaggeration. The bulls alone, which were introduced as an afterthought on the part of Alexander, in order to tear the criminal asunder, perhaps belong to the original tale. Some specially shocking detail is needed as a cause for Tryphæna's fainting ; and this seems a device which might be easily suggested and acted on in real life. The preparation of this mode of execution so affected the Queen that she fainted. Alexander was terrified lest he should be considered by the Emperor, her relative, as guilty, if Tryphæna suffered seriously. He hastened to release Thekla. The governor, who is represented as having consented rather reluctantly to the last

---

* Camel fights are now a recognised sport at festivals. A lion-and-bear fight is reported in *Scotsman,* about January 2nd, 1893.

† Lightfoot, *Ignat.,* i., p. 412 ; ii., p. 212. Syrian and African leopards were the two species used in *venationes* by Probus, *Scr. Hist. Aug.,* xxviii., 19.

‡ They are often mentioned in Cicero's letters from Asia Minor.

act of barbarity, at once pardoned her, and she returned home with Tryphæna.

In the scene at Antioch few traces are found which imply that Thekla was known to be a Christian. The women sympathise with her in a most thorough and enthusiastic way. Her cause was theirs : what she is condemned to suffer they may in ordinary course deserve. This is most strongly expressed in the Latin version, § 32, but the Greek also has it less plainly. Such a view was impossible if they thought her a Christian; they believed her to be a devotee, bound by some unusual conditions.* Only in the passage referring to Falconilla is Thekla's religion known to other persons. But the name Falconilla† shows that the passage is not original ; and its inconsistency with its surroundings in this feature confirms the inference. Moreover, the prayers for the soul of the deceased Falconilla have a formal and developed tone, which suits the second century better than A.D. 50.

The words of the governor's *act*,‡ setting Thekla free, have not been left uninterpolated by later taste ; at least, the epithet God-fearing ($\theta\epsilon o\sigma\epsilon\beta\hat{\eta}$, *metuentem dominum*) is due to a later age, and to the desire to use this opportunity of making the governor bear witness to the truth. The phrase "the servant of God," however, is probably

---

* Much allowance, they might contend, ought to be made for an inspired servant of " the God " ; she differed from the usual type, but that is a matter between " the God " and herself.

† It could not occur in the *gens Antonia* : it became familiar in Asia when Falco was proconsul, about 130.

‡ F and G retain the term *actum*, which is correct, though the plural is much commoner than the singular.

original, for, in the Latin * form *ancillam dei*, it is susceptible of a sense perfectly consistent with the original scene. The governor knew that the women defended Thekla as a devotee of unusual style acting in obedience to the commands of "the God," who had imposed on her a special service; and he therefore says, "I release to you Thekla, the servant of 'the God'"—*i.e.*, "I accept your explanation of her action towards Alexander as a ground for freeing her from punishment."

M. Le Blant (*Actes*, p. 174) finds in the use of the correct term *dimitto* in the Latin version evidence that the scene is of early character. But it is obvious that the use of such a term in a translation from the Greek cannot be taken as evidence of anything more than the translator's skill. Moreover, in this case, M. Le Blant makes the mistake of taking Grabe's Latin rendering of the text of G for the old Latin version. Grabe uses a formula which M. Le Blant considers to be strikingly accurate; but the old Latin version is far looser and freer in its expression. This is one of the cases in which G has preserved the original form better than the Latin version. The ease with which Grabe renders it into a Latin phrase that has deceived M. Le Blant, shows that the Greek is a literal translation of the Latin original.

---

* The proceedings were of course in Latin, except where evidence had to be taken in Greek; and the original *actum* was couched in Latin. There can be no doubt that Lipsius has been led astray by his false view as to the excellence of E, when he prefers its text, λέγων, to that of F and G, γράψας οὕτως. The rule was that the sentence must be written out first, and then recited from the document. See Le Blant, *Actes*, pp. 168, 176.

7. THE ORIGINAL TALE OF THEKLA.

Starting from the arguments advanced in the preceding sections, we must next try to determine the chief features of the original tale, selecting those incidents which are inexplicable except as having been written in the first century, and adding to them others which are needed to connect and complete them, and which bear obvious marks of high antiquity. It would be best to try to preserve the original language as far as possible; but this attempt would involve a minute study of the text and comparison of the various versions and manuscripts. Perhaps it would prove an impossible task, owing to the great changes that have been introduced during later ages; but even the attempt is precluded to one who has not access to more materials than I have before me.* A brief outline is all that can now be ventured on.

When Paul was expelled from Antioch, a citizen of Iconium, a just man (Onesiphorus†) was warned (in a dream‡) that Paul was about to come to that city, and was told where he should find him, and how he should recognise him. He went forth to the place where the roads met, and watched those who were passing by along the Royal Road that leads to Lystra, until he saw Paul approach, and recognised his appearance (see p. 31). Paul returned with Onesiphorus, lived in his house, and declared the word of God. Meetings were held in the house, with bending of the knees and breaking of bread.

---

* On the text see the note at the end of this chapter.

† The name Onesiphorus was introduced in the second century. See next section.

‡ Perhaps the warning was originally given in a dream. The name of Titus is certainly a later addition. See next section.

A noble Iconian family, rich and influential, lived in an adjoining house. A chamber in an upper story of this house overlooked the humbler home of Onesiphorus; and Thekla, to whom this chamber belonged, could thus easily hear Paul's teaching. She was fascinated; and her mind was alienated from her ordinary pursuits, from her family, and from her affianced husband Thamyris. This soon became obvious, and drew on Paul the enmity of the two powerful families of Thamyris and Thekla. Paul was, at their instigation, imprisoned by the magistrates, the charge against him being that he had influenced the minds of women by magical arts, and caused disorders in the city.

At night Thekla bribed the porter with her bracelets to let her go out of the house. She went to the prison, and, by giving the gaoler a silver mirror, induced him to allow her access to Paul. She was instructed by him throughout the night, and was found there next morning, in the way already described. Paul was then scourged and expelled from the city by the magistrates, the severest penalty within their competence. Thekla was taken to her own home; and it was hoped that in course of time she would recover her reason, and be free from the influence of the magician who had bewitched her. Some interval elapsed,* during which her family used persuasion and

---

* It is clear that the course of events required some time, because the interpolator of the Myra episode was under the impression that several years elapsed; and when he wished to bring about a subsequent meeting with Paul he thought it necessary to put the meeting at a late period. He must, however, have exaggerated the lapse of time, as all the events belong to the reign of Claudius. The homily attributed to Chrysostom is the authority at this point.

moral influence : her parents, lover, relatives, and attendants tried all their arts to bring her back to her old
ways, but in vain. She could think only of Paul.

They then resorted to more severe measures. One of
their means was to bring her before a tribunal of the city,
in which the judges (*dikastai*) threatened her with severe
penalties. Thekla at last escaped (or was allowed to
escape), and was pursued by Thamyris ; and presumably
it was believed that, if he once forced her to his will, she
would thereafter be under his influence, and freed from that
of Paul. She fled into the bare level plains that stretch
away from Iconium on all sides except the west.
Thamyris overtook her : there seemed no escape from
his violence : she prayed, and was saved in some way
unknown.

Thekla, trying to find Paul, finally came to Antioch.
As she entered the city, she was accosted by (Alexander)*
the high-priest, president of the festival which was just
beginning. In order to give dignity to this festival, which
was of an official character, and formed part of the Roman
plan for consolidating the province and strengthening the
feeling of loyalty in it, the governor of Galatia had come
on a visit to Antioch ; and all the most influential and
wealthy citizens of the southern parts of the province had
come to pay their respects to him.† Alexander, struck
with the beauty of this young woman, whose appearance,

---

* The name was introduced, perhaps, in the second century.

† The statue of Concord, presented by Lystra to Antioch, may
have been given on some such occasion as this. (See p. 50.) Dio
Chrysostom's description of the crowds at Apameia, when the
Roman proconsul of Asia came to hold the *conventus*, may be read
in illustration of this description. See his Apameian oration.

unescorted, in the street seemed to indicate her status out-side of the pale of respectability, accosted and kissed her. Thekla repelled his advances, appealing to the right of a stranger and guest, noble in her own city, and engaged in the service of "the God"; and on his continued im-portunity, she tore his outer garment (*chlamys*), and pulled from his head the crown that marked his priestly office. He ordered his attendants, who were of course numerous, to arrest her. She called on Paul to help her.

Being brought before the Roman governor straight from the scene of the offence, she was judged forthwith at the festival in view of all the spectators. The charge was sacrilege, in that she had assaulted the high-priest while wearing his sacred official dress. The offence being proved by the admission of the accused, she was condemned to be exposed to the wild beasts, which the president was going to exhibit on one of the later days of the festival. Much feeling was aroused in the city; and the women especially took the part of Thekla, as being in the service of "the God," and carrying out the conditions imposed on her by his commands. Thekla was permitted to continue to observe the rule of purity; and, through the general sym-pathy, the noblest lady in the assembly, Queen Tryphæna, became guarantee for her appearance when required, and took her meantime to her own house. On the day of the procession with which the games in the stadium opened, Thekla was placed on the top of a cage, in which was confined the chief ornament of the exhibition, a lioness. The lioness licked her feet, protruding its tongue between the bars. After the procession Thekla returned to Try-phæna's charge to spend her last night.

During the night Tryphæna, whose sympathies had been

already strongly excited in defence of the young woman, was still further moved in her favour by a dream, in which her own deceased daughter directed her to receive Thekla as a new daughter.* In the morning Tryphæna refused to give up Thekla to her fate, until the appearance of soldiers sent by the governor showed her that it was vain to resist. She then led Thekla by the hand to the stadium, escorted by her numerous train of attendants. The feeling of the crowd had in part changed, and many were eager for the spectacle. But the women were still true to Thekla, and loudly upbraided the governor, sarcastically bidding him slay them all.

In the arena Thekla, wearing only the cincture, according to the Roman practice at such executions, was bound to a stake.† She prayed, saying, " My Lord and my God, the Father of our Lord Jesus the Messiah, Thou art the helper of the persecuted, and Thou art the companion of the poor ; behold Thy handmaiden, for lo, the shame of women is uncovered in me, and I stand in the midst of all this people. My Lord and my God, remember Thy handmaiden in this hour."

In the *venatio*, which followed, the lioness, which had already become acquainted with Thekla, recognised her (perhaps by smelling, as in the case of Marciana) and did her no harm When a bear was introduced, the lioness fought with it. Alexander then suggested that Thekla should be fastened to bulls and thus torn asunder, and the

---

* The incident was greatly elaborated in the growth of the tale ; but something of the kind seems required to explain the action.

† This, as M. Le Blant has shown, was the regular practice. Some of the additions to the scene are inconsistent with this, which constitutes an additional argument against them.

governor reluctantly consented.   As the preparations were
being completed Tryphæna fainted away from horror.

Then followed the release of Thekla, as already related.
She returned home with Tryphæna, lived as her daughter,
and converted her and her household.

These incidents, in their simple and vivid character, take
us back to the age of Claudius, or the earlier part of Nero's
reign ; and they are so true to the circumstances of that
period, that they could not possibly have been constructed
in an age when Christianity had come to be a proof of
disloyalty, and the old procedure was forgotten.   We are
carried back to the first century, and to a writer who
remembered at least the local surroundings (see p. 31 ff.),
the actual characters (Paul's appearance, Tryphæna), and
the species of charges made about A.D. 50–64.   Finally, we
consider that the easiest supposition is that Thekla was
a real person, and her actual fortunes were related by the
original author, with perhaps a certain amount of selection
and idealisation.   Like Zahn, we should find no chronological difficulty in accepting Jerome's statement that the
original author, a presbyter of Asia, was degraded from
his office by St. John.   The statement is quite a possible
one ; but it rests on too poor authority to be accepted, for
Jerome quotes from Tertullian, and Tertullian does not
name John.   Now it is plain that Jerome's words are at
least partly taken from the extant passage of Tertullian ;
and, unless some further support can be found, we must
treat what he adds to Tertullian as void of authority
(see also p. 403 *f*).

The question naturally suggests itself,—Why was the
author of this tale degraded from his office?   We might
explain it, partly because he represented the action of Paul

as causing a disturbance of family life and family ties
which the Church in early times discouraged (see pp. 246,
282), and partly on the hypothesis that some points in
his teaching were considered to be dangerous, and were
subsequently eliminated, and cannot be recovered. Moreover, there remain even in the mutilated and re-written
tale some traces of a view of women's rights and position,
which is thoroughly characteristic of the Asian social
system, and thoroughly opposed to the ideas favoured by
the Church (see p. 161 f.). But I believe the answer lies
in another direction. This original edition is not the one
alluded to by Tertullian. It is not written by a native
of Asia, but is native to Galatic Phrygia, where the scene
lies, and redolent of the soil from which it sprang. It is
an old tale about Thekla, in which Paul appears only for
a brief space at the beginning of the action, and from
which a presbyter of Asia, as Tertullian says, constructed
the document popularly known and appealed to by some
as an authority in his time. Tertullian was clearly aware
that this presbyter was not the original author. He does
not say that he composed the tale, but that he constructed
it from previously existing material.* The material consisted of the tale which has just been given, and additions
were made by the presbyter.

---

* This statement of Tertullian (*de Baptismo*, 17), " . . . *eam
scripturam construxit, quasi titulo Pauli de suo cumulans,*"
has been singularly misinterpreted by writers on the subject. It
clearly implies additions made by the presbyter from his own store
to a document, the result being that he "augmented it with the
title of Paul." His additions were from "love of Paul," and greatly
increased the part played by Paul in the action. Such seems the
plain inference from Tertullian's words

8. Revision of the Tale of Thekla, A.D. 130–150.

About A.D. 130, or soon after, the tale of Thekla was enlarged by a reviser,[*] who accepted it as true, and wished to connect it with the incidents and personages recorded in Acts and the Epistles of Paul. This person had never seen either Antioch or Iconium, but probably lived in the province of Asia ; and the country from Thyatira to Troas best suits the conditions prescribed by the following view of his action. He belonged to the Church in the period before the differences which led to the Montanist quarrels began. Hence we find in the work, as he left it, no references to the questions that developed soon after A.D. 150 ;[†] but its tone is that of the conditions amid which Montanism grew.

This reviser introduced into the tale the teaching, which, while of a strongly ascetic tendency, never actually goes so far as actual disapproval of marriage, but which might readily be pushed to that extreme. Abstaining from wine and flesh is implicitly recommended ; for Paul's food, § 25, consists only of bread, herbs, water, and salt (the last only in the Syriac version). Lipsius, pp. 448–57, has discussed these indications carefully, though his conclusions are different. These views are not expressed in a way so extreme as to have been expelled by later revisers, but belong to a simpler period of thought, when a Catholic writer indulged in an " extravagance of statement " that has almost a " heretical aspect."[‡] " Such skill as the

---

[*] For brevity's sake I state opinions dogmatically, and without argument.

[†] Zahn puts this clearly and well, *Gött. Gel. Anz.*, 1877, p. 1305.

[‡] So Dr. Gwynn, p. 891, following Dr. Salmon, *Introduction to New Testament*, 2nd ed., p. 420.

writer possessed appears chiefly in the ingenuity with which he works in genuine Pauline phrases, all of them in some degree turned from their proper bent." [*]

Demas and Hermogenes belong to this period. Their action in Iconium is an anachronism ; but, as M. Le Blant shows (*Actes*, p. 97), does not belong to a late period. Their appearance in § 1 is inconsistent with § 3, where Paul seems to advance alone towards Onesiphorus. They belong to a series of interpolations, intended to connect *Acta Theklæ* with circumstances and personages mentioned in 2 Tim. Demas "forsook Paul, having loved this present world" (iv. 10) ; and Hermogenes "turned away from" him (i. 15). The name of Paul's host at Iconium, Onesiphorus, was also introduced at this time, being suggested by the words, "the house of Onesiphorus, for he oft refreshed me" (i. 16, cp .iv. 19). Probably the host bore in the original tale a native, non-Greek, name, like Thekla.[†] As Lipsius has remarked, the allusion to Paul's sufferings at Antioch, Iconium, and Lystra, in 2 Tim. iii. 11, probably directed the reviser's attention to that Epistle, when he was seeking to connect a tale whose scene lay in these towns with Paul's own words. Moreover, as Timothy was a native of Lystra, it seemed to the reviser natural that the characters of the tale should be mentioned by Paul in writing to him. The reviser also found in the same Epistle an allusion to a coppersmith (which he used in § 1), and to Titus as travelling apart from Paul (which made him introduce Titus as describing Paul to Onesiphorus in § 2).

---

[*] Gwynn, p. 890.

[†] The name of Onesiphorus' wife and of one son seem also to be non-Greek ; but they have been much corrupted in the MSS.

In the original tale Paul played too slight a part, and this the reviser corrected. He introduced the residence of Onesiphorus and his family with Paul in the tomb on the road to Antioch,* praying for Thekla's deliverance, and the journey of Thekla to Myra for a last meeting with Paul.

Part of the scene in the tomb, with its ascetic diet, is distinctly of this period. M. Le Blant has argued also that the residence in a grave by the roadside is a sign of early date (*Actes*, p. 269); and he illustrates this detail by similar real events. The second century is the date to which M. Le Blant inclines on p. 97.

The journey to Myra is due to the desire for a final recognition of Thekla's faith by the Apostle. It was introduced by one who had a certain acquaintance with the topography of Asia Minor, and who selected the nearest point on the south coast visited by Paul. This was Myra according to the text of Acts xxvi. 30, as preserved in *Codex Bezæ.*† But this person cannot have had any personal acquaintance with Antioch; for he evidently imagined that the journey to Myra from Antioch was quite a short one.‡ Such imperfect knowledge of the topography implies that he belonged to a district out of direct

---

* Daphne was substituted when the Syrian Antioch was introduced.

† See p. 155. In one Latin version, D, the more familiar name Smyrna is substituted for the unknown Myra by a translator ignorant of Asia Minor, and of the very name of Myra.

‡ This we see because (1) Paul's stay at Myra could not be long, and there was no time for news of his arrival to spread far, and for Thekla to go to him; (2) Tryphæna heard that Thekla was going from Myra to Iconium, and sent offering her gifts. Both considerations imply rapid communication between the two places.

communication with Antioch, such as Mysia or the Troad ; and that Myra and Antioch were vaguely known to him as distant cities, one on the south coast, and the other connected by road with the same coast.

The Myra episode has several marks of early character. M. le Blant quotes from M. Heuzey * the explanation of the alteration which Thekla made in her dress. By a change in the arrangement of her tunic at the girdle, and by some use of the needle, she so transformed it, that it passed for a man's tunic.† This description, so brief yet so particular, was perfectly clear in the second century to readers familiar with the old Greek dress ; but it was unintelligible to persons living in a later period, when the style of dress had changed. We can now understand it by an effort of archæological imagination. Thekla wore the woman's long tunic, reaching to the feet and confined by a girdle round the waist. Ordinarily, when a woman wished to take active exercise, she took hold of the tunic above the girdle, and pulled it up, so that it formed a wide loose fold, which hung down over the girdle round her body, and which she usually confined by a second girdle ; thus the tunic, even though as short as a man's, still continued distinguishable as a feminine garment. Thekla, instead of allowing the fold to hang down outside, kept it inside, so that it was unseen ; and she sewed the tunic together in this position, thus shortening it by a broad " tuck." Her girdle would conceal the seam, and the garment would resemble a man's short tunic. The description was evidently quite unintelligible to the Latin translators.

It is also clear that the Myra episode was inserted before

---

* *Actes des Martyrs*, p. 322.

† ἀναζωσαμένη τε καὶ ῥάψασα τὸν χιτῶνα εἰς ἐπενδύτου σχῆμα ἀνδρικόν.

the confusion with the Syrian Antioch had been caused ; for it would be absurd to make Thekla go from the Syrian Antioch to Myra to meet Paul.

The reviser evidently connected the tale with Paul's third journey. His reasoning, apparently, was that the action could not be conceived as taking place at Paul's first visit to Iconium, for he disappears from the action so quickly ; whereas Paul remained in the country, and soon returned to Iconium after his first expulsion or flight from it. Moreover, neither Barnabas nor Timothy, Paul's companions on his first two journeys, played any part in the tale ; and the reviser could imagine that unimportant characters should be omitted, but not important personages like these. On the third journey nothing is recorded in Acts about Paul ; and there was therefore a suitable gap in which to introduce the tale of Thekla. Allowing a fair interval to elapse, he found that, by the time Thekla was victorious over all her trials, Paul might have arrived at Myra on his way to Jerusalem.

The reviser showed some skill in connecting the tale of Thekla with the record of Paul's life ; and in the case of Titus this is conspicuous. The argument has often been advanced that Titus is spoken of in Gal. ii. 1 as if he were familiar to the Galatians. The presbyter apparently believed that Titus (who, as appears from Acts, did not travel along with Paul on the third journey) went before him through Iconium to Corinth, whence he returned to meet Paul in Macedonia (2 Cor. ii. 13, vii. 6).

The name of Falconilla was introduced at this time (see p. 407), and the scene in the stadium at Antioch was modified in some details. The self-baptism of Thekla is inconsistent with her being fastened to the stake, which was probably the original attitude ; and the cloud that veiled Thekla was probably inserted at the same time. The references to baptism may probably all be taken as insertions of this period, except that in § 25 (p. 422).

The attitude assumed by Thekla, both in the theatre at Iconium and in the stadium at Antioch, was with hands outstretched in the attitude of crucifixion. M. le Blant (*Actes*, p. 297) quotes various passages, showing that this attitude was common for martyrs and for persons praying.*
But the custom seems to belong to the second and later centuries, and the statements about Thekla's attitude (which vary greatly in different MSS.) must be all considered interpolations, probably of this period.

Lipsius quotes a number of characteristics which prove that the *Acta* belong to a date not later than A.D. 190. These seem to me to fall into two classes: (1) those which are consistent with a first century date—*e.g.*, the simple formula of baptism in the name of Jesus Christ (§ 34), the simple forms of worship (bending the knee, breaking of bread, declaring the word of God, § 5), the meeting in private houses (§§ 5, 7). (2) Those which rather point to the second century, or at least a period of more developed forms than the middle of the first century—*e.g.*, prayers for the heathen dead (§ 29), designation of baptism as " the seal " (§ 25), the conception of baptism as a safeguard against temptation (§§ 25, 40). It will be found that the division to which the investigation has led us independently, corresponds well with this evidence.

* The Christians would not pray in the heathen attitude, *palmas ad cælum tendentes.* Tertullian, *de Orat.*, 17, says the Christians, from a feeling of humility, did not raise their hands high.

M. le Blant's chapter (*Actes*, p. 80) on the method of interpolation of some hagiographical documents is most instructive in regard to the history of the *Acta*, and he gives some striking examples of the way in which old texts were worked over, additions being made in some places and complete changes in others (the changes being sometimes almost motiveless in their inanity, sometimes conditioned by a distinct purpose).

The author of this revised edition may be identified as the Asian presbyter said by Tertullian to have constructed the document by adding to older material. His date is determined both by internal evidence (1, character of the teaching of Paul, already described ; 2, he still seems to consider Antioch and Iconium as in the same province), and by inference from Tertullian, who implies that the work was known and quoted as an authority and not as a work of yesterday. It seems hard to think that Tertullian could have written as he did, if the work had not been "constructed" at least twenty-five or thirty years previously—*i.e.*, the revision was older than 165 or 170.

We gladly acquit the presbyter of making Paul go with Thekla to Antioch and play the disgraceful part assigned to him there ; for this episode is necessarily connected with the trial and attempted burning of Thekla, and is inconsistent with the flight of Thekla to the wilderness. Moreover, when Thekla asked for baptism, there was at this stage of the growth of the legend no reason why it should be refused ; whereas at a later stage it must be refused in order to preserve the self-baptism at Antioch. Again, the presbyter did not object to Thekla's dressing like a man ; but the composer of her interview with Paul did evidently object to it, and makes Paul formally express disapproval of it. In the presbyter's revision, then, Paul, after fasting and praying for Thekla's deliverance, went on to Antioch and Ephesus (see chap. v.).

9. THE ICONIAN LEGEND OF THEKLA.

About A.D. 140-160 Lycaonia was united with Cilicia and Isauria, and the "three Eparchies" were governed by an official of consular rank. Iconium was henceforth a city of higher dignity, metropolis of an eparchy, and a colony. As it was now completely separated from Antioch, the situation implied in the tale of Thekla was no longer suitable to existing conditions. Moreover, when Christianity became the strongest element in the city, the close union between the Christians and their co-religionists in other towns was replaced by a certain emotion of municipal patriotism and a feeling of distinction from other cities. Thekla was the heroine of Iconium, and it seemed right that the city should be signalised as the scene of her triumph, and it had more right to the presence of a Roman governor than Antioch, which was not a metropolis. Thus an Iconian legend grew up, and was finally incorporated in the tale, to the effect that Thekla was tried, condemned by the governor to the flames, and miraculously rescued. This legend involved the dropping out of the older tale of Thekla's sufferings and flight. The meeting with Paul in the tomb and journey with him to Antioch were substituted for the episode in the wilderness.

It is clear, however, that the scene in the theatre developed separately from the meeting with Paul. These were two independent floating legends, which were awkwardly put side by side in the text without being properly worked into one another. The literary form of these additions is defective; and they show a vulgarity of conception and poverty in creative power which places them below the work of the presbyter.

The Iconian legend was familiar to Gregory of Nyssa, and other writers of the fourth century;* and appears even to be older than A.D. 300, to judge from the account given by Dr. Gwynn of the evidence of Methodius.† Probably there were for a time copies of both the presbyter's and the Iconian revision in circulation; but the latter soon prevailed, for the deliverance from fire was too striking a detail to be omitted.

A general revision of the text, with slight modifications, additions, and modernisations, also continued to be made as time went on. A proof of this appears in the title *proconsul*, which is applied in most MSS. to the governors. Now there never was a time when a proconsul was resident at Iconium or Antioch, or was governor of the province in which either city was situated. We often find anachronisms in the way of giving to an officer a title appropriate to the period in which the writer lived, but inappropriate to that in which his scene lay; here the anachronism cannot be explained in that way. Dr. Gwynn suggests that a writer, who lived in Asia before A.D. 190, named the governor of Galatia proconsul, "because he had himself been accustomed to see a pro-

---

* The Iconian revision was unknown to the author of the *Homily* attributed to Chrysostom; but the date of the *Homily* is not known.

† I have not access to his dialogue *de angelica virginitate et castitate*. Photius is said to declare that the work had been adulterated.

consul at Ephesus or Smyrna."* But no parallel is known
at that period, for titles are generally given very accurately
in documents of the second century ; and such accuracy
is usually taken as a test of date. The title *proconsul* is
found in a very uncertain way in the MSS.,† and has
probably crept gradually into the text, after the meaning
and distinction of the Roman titles had been forgotten,
through a process of ignorant archaising under the influence of other old *Acta*, in which the title was rightly used.
Apparently the false title was first introduced in speeches
addressed to the governor, and gradually spread to some
other cases ; and it is far more generally used in the
late Iconian narrative than in the old Antiochian scene.
If, as is not improbable, the Latin text *c*, in which the
title is often used, was of African origin, the writer would
be familiar with similar tales in which proconsuls were
prominent.

M. Le Blant (*Actes*, p. 109) points out that the governor

---

* *Dict. Chr. Biogr.*, iv., p. 893-4, where he has not noticed that
at the period in question Antioch and Iconium were in separate
provinces. See above, p. 111.

† The correct titles, *Hegemon, Præses*, are commoner in the MSS.
In the scene at Antioch one of the Latin MSS., D, uses only *præses*,
while another, *c*, uses *proconsul* very often, and the third, *m*,
occasionally. In the same scene the term *proconsul* occurs only
once in the Greek MSS., which have it frequently in the Iconian
scene. Again, we find cases where the title *proconsul* occurs only
in the poorer Greek MSS., while the better have *hegemon—e.g.*,
§ 16, l. 6, where two MSS., F and G, read *hegemon* with the
Syriac version, while all Lipsius' other MSS. have *proconsul*.
Lipsius includes the Latin MSS in this latter class, but D has
præses. Moreover, *proconsul* in the Greek MSS. is rarely used,
except in the vocative, in which it is least likely to belong to the
original text, and most likely to be a later insertion. Basil uses
proconsul at Iconium, hegemon at Antioch.

at Iconium was assisted by a council. Such assessors are a well-known feature of Roman procedure (pp. 223–28). Undoubtedly accuracy in such points is a proof of good character in a tale; but the Iconian reviser was quite as likely as the Asian presbyter to introduce the procedure by assessors (*consilium*), which was in regular use at the time when he was writing.

In subsequent history, the worship of Thekla as a saint became established widely in Asia Minor; first of all in the southern parts, and especially in Seleuceia of Isauria. There grew up at each shrine, doubtless, a foundation legend (ἱερὸς λόγος),* and such legends found their way into the text. In this way Thekla was made to travel to Seleuceia, and to pass through various adventures there. In some MSS. she is even described as going to Rome and dying there. But we need not enter on these Seleucian and later developments, nor touch on the statements about her age, which are devoid of authority.

Note i. Pauline Chronology.—Assuming a historical element in the tale of Thekla, we must try to fix the date. My view is that, after his first journey, Paul was possessed with the idea that his work lay towards the west (Acts xv. 38; Gal. *passim*); and no long interval is likely to have occurred in his work. Particularly after the trial before Gallio his views developed rapidly. He recognised that his work lay in the Empire, which protected the Christians against the Jews; and his thought developed from the stage seen in *Thessalonians* to that in *Galatians*. Accepting Spitta's view that Acts xv. 1–33 precedes Acts xiii., xiv., we date Paul's first journey April, 49–July, 51; his second began in April, 52. He came to Corinth, and wrote to the Thessalonians in autumn 53. The rupture

---

* Any one who wishes to study the formation of such legends in the country should go to Sasima in Cappadocia, now called Hassa Keui, and ask the priest to tell the story of the foundation of the village church by St. Makrina, to whom it is dedicated.

with the Jews took place, as usual, soon after his arrival; Gallio
was proconsul 1 July, 53–30, June, 54. In spring 55 Paul went to
Ephesus, whence he wrote to the Galatians (see p. 167); after visiting Jerusalem and Antioch, he resided in Ephesus from autumn
55 till the end of 57 (the three months, Acts xix. 8, are probably
included in the two years, xix. 10). Then, after visiting Macedonia
and Greece, he reached Patara and Myra in late summer 58. His
first residence in Iconium was in winter 49–50; and the story of
Thekla belongs to the spring, summer, and autumn of A.D. 50.

Note 2. Family of Antonia Tryphæna, Queen-Consort in
Thrace, Queen of Pontus (Mommsen, Eph. Ep. II. p. 259ff. :—

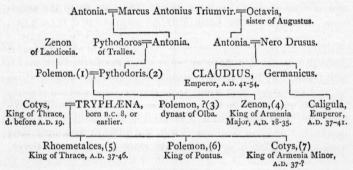

(1) Polemon Eusebes was made King of Lycaonia and perhaps part
of Cilicia in 39 B.C.; but this territory, soon afterwards, was seized
by Amyntas. Polemon became King of Pontus 38 or 37, King of
Armenia Minor 33, and King of Bosporus 14. He died about 8 B.C.
(2) Pythodoris, born about 33, married King Polemon B.C. 13 or 12,
and reigned as Queen of Pontus after his death till some unknown
date after A.D. 21. (3) The eldest son of Polemon and Pythodoris
was probably M. Antonius Polemon; but Strabo (p. 556) does not
mention his name. He aided his mother in governing Pontus without the title of king; and, soon after the death of Archelaus in
17 A.D., he became dynast of Olba. In the passage of Strabo the
words δυναστεύει δ' ὁ πρεσβύτ[ερ]ος αὐτῶν are to be taken as a subsequent
addition made by the writer to the following line. He wrote
originally συνδιοικεῖ, and altered it to συνδιῴκει, when the change
occurred; the words δυναστεύει κ.τ.λ. have got into the wrong place,
and are incorrectly applied to the son of Tryphæna. The sense is
"of the sons of Pythodoris one used to govern along with his

mother without regal title, and is now a dynast—viz., the older of them." Polemon ruled at least eleven years at Olba, as we learn from coins.* (4) M. Antonius Zenon was no doubt his full name. (5–7) The brothers were taken to Rome on the death of their father, and educated there along with the young Caligula. Tiberius was too jealous to allow them to reign. Caligula, as soon as he came to the throne, made them all kings, A.D. 37. (6) Polemon became King of Pontus and Bosporus 37, lost Bosporus and received Olba in exchange 41, lost Pontus 63, died probably before 72.

NOTE 3. TEXT.—Lipsius, *Proleg.*, p. cv, justly praises the Syriac version as retaining much that the Greek MSS. have lost or altered, and as often approaching more closely than they do to the archetype. Among the three Latin MSS. he assigns the first rank to *c*, as approaching nearest in character to E, to which he attributes a similar rank among the Greek MSS., and he puts *m* second in point of excellence. It is difficult to judge about the Latin texts, for the plan followed by Lipsius often leads him to omit variants. But, so far as I can judge from using D, it retains some original features which are not quoted by Lipsius from *m* and *c*. Occasionally, however, the latter are preferable to D; and they seem to be independently translated from the Greek, but perhaps at a little later date, and therefore they approximate more closely to the Greek. Schlau believes that D may represent a translation of the second century (Zahn, *Gött. Gel. Anz.*, 1877, p. 1293); but its Latinity is rather of the fifth than the second journey. There was probably no Latin version till after Jerome's time, when Thekla's worship had spread to the west. The Syriac version seems earlier than the Latin; one of the MSS. belongs to the sixth century. Among the Greek MSS., G, F, and M show archaic touches lost in the others.

NOTE 4. CASTELIUS.—This fictitious governor, resident at Iconium, is supposed by Gutschmid to be historical, and his name to be really Cæsellius (*Rhein. Mus.*, 1864, p. 397); and this impossible suggestion (no officer Cæsellius is known about A.D. 50) has been quoted on a par with his brilliant identification of Tryphæna. The form Castelius is as old as Basil; but the Latin variant Sextilius points perhaps to Statilius as the original form.

---

* This account of Tryphæna's brother is a hypothetical addition. He died certainly before 41.

CHAPTER XVII.

THE CHURCH FROM 120 *TO* 170 *A.D.*

WE have seen that, before the end of the first century, there was, as a rule, an individual *episkopos* in each community, who tended, in fact, to be permanent, but who possessed no official rank except as a *presbyteros*. It may be argued that the account we have given of his position is inconsistent and self-contradictory. We acknowledge that this is so ; but this does not prove it to be untrue. The office was in process of rapid growth, and no account of it can be true which makes it logical and self-consistent in character. It had vast potentiality, for the whole future of the Church was latent in it ; yet, in its outward appear-ance and its relation to the past, it was humble, and the *episkopos* was merely a presbyter in special circumstances.* His actual influence depended on his personal character. The order of prophets still existed ; but, to take an example, what influence was any prophet likely to have in Smyrna except with Polycarp's approval? But if the idea had been possible in Smyrna that Polycarp's action was guided to the faintest degree by thought of self, his influence would never have existed. His personal

---

* If the view we have taken is correct, the question whether an *episkopos* exercised any teaching or religious duties shows a mis-apprehension of the situation. The *episkopos* may do anything that a presbyter may do, for he is a presbyter. He may be a prophet and speak with inspiration, for inspiration may come to all.

influence, however, was undoubtedly increased by the
important administrative duties which he performed as
episkopos; and, in all probability, his position in Smyrna
did much to impress on the mind of his contemporaries
in general, and of Ignatius in particular, a new conception
of the episcopal office. Yet, even after his death, the letter
to the church at Philomelion, written, as we must understand, by the *episkopos* who succeeded him, is couched in
the old style. The writer is merely the impersonal mouth-
piece of the community at Smyrna.

An important step was made when the Christian communities began to accommodate themselves to Roman law
by enrolling themselves as Benefit Clubs. That this step
had been taken by the third century is certain in a considerable number of cases, and may safely be assumed as
general.* As to the time when the custom began no evidence remains; but I see no reason why it should not have
begun as early as Hadrian's reign, simultaneously with the
outburst of Apologetic literature and the general *rapprochement* between the Church and the Empire, A.D. 130–40.†

---

* Le Blant, *Actes*, pp. 282, 288; De Rossi, *Roma Sotterr.*, ii.,
p. 82; and my papers in *Expositor*, December 1888, February 1889.
Hatch, *Bampton Lectures*, p. 152, collects the facts well, but
states them without sufficient legal precision. The right of forming
associations, provided these were not in themselves illegal, belonged
theoretically to all except soldiers; but practically almost all associations were illegal. The exception in the case of poor persons,
chiefly for purposes of burial, came to be important under Hadrian,
Digest, 47, 22; *C. I. L.*, xiv., 2112. The technical name is *collegia
tenuiorum*, or *funeraticia*, p. 359*n*.

† In 1882 (*Journal of Hellenic Studies*, p. 347), unaware of the
bearings of the case, I tried to prove that a benefaction to the poor,
mentioned in the fourth-century legend of Avircius Marcellus as
taking place in Hieropolis of Phrygia, and beginning as early as
the second century, was historical.

The general development of such *collegia* over the Empire was quite in accordance with Hadrian's broad views and his superiority to the narrow Roman idea.

Christian communities, registered as *collegia tenuiorum*, held property. The *collegium* had to be registered in the name of some individual, who acted as its head and representative, and who held the property that belonged to it. We can hardly doubt that the *episkopos* was the representative of the *collegium*, for he already acted as representative of the community in its relation to others. About 259 Gallienus granted to the bishops the right to recover the cemeteries, which had been seized in the recent persecutions, and which had therefore been registered in the name of the bishops a considerable time previously. This being the case, the community would be unable to recover such property by ordinary legal process from the bishop, if he were deposed or changed ; for it could not appear before a court except through its bishop.* Permanence in the discharge of episcopal duties was usual long before 130 ; but the new character of the bishop must have greatly strengthened his official character. If the impression I have as to the numbers and power of the Christians in Asia Minor is correct, the property of the communities must have been considerable. Doubts were sure to arise as to boundaries and other points ; and in such cases the community must either submit to external claims, or appear by its bishop before a tribunal. The bishop thus became the regulator of the property of the community. Similarly in modern

---

* For example, in A.D. 270, when Paul of Samosata, Bishop of Antioch, was deposed, he retained the church building and property until the whole church appealed to Aurelian against him (Eusebius, *H. E.*, vii., 30).

Turkey, a religious community can have a legal position only as represented by an individual head ; but, if it thus legalises itself, the head has *ex officio* a seat on the district council.*

Such associations were commonly for sepulchral purposes, and cemeteries were the most widely spread form of property. Bequests of such property are well known.†

With Hadrian a new period begins in the Church. Not merely did Apology arise, as an immediate consequence of his wiser policy. The Church as a body responded to his action, and a marked distinction in its policy and its utterances appears to have taken place about 130. The uncompromising spirit of Ignatius did not long survive him.‡ That amount of concession to the State, which was implied in pleading before the Imperial tribunal or the bar of public opinion, probably became universal soon after his time. But there was much disagreement as to the extent to which concession should go ; and the disagreement increased as time went on. It is quite impossible, owing

---

* In this way the pastor of a small Armenian community in Cæsareia of Cappadocia is a member of the Mejliss of that important city, and has at least once, by his solitary resistance, prevented an arbitrary act of the Pasha. My authority is Dr. Farnsworth, whose mission is not connected in any way with this Protestant community.

† One of the most curious is published by me in *Revue des Études Grecques*, 1889, p. 24, where we must read in A (as Mommsen writes) πη(χέων) δέκα ἐπὶ δέκα, and in B δικε[λ]λα[τὰ] δύο and ἀ[γωγὸ]ν ὀρυ[κ]τόν.

‡ From this point of view we must date the *Shepherd* of Hermas before the era of the charge—*i.e.*, before c. 130. In every aspect that I can appreciate, it belongs to the age 100–120, and is earlier even than Ignatius' letters. 2 Peter seems to belong to the same period as Hermas : I cannot, *e.g.*, imagine iii. 1, 2, being written at an early period.

to the dearth of works of the period, to say when the
disagreement began to be apparent; but it is a striking
feature of Christian documents (except the purely Apologetic) in the period that follows A.D. 150. In the Letter of
the Smyrnæans about the death of Polycarp in 155, it
is strongly marked, and evidently is a question that has
existed for some time, but on which peaceable discussion is
still possible. The *Acta of Carpus*, a document of uncertain
date, but probably very little later, shows a similar state
of the discussion, in which it takes the opposite side.

In the former document, as Keim has rightly observed,
there is a strong though veiled protest against voluntarily
offering oneself for martyrdom. The Christian should wait
till he is arrested, and should consider the safety of his co-
religionists. Keim * rightly urges that such a protest is
not in keeping with the earlier tone of the Church; but he
wrongly adduces it as an argument that the document is a
late forgery. In this protest we catch the new tone that
grew up after Hadrian's time. Hence marked blame is
cast on the Phrygian, Quintus, who voluntarily gave himself up; and the drawing of a triumphant moral is implied
in the way in which his subsequent weakness is described.
On the other hand, Polycarp's withdrawal from the city
is described as arising, not from cowardice, but from the
belief that it was the right course; and the intention to
paint Polycarp's action as a law to others is proved by the
straining after analogies, some rather far-fetched, between
his death and that of Christ (p. 374; Lft., *Ign.*, i., p. 610).

In *Acta Carpi*, especially in the concluding episode of

---

* *Aus dem Urchristenthum*, p. 119. In his reply to Keim
Lightfoot seems to me not to show his usual historical insight when
he inclines to dispute the fact, i., p. 619.

Agathonike, the opposite principle—viz., that the Christian ought to proclaim openly his religion, and even to rush upon martyrdom *—is insisted on. This document shows the same type of feeling, though not so developed, as appears in *Acta Perpetuæ*, in which Professor Rendel Harris has rightly recognised the controversial character. But, though in *Acta Carpi* the tone is more developed than in the Smyrnæan letter, it is still peaceable, and free from the rancour that characterised the bitter controversy of the years after 170.† In that period Catholic prisoners would have no intercourse with Montanists, and in *Acta Perpetuæ* the Montanist Saturus in a vision saw the bishop of his church shut out from heaven. *Acta Carpi* is still far from that extreme.

The bishops were the chief agents in carrying out the policy of conciliation towards the State, which the Catholic Church, as a whole, resolved on, but which a strong party in it considered to be a secularisation of

---

* This episode, as Harnack well shows, wants the striking individualism shown in the characters of Carpos and Papylos, and the incidents seem even coloured in imitation of the tale of Thekla. Where he preaches most, the writer is more remote from bare narrative of facts (p. 399).

† The chief point in which I differ from Dr. Harnack's admirable edition of *Acta Carpi* is his inference, founded on a comparison between the later and the earlier *Acta*, that it is impossible to recover from late *Acta*, by such subjective criticism as M. Le Blant has used, any real historical facts. The inference I would draw is different. In the late *Acta Carpi* there is not a single point that would be quoted as indicative of real foundation, and there is not a trace of local colour; yet we now find that this miserable legend is only a distortion of fact. This case seems to lend strength to the argument of those who take any points of finer character in these late legends as survivals of real history on which the legends are founded.

that the Phrygian Montanist prophetesses, Prisca and Maximilla, must have gone far further.

The subject would soon carry us far beyond our limits. We must not, however, pass from it without referring to the one great figure on the Catholic side produced by the Phrygian Church during this period, Avircius Marcellus, born about A.D. 120–130. We are fortunate in possessing two accounts of his life and action ; one written by himself, in his seventy-second year, the other a legendary biography, composed, probably, about A.D. 400. In the former he appears as an upholder of what he believed to be the truth, in a controversy that took place within a powerful and world-wide church ; in the latter he is the missionary who converted a heathen land. From the latter alone it would be impossible to discover the real character and position of Avircius Marcellus ; and yet the original document, combined with the information given by Eusebius, shows how most of the legendary adventures originated. It would be most instructive in regard to the nature of these late *Acta* in general, and also in regard to the difference between the tone of the Church in the second century and A.D. 400, to study in detail the legendary biography. But such a study would be premature until a MS. of the *Acta* in the National Library in Paris is published.* An important MS., now in Jerusalem, is said by Professor Rendel Harris to be on the eve of publication by M. Papadopoulos Kerameus. For the present I need only refer to what I have written on the subject in *Expositor*, 1889 ; further reflection and study have confirmed me in the opinions there expressed. In par-

---

* No. 1540. Rev. H. Thurston, *S. J.*, has kindly sent me some highly interesting passages from it.

ticular, the name Avircius Marcellus still seems to me to imply Western origin. If the name occurred in a pagan inscription, no one would have a moment's hesitation in accepting it as belonging to an Italian settler in Asia Minor, one of the numerous Roman traders who swarmed in the great cities of the provinces, and who played in ancient times a part similar to that played by British commerce in spreading national influence at the present day. I feel obliged to interpret the names of Christians on the same principles as those of pagans, and to recognise Avircius Marcellus as a Roman citizen (the *prænomen* being, as often, omitted) belonging to a Western family settled in Asia Minor.*

The Catholic champion's fame naturalised the name Avircius in Phrygia in its Greek forms, Ἀουίρκιος, Ἀβίρκιος, Ἀβέρκιος. Examples of its use occur as late as the tenth century, when it was borne by an official mentioned in the treatise of Constantine Porphyrogenitus *de Adm. Imp.*, 50. It is found in Phrygian inscriptions of the fourth century † (see *Expositor*, 1889, p. 395, and Lightfoot, *Ignatius*, i., p. 501). One of these, shown in the accompanying illustration, deserves more notice; it is the epitaph on the gravestone that marked the tomb of Abirkios, son of Porphyrios, a deacon at Prymnessos. His name is a

---

* Aburcus at Falerii, Deecke *Falisker*, p. 214; Avircius in Rome, *C.I.L.*, vi., 12923-5; Avercius in Gaul, xii.,1052; it spread to Cappadocia as Abourgios, Basil, *Ep.*, 33. Ignatius Theophorus is not Roman: he belonged to a Syrian family, strongly affected by Western civilisation, which had discarded native names and used the double nomenclature, Italian and Greek. The unusual name Ignatius has some historical explanation.

† They mark the period when Avircius was remembered as the old Christian hero, and the legend was growing in Catholic circles.

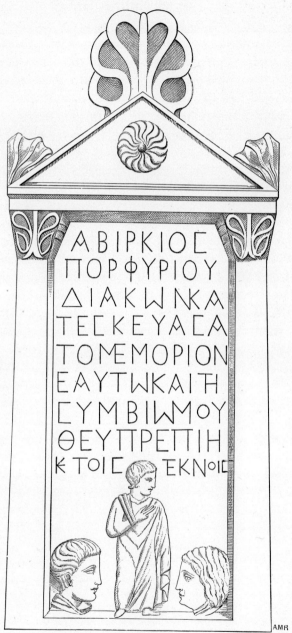

EARLY CHRISTIAN MONUMENT FROM PRYMNESSOS. [p. 441.

sufficient proof that he belonged to the Catholic Church, and therefore that there was a Catholic Church at Prymnessos, in the anti-Catholic part of Phrygia.*

The sculpture on the gravestone is interesting, as giving one of the earliest known representations of the Saviour, who, as in other early sculptures, is represented as a youthful figure. In all probability a Montanist would have regarded the representation of the Saviour as idolatrous ; but the Iconodoulic tendency was already beginning in the Orthodox Church. He stands, facing, but with the head turned to the right, with the thumb and two fingers of the right hand extended. The attitude is that of admonition and instruction. The figure has the squat proportions that mark the declining art of the late third and the fourth century. The features are those of the conventional male youth of later art, insipid but retaining the Greek type and character. The artist was used to represent the face in profile, and therefore put the head in that position, though the body is differently placed.

The heads of Abirkios, and his wife, Theuprepia, are shown on a larger scale, one on each side of the central figure. That of Abirkios is of the conventional, expressionless type ; but in the face of Theuprepia there appear individuality and beauty, which are lost in the reproduction. It is the portrait of a matron, plump, with a slight tendency to double chin ; the features are graceful, dignified, and

---

* An inscription of Sinethandos or Laodiceia Combusta, probably of the end of the fourth, or early fifth, century, mentions the Church of the Novatians there. The phrase τῶν Ναυατῶν has been misunderstood in the *Corpus*, No. 9,268, and treated as a single word even by M. Waddington, No. 1,699. The article τῶν has been doubled by error of the engraver.

noble, and wear the placid and contented expression which indicates comfortable circumstances and a happy life. I can hardly imagine this face to be the work of a fourth-century artist.

The official title deacon, on the other hand, points to the period when the Christian religion was recognised and legal after the triumph of Constantine. The Catholic principle seems to have been to avoid the public use of official terms before the Church was explicitly legalised. It is, however, not impossible that we have here an instance of the title being used even earlier—*e.g.*, in the early years of Diocletian's reign, when he was favourably inclined towards the Christians.* The use of *memorion* to indicate an ordinary grave also, perhaps, points to a third rather than a fourth century date. It was afterwards appropriated to the holy grave and shrine of a martyr or saint.

We notice that, as in almost all Asian epitaphs, the wife precedes the children. The regular order in Greek literature was to mention the children before the wife.

NOTE.—A document, published too late for Lightfoot to use, gives a clue to the proper form of the inscriptions about Philip the Asiarch, published in his *Ignat.*, i., p. 629 f. : the words perhaps are [κατὰ τὰ τῆς βουλῆς δόγματα, ἀναγνωσθέν]τ[α] καὶ ἐπικυρ[ωθέν]τα ὑπὸ τοῦ θειοτάτου αὐτοκράτορος Ἀντωνείνου, κ.τ.λ. ; or possibly [κατὰ τὰ ὑπὸ τῆς βουλῆς ψηφισθέν]τ[α], καὶ ἐπικυρ[ωθέν]τα, κ.τ.λ. *Bull. Corr. Hell.*, 1887, p. 299.

* The form διάκων for διάκονος occurs in a pagan inscription giving a list of the officials of a temple at Metropolis in Ionia, and therefore not later than the end of the third century : *Mous. Smyrn.*, iii., p. 93.

CHAPTER XVIII.*

GLYCERIUS THE DEACON.

WE have now treated in brief outline the position of the Church in the Empire during the period when its organisation was in process of formation. By the time which we have reached (170–180 A.D.), all the elements of the consolidated Church had assumed the form and the mutual relations which on the whole characterise its subsequent development.

From this date onwards the subject which has occupied our attention becomes more complicated, far more evidence bearing upon it is accessible, and it is hardly susceptible of treatment as a whole. The development of the Catholic Church was indeed an element of unity over the whole Empire ; but in each province the situation of the unified and universal Church varied. The elements within the pale of Christianity which opposed the tendencies of the universal Church varied in each province ; the character of the people, the type of their religious feeling and attitude, the relation in which they stood towards the Roman Government and society, differed widely in different lands. In the history of each province this subject should occupy

---

* This chapter, published in great part in *Expositor*, 1891, was originally a lecture delivered in Cambridge at the invitation of Dr. Westcott in 1889. Traces of the original form remain on pp. 448, 450.

some place—even a prominent place; * and until the local
varieties are better understood and more clearly described
than has hitherto been the case, it will be impossible to
attain a trustworthy conception of the position of the
Church within the Empire, between the point which we
have reached and the final triumph of the new religion.

To come to the particular case of the country with which
I am most familiar, we want to catch the Cappadocian
Christian of the fourth century, the Phrygian Christian of
the second and third centuries, and to acquire some conception of his character, his ways, and his thoughts, and
of how he got on with his non-Christian neighbours. In
studying this subject, one is led to the opinion that a
distinction in social type must be drawn among the
Christians. In the period following A.D. 130 the history
of Christianity in Asia Minor, when treated as a branch
of the history of society, is a long conflict between two
opposing tendencies, leading to the formation of sects
or churches. From the theological point of view, these
provincial churches belong to various classes, and are
called by many names; but they have all certain common
features,—they tended towards separatism and diversity,
in opposition to the unity of the Catholic Church, and
they arrived at this diversity through no intentional rejection of the unity of all Christians, but through the
gradual and unmarked development of native characteristics in what they considered to be the true and original
form of their common religion.

---

* In Mommsen's *Provinces of the Roman Empire* it did not
enter into his plan, and the social conditions of each province
are described almost as if there had been no Christians in it, or, at
least, as if they exerted no influence on it.

The history of the Catholic Church varied greatly in different districts of Asia Minor. In some it never touched the popular heart, and was barely maintained by external influence ; in others it achieved a complete victory over the forces that tended to cause disintegration ; and in some cases only a faint echo of any conflict has reached us. My position is, that there was, in every case throughout Asia Minor where any evidence is known, such a conflict ; that the first Christians of the country were not organised in a strict fashion, but were looser communities, in which personal influence counted for much and official station for little ; and that the strict discipline of the Catholic Church was gradually framed to counteract the disintegrating tendency, in a political and a religious view alike, of the provincial character, organised the whole Church in a strict hierarchy of territorial character, parallel to the civil organisation, and enabled the Church to hold together the Roman Empire more firmly than the worship of the Emperors could ever do. Politically the Church was originally a protest against over-centralisation and against the usurpation by the Imperial Government of the rights of the individual citizen. It ended by being more centralised than the Empire itself ; and the Christian Empire destroyed all the municipal freedom and self-government that had existed under the earlier Empire.

We should be glad if we could answer the question why some districts of Asia Minor resisted the Catholic Church so persistently, and others followed it so readily ; why, for example, if I may use the question-begging terms, Cappadocia was orthodox and Phrygia heretical ?

The answer seems obvious in the case of Cappadocia. The group of great Church leaders, Basil, Amphilochius,

and the three Gregories (for I think Gregory, the Bishop
of Nazianzos, may fairly be mentioned along with his far
more famous son),—this group of leaders carried the
country with them. But this answer only puts the difficulty
one step back.   Can any reason be suggested why the great
Cappadocian leaders followed the Roman Church, whereas
almost all the most striking figures in Phrygian ecclesiastical
history opposed it ?

Partly, no doubt, the reason was geographical or racial—
i.e., it depended on the character produced in the inhabitants by the situation, the atmosphere, the scenery, and the
past history of the two districts respectively; but partly it
was due to influences acting at the time on the general
population and on the leaders of thought in each country.
These influences are an interesting study.   In Phrygia the
evidence is almost entirely archæological, for no historian
does more than make an occasional passing allusion to the
country; but in Cappadocia much light is thrown on the
subject by the biographies and writings of a series of great
historical figures; and a study of these documents in
their relations to the archæological evidence is the first
preliminary in carrying out the purpose that has just been
indicated.   This book cannot be better concluded than by
a few specimens of the work that remains to be done for
the later history of Christianity in the country with which
we have been chiefly concerned.

The history of Basil of Cæsareia, Gregory of Nyssa, and
the distinguished family to which they belonged, is closely
connected with the city of Ibora in Pontus. A glance at
the biography of the various members of the family shows
that a number of questions with regard to the circumstances of their life, and the exact meaning to be placed

on the language of many of their letters and the incidents
they describe, depend on the locality and surroundings.
But the name Ibora was long floating in air, and had
not set foot on the ground; and for all reasoning that
depends on local circumstances, on the relation of city
with city, district with district, and civil governors or
bishops with each other, it would have been as useful to
say that Basil's family owned an estate beside Cloud-
Cuckoo-Town, as to say that they were landed proprietors
near Ibora. But, if any one were to attempt the task of
reconstructing a picture of the society in which Basil, the
Gregories, and Amphilochius moved, and of their relations
with it, the state of education in the country, and the
attitude which young graduates of the University of Athens
assumed to the home-trained Cappadocians or Pontians—
an historian of that class, if such a one should arise, would
find many investigations stopped, unless he could attain
certainty as to the situations in which the events were
transacted. The operations of the English Asia Minor
Exploration Fund have now cleared away much of the
uncertainty that hung over the localities in which the great
events of Cappadocian religious history took place, and
have made it possible to face fairly the problem of describing the circumstances of that critical period, 350–400, when
the character of the Cappadocian Church was determined.
Here is a period about which a great body of evidence
remains, in the writings of the principal agents on the
victorious side. The account of their opponents, of course,
has to be accepted with caution; but in weighing it we
can, at least, always have the certainty that they are not
too lenient in their judgment, or flattering in their description, of the opposite party.

In the year 370, Basil was appointed bishop of Cæsareia, metropolitan of Cappadocia, and exarch or patriarch of the Pontic *diæcesis.* He was appointed in spite of the resistance of the majority of his bishops, in spite of the dislike and dread of many of the people, in spite of the open opposition of the Government. He was elected by the strenuous exertions of a few influential individuals ; and the authority of the Church outside the province was needed in order to put down the disaffected within it. The cause of the Catholic Church was involved in his election : without the hand of a vigorous organiser there was extreme danger that " heresy "— Eunomianism, Arianism, and so on—would triumph in Cappadocia. We want to learn what this means to the student of society. Did the Eunomian differ from the Catholic only in certain points of doctrine, being otherwise undistinguishable from him ? or do these words indicate a difference in private life, in political feeling, and in Church organisation ? The question may be answered fully, when the historian is found who will face the problem as it has just been sketched.* I can only express the hope that in this university something may be done to solve it. The later Greek and Latin writers are full of material, uncollected and unvalued, for the history of society. Why should almost all the natural ability and admirable training of the classical scholars of Cambridge be directed towards such a narrow range of authors ? Every one who has toiled through a Byzantine historian in the edition of the Berlin Academy—that *dauernde Schande der deutschen Philologie*

---

* The following sentences are left in the same form as they had in the lecture addressed to a Cambridge society. So also on p. 450

—compelled, as he does so, slowly and without critical material, to remake his edition for his own use, and has then run joyously through De Boor's admirable Theophanes—every one who has done that knows what need there is for the wider employment of learning and skill. Why should traditional belief—or, shall I say, traditional ignorance?—exclude all Christian Fathers or Byzantine historians from the classical scholar's interests, and almost confine him to producing the 43rd edition of one out of about a score of writers? When he has something to say about Homer or Cicero that he must say, then let him say it; but might not some of the good scholarship of this university be more profitably employed? I am not ungrateful for the large amount of help that I have had from Cambridge scholarship, but what I have had only makes me wish for more.

I shall try to give an example of the importance and the human interest of this subject, by examining one single episode in Cappadocian history, about A.D. 371–374, and showing what light is thrown by it on the character of the Cappadocian Christians at the time. The incident is related by Archdeacon Farrar in his *Lives of the Fathers* as follows. His account agrees in all essential points with that given by Canon Venables in the *Dictionary of Christian Biography*, with Tillemont, and with the Migne biography, and may fairly be taken as representing the usual interpretation.

" The extraordinary story of the deacon Glycerius illustrates the aberrations due to the fermenting enthusiasm and speculative curiosity which marked the Eastern Church, and which were fostered by the dreamy idleness of innumerable monks. Glycerius was a young man whose early vigour

29

Basil viewed with so much favour, that he had ordained him deacon of the church of Venesa (?)* about 372. Puffed up by his ordination, the young deacon proceeded to gather round him a band of devoted young ladies, whose admiration he won by sleek and soft religious arts, and who supported him by their offerings. Severely reproved by his presbyter, his *chorepiscopus*, and lastly by Basil, Glycerius left the town by night with a band of these girls and some youths, and scandalised the country by wandering about with them in a disorderly manner, dancing and singing hymns, amid the jeers of the coarse rustics. When their fathers came to rescue the girls Glycerius ignominiously drove them away. Finally, the whole band took refuge with a bishop named Gregory, whom even the Benedictine editor is inclined to think *may* have been Gregory of Nyssa. Basil treated the vain, mischievous, and deluded deacon with much fatherly forbearance, and promised to deal with him kindly if he would dismiss the votaries he was leading, not to God, but to the abyss. Strange to say, the bishop, whoever he was, either failed to second Basil's efforts, or only did so in a lukewarm and inadequate way."

Let me now read to you the letters from which all our knowledge has to be gathered. I hope that, through my bald translation something of the fire and vigour of the original may appear. Few writers can compare with Basil in directness; not a word can be spared without a distinct loss of effect. He does indeed use ἵνα with conjunctive in a way to make a classical scholar's hair stand on end; but, if the classical scholar disdains the usage, so much

---

* The interrogation is left as in the original.

the worse for him.* It is true that the usage does not occur in Demosthenes, but it is stamped by a greater than that man of words, the man least capable of understanding his time of all that have ever figured in history as statesmen, unless Cicero be taken into account.

I. BASIL TO GREGORY (EP. CLXIX. [CCCCXII.]).

" THOU hast taken a reasonable and kindly and compassionate course in showing hospitality to the captives of the mutineer Glycerius (I assume the epithet for the moment) and in veiling our common disgrace so far as possible. But when thy discretion has learned the facts with regard to him, it is becoming that thou shouldst put an end to the scandal. This Glycerius who now parades among you with such respectability was consecrated by ourselves as deacon of the Church of Venasa, to be a minister to the presbyter there and to attend to the work of the church ; for though he is in other respects unmanageable, yet he is clever in doing whatever comes to his hand. But when he was appointed, he neglected the work as completely as if it had never existed. Gathering together a number of poor girls, on his own authority and responsibility, some of them flocking voluntarily round him (for you know the flightiness

---

* There is too great proneness to stamp one period of Latin, one period of one dialect of Greek, as correct, and everything that differs as wrong. But the real cause of the inferiority of style in later pagan writers lies, not in the words, but in the want of life and spirit in the men. The question has yet to be asked and answered, how far the language used by Basil is less fit to express clearly and vigorously his meaning than that used by Demosthenes, and, if so, what are the real reasons for the inferiority ? Those who have read least of such authors as Basil are most ready to condemn their style.

of young people in such matters), and some of them unwill-
ing, he set about making himself the leader of a company ;
and taking to himself the name and the garb of a patriarch,
he of a sudden paraded as a great power, not reaching this
position by a course of obedience and piety, but making it
a livelihood, as one might take up any trade ; and he has
almost upturned the whole Church, disregarding his own
presbyter, and disregarding the village-bishop and ourselves
too, as of no account, and ever filling the civil polity and
the clerical estate with riot and disorder. And at last,
when a slight reproof was given by ourselves and by the
village-bishop, with the intent that he should cease his
mutinous conduct (for he was exciting young men to the
same courses), he conceives a thing very audacious and
unnatural.   Impiously carrying off as many young women
as he could, he runs away under the cover of night. This
must seem to thee quite horrible.

"Think too what the occasion was. The festival of Venasa
was being celebrated, and as usual a vast crowd was flocking thither from all quarters. He led forth his chorus,
marshalled by young men and circling in the dance, making
the pious cast down their eyes, and rousing the ridicule of
the ribald and loose-tongued.   Nor is this all, serious as it
is ; but further, as I am informed, when the parents could
not endure to be orphaned of their children, and wished to
bring them home from the dispersion, and came as weeping
suppliants to their own daughters, he insults and scandalises
them, this admirable young fellow with his piratical
discipline.

"This ought to appear intolerable to thy discretion, for it
brings us all into ridicule. The best thing is that thou
shouldest order him to return with the young women, for he

would meet with allowance if he comes with letters from thee. If that be impossible, the young women, at any rate, thou shalt send back to their mother the Church. Or, in the third place, do not allow them that are willing to return to be kept under compulsion, but persuade them to come back to us.

" Otherwise we testify to thee, as we do to God and men, that this is a wrong thing, and against the rules of the Church. If Glycerius return with a spirit of wisdom and orderliness, that were best ; but if not, he must be removed from the ministry."

II. BASIL TO GLYCERIUS (EP. CLXX. [CCCCXIV.]).

" How far wilt thou carry thy madness, working evil for thyself and disturbance for us, and outraging the common order of monks ? Return then, trusting in God and in us, who imitate the compassion of God. For, though like a father we have chidden thee, yet we will pardon thee like a father. Such are our words to thee, inasmuch as many supplicate for thee, and before all thy presbyter, whose gray hairs and kindly spirit we respect. But if thou continuest to absent thyself from us, thou art altogether cast out from thy station ; and thou shalt be cast out from God with thy songs and thy raiment, by which thou leadest the young women, not towards God, but into the pit."

These two letters were obviously written at the same time, and sent by the same messenger ; the third was written after an interval, and apparently after receipt of a letter from Gregory asking for assurance of full pardon for Glycerius.

III. BASIL TO GREGORY (EP. CLXXI. [CCCCXIII.]).

" I WROTE to thee already before this about Glycerius
and the maidens. Yet they have never to this day returned,
but are still delaying ; nor do I know why and how, for I
should not charge thee with doing this in order to cause
slander against us, either being thyself annoyed with us or
doing a favour to others.* Let them come then without
fear ; be thou guarantee on this point. For we are
afflicted when the members of the Church are cut off, even
though they be deservedly cut off. But, if they should
resist, the responsibility must rest on others, and we wash
our hands of it."

For the right understanding of this incident the only
evidence available is contained in (1) these three letters of
Basil ; (2) a sentence of Strabo (p. 537), describing the
village and district of Venasa ; (3) an inscription found in
1882 on a hill-top near the village ; (4) the map of Cappadocia as now reconstructed. A first glance at the evidence
is enough to reveal various details inconsistent with the
accepted account ; and we may be sure that Basil has not
coloured in favour of Glycerius those details that give a
different complexion to the incident.

In the first place, the very evident sympathy of Gregory
for Glycerius disquiets all the modern interpreters ; his
sympathy cannot be due to ignorance of the facts of the
case, for he was far closer to the spot than Basil himself,
and the acts were not hid under a bushel, but done openly,

---

* The reference is to Basil's numerous enemies, who would be
delighted that the Bishop of Nazianzos should refuse to comply with
his wishes.

and no doubt widely talked about. The only explanation that can be devised by the interpreters is to deny part of the evidence. The MS. evidence, so far as quoted in the Migne edition, is that two of the letters are addressed to Gregory of Nazianzos. Most of the interpreters say that Gregory of Nyssa must be meant, and that Gregory of Nyssa was guilty of many weak and foolish acts. The answer lies in the map, which confirms the old authority, and disproves the modern suggestion.*

In the next place, the presbyter, whom Basil represents as having been disregarded and set at nought, is in favour of the offender, and beseeches Basil to act kindly to him. Canon Venables indeed says that the presbyter " gravely admonished" Glycerius; but this misrepresents the evidence. The " village-bishop " and Basil himself censured Glycerius ; but though Basil says Glycerius showed disrespect to the presbyter, he drops no hint that the presbyter complained about this, but rather implies the opposite. Basil himself does not even hint at any darker crime than injudiciousness and ambition in the relations of Glycerius to the devotees ; and there can be no doubt that the letters omit no charge that could be brought against the rebellious deacon. The evident purity of conduct in this strange band may fairly be taken as necessarily implying that the strictest religious

---

* If any change is permitted in the MS. authority, I should understand the elder Gregory, Bishop of Nazianzos, and date the letters A.D. 373. The Gregory to whom these letters were addressed was obviously not under Basil's authority, and was therefore under Tyana; but Nyssa was under Cæsareia, subject directly to Basil, as Venasa also was. The tone of the letters also is more respectful and less peremptory than Basil would probably have employed to his brother, or even to his friend Gregory. On the map, see *Historical Geography of Asia Minor*, p. 293.

obligations were observed by the devotees. In such a difficult situation there is no alternative but either strict asceticism, springing from fanatical or enthusiastic religious feeling, or license and scandal.

Now the evident sympathy both of the immediate superior, the presbyter, whose influence had been apparently diminished by the popularity of the deacon, and of the Bishop of Nazianzos (whether the older Gregory or his son, who filled his place for a short time after his death in 374), is quite unintelligible if Glycerius had introduced some new and startling features into the religion of the province. It is, of course, certain that the principles of both the Gregories, father and son, were opposed to such manifestations, as being contrary to the whole spirit of the Catholic Church. The reason why Gregory sympathised must be that Glycerius was only keeping up the customary ceremonial of a great religious meeting. Canon Venables indeed says that the band "wandered about the country under the pretence of religion, singing hymns and leaping and dancing in a disorderly fashion," and Archdeacon Farrar agrees with him. But there is no warrant in the letter of Basil for this account. The band is not said either to wander about the country or to dance in a disorderly way. Accurate geography is useful in studying these writers, but accurate translation is not without its advantages. Let us scrutinise the facts a little more closely, examining the situation and the probabilities of the case; and I think we shall have to admit that Basil is giving us a picture, coloured to his view, of a naïve and quaint ceremony of early Cappadocian Christianity, which he regarded with horror, and was resolved to stamp out.

One of the most striking features in the whole incident

is the important part played by women. Now this is the
most striking feature also in the native religion and society
of Asia Minor. (See pp. 161, 398.)

The occasion when the most extreme features of this
Cappadocian " heresy" were displayed was the great
festival at Venasa, when a vast concourse was gathered
there. This festival is called by Canon Venables a " fair " ;
but this is not an accurate translation. The *synodos*, which
was held there, was certainly similar to the Armenian
synodos, held at Phargamous. At Phargamous, in the
month of June, a great festival was held in honour of
certain martyrs ; and such dignitaries as Basil himself,
Eusebius of Samosata, and Theodotus of Nicopolis, might
be expected at it.

Moreover, the *synodos* of Venasa was one of the most
ancient and famous religious meetings in Cappadocia.
The priest of Zeus at Venasa was second in dignity and
power only to the priest of Komana; he held office for
life, and was practically a king. A village inhabited by
3,000 *hierodouloi* was attached to the temple, and round it
lay a sacred domain that brought in an annual income of
fifteen talents (nearly £4,000). Christianity directed the
religious feeling of the country towards new objects, but
preserved the old seasons and methods. A Christian
festival was substituted for the old festival of Zeus, doubtless the occasion when the god made his annual ἔξοδος, or
procession round his country. Basil, unluckily, pitiless of
the modern scholar, does not name the month when the
festival took place, and the sole memorials of it that remain
to complete the account of Strabo are, first, a brief invocation to the heavenly Zeus, found on a hill-top, to guide us
(along with other evidence) to the situation (see p. 142) ;

and, secondly, these letters of Basil, to show how the Cappadocian Christians developed the pagan festival.

At this great religious ceremony of the whole country, Glycerius brought forth his followers, singing and dancing in chorus. Such ceremonies were necessarily a part of the old religious festival of Zeus, and their existence in it, though not attested, may be safely assumed; accordingly there is every probability that they were not novelties introduced by Glycerius, but were part of the regular Cappadocian custom. They are a natural and regular concomitant of the earlier and simpler forms of religion, whether Pagan or Jewish; and at Venasa they were retained, with some modifications in the words and the gestures. Hymns undoubtedly were substituted for the pagan formulæ, and not a hint is dropped by Basil that the dancing and singing were not of a quiet and modest character. The license of the old pagan ceremonies had been given up; but in many respects there was no doubt a striking resemblance between the old pagan and the new Christian festival. Probably the dancing of the great dervish establishments of Kara Hissar and Iconium at the present day would give the best idea of the festival at Venasa in the time of Basil, though the solemnity and iconoclastic spirit of Mohammedanism have still further toned down the ecstasy and enthusiastic *abandon* of the old ritual. But the strange, weird music of the flute and cymbals, and the excited yet always orderly dancing, make the ceremony even yet the most entrancing and intoxicating that I have ever witnessed. Through this analogy we can come to realise the power that might be acquired by a man of natural ability and religious fervour over numbers of young persons. This influence was increased by the character which Glycerius assumed and the robes which he wore. In the old pagan festival the leader of the festival wore the dress and bore the name of the deity whom he represented. The custom is well known both in Greece (where the Dionysos festival is the most familiar, but far from the sole, example) and in Asia Minor.* Glycerius, as Basil tells us, assumed the name and the dress of a "patriarch." The meaning of this seems to be that the director of ceremonies (who, like the modern dervish sheikh, never danced himself) was equipped in a style corresponding to the pagan priest, and assumed the character of the highest religious official, the patriarch.

But a new era began in Cappadocia when Basil became head of the Church. It is obvious that abuses might readily, almost necessarily, creep into such ceremonies; and clearly the edict went forth that they must cease. Basil does not say that any real abuses had occurred. He speaks only of the downcast looks of the pious spectators, and the jests of the ribald and loose-tongued; but he is clearly describing what he conceives to be the inevitable outcome of such ceremonies. The spirit of the Church, whose champion Basil was, was inexorably opposed to such exhibitions. For good or for evil, such prominence given to women in religious ceremonial was hateful to it. The influence acquired by a deacon, his assumption of the robes and name of a patriarch, were subversive of the strict discipline of the Roman Church. The open association of a monk with a band of young women was contrary to the rules of the monastic order. The village-bishop, acting doubtless on previous general orders of his superior,

---

* *E.g.*, at Pessinus the priest took *ex officio* the name Attis.

reprimanded Glycerius, and his action was confirmed and enforced by Basil.   Glycerius, when thus treated, took advantage of the recent changes which had curtailed the power of Basil.   He crossed the frontier into the adjoining bishopric of Nazianzos, which was now included in the province of Second Cappadocia, under the metropolitan of Tyana.   The young women that followed his ministrations fled with him ; and, as Gregory received and sheltered them all, we cannot doubt that the flight was made in an orderly way, without scandal, and with the air of pious but persecuted Christians.   Basil then complained to Gregory in the letter quoted.   The reply of Gregory unfortunately has not been preserved ; but we can imagine that he gave a different version of the case, stated his views as to the character of Glycerius, and urged Basil to promise complete forgiveness on condition of the immediate return of all the fugitives.

We have the reply of Basil, giving the required assurance, though not with the best grace.   One motive that evidently weighed with him was apprehension of the talk that he would give rise to, if he persisted in an intolerant policy. Now all this is inconceivable except on the supposition that, according to the above description, Glycerius was acting in accordance with established custom and the general feeling of the Cappadocian Church, while Basil was too hastily and sternly suppressing the custom of the country.   The incipient schism, roused by the sternness of Basil, was healed by the mild mediation of Gregory.

The fault in Glycerius which most offended Basil was evidently his transgression of the Church discipline.   The full significance of this can be grasped only in its connection with the whole policy of Basil.

The powerful personality, the intense, uncompromising zeal, and the great practical ability of Basil were of the first consequence in insuring the triumph of the Catholic Church in Cappadocia. But one man, however powerful, cannot do everything by his own immediate effort, especially when his personal influence is interrupted by a too early death, as Basil's was. The organising power which has always been so conspicuous a feature of the Church, exercised as powerful an influence in Cappadocia as elsewhere. The organisation which Basil left behind him completed his work. One great object of Basil's administration was to establish large ecclesiastical centres of two kinds : first, orphanages, and, secondly, monasteries. An orphanage was built in every district of his immense diocese ; the one at Cæsareia, with its church, bishop's palace, and residences for clergy, hospices for poor, sick, and travellers, hospitals for lepers, and workshops for teaching and practising trades, was so large as to be called the " New City." Such establishments constituted centres from which the irresistible influence of the Church permeated the whole district, as, centuries before, the cities founded by the Greek kings had been centres from which the Greek influence had slowly penetrated the country round. The monks and the monasteries, which Basil established widely over the country, were centres of the same influence ; and though the monks occasionally caused some trouble by finding even Basil himself not sufficiently orthodox, they were effective agents of the Catholic Church, whereas the solitary hermits and anchorets, whom Basil rather discouraged, though he had been one himself, were perhaps more favourable to the provincial Church, and were certainly a far less powerful engine for affecting the country.

That the monk Glycerius should break through the gradations of office and the spirit of the Church, should parade in the robes of the patriarch, and flee from his superior's jurisdiction in the company of a band of women, was a thing intolerable to Basil.

One other point requires notice : is any external circumstance known that is likely to have directed such men as Basil and Gregory away from the line of native development in religion ? A strong impulse probably was given them by their foreign education. They lost the narrow, provincial tone ; they came to appreciate the unity and majesty of the Roman Empire ; they realised the destiny of the Church to be the unifying religion of the Empire— *i.e.*, of the civilised world. They also learned something about that organisation by which Rome ruled the world, and they appreciated the fact that the Church could fulfil its destiny and rule the Roman Empire only by strict organisation and rigid discipline. Men like Glycerius could not see beyond the bounds of their native district with its provincial peculiarities; men like Basil were perhaps intolerant of mere provincialism.

Perhaps a clearer idea of the causes which made Cappadocia orthodox may be gained by looking at Phrygia, which was mainly a heretical country. The cities of the Lycus valley, and of the country immediately east and north-east of it, which were most under the Roman influence, were of the dominant Christian Church ; but the mass of the country adhered stubbornly to the native forms of Christianity. Probably this has something to do with the fact that in Phrygia so few Christian communities have maintained an unbroken existence through the Turkish domination, whereas in Cappadocia a fair proportion of the whole population has preserved its religion to the present day. Many of the Phrygians were always discontented with the Byzantine rule, except under the Inconoclast emperors. When John Comnenus was invading the Seljuk dominions, he found Christian communities, who so much preferred Turkish rule to Byzantine, that they fought against him, even without support from the Turks, and had to be reduced by force of arms. To a certain extent this was perhaps due to their preferring the easy Seljuk yoke to the heavy Byzantine taxation ; but it is very probable that religious difference was the chief cause.

How far then can we trace in Phrygia the presence or absence of the causes that made Cappadocia orthodox? Little or no trace of such organisation as Basil made in Cappadocia can be found in Phrygia. In the life of Hypatius written by his disciple Callinicus, and corrected by another hand in the time of his third successor, we read that he was born in Phrygia, but was obliged to emigrate to Thrace in order to gratify his wish to live in a church or monastery where he might associate with discreet men ; "for there were then no such persons, except isolated individuals, in Phrygia, and if a church existed anywhere, the clergy were rustic and ignorant, though the country has since become almost entirely Christian " (*i.e.*, orthodox).

Hypatius flourished in the first half of the fifth century ; so that the apparent reform here described belongs to the period 450–500.* The organisation of Phrygia on the

---

* The revision of the biography as composed by Callinicus is said expressly to have extended only to a correction of the bad Greek of a Syrian dialect. The reviser neither added nor took away anything, though he knew various things that might be added (*Acta Sanct.*, June 17th, p. 308).

orthodox model therefore is much later than that of Cappadocia, and it was probably not so thorough. It seems to have been only superficial, caused by the Government imposing on the country the forms of the Catholic Church.*

NOTE.—The "New City" of Basil, p. 461, seems to have caused the gradual concentration of the entire population of Cæsareia round the ecclesiastical centre, and the abandonment of the old city. Modern Kaisari is situated between one and two miles from the site of the Græco-Roman city. Here we have a type of a series of cases, in which population moved from the older centre to cluster round an ecclesiastical foundation at a little distance; and this cause should be added to those which are enumerated in *Hist. Geogr.*, ch. viii., "Change of Site."

* In writing to Gregory, Basil had to give details; and from these we learn the real character of Glycerius's action. But, if we had only some brief reference to him, made by Basil in writing to a sympathetic foreign friend, we can imagine that it would have been prejudiced and unfair. The letter of Firmilian, Bishop of Cæsareia, to Cyprian (Ep. 75) is a document of the latter class; and we cannot take his description of the unnamed Cappadocian prophetess as fully trustworthy. The general facts are true; but the colour is prejudiced. One detail has been recently confirmed by Mr. Hogarth: he has found an inscription stating that Serenianus (mentioned by Firmilian as *præses temporibus post Alexandrum*) was governor of Cappadocia under Maximin, Alexander's successor.

CHAPTER XIX.

THE MIRACLE AT KHONAI.

IN Asia Minor the result of the contest between the unifying principle of the Catholic Church and the tendency towards varieties corresponding to national character, was that the former succeeded in establishing itself as the ruling power. But it could not entirely extirpate the development of varieties. The national idiosyncracies were too strongly marked, and these Oriental peoples would not accept the centralised and organised Church in its purity, but continued the old struggle of Asiatic against European feeling, which has always marked the course of history in Asia Minor. The national temper, denied expression in open and legitimate form, worked itself out in another way—viz., in popular superstitions and local cults, which were added as an excrescence to the forms of the Orthodox Church. A growing carelessness as to these additions, provided that the orthodox forms were strictly complied with, manifested itself in the Church. The local cults grew rapidly in strength ; and finally the Orthodox Church in Asia Minor acquiesced in a sort of compromise between local variety and Catholic unity, which showed much analogy with its old enemy, the State religion of the Roman Empire. The latter, so far as it had any reality, was, as we have seen, founded on the principle (which was indeed never fully developed, but which is quite apparent underneath most of the fantastic varieties of the Imperial cultus) that the incarnate God in human form who ruled the State was in each district identified with the deity special to the district. The Orthodox Church acquiesced in the continuance of the old local impersonations of the Divine power in a Christianised form. The giant-slaying Athena of Seleuceia is dimly recognisable beneath the figure of Saint Thekla of Seleuceia ; the old Virgin Artemis of the Lakes became the Virgin Mother of the Lakes, whose shrine amid a purely Turkish population is still an object of pilgrimage to the scattered Christians of southern Asia Minor ; the god of Colossæ was represented as Michael. In one case (unique, so far as my knowledge extends) we find in A.D. 1255 even the Christ of Smyrna, *Hist. Geogr.*, p. 116.

The tendency to localise the Divine power and to find a special manifestation of the Divine nature in certain spots can nowhere be better studied than in Asia Minor. A succession of conquering races has swept over the land, coming from every quarter of the compass, by land and by sea, and belonging to diverse branches of the human family. Time after time the language, the government, the society, the manners, the religion of the country have been changed. Amid all changes one thing alone has remained permanent and unchanging—the localities to which religion attaches itself. In the same place religious worship continues always to be offered to the Divine power: the ritual changes, and the character attributed to the Divine Being varies, according to the character of the race, but the locality remains constant. The divinity is more really present, more able to hear or to help, in certain spots than he is elsewhere ; he assumes a distinct and individualised character in these spots, and takes on himself something of humanity, becoming more personal and more easily conceived and real to the ordinary mind. After a time this law was accepted by the Orthodox Church, and became a strong determining force in its future development. The country was divided and apportioned to various saints, who were not merely respected and venerated, but adored as the bearers and embodiments of the Divine power in their special district. We would gladly know more about the attitude in which the later heresies of Byzantine history, the Iconoclastic movement, Paulicianism, etc., stood towards this tendency of the Orthodox Church.

But we must not lose sight of the fact that above all these local differences there was a rather empty, but still very powerful, idea of unity. So strong was this idea that it alone has held together that which is now called the Greek race. The Greeks of to-day have no common blood. They include Cappadocians, Isaurians, Pisidians, Albanians, as well as Greeks by race. They have little common character; they are divided by diversity of language. They are united by nothing except the forms of the Orthodox Church; but in spite of a low standard of education in its priests and no very high standard of morality in its teaching, these have been strong enough to maintain the idea of a united people. For old Rome as its centre was substituted the new Rome of Constantine. The political changes of the present century have even destroyed to appearance the unity of the Church; but still the idea remains, and every Greek looks forward to a future unity of the Church and its adherents, with free Constantinople as its metropolis.

To understand the character of this later development of Christianity in Asia Minor, it is best to study it in individual cases, and we shall find a typical instance in the narrative of the miracle wrought at Khonai by the archangel Michael. Our authority is a document, which, in its existing form, is a very late fabrication, probably not earlier than the ninth century. It shows a strange mixture of knowledge and ignorance of the localities, and, while purporting to be strongly individualised in its account of persons, it is a tissue of general platitudes and marvels applied to individual names. The author was perhaps a monk of the ninth century. I shall speak of him as the redactor. He was not uneducated, but his knowledge was very inexact and of a low order. He was in some way acquainted with a tale current at Khonai, the town which succeeded the older Colossæ, with regard to an apparition of Michael there. This tale was the foundation legend (ἱερὸς λόγος) of one of the most famous churches of Asia Minor, the church of St. Michael of Khonai.

The redactor confused this apparition of Michael with another, which he found in the Menologia. It is there mentioned on the 6th day of September that Michael of Khonai was manifested at Khairetopa or Keretapa. The redactor concluded that the apparition at Keretapa was the apparition at Khonai, and that Keretapa was the name of the exact spot beside Khonai where the apparition had occurred. Thus he made out the extant version of the legend.

He also knew that Khonai was situated in the Lycus valley, not far from Laodiceia and Hierapolis ; and, wrongly supposing Keretapa to be a spot in the territory of Khonai, he fancied that the Lycus flowed towards Lycia. The real Keretapa is not far from the watershed of the Indos valley. About six miles west of Keretapa one reaches the extreme waters of the Indos, which flows towards Lycia.

Having thus arranged the localities for his tale, he begins from the apostle of Hierapolis, Philip, and as a suitable introduction works in the Apostle John and the Echidna, taking his facts from a different set of documents, examples of which are preserved.* From Hierapolis the two apostles went to Khairetopa, and, after working wonders there and predicting the apparition of Michael, they proceeded to other cities. Then there gushed forth a healing spring at Khairetopa. Long before the church was built, a small chapel † existed on the spot. It was the work of a pagan, a native of Laodiceia, who became a convert after his dumb daughter was cured and made to speak by the miraculous fountain. The father and daughter are introduced for this one purpose, and remain nameless. Ninety years later the first guardian ($\pi\rho\sigma\mu\rho\nu\acute{a}\rho\iota\sigma$) of the holy fountain came to it. His name was Archippos, and he was a child of ten years old, born of pious parents in Hierapolis. The name comes from Coloss. iv. 17, cp. 13.‡ Archippos, a hermit of the strictest austerity, guarded the sanctuary for sixty years; and it required a series of miracles to preserve it from the attacks of the heathen, though during the ninety years preceding his arrival it needed no guardian. The heathen natives were determined to pollute the sacred fountain, or Ayasma,§ by turning into it the water of some other stream. They first tried to mix the river Chryses with the Ayasma, but it parted into two branches, flowing right and left of the sacred water.

---

* Lipsius, *Apokryphal Apostelgeschichte*, ii., 2, 24.

† εὐκτήριον, θυσιαστήριον.

‡ According to Batiffol, *Stud. Patrist.*, i., 33, this is perhaps a genuine tradition about the true Archippos.

§ ἁγίασμα : so also at Lystra (p. 50) and Tymandos, *Hist. Geogr.*, p. 402.

After this five thousand heathen collected at Laodiceia, and resolved to overwhelm the Ayasma with the united waters of the Lykokapros and the Kouphos. These rivers flow about three miles distant from the Ayasma, and after uniting beside the great mountain flow away into the country of Lycia. To ensure that the rivers should be full, the five thousand began by damming them up for ten days. But when they opened the dams and let the waters run into the new channel which they had cut to divert the rivers into the Ayasma, Michael himself came down to defend the holy fountain. He stood upon a rock beside the sanctuary, and, after bidding the waters stand still until they were as deep as the height of ten men, he caused the rock to open, and leave a path for the united streams to flow through. And the rock split open with a noise like thunder and a shock as of an earthquake; and the waters flow through the cleft to the present day.

There is a curious mixture of knowledge and ignorance, of local accuracy and inaccuracy, in this legend. The name Lykokapros is a mixture of the two rivers Lykos and Kapros, which bounded the territory of Laodiceia on the north and west.* The Kouphos also may be a real river, perhaps one of those which flow from Mount Cadmos northwards into the Lycus. The great mountain of course is Cadmos, which rises from the valley 6,000 feet over Colossæ, and 7,000 above the sea ; it is called the great mountain to distinguish it from the low ridge which im-

---

* Just as one of the western Χῶροι of Laodiceia was called Eleinokaprios from the two rivers Eleinos and Kapros, so the north-western Χῶρος, beside the junction of Lykos and Kapros, may have been called Lykokaprios, and thus have misled the author into the idea that there was a river Lykokapros.

pedes the exit of the Lycus from the valley. That the
Lycus ever flowed to Lycia is of course absurd ; but the
legend had to explain what happened to the river before
its new course was opened for it by the archangel.
Whether from some vague idea that Khairetopa was near
a stream that flowed to Lycia, or from the mere pseudo-
etymological fancy that the names Lycus and Lycia were
connected, the explanation suggested itself that the Lycus
originally flowed away towards Lycia. Whether this detail was added by the redactor or belonged to the older
local legend, no evidence remains.

The name Chryses is perhaps a relic of an older form
of the legend distinguished by better local knowledge.
Names of this form are not uncommon in Asia Minor ;
and it is quite probable that some branch of the Lycus
beside Colossæ was called Chryses. The sacred stream at
Hierapolis is called on coins the Chrysorrhoas, so that
a name of the same stock, at any rate, occurred in the
Lycus valley. It is remarkable that two branches issuing
from the same source flow on the right and the left of the
sacred spring at the present day, as may be seen on the
map. The northern one is artificial, but ancient.*

Legends of this kind may originate in three ways :
(1) Some are mere inventions to explain a name.† In this

---

* In Maspero's *Recueil de Travaux*, xiv., 1891, Hogarth and
I have described the irrigation works at Heracleia-Cybistra, which
are probably very ancient.

† One case bears on our subject. The name Κερέταπα was sometimes misspelt Καιρέταπα and Χαιρέταπα ; a legend arose of the
apparition of Michael, saying Χαῖρε, Τόπε, and this has found its
way into some MSS. of the Miracle at Khonai. A different legend
connected with Keretapa and St. Artemon exists, see *Expositor*,
1889, i., p. 150.

way a tale might be made to explain the name Khonai, "*funnels*," as derived from a channel or funnel through which a neighbouring river flows. (2) In many cases old legends, told originally of some pagan deity, were transferred to a Christian saint. (3) Some legends were founded on historical facts, which occurred in Christian times. The last class is far the most interesting ; and it is possible that the miracle at Khonai belongs to it.

Colossæ was situated at the lower western end of a narrow glen some ten miles long. On the north and east the broken skirts of the great central plateau hem in the glen. On the south Mount Cadmos rises steep above it. On the west a low rocky ridge about two miles in breadth divides it from the lower Lycus valley. This glen forms a sort of step between the lower Lycus valley, which is an eastern continuation of the long narrow Mæander valley, and the central plateau, to which it affords the easiest approach ; and the great highway from the western coast to the Euphrates valley traverses it. The river Lycus flows down through the glen, rising in a series of vast springs at its upper eastern end. The largest set of springs forms a lake now called Kodja Bash (Big Head, or Source). According to popular belief, this lake is a *duden* (κατάβοθρον), a term which denotes a place where a river either rises out of or disappears into the ground. Such *dudens* are numerous in Asia Minor.*

East of the Colossian glen, on the upper plateau, is the salt lake Anava. Popular belief sees in the Lycus springs the outlet of this lake ; and the Lycus water, though not salt, is bad in taste and not drinkable. Similar

---

* The Mæander, the Sangarios, and many other rivers rise in *dudens*, forming small lakes like Kodja Bash.

connections between rivers and high lakes behind their sources are often traced in Asia Minor, the typical example being between the Mæander and the lake of Bunarbashi, the ancient *Aurocreni Fontes*. Such *dudens* are commonly found where a ridge separates two plains at different levels. At the western end of the Colossian glen the Lycus has a good opportunity for another *duden*, for a ridge separates the glen from a plain three hundred feet lower ; but the Lycus traverses the ridge by a narrow open gorge in place of a *duden*. Now Herodotus says that the Lycus at Colossæ enters a rift in the earth within the very city, and reappears at a distance of five stadia. Colossæ was situated on the south bank of the river, but the buildings extended to the north bank ; and a glance at the map shows that the Lycus enters a rift in the ridge within the circuit once inhabited. The question then arises, did Herodotus describe rather inaccurately the scenery as it at present exists, or has any catastrophe occurred to change a former *auden* into an open gorge ? It must be granted that the phenomena of the legend are strongly suggestive of such a catastrophe : the noise like an earthquake, the inundation caused by the blocking of the passage, and the subsidence of the water when the gorge was cleared, would all be explained by Hamilton's supposition, that the two cliffs of the gorge were once connected over the stream, and that the crust was subsequently broken by an earthquake. The breaking of the crust would necessarily block the stream till the accumulated waters carried away the fallen *débris*. If such an event took place it must have been after the time of Strabo and Pliny, otherwise they would have mentioned such a remarkable phenomenon in alluding

to Colossæ. If it happened at all then, the change happened when a Christian community existed at Colossæ.
These considerations prompt us to examine the evidence
more closely, taking as guides M. Bonnet's excellent
edition of the Greek text of the legend (with his useful
essays prefixed), and M. Weber's careful description of
the gorge.*

No clear confirmation of Herodotus' statement has
come down to us. The chief witness is Strabo, who,
unlike Herodotus, had actually seen both Colossæ and
Apameia : " (the Lycus) flowing for the greater part of
its course underground, thereafter appears to view, and
joins † the other rivers (Mæander, Cadmos, Kapros),
proving at once the porous character of the country and
its liability to earthquake." The passage has frequently
been misunderstood ; the words cannot be explained as
a reference merely to this *duden*, for Strabo is a careful
writer, and the Lycus has a course of considerably more
than twenty miles. Obviously Strabo refers to the connection of the Lycus with Lake Anava ; and thus he
is correct in saying that most of its course is underground, and that after its underground course it appears
to view, and flows to join the Mæander. The description
is illustrated by Hamilton's description of the source
near Dere Keui. It issues from beneath the rock ; and
when Hamilton penetrated further up a cavern or " deep
chasm in the rock, . . . the sound of a subterranean
river rushing along a narrow bed or tumbling over pre-

---

* Bonnet, *Narratio de Miraculo Chonis patrato*, Paris, 1890 ;
Weber, *der unterird. Lauf des Lykos*, in *Athen. Mittheil.*, 1891,
p. 195.

† The aorist, συνέπεσεν, is remarkable here, *Strab.*, p. 586.

XIX. The Miracle of Khonai.

cipices . . . was distinctly heard" (i., p. 507).* Now it
is probable that Strabo, who certainly knew Herodotus'
description, would tacitly correct anything in it which
he disapproved of; and when he says so emphatically
that the river runs underground for many miles, and
then emerges to view and joins the Mæander, he must
be interpreted as expressing dissent from Herodotus.

No other passage known to me seems to possess any
value as independent evidence about the localities; and
especially the words of Scylitzes are obviously a mere
report of the legend, connecting it with the derivation
of the name Khonai.

Such is the ancient evidence—scanty and inconclusive.
We are brought face to face with the old question as to
Herodotus' credibility. Can we accept his evidence un-
supported, even supposing that it were not contradicted
by Strabo? Is his statement of that strikingly accurate
and vivid character, which in many cases leads us to
accept a description even against other witnesses?

We turn, then, to the archæological or topographical
evidence. Here scientific training as a practical geologist would be of high value in a witness. Hamilton
had training and practical experience, but he saw only
the lower and upper ends of the gorge. The engineers
of the Ottoman Railway traversed and surveyed it
some years ago, and I have talked with them. M.
Weber, of Smyrna, has printed in *Athen. Mittheil.*, 1891,
p. 197 ff., a clear and accurate account of the gorge;
but he did not extend his researches over the whole
territory of Colossæ, nor attend specially to the points

---

* I explained what I believed to be Strabo's meaning in *Amer.
Jour. Arch.*, 1887, p. 358*f*, but have failed to convince M. Bonnet.

raised by the legend. So far as he goes I agree with him; * but only a practical geologist can answer the further questions that arise.

The gorge, as a whole, has been an open gap for thousands of years; on that all are agreed who have seen it; and the grave chambers in the north wall of the gorge near its northern end, as M. Weber acutely argues, prove this conclusively. This statement, however, does not imply that the stream was always ópen to view. It is still in some places half concealed from view, as M. Weber says; and we must admit the possibility that incrustation from the streams that join it, both on north and south, may have at a former period completely over-arched it for a little way. But such a bridge would not justify Herodotus, who describes a *duden* more than half a mile long. His description fails in minute accuracy; and we must, so far as the evidence goes, consider his words as less accurate than Strabo's, and due to misconception in reporting an account given him by an eye-witness. †

The character of the localities shows that an inundation might readily occur at Colossæ; though we must abandon the theory that it was caused by the collapse of Herodotus'

---

* I cannot, however, accept his statement, p. 197, "*sein Lauf hat sich nie geändert, wie es Hamilton annimmt.*" Hamilton is quite right; M. Weber has not observed quite carefully.

† An idea, more favourable to Herodotus, occurred to me in 1891 (*Athenæum*, August, p. 233); but I have been forced by M. Weber's clear argument to abandon it. Sacrifice of this idea spoils the view with which I planned this chapter; and brings me back to the conclusion I stated in *Amer. Jour. Arch.*, 1887, p. 358, that Herodotus confused the *duden* at the source of the Lycus with the gorge at Colossæ. Vast incrustations are made by these streams.

duden. Deliverance from such an inundation would inevitably be construed as a miracle by the inhabitants. In the Pagan time they would have attributed their safety to the Zeus of Colossæ; in the later Christian period they attributed it to one of the angels—a proof how little removed was the later Christianity of Colossæ from the old paganism. The worship of angels was strong in Phrygia. Paul warned the Colossians against it in the first century. The Council held at Laodiceia on the Lycus, about A.D. 363, stigmatised it as idolatrous.* Theodoret, about 420-50 A.D., mentions that this disease long continued to infect Phrygia and Pisidia.† But that which was once counted idolatry, was afterwards reckoned as piety.

Michael, the leader of the host of angels, was worshipped very widely in Asia Minor. Akroinos-Nikopolis, the scene of the great victory over the Saracens in 739, was dedicated to him; and his worship is implied in an inscription at Gordium-Eudokias in Galatia.‡ A church of Michael was built by Constantine on the north coast of the Bosphorus; § and here Michael was believed to manifest himself, and miraculous cures were to Sozomen's own knowledge wrought. The origin of Christianity at Isaura, in the legend of Conon,

---

* Coloss. ii. 18, ἐν θρησκείᾳ τῶν ἀγγέλων; Concil. Laod., οὐ δεῖ χριστιανοὺς ἐγκαταλείπειν τὴν ἐκκλησίαν τοῦ θεοῦ καὶ ἀγγέλους ὀνομάζειν καὶ συνάξεις ποιεῖν, ἅπερ ἀπαγορεύεται. εἴ τις οὖν εὑρεθῇ ταύτῃ τῇ κεκρυμμένῃ εἰδωλολατρείᾳ σχολάζων, ἔστω ἀνάθεμα, ὅτι . . . εἰδωλολατρείᾳ προσῆλθεν, Canon 35.

† ἔμεινε δὲ τοῦτο τὸ πάθος ἐν τῇ Φρυγίᾳ καὶ Πισιδίᾳ μέχρι πολλοῦ . . . καὶ μέχρι δὲ τοῦ νῦν εὐκτήρια τοῦ ἁγίου Μιχαὴλ παρ' ἐκείνοις καὶ τοῖς ὁμόροις ἐκείνων ἔστιν ἰδεῖν Interpret. Ep. Coloss. ii. 16 (Ed. Hal., iii., 490).

‡ *Athen. Mittheil.*, 1883, p. 144; *Bull. Cor. Hell.*, 1883, p. 23 (read [τ]ῷ Ἀρχιστρατήγῳ ἑ[αυτὸν ?] παραδοὺς ἐνθάδε κ[εῖται?] Σωτήριχος).

§ It replaced the temple of Zeus, erected by the Argonauts, 35 st. from Constantinople; Sozomen, ii., 3; Cedrenus, ii., p. 210.

is ascribed to the action of Michael ; and his intervention is considered by M. Batiffol a reason for assigning to the " Prayer of Aseneth " an origin in this region (*Stud. Patrist.,* i., 34).

As to the legend, we cannot date it in its extant form before the ninth century. This is proved by the local names employed. Colossæ was a city of the plain, exposed to sudden attack ; though, if carefully fortified and well guarded, it was easily defensible against a regular siege. In the Sassanian and Saracen inroads sudden assaults, and not formal sieges, were the danger ; and fortresses on peaks of extraordinary natural strength, safe against raids, though difficult to provision for a long siege, suited the period. Khonai was then built on a steep spur of Mount Cadmos. The castle must be near 3,000 feet above the sea, and the village is situated on a lower shelf, overlooking the rich little glen, and commanding a beautiful view of the Lycus valley. It was founded probably by Justinian, as part of his general defensive scheme of roads and forts ; but Colossæ, in its convenient position, long continued to be the centre of population. But, after the Arab invasions became a constant dread, the population sought the safer site ; and in 787 the bishop resided at Khonai, though bearing the title of Colossæ, since the church on the north bank of the Lycus at Colossæ continued to be the great sanctuary of the district. But in 868 and later the bishop bore the title of Khonai, the name Colossæ had disappeared, and the whole territory, once called Colossæ, was now termed Khonai. The great church by the Lycus still existed, till it was burned by the Turks on a raid in the twelfth century ; but it was now known as the church of Michael of Khonai. Now in the miracle-legend the church and the whole glen bear the name of Khonai; and it therefore cannot be earlier than the ninth century in the present form.*

That the legend relates to the church at Colossæ, and not to a church on the actual site of Khonai, seems indubitable. No one after reading the legend, and looking at the remains of the large and splendid church (whose walls barely projected above the soil in 1881), can doubt that the tale is the foundation legend of the church. But so utterly was the name Colossæ lost, that the redactor, through the confusion described, calls the site Khairetopa.

The words quoted above from Theodoret prove that there was only a chapel of Michael at Colossæ, about A.D. 450. On the other hand, the church at Colossæ must have been built before the centre of population was moved to Khonai, about 700. † The legend, then, had several centuries to grow before the redactor put it into the extant form; but he evidently had an older form to work on, a genuine local legend, free from the topographical confusion of Keretapa and Khonai.

We have then failed to find evidence to show with certainty which of the three classes enumerated above the legend of Colossæ belongs to. It may arise from a real fact of history, an inundation that occurred in Christian

---

* A similar date may be inferred from the form Khairetopa, which is found in 787 and 879; but in earlier times the name, though corruptly spelt, has not lost the memory of *a* in the penult (which was probably long). This test admits an eighth century date, but is inconsistent with the seventh century, the date favoured by M. Bonnet and by M. Batiffol, *Stud. Patrist.*, i., 33.

† No reference to the miracle or the church of Khonai occurs before the ninth century, Bonnet, p. xxxix., *Act. Sanct.*, September, vol. viii., p 40, § 198.

times, or it may be an artificial legend, founded on the strange natural cleft through which the Lycus flows, and probably giving in Christian form an older pagan myth.

NOTE 1.—A remarkable example of the worship of angels is contained in an inscription of Miletos. In this strange instance of superstition, inscribed (necessarily by public permission) on the wall of the theatre, the seven archangels who preside over the seven planets are invoked to protect the city. The names of the archangels are not given, but each planet is denoted by mysterious symbols, with the same inscription beneath, ἅγιε, φύλα[ξ]ον τὴν πόλιν Μιλησίων κ.τ.λ. Underneath the seven inscriptions is the single line ἀρχαγγέλοι[s] φυλάσσεται ἡ πόλις Μιλησίων κ.τ.λ. C. I. G., 2895. The words quoted from Theodoret illustrate this curious piece of superstition, οἱ δὲ ἀρχάγγελοι τὰς τῶν ἐθνῶν προστασίας ἐνεπιστεύθησαν, *interp. in Dan. c. x.*

NOTE 2.—The length to which this work has already been carried prevents me from saying more about the Jews in Asia Minor; but one point must be alluded to (p. 46*n.*). M. Salomon Reinach has inferred from a Smyrnæan inscription that the *archisynagogoi* (women as well as men) in Asia Minor were not officials, but merely persons of rank in the community, who exercised, by virtue of their social weight, a certain influence on the religious practices. *Codex Bezæ* confirms his acute conclusions. The inscription which he comments on must be probably older than A.D. 70 (p. 349).

NOTE 3.—The British Museum inscription, No. 482, "begins by complaining that the Ephesian Goddess was now being set at nought," about A.D. 161. This document would appear to have an important bearing on Chap. XIV., § 3 ; but I have tried to show in *Classical Review*, January 1893, that the text is wrongly restored, and that the meaning is different.

NOTE 4.—It resulted from the requiring of a specific accuser, and still more from the rewards given to the accuser out of the property of the accused (p. 336), that a class of lawyers arose, who made a speciality of cases against Christians. Just as *delatores* in charges of treason arose in numbers from the policy of Tiberius and Domitian, so *delatores* in Christian cases necessarily sprang from the circumstances of the second and third centuries. Allusions to such *advocati* often occur (Le Blant, *Actes*, p. 306).

INDEX.

ILLUSTRATIONS AND MAPS.

1 (p. 47). View of Lystra, from a photograph by Mr. D. G. Hogarth, 1890. The view is from the south; Ayasma with trees in the foreground.

2 (p. 55). View of Derbe, from a photograph by Mr. Hogarth, 1890. The view is from the south-west.

3 (p. 441). Gravestone, in possession of a Turk, native of Seulun, drawn by Mrs. Ramsay, August 1884. I tried vainly to induce some rich Armenians of Kara Hissar to bring the stone to their church for preservation.

4. The Map of Asia Minor is intended chiefly to show the political divisions A.D. 50-70, and, secondarily to aid the comprehension of the history of Christianity in the country during the early centuries. By a mistake the hills bounding the valley of Lystra on N.E. are represented too near Iconium.

5. The Map of the Lycus valley depends on the Ottoman Railway Survey, kindly given me by Mr. Purser. The route from Denizli to Khonai is added by me: I traversed it in October 1891.